# NORTHERN IRELAND

# NORTHERN IRELAND

## IRELAND

### THE RELUCTANT PEACE

**FEARGAL COCHRANE**

YALE UNIVERSITY PRESS
NEW HAVEN AND LONDON

For information about this and other Yale University Press publications, please contact:
U.S. Office: sales.press@yale.edu    yalebooks.com
Europe Office: sales@yaleup.co.uk    www.yalebooks.co.uk

Set in Janson Text by IDSUK (DataConnection) Ltd
Printed in Great Britain by TJ International, Padstow, Cornwall

Library of Congress Cataloging-in-Publication Data
Cochrane, Feargal.
  Northern Ireland: the reluctant peace / Feargal Cochrane.
     pages cm
  Includes bibliographical references and index.
  ISBN 978-0-300-17870-8 (cl : alk. paper)
1. Northern Ireland—Politics and government—20th century. 2. Northern Ireland—Politics and government—21st century. 3. Northern Ireland—Foreign relations—Great Britain. 4. Great Britain—Foreign relations—Ireland. 5. Political violence—Northern Ireland—History. 6. Peace-building—Northern Ireland. I. Title.
  DA990.U46C628 2001
  941.6082—dc23

                                                                    2012047267

A catalogue record for this book is available from the British Library.

10 9 8 7 6 5 4 3 2 1
2017 2016 2015 2014 2013

# CONTENTS

# LIST OF ILLUSTRATIONS

For Oisín

# ACKNOWLEDGEMENTS

THERE ARE A number of people whose advice, encouragement and support have been critical during the writing of this book. My editor at Yale, Phoebe Clapham, has steered the project from its inception and has guided me with consummate professionalism and care through the process of producing and refining the manuscript; for this I am truly thankful. Thanks are also due to my copy-editor, Clive Liddiard, for his sharp eye and attention to detail.

I began writing the book while working at Lancaster University, and am indebted to my former colleagues and friends at Lancaster, in particular Professor David Denver, who provided encouragement, friendship and, at times, useful critical engagement throughout the project. I would also like to thank all my students at Lancaster over the last fourteen years for their engagement with the themes at the centre of the book.

I moved jobs while writing the book, and I would like to thank my new colleagues at the School of Politics and International Relations at the University of Kent for their friendship and collegiality. I would particularly like to thank my Head of School, Professor Richard Sakwa, and Professor Richard Whitman for easing me into my new role at Kent and for helping me to balance my responsibilities within the School with the process of finishing the book. My new colleagues at the Conflict Analysis Research Centre at Kent have also provided me with new perspectives on Northern Ireland, as well as on wider issues relating to political violence. I would particularly like to thank Dr Gulnur Aybet, Dr Ruth Blakeley, Dr Govinda Clayton, Dr Philip Cunliffe, Dr Andrea den

Boer, Dr Neo Loizides, Professor Hugh Miall, Dr Doug Stokes and Dr Harmonie Toros.

I would also like to thank a number of other colleagues and friends who have helped me to clarify my thoughts on the wider debates surrounding the dynamics of violent political conflict and the potential for overcoming it, including: Dr Patrick Bishop, Dr Kynan Gentry, Dr Alan Greer, Professor Terence Lyons, Dr Vicky Mason, Professor Gerd Nonneman, Dr Eamonn O'Kane, Dr Graham Smith, Professor Ashok Swain and Professor Jonathan Tonge. I would also like to thank Greg and Kathie Irwin, Donald and Deborah McWhirter and Dr Alison Montgomery for their friendship and advice. The anonymous readers of the initial proposal and draft manuscript also provided useful criticisms and suggestions, for which I am extremely grateful.

A number of people were kind enough to be interviewed in relation to some of the themes within the book, and I would like to thank in particular Noel Doran, Stephen Farry, David Ford, Ciarnan Helferty, Conall McDevitt, Joe O'Donnell, Quintin Oliver, Nigel Smyth and Peter Weir for their time and valuable insights.

On a personal note, I want to thank family members Niall, Geraldine, Eamonn, Peter and Sean and my mother and father, Roisin and Gerry Cochrane, for their love and support. The most heartfelt thanks go to my wife, Professor Rosaleen Duffy, who has perhaps suffered more than I have through the writing process. Apart from acting as a constant sounding-board for my arguments, she has had to endure listening to the minutiae of Northern Ireland's painful political history more than any person should reasonably be expected to. Rosaleen has been particularly tolerant of the time the book has taken to write when there have been other priorities in our lives, such as a new-born baby to feed, nappies to change and new jobs to start. I thank Rosaleen for her constant patience, advice, love and encouragement. The book also benefits from Rosaleen's talent as a photographer, though spending New Year's Day 2013 on the Newtownards Road was not the holiday she had initially envisaged.

The book is dedicated to our beautiful son Oisín, who arrived midway through the writing of Chapter 3. As Gaelic legend has it, Oisín was both a warrior and a poet. While he was not thus christened with this book in mind, these two traits seem particularly appropriate for the subject matter contained within its pages.

# ABBREVIATIONS AND ACRONYMS

| | |
|---|---|
| ANIA | Americans for a New Irish Agenda |
| AOH | Ancient Order of Hibernians |
| CLMC | Combined Loyalist Military Command |
| CRC | Community Relations Council |
| CRM | Civil Rights Movement |
| CSI | Cohesion, Sharing and Integration |
| DSD | Department for Social Development |
| DUP | Democratic Unionist Party |
| EPA | Emergency Provisions Act |
| ERM | Exchange Rate Mechanism |
| FAIT | Families Against Intimidation and Terror |
| FARC | Revolutionary Armed Forces of Colombia |
| FRU | Force Research Unit |
| GAA | Gaelic Athletic Association |
| GFA | Good Friday Agreement |
| HET | Historical Enquiries Team |
| IMC | Independent Monitoring Commission |
| INC | Irish National Caucus |
| INLA | Irish National Liberation Army |
| IPP | Irish Parliamentary Party |
| IRA | Irish Republican Army |
| IRB | Irish Republican Brotherhood |
| JRRT | Joseph Rowntree Reform Trust |
| LVF | Loyalist Volunteer Force |

| | |
|---|---|
| MLA | Member of the Legislative Assembly |
| MLK | Maze/Long Kesh |
| MLK DC | Maze/Long Kesh Development Corporation |
| NICRA | Northern Ireland Civil Rights Association |
| NILT | Northern Ireland Life and Times |
| NIO | Northern Ireland Office |
| NORAID | Irish Northern Aid Committee |
| NUM | National Union of Mineworkers |
| NUS–USI | National Union of Students–Union of Students in Ireland |
| OFMDFM | Office of the First Minister and Deputy First Minister |
| PD | People's Democracy |
| PfG | Programme for Government |
| PIRA | Provisional IRA |
| PLO | Palestine Liberation Organization |
| PSNI | Police Service of Northern Ireland |
| PTA | Prevention of Terrorism Act |
| PUP | Progressive Unionist Party |
| RAAD | Republican Action Against Drugs |
| RCN | Rural Community Network |
| RHC | Red Hand Commando |
| RNU | Republican Network for Unity |
| RUC | Royal Ulster Constabulary |
| SDLP | Social Democratic and Labour Party |
| TUV | Traditional Unionist Voice |
| UDA | Ulster Defence Association |
| UDP | Ulster Democratic Party |
| UDR | Ulster Defence Regiment |
| UFF | Ulster Freedom Fighters |
| UKUP | UK Unionist Party |
| UUC | Ulster Unionist Council |
| UUP | Ulster Unionist Party |
| UUUC | United Ulster Unionist Council |
| UVF | Ulster Volunteer Force |
| UWC | Ulster Workers' Council |

Portrush
Ballycastle
Coleraine
Limavady
Derry/Londonderry
Larne
Strabane
NORTHERN
IRELAND
Ballymena
Carrickfergus
Antrim
Bangor
Cookstown
Belfast
Holywood
Omagh
Newtownards
Kesh
Dungannon
Lurgan
Lisburn
Irvinestown
Aughnacloy
Hillsborough
Enniskillen
Portadown
Armagh
Downpatrick
Newry
Newcastle
Warrenpoint
Crossmaglen

*Atlantic Ocean*

*Irish Sea*

R E P U B L I C
O F
I R E L A N D

Galway
Dublin

Limerick

Waterford

Cork

| 0 | miles | 50 |
| 0 | km | 80 |

# INTRODUCTION

FEW WOULD DISPUTE that Ireland has had a troubled history, though of
course it is not unique in that respect. However, it presents a fascinating
example of the overlapping layers of conflict and of how they seep into the
history, politics and culture of the people caught up in it. Centuries of
troubled history were crystallized into a generation of political violence
from the 1960s until the 1990s. This helped to fuse historical, political,
cultural and social divisions into a heady cocktail of sectarian violence
that grabbed international media attention, while dislocating the region
and those who lived there. At the end of the 1960s, Northern Ireland
had shot from being a forgotten political backwater within the United
Kingdom to an international conflict zone and a policy priority for the
British government.

As the political violence evolved over three decades, a number of
emotions swirled around Northern Ireland and beyond: fear, confusion,
anger, guilt – and eventually hope that peace could be built out of the ashes
of conflict. Sheer bafflement was the conclusion of many people who did
not have an intimate knowledge of the region. Why could these people not
live together peacefully? Why could they not move beyond historic
episodes from the seventeenth century or their religious faiths (divided as
they were by their common Christianity)?

Bafflement and hope gave way to boredom as the peace process edged
into view in the late 1990s, not to a fanfare of trumpets so much as to a
few weedy notes from an asthmatic busker. Many people wondered (not
unreasonably) whether the conflict was not supposed to have been sorted

out at this point, as a political agreement had finally been reached by the main political parties and endorsed in a referendum by the vast majority of the population. Despite the international media focus on Northern Ireland during the 1990s and the general optimism that generations of sectarian hatred and violence could now be consigned to the history books, the problem was that history has not been an inert subject in Ireland. History was alive, and it prowled the imaginations of those who wanted to use it to justify their politics or their belief systems, or even to explain why they had no choice but to kill other members of their community.

Of course, there is more than one version of history, and there is more than one community in Northern Ireland. So one person will use *their* history to defend *their* community against *the other*, and as a way of protecting *their* heritage and that of *their* ancestors against those they believe are trying to destroy it. In other words, the past is woven into the present in Northern Ireland because the argument upon which it was founded has never really been resolved. On several occasions in the past hundred years it has been forgotten; at times it has been disguised; but never has it fully been confronted and dealt with. George Bernard Shaw is famously attributed as saying that Irish history was something no Englishman should forget and no Irishman should remember. However, neither collective amnesia nor obsession would be as beneficial as a general realization among all those concerned that in Ireland the present is informed by the past to an extraordinary degree. It colours and shapes current attitudes, grievances, belief systems, hopes, fears and desires.

The intention here is to demonstrate the different ways in which political attitudes in Northern Ireland are informed by the past and have been shaped through conflicting readings of a shared history. The purpose is to dispel the confusion about why political violence exploded in Northern Ireland in 1969, why it continued for so long and why it remains a feature of the political landscape today. The belief that the political system was incapable of delivering reform and that community grievances could best be addressed outside the formal political process has plagued the region since the creation of Northern Ireland in 1921. It is argued here that unless the current political generation understands and learns from this history (and specifically makes a meaningful connection between the formal political system and the people) then it may be doomed to repeat its troubled past in the years ahead.

So, in order to comprehend Northern Ireland today we have to under-stand where it has come from and how the main community divisions were built and sharpened to the extent that violence became the cutting edge of political activism. An obvious (and rudimentary) question suggests itself here: why did violence become such a feature of political exchange in Irish politics? If Canadians and Belgians can manage their political differences without resorting to murdering one another, then why have we on 'these Islands' taken to doing so with such apparent ease?

The answer to this lies not with any primordial forces that consigned the unfortunate Irish to centuries of conflict, but is to be found in more rational explanations. In short, violence has worked. More precisely, it has worked for *some* people, on *some* occasions, to further a particular set of political and economic interests. While Northern Ireland has sometimes been portrayed in the popular media as a seventeenth-century throwback to unyielding religious hatreds and contradictory political goals, mediated by warring Gods, this is a simplified stereotype of more complex political and economic forces.

This portrayal of Northern Ireland also conveniently casts the people who live there as the 'problem' and absolves those on the outside of blame or guilt for the political violence that has occurred. The worrying policy implication of this view for many years was that a 'solution' or settlement of the conflict was impossible, as the circle dividing Catholics and Protestants could never be squared. In religious terms, each regarded the other as heretics who were going to Hell; while in political terms they adhered to apparently mutually exclusive identities. Northern Ireland would either be British or it would be Irish, and this constitutional tug-of-war over rival nationality claims meant that victory for one side meant automatic defeat for the other.

'Solutions are for chemists' was the fatuous response of those who could not (or would not) believe that the 'mad Irish' could be 'civilized' into peace. While there certainly have been times when sectarian bitterness has reached levels that makes dialogue and negotiation unrealistic for all except the most idealistic, more frequently the notion that 'nothing could be done' to end the conflict was a do-nothing charter, promoted largely by those who wanted to do nothing.

A prerequisite for doing something was to understand the political context and the way in which the past was hard-wired into the present in Northern Ireland. The roll call of key dates in Irish history (1641, 1690, 1798, 1849, 1916, 1969, 1972, 1994, 1998) is saturated in blood, and few of those dates are without political significance. The same goes for the rogues' gallery of personalities who have bestridden the Irish stage, whether in a leading role or as bit-part player (Cromwell, Tone, Carson, Collins, Paisley, Thatcher, Adams). These names and dates illustrate the way in which history, religion, politics and identity have overlapped in Irish history and have shaped relations between the people who live there. The connections between history, politics and identity have endured and strengthened to the point that the past is alive in Northern Ireland – a contemporary reality rather than a cultural remembrance, and a means of connecting what is (and what might be) to what has gone before.

Religious difference/intolerance is, of course, an important aspect of the story; but it is not, in itself, a cause of conflict in Ireland. In order to appreciate why religion matters so much, we have to understand how it intersects with the region's historical, political, economic and cultural development. Although it might appear that violent conflict in Northern Ireland has been the consequence of ancient religious hatreds between Protestants on the one hand and Catholics on the other, this does not mean that religion has been the cause of such division. It would be more accurate to say that religious identity became a key aspect of division between a powerful majority and a relatively powerless minority. This grafted onto political and cultural identity through civic associations such as the Orange Order and, later, the Gaelic League and Gaelic Athletic Association (GAA) in ways that brought religion, culture and politics together for the Protestant/British/unionists and the Catholic/Irish/ nationalists. A form of ethno-nationalist division emerged, where religion served to define and identify the sides, rather than to create those divisions in the first place. To know someone's religion was to know their politics and their culture, and so began a deadly reductionist tango, where beliefs were assumed rather than verified. There is an old joke: A Jewish man stopped on the street in Belfast is asked whether he is a Protestant or a Catholic. When he responds that he is Jewish, the rejoinder comes: 'Aye, but are you a Catholic Jew or a Protestant Jew?'

This emphasizes the point that, rather than theological, it has been political and cultural differences that have divided people in Northern Ireland. Indeed, sectarianism became such an internalized system that few actually rationalized the causes of their antipathy. It was our side against theirs; two communities, unionist and nationalist, that defined themselves by who they were not, as much as by who they were. An ethno-national co-dependency developed, where political and cultural identities were understood and defined in zero-sum terms, with gains for the unionist British 'tradition' coming necessarily at the expense of its Irish nationalist counterpart. The tragic irony in all of this is that to outsiders (including the majority of people in the Republic of Ireland) the two sides were indistinguishable from one another: small-c conservative; politically aware (if a little paranoid); literate; generously communitarian; and endemically suspicious. One aspect of the violent conflict that made it so deadly was that both sides understood the rules all too well and could sniff out an insult as surely as a pig scents a truffle. This fatalism was grounded in the reality of community sectarianism, of course; but it created a bunker mentality that was extremely difficult to get out of and that created self-fulfilling prophecies of mistrust.

One of the reasons why the violence became so visceral and bitter relates to the geography of the region. Northern Ireland is – in the greater scheme of things – a tiny place. With a population of 1.8 million, it is the equivalent of a decent-sized city in UK terms (though smaller than Greater Manchester or London). But some regard it as a 'state' (which it is not), and it is commonly referred to as a 'country' by many of those who live there – and not all of them would define themselves as unionists. This owes something to the fact that, despite its relatively small size, Northern Ireland is different. It was so even before it was called Northern Ireland, since the industrial revolution and the large concentration of Protestants combined to separate Ulster from the other three, more agricultural provinces of Ireland.

While Northern Ireland emerged at the end of 1920 as a political acci- dent – everyone's least-worst option, loved by no one but accepted by sufficient numbers on all sides – it did define an existing reality. It had a particular political character: the unionists were not as British as in the rest of the UK, and Northern nationalists were not quite as Irish as on the rest of the island. Both sides were defined by a blunt and abrupt directness not found as readily elsewhere in Ireland or Britain. Our accent is more a guttural bark than the lilting brogue of the Southern Irish – though none- theless beautiful in its ruggedness. Our humour is blacker than a depressed Glaswegian's, honed from years of sectarianism, violence, poverty and periodic rejection by the two alternative states to which we gave allegiance and craved it back in return. Perhaps this subliminal realization lies at the heart of the insecurity that is stamped indelibly on the political psyches of both communities. In the end, we are on our own, joined at the hip to the very people we most mistrust and in and out of (unrequited) love with our would-be suitors in Britain and the Republic of Ireland.

This book explains how Northern Ireland was forged out of centuries of division – religious, economic, political, cultural and physical. A conflict that simmered for a generation is slowly cooling down, but it is still scalding those who live there. Despite all the hoopla surrounding periodic agreements between the political parties, little has changed on the ground for many people. The 'peace dividend' has been slow to percolate down from the elites to the wider community. Clashing memories of a shared history resonate, like the tolling of a submerged bell, at once amplifying and distorting reality.

In a society shaped and damaged by its violent inheritance, there is a tendency to explain and interpret both the present and even the future through the lens of history. This historical view is distorted and contested by today's generation, entwining the present with the past in ways that frequently force people to look backwards rather than forwards. This book examines and unravels these contested readings of history and tries to explain how the past connects with current relationships and political attitudes in Northern Ireland.

It also emphasizes how generations of sectarian division have complicated the relationship between the formal political system and the wider community in Northern Ireland. The region has either had partisan government (1921–72), an absence of government (1972–98) or an evolving government (1999–present), and all of these have led to varying degrees of scepticism about the value of politics among those on the receiving end. This book argues that politics in a place such as Northern Ireland is shaped by communities themselves, as well as through the formal political structures forged from violence and subsequent negotiated agreements. Power relationships and hierarchies are informal as well as formal, malleable as well as structured, and these have evolved over time in complex and fascinating ways. Martin McGuinness has had a powerful political influence on Northern Ireland from the early 1970s to the present day, but the context of this influence and the means by which it has been demonstrated have evolved enormously across that period. This book demonstrates that we cannot understand politics in Northern Ireland unless we grasp the fluid interactions between political elites and the wider constituencies within which they are located.

It seeks to explain that we cannot interpret Northern Ireland's current reluctant peace unless we understand where the place and its people have come from. Without this context, we may hear the words spoken but fail to understand the pauses in between them, wherein real meaning lies.

CHAPTER ONE

# THE COLLISION OF RELIGION AND POLITICS, 1690–1920

IN 1995, DURING the period popularly known as the 'peace process' in Northern Ireland, British Prime Minister John Major sat down to be interviewed by a local television journalist. 'Okay Ken,' he enquired, 'where do you want me to begin?' In a deadpan but mischievous response, the reporter quipped, '1690, Prime Minister'.[1]

This exchange epitomizes the fact that where we begin any account of history is selective and is, to some extent therefore, a political act in itself. The first of July 1690[2] was a pivotal moment in Irish (and British) history. It was the date of the Battle of the Boyne when the Protestant Dutch Prince William III defeated his Catholic rival James II, vanquishing his ambitions to regain the English throne he had lost two years earlier. This event was important in that it helped to ensure that Ireland remained under Protestant control. Many Protestants saw it as protecting their religious, economic and political position in Ireland, and in turn damaging that of the Catholic population. Inevitably the reality was more complicated, but ever since then the Battle of the Boyne has been hard-wired into Irish Protestant folklore, and the slogan 'Remember 1690' can still be seen in graffiti and wall murals today. The reason why this battle is remembered and celebrated in Northern Ireland today, in a way that, for example, the Boston Tea Party in America is not, is that it still defines the current political divisions in the former, while they have receded into the cultural archives of the latter. In a facetious (but nonetheless telling) example, one renowned Irish academic colleague revealed to a friend in an unguarded moment that he had set his ATM bank pin-code to '1690', as it was the one sequence of numbers that he could be sure to remember.

## RELIGION, POWER AND POLITICS

As the political history of Ireland evolved during the seventeenth century, the struggle for power connected religion to politics and to nationalism in ways that made it relatively easy to define and recognize in-groups and out-groups, loyal and disloyal, friend and enemy. As a result of the Protestant reformation in England, religion became a key divider between the dominant and the dominated sectors of society, this in itself being linked to attempts by the Protestant English state to colonize and Anglicize Ireland for both political and economic advantage. Ireland had resources, such as land, that could be given in reward for service by the English Crown to its soldiers. Ireland was also a potential security threat to Britain as a launch pad for foreign invasions from Spain and elsewhere, and its stubborn adherence to Catholicism increased this perceived threat considerably. As a result, resources were confiscated from the 'native' Catholic population and given to the newer Protestant community. This was done in a number of ways, through a combination of bribery and force, as the English Crown attempted to colonize and control Ireland, and thereby to enhance its own political and territorial security.

The most overt example of this policy was the plantation of Ulster in the early seventeenth century, when Scottish and English Protestants were encouraged to go to Ireland and were given land in return for their loyalty to the Crown. It is difficult to imagine the scale of this initiative in today's era of global capitalism and retreat from command-style economics. Given that we are talking about the year 1609, the plantation of Ulster was a staggeringly ambitious project. Over just a few years, 170,000 English and Scots settlers were given land in Ulster, twenty-three new towns were established, and varying levels of protection were provided against the understandably unhappy Catholic natives who had been dispossessed.

In modern jargon we might refer to the plantation as an early example of a public-private partnership, where the government provided some resources and the settlers put in their own capital as well, in order to farm the land and establish new communities. The London Corporation poured significant money into the establishment of a new town in the north of Ulster that was henceforth to be known officially as 'Londonderry'. Here we have another example of the way in which the past connects with the present, as the current official name for Northern Ireland's second-largest city is a linguistic throwback to the plantation itself and to the moment when the Gaelic Catholics were dispossessed and England finally managed some level of political control over Ireland. Use of 'Londonderry' in casual conversation positions the speaker as a unionist, while the non-official 'Derry' is more likely to indicate a Catholic.[3]

While the impact of the plantation has been overstated in the subsequent political development of Ireland, it helped to provide a critical mass to the existing Scottish Protestant community that had built up in Ireland over previous generations. This connected the issue of religion to economic grievance and citizenship in a way that defined Catholics and Protestants in oppositional terms. More broadly, the arrival of such a large body of Scots and English settlers changed the pattern of agriculture, as well as Irish educational and legal structures, making them more compatible with those in England.

A series of 'Penal Laws' was also enacted at the end of the seventeenth century in an attempt to subjugate the Catholic population, deprive them of citizenship, religious freedom and economic means. These laws removed the right of Catholics to bear arms, hold public office, vote in elections, be members of parliament, educate their children and (more bizarrely) own a horse worth more than £5. One of the over-riding themes of the penal laws, in addition to confiscation of Catholic property, was the obsessive fear of the Catholic Church and its clergy. While this might seem a little paranoid today, England was still recovering from the reign of 'Bloody Mary', who had attempted to reverse the Protestant reformation in England and the religious revolution initiated by her father, Henry VIII.

Much of this effort to control and Anglicize Ireland involved confiscating the property of the Gaelic Catholic population and then giving it to the Scots and English Protestant arrivals. Another technique was to legally disinherit Catholics, so that land and other property transferred into Protestant hands. However, the picture was a complicated one, and it is too simplistic to paint all Protestants as land-grabbing zealots and all Catholics as hapless victims of legal theft. The main story of the period, however, was the enormous transfer of property ownership from Catholic into Protestant hands and the creation of what became known as a Protestant 'Ascendancy' and a Gaelic Catholic underclass. As a result of English government policies, Catholic land ownership fell from around 60 per cent in 1641 to 14 per cent by 1703, following William's victory over James II and the subsequent 'Act of Settlement'. By the 1750s, the figure is estimated to have fallen to around 5 per cent.[4]

Regardless of the rights and wrongs of England's policies in Ireland throughout this period, the transfer of property from the Catholic to the Protestant population simplified a series of quite complicated political dynamics within these groups into an antagonistic binary relationship between the two. Assimilation between these contradictory groups was next to impossible, and a form of religious/political apartheid evolved between the Protestant Ascendancy (and eventually the Presbyterian Dissenters) on the one hand and the dispossessed and disenfranchised Catholics on the other. The general picture from the Act of Settlement in 1701 through to the 1780s was one of domination by the Protestant Ascendency. The Catholic population was marginalized economically and excluded politically. They were effectively non-citizens, although, as their political and economic fortunes declined, their grievances crystallized into increasingly vocal demands for reform, especially over the rising rents being charged by their Protestant landlords.

## THE FUTURE'S ORANGE

As the relationship between Protestants and Catholics became more polarized, so historical events such as the Battle of the Boyne became more relevant and divisive. The twelfth of July – known simply as 'the Twelfth' – is a public holiday in Northern Ireland (though it is only celebrated by one section of the community). It is a day when many unionists have traditionally connected their Protestant religion to their loyalty to the British Crown via a series of parades and speeches led by the 'Orange' Institutions, which emphasize their position as British citizens in Northern Ireland. While these celebrations might seem anachronistic to outsiders, they have an internal code that is understood by everyone who lives there. In addition to signalling an historic military and political victory, this is more than a religious or cultural self-validation. One of the reasons why the Orange Order and its commemorations have survived into modern times is that they go beyond the personal into the public sphere, and are a re-statement of the region's current political and cultural status.

This is not to lay all of the problems of Irish history at the door of the Orange Order or its supporters. There have been many cases where sectarian Catholic societies, such as the 'Defenders' and 'Ribbonmen' (groups active in their opposition to the Orange Order in the eighteenth century), connected their religious traditions to more material self-interest and sectarian hatreds. A loose grouping known as the Whiteboys (due to their habit of wearing white clothes during attacks) emerged in the 1770s in response to attempts by landlords to raise rents and clear tenants from their estates in order to move to pasture farming. These groups were part trade union, part freemason and part gang, enforcing oaths of allegiance, holding kangaroo courts and carrying out the execution of those deemed to have broken the code. There are countless examples of local skirmishes developing into extreme violence perpetrated by the Whiteboys and other militant secret societies, even before the Orange Order was formed. One particularly unpleasant instance was when Catholic Defenders attacked a schoolteacher's home in the small town of Forkhill in Co. Armagh in 1791. The local Presbyterian minister wrote an account of the attack:

> You know Barkeley, who was stabbed by Donnelly – he is one of the schoolmasters of Forkhill . . . in rushed a Body of Hellhounds – not content with cutting and stabbing him in several places, they drew a cord around his neck till his Tongue was forced out – It they cut off along with three fingers of his right hand – They then cut out his wife's tongue and some of the villains held her whilst another with a case knife cut off her Tongue and four of her fingers one after another –They cut and battered her in different places – She I fear cannot recover.[5]

The point of this example is not its extreme violence, nor the background of the attackers or the victims; rather it is emblematic of the fact that, by this point in Ireland's history, religious identity had become a badge of economic and political division. While this grisly tale depicts an attack on a group of Protestants by a sectarian Catholic gang, it was actually a small incident in a period of wider community unrest in Co. Armagh. This friction had been caused by economic competition between Catholic and Protestant groups in the area, due to overpopulation in Armagh as a result of the expansion of the linen industry. The pressure on land resulted in trading rivalries between mainly Protestant linen drapers and Catholic linen weavers, as well as competition over land rents. This was made all the more combustible by the dramatic fluctuations in the price of linen at the time, which added to the economic insecurity of all concerned. That Catholic and Protestant communities were already separated along religious lines, had a divided historical inheritance and differing economic interests all made it extremely easy for economic feuds to become religious ones.

The Orange Order was founded in Co. Armagh in 1795 as a direct result of sectarian unrest between Catholics and Protestants, who had different political grievances and economic interests, as well as different faiths. When they looked for a group identity – what might today be called a 'brand' – that could unite the various Protestant sectarian societies, they looked back to the iconic event of a century before, when the Protestant King William (Prince of Orange) defeated the Catholic former King James II.

There are many examples of Catholic activism during the last few centuries, but the Orange Order has probably been more active than most in bridging the gap between religion, history and politics, and it continues to play a role today that is not seen to the same degree elsewhere. An oft-quoted example is the fact that from the creation of Northern Ireland in 1921 until the suspension of the unionist-dominated regime in 1972, only three members of the Northern Ireland Cabinet were not members of the Orange Order (and one of those was a Catholic and therefore ineligible to join, even had he wanted to). While the tradition of Orangeism emerged in response to squabbles over economic resources in the late eighteenth century, over the next two hundred years it became the social and cultural glue that bound religious Protestantism to political unionism and that maintained the bonds of loyalty and solidarity to Britain and the Crown in the face of external threats to their position. They were kin, blood-brothers even, not just friends, acquaintances or temporary political allies.

There are a number of apocryphal tales linked to Orange commemorations and the way in which historical events have been refracted and distorted through time into a new mythology. The following exchange between an Orangeman and an English tourist is facetious, but all the same it hints at the way in which politics, culture and religion have been collapsed inwards to the point that they possess their own logic and meaning:

> The tourist watching the Twelfth parades turns to a local Orangeman and says: 'I say, old chap, could you tell me what this means?' The 'native' stared at him and muttered 'The Twelfth'. 'I know' persisted the Englishman, 'but what does the Twelfth mean?' 'Man are you ignorant,' replied the Ulsterman, 'away home and read your bible.'[6]

Whether or not the story is true, the point remains that religion, history and politics are entwined in Ireland to an unusual degree, and have been twisted and distorted over time to the point where the myth itself contains its own legitimacy. In reality, the idea that William of Orange fought and defeated James II to protect the Protestantism of the English Crown and to save Irish Protestants from the clammy hands of the Vatican is about as accurate as John Wayne's role in *Stagecoach* in terms of understanding the early US settlers' relations with Native Americans. The fact that William was really fighting a larger battle against the growing threat of Louis XIV and had the blessing of Pope Innocent XI in his campaign has been conveniently airbrushed out of Irish Protestant folklore ever since. A more recent suggestion that King Billy was gay (by British gay rights activist Peter Tatchell in 2008) also opens up an avenue that many unionists would prefer not to go down, preferring to see the claim as 'deliberately offensive and provocative'.[7]

Whatever his sexual orientation, in truth Ireland was a relatively insignificant but useful battleground where William could assert his influence by attacking and defeating James, who had allied himself politically to Louis XIV. This gap between myth and reality is the reason for the consternation expressed when a portrait entitled *The Entry of King William into Ireland* by the Dutch painter Pieter Van der Meulen was unveiled in 1933 in the newly built Stormont, home to the Northern Ireland Parliament. Oblivious to important local sensitivities, the painting depicted King William alongside the Pope, and it had to be hastily removed from the chamber after angry complaints from the unionist contingent.[8]

Of course, Catholic nationalists are equally capable of being seduced by the Chinese Whispers of history, and it has frequently been remarked that the Irish do not let the facts get in the way of a good story. The Irish are not alone in this respect, though they have perhaps more history and more stories than most.

It is difficult to understand the political relationship between unionists and nationalists in Northern Ireland these days without coming to terms with this historical inheritance. Obviously unionist and nationalist political behaviour today is not driven by the past in any active sense, but it is certainly subliminally informed by it. Protestants (or more precisely, Anglicans who formed the Church of Ireland) were given a privileged position within society and quickly gave their political allegiance to the English Crown and, in due course, to the British Parliament. The Gaelic Catholic population were conversely penalized, disenfranchised and condemned to a second-class form of existence, as a result of which the majority felt little by way of allegiance or loyalty to the political system they found themselves imprisoned within.

This blunt political geography by no means negates the fact that, over many generations, Protestants forged their own destiny through sheer hard work, in the face of hostility from Catholics in Ireland and periodic British neglect or political mendacity. Similarly, it needs to be remembered that not all Protestants were equally rewarded for their loyalty and hard work, especially (ironically) after the Battle of the Boyne and the Williamite Settlement that followed it. While Presbyterians formed the dominant Protestant denomination in Ulster after the Plantation, these 'dissenters' were themselves caught up in a net of discrimination, targeted primarily at the Catholic population. After the introduction of the penal laws for example, Presbyterian marriages were not legally recognized unless the ceremony had been performed in the Church of Ireland – a restriction that lasted until 1782. The 1704 Test Act to 'prevent the further spread of popery' included the 'Sacramental Test', which required all those holding public office in Ireland to take communion in the Church of Ireland. While the primary target of this legislation remained the Catholic population, its introduction saw the mass resignation of Presbyterians from publicly elected office, as the alternative would have required a renunciation of their faith.

The Test Act excluded many Presbyterians from holding public office until it was rescinded in 1780, and it had very practical economic and legal implications. Given that marriages carried out by Presbyterian ministers were regarded as invalid by the state, the offspring of such marriages were deemed to be illegitimate, which had obvious knock-on effects for inheritance entitlements.

This puts the legacy of the Battle of the Boyne and the victory of Protestant King William over Catholic King James into a different perspective and casts a rather unforgiving light on the fact that, throughout most of the eighteenth century, religious tensions were not so much between Catholics and Protestants as between the Church of Ireland and its Presbyterian cousins. A mere fourteen years after William of Orange 'saved' them from the clutches of Catholic King James, therefore, Presbyterians found themselves deprived of some of the most basic principles of citizenship. This poetic irony was not lost on the Presbyterian community, with one contemporary writer pointing out the injustice of the situation:

It seems somewhat hard, and savours of the most scandalous ingratitude that the very people who drank deepest of the Popish fury, and were the most vigorous to show their zeal and their courage in opposing tyranny and Popery, and on the foot of whose forwardness and valour the Church of Ireland recovered herself from her low condition, should now be requited with so injurious a treatment as to be linked with these very Papists they fought against. This will certainly be no encouragement to those Dissenters to join with their brethren the next time the Papists shall please to take arms and attempt their throats.[9]

This indignation is understandable. However, it was driven not by internal theological disagreement between Protestant denominations, but by different economic interests: Presbyterians were merchants, manufacturers and businessmen, while the Church of Ireland had its power base in land-ownership and agriculture. The latter group felt increasingly threatened by the former (especially in Ulster, where Presbyterians were numerically strong and as Belfast began to industrialize) and attempted to exclude them through its control of the political system. The Church of Ireland even suggested that landlords should not give leases to Presbyterian tenants; or, if they did, to charge them higher rents than their Church of Ireland neighbours.

The other interesting aspect of the above quotation is that it shows how the past can be both remembered and deployed as a political argument. This becomes a recurring theme within the development of unionist and nationalist political behaviour over the next two centuries. The sense of entitlements due as a result of past sacrifices was to become a familiar refrain and helps to explain why history – or a particular narrative of the past – retained such political currency within contemporary events.

The disadvantage experienced by Presbyterians during this period is one of the reasons why so many of them migrated to America and established such a strong bond with those fighting for independence from the English Crown. By the time of the American War of Independence, it is estimated that around 200,000 Presbyterians had arrived in America seeking relief from the penal laws and joining the democratic fight against English Crown forces. Their enthusiasm for the American cause subsequently caused President Theodore Roosevelt to remark that 'the fiercest and most ardent Americans of all were the Presbyterian Irish settlers and their descendants'.[10]

While such discrimination led to a brief alliance between Presbyterians and Catholics at the end of the eighteenth century, with the emergence of the 'United Irishmen' in the 1790s, this was a relatively short interlude. Irish Presbyterians were relatively wealthy but politically powerless, with a leadership that was educated, literate and remarkably internationalist, enthused by the French and American revolutions:

> What is that in your hand?
> – It is a branch
> Of What?
> – Of the Tree of Liberty
> Where did it first grow?
> – In America
> Where does it bloom?
> – In France
> Where did the seed fall?
> – In Ireland
> When will the moon be full?
> – When the four quarters meet.[11]

Despite the energetic leadership the Presbyterians brought to the United Irishmen, the movement eventually dwindled due to a combination of political naivety, military failure and legislative reforms introduced by the British government that reduced the discrimination suffered by the Presbyterian community in Ireland.

But they would not go down without a fight. The activism of the United Irishmen came to a head with the 1798 Rebellion, an armed insurrection of Catholics and some Presbyterians against British rule in Ireland. The rebellion raged for most of the summer months of 1798 and resulted in over 10,000 fatalities, but the battle was lost before it had even begun. The insurgents were split politically by this stage over their aims and objectives and were a shambles militarily. Wolfe Tone, one of the figureheads of the movement, had earlier gone to America and France to recruit soldiers to fight in support of the United Irishmen's cause. He returned in 1796 with a force of over 14,000 French troops, but due to calamitous seamanship and atrocious weather off the coast of Ireland, they were unable to land and returned home to France. By 1798 the movement was riddled with British informers who knew much of what was being planned and could prepare accordingly. The 1798 Rebellion could be said to have been a military failure, but a political success, in that it demonstrated the potential for a joint manifesto for change.

The mythology of 1798 remains strong within the contemporary republican tradition, as (however fleetingly) it provided evidence of a secular liberal and internationalist potential, where Protestant, Catholic and Dissenter could overcome their sectarian pasts, recognize their shared commonality as Irishmen, and fight British interference in their common political and economic interests. That such romantic notions were to be dispelled by the harsh winds of political and economic reality did not diminish the extent to which they were cherished within the bosoms of Irish nationalists for generations thereafter.

The combination of religion and economic and political self-interest proved to be a heady brew in the formation of both unionist and nationalist political identities from this point onwards. Contemporary political and economic pressures promoted separation rather than integration between the Protestant and Catholic populations of Ireland – populations that were divided by religion, by different versions of history, by economic interests, by political ideology and even by geography, with the Protestants strong in the industrializing northern counties of Ulster and the Catholics more numerous in the agricultural southern regions of the island.

## FAMINE, PROTEST AND RADICALIZATION

We must not aim at giving more than wholesome food.
Charles Edward Trevelyan[12]

The Irish potato famine of 1845–49 – known in Gaelic as *An Gorta Mor* (The Great Hunger) – ravaged and radicalized the country. The effects of a new and deadly potato disease, *Phytophthora infestans* (commonly known as the 'blight'), were exacerbated by the fact that nearly a third of the Irish population had become dependent on the potato for food. Some estimates suggest that, when the disease first hit Ireland in 1845, up to half of the entire potato harvest was lost. The following year, up to three-quarters of the potatoes grown in Ireland were destroyed by blight, condemning over 750,000 people to hunger and destitution. To add insult to injury, though the blight did not hit Irish subsistence farmers as hard in 1847 or 1848, they had fewer seed potatoes available to plant, and so the harvest remained low. Already weakened by hunger and disease, their suffering thus intensified during these years.

The overdependence of subsistence farmers on this one crop meant that starvation, disease and famine were inevitable. People started dying of hunger and associated disease (such as typhus and dysentery) in autumn 1846, and there was no let-up for the next five years. Those who had the means to leave did so, while the less fortunate were, in some cases, worked to death in badly conceived poor-relief public works schemes. It was a desperate and devastating situation, and by 1847, following a particularly harsh winter, many of the dead were simply being buried in mass graves and covered in quicklime. Stories of gaunt, ghostly and haggard figures eating grass to survive were recorded by eye-witnesses and visiting writers and eventually became the stuff of legend within Irish popular culture. The deaths continued through 1848, 1849 and 1850, as a combination of British government policies failed to tackle the famine effectively.

While precise figures are not available, it is generally agreed that around 1 million people died, while another million left Ireland between 1845 and 1851. Up to 2 million more left over the next twenty years. Even when the famine was over, the high level of emigration continued, so that in the following sixty years an additional 6 million left. The principal destination of the emigrants was the United States, with approximately 80 per cent choosing to go there.[13]

Quite apart from the immense suffering it inflicted on the unfortunate people at the sharp end, the famine was crucial to the future political development of Irish nationalism for a number of reasons. For one thing, the exodus from Ireland in the middle of the nineteenth century sowed the seeds of the Irish diaspora, which today is believed to number some 70 million people. While the depth of this ethnic inheritance needs to be treated with extreme caution, large numbers of Irish emigrants went to the United States and maintained a sense of Irish identity. This was handed down through several generations, and when political violence erupted in Northern Ireland in 1969, some of these Irish-Americans took a close interest in events and played an important role in the conflict itself, as well as in the peace process that followed in the 1990s.

While there had been previous famines and earlier waves of migration from Ireland, it was the Great Hunger and its aftermath that provided the critical mass to Irish-America that sustained it as a viable ethnic community in cities such as New York and Boston and that led to external interventions in Irish politics at critical periods in the twentieth century.

Given that Ireland's population before 1845 was in the region of 8–9 million, the numbers involved represent a massive social dislocation, and the population to this day has not recovered to pre-famine levels (currently standing at under 7 million in the Irish Republic and Northern Ireland combined).

The exodus of people from Ireland to North America provided the raw material for the establishment of ethnic networks that remain today. This quickly translated into the formation of social co-operation, political alliances and eventually to a re-involvement in the politics of their home-land. The most radical elements formed the Irish Republican Brotherhood in the United States, which provided an early model for the type of militant Irish republican violence that was to emerge in the twentieth century. More immediately, the famine period left a lasting and visceral grievance within Catholic Ireland against the predominantly Protestant landlord class and against the British in particular, who were seen as callous and vindictive in their treatment of those who starved to death:

> Weary men, what reap ye? – Golden corn for the stranger.
> What sow ye? – Human corpses that wait for the avenger.
> Fainting forms, hunger-stricken, what see you in the offing?
> Stately ships to bear our food away, amid the stranger's scoffing.
> There's a proud array of soldiers – what do they round your door?
> They guard our masters' granaries from the thin hands of the poor.
> Pale mothers, wherefore weeping – Would to God that we
> were dead;
> Our children swoon before us, and we cannot give them bread.[14]

This is a simplification of what was a complicated set of political and economic relationships, but no one wants a lesson in political economy when they are starving or facing destitution. Nevertheless, the contemporary cliché of the 'perfect storm' is an appropriate metaphor to describe the period: a disinterested British government that was more concerned about economic policy than the plight of starving peasants in Ireland; repeated failure of the potato harvest over successive years; a landlord class, many of whom were also suffering due to lack of income; and an Irish economy that was itself blighted for a number of years and had increased poverty well before the famine hit. The population was at a high, which served to increase pressure on the land and on jobs; rents were rising because of a lack of housing; and wages were falling due to a dip in the economy.

Opinion differs on whether the famine represents a watershed moment in Irish history, after which the dynamics of economic and political mobilization fundamentally changed course, or whether it simply sharpened and accelerated trends that had been established earlier in the nineteenth century. While the broad brushstrokes are relatively obvious, the fine detail is more obscure. Why did the 1845–49 famine wreak such human havoc when previous famines had not?[15] Why were some agricultural regions more dependent on the potato crop than others? Why did some villages receive more assistance than others? Crucially, who was ultimately responsible for the famine – the landlords or a British government that was more interested in preaching the bible of self-help economics than in the human cost of its non-interventionist policies?

Perhaps more fundamentally, was it even a 'famine' at all? It certainly was for those who starved to death and for those who had to board the 'coffin-ships' to America and elsewhere. But it was only a famine for some – those who depended on the potato crop to live, those who had no other means of survival, and those whom the wider community structures (particularly the Protestant landlords) either could not or would not help. But in fact, there was plenty of food in Ireland in the middle of the nineteenth century, and much of it was exported during the famine period – a time that saw livestock numbers in Ireland increase. The British government knew that large sections of the Irish population relied on the potato for survival, and it knew that the potato was a notoriously unreliable crop. Yet no restrictions were placed on food exports by the government during the famine period. Again this has been taken as evidence that it regarded those starving to death as 'expendable'.

Thus, there was no shortage of food and no lack of warning. But there was a lack of political will to save these 'undeserving poor' – a concept that had been hard-wired into the English mentality since the days of Henry VIII and that persisted long after, aided and abetted by the anti-Irish racism of the time, which held that the Irish were a savage sub-species.

At its radical edge, the famine was seen as the fault of the feckless, lazy and weak elements of Irish society, whose eradication, though perhaps unfortunate at a human level, would produce a leaner, fitter and more economically responsible society. This was social Darwinism, red in tooth and claw.

Clearly, the famine was not an unforeseeable act of God. Nor was its *cause* an unfortunate dependence of the poorest sections of society on a notoriously unreliable crop and even more unreliable weather. These, along with the blundering responses of both landlords and government, were actually symptoms of a more fundamental and frightening reality.

This amounts to an allegation (not shared by all historians) that the famine was allowed to happen by an English government that was obsessed by the Malthusian logic that Ireland was overpopulated and that was devoted to liberal economic values. Equally damning is the suggestion that the English response to the famine was directed not at keeping as many people as possible alive within the financial constraints of the time, but at consolidating property ownership and fast-tracking more commercial forms of farming. In other words, the English response to the famine was wilful, not negligent.

According to this line of argument, then, the reason that over a million people died and another 1–2 million emigrated was not a lack of food in Ireland, but a structural inequality within the Irish economy, where large sections of those at the bottom of the economic food-chain were forced into dependence on one unreliable crop by a government that did not prioritize their survival. While the fundamental causes of, and responsibility for, the famine remain a matter of some debate between historians, it is reasonable to conclude that too little was done too late, and much of what was done was inadequate to deal with the scale of the problem, especially from 1847 onwards.

British government complicity in the Great Hunger became a piece of received wisdom for succeeding generations who survived in Ireland and who spilled out beyond its shores. It joined the dots between the British government's 'voodoo economics' of self-help at a time of destitution and all the previous efforts to subjugate, Anglicize and dominate the Irish Catholic population. This bitter enmity hastened – rather than created – a political radicalization against the nature of land ownership, and also increased agitation for Irish self-government to ensure that such a calamity did not reoccur.

New militant groups emerged after the famine, such as the Young Irelanders or the Fenians/Irish Republican Brotherhood (IRB), which successfully connected resentment over land ownership and the behaviour of landlords to the desire for local political control. The Fenians – from the Gaelic word *Fianna* (warriors, army) – emerged around 1858 and combined recruitment drives (especially in the United States, where, of course, many people had recently arrived to escape the potato famine) with an ideology that was overtly separatist. Fenian agitation and political campaigning helped to crystallize the key issues of agrarian unrest and political grievance, with a strategy of unconstitutional activity, including violent confrontation.

The result was modern Irish nationalism, with two dominant strands that remain in evidence to this day. The first strand was a form of Irish nationalism that sought political separatism from Britain through constitutional action. This led directly to the home rule movement and, more recently, to the constitutional nationalism practised by the Social Democratic and Labour Party (SDLP) and, eventually, by Sinn Fein. The second strand led to a form of unconstitutional militant republicanism that pursued physical force as its dominant strategy, leading to the formation of the Irish Republican Army (IRA) and the guerrilla war against British rule in Ireland masterminded by Michael Collins, through to the formation of the Provisional IRA in 1969 and other militant republican groups thereafter.

As Catholics began to cluster around a political agenda that sought political autonomy and self-government – colloquially known as 'home rule' – unionists opposed it, fearing instead 'Rome rule' (see below). The battle lines between unionists and nationalists had long since been drawn, and the issue of 'home rule' became the anvil on which Northern Ireland was hammered into existence.

## HOME RULE AND THE STRUGGLE FOR POLITICAL CONTROL

> Life springs from death, and from the graves of patriotic men and women spring living nations.
>
> Patrick Pearse, 1915

The issue of 'home rule' dominated the Irish and British political landscape from the 1870s until the signing of the Anglo-Irish Treaty and the partition of Ireland in 1921. While unionists were overwhelmingly opposed to it, this was not actually a campaign for Irish separatism, but merely for regional self-government within the British Empire. In essence, it meant that Ireland would have a parliament that would deal with local matters, while the imperial parliament in London would retain overall sovereignty. Its nationalist advocates saw it as a means of achieving moderate political reform that could protect the Irish Catholic population from the worst aspects of British policy in Ireland. Moderate Irish nationalists also saw home rule as a means of drawing support away from the more militant groups that had emerged and that had more radical demands based on Irish independence.

Unionists were opposed to home rule on religious, political and economic grounds. They saw it as the first stage in the disintegration of the political union of Ireland and Britain, and while it might begin as a form of local government, it would end in the complete separation of the two countries. The fact that the parliament would be established in Dublin, while the unionist population was predominantly located in the northern counties of Ulster, reinforced their fears that it would be a Catholic nationalist-dominated regime that would be ruinous to the Protestant unionist position. There was also a worry that the religious freedom of the Protestant population would not be tolerated in a home rule-Ireland, and this led to the slogan 'Home rule is Rome rule'. Unionists were also opposed to the policy on economic grounds, as they felt that the industrialized northern counties of Ulster would end up subsidizing and being dragged down by the agricultural South.

By the 1870s, the Catholic nationalists had become politically organized, forming the Irish Home Government Association, which became the Home Rule League in 1873. By the end of the decade, Charles Stewart Parnell had reconstituted this group as the Irish Parliamentary Party (IPP) and had begun fighting and winning elections. Under Parnell's leadership, the IPP became a political force at Westminster and began to lean on the British political elite to deliver political reform.

Under pressure from the IPP, British Prime Minister William Gladstone introduced the First Home Rule Bill in January 1886. This caused convulsions within the British political system and led Lord Randolph Churchill to resign from the Conservatives to form his own 'Fourth Party' in protest at what he saw as Conservative dithering over the issue. In February, Churchill made an explosive visit to Belfast, in order to, as he put it, 'play the Orange card'. By May of 1886, he was warning people in Britain that unionists in Ireland would resist by force if necessary, claiming that 'Ulster will fight, and Ulster will be right'. This warning bell has since resonated down through generations of unionists in Northern Ireland whenever they have felt their constitutional position within the United Kingdom being undermined by the actions of British government policy.

As the nineteenth century drew to a close and the twentieth century dawned, the future of home rule became a captive of British parliamentary arithmetic and manoeuvring between the Liberals on the one hand and the Conservatives on the other, with the Irish Parliamentary Party attempting to play one off against the other when they held the balance of power.

With the failure of the First Home Rule Bill in 1886 and of the Second in 1893, Irish nationalist opinion became increasingly frustrated, while unionists lived in a semi-permanent state of insecurity, fearing that it was only a matter of time before Irish home rule would be accepted by the British parliament. Despite the rather modest framework of the Third Home Rule Bill of 1912, which proposed the devolution of limited powers to a new Irish parliament (excluding policing, taxation and defence policy), many unionists regarded it as a threat to their British identity, their religious liberty and their political and economic interests. The Conservative leader, Andrew Bonar Law, reacted by implicitly defending the unionist right to resist home rule by force, commenting in a landmark speech that: 'I can imagine no length of resistance to which Ulster can go in which I would not be prepared to support them'.

The unionists were now led by Dublin barrister Edward Carson and his close ally from Ulster, James Craig, both of whom spearheaded a popular unionist mobilization against home rule. Carson was mainly an orator and flamboyant propagandist, while Craig was an organizer and a 'details man': 'Each had what the other lacked. Pooling their resources, they became a third and undeniable person. Effective apart, they were irresistible together.'[16] Their co-ordination of unionist opposition to the Third Home Rule Bill certainly presented a formidable leadership, around which their supporters in Ireland and Britain could rally. They announced that 28 September 1912 was to be 'Ulster Day', when a solemn covenant would be entered into by the people. This would demonstrate that the British government had broken the contract from which it derived its legitimacy to govern. The text of the Ulster Solemn League and Covenant has become an iconic statement of unionist conditional loyalty, suggesting a continuing allegiance to the *theory* of the British Empire, but a readiness to break with the *practice* of government policy. At a more basic level, it represented a threat to the British government that unionist resistance to home rule would include a resort to violence, if necessary:

> Being convinced in our consciences that Home Rule would be disastrous to the material well-being of Ulster as well as the whole of Ireland, subversive to our civil and religious freedom, destructive of our citizenship, and perilous to the unity of the Empire, we, whose names are underwritten ... hereby pledge ourselves in solemn

Covenant throughout this our time of threatened calamity to stand by one another in defending for ourselves and our children our cherished position of equal citizenship in the United Kingdom, and in using all means which may be found necessary to defeat the present conspiracy to set up a home rule parliament in Ireland. And in the event of such a parliament being forced upon us we further solemnly and mutually pledge ourselves to refuse to recognise its authority.

. . . God save the King.[17]

In essence, Ulster Day was a carefully stage-managed publicity stunt, as nearly 250,000 men signed the Covenant and 230,000 women signed a similar declaration. Today, this might be regarded as an exercise in 'people power', where mass protest signals a breakdown in the relationship between government and people. At the time, it provided a very public demonstration to the outside world of unionist determination, solidarity and commitment to resist the home rule policy.

More ominously, unionists had been preparing for physical resistance by establishing a volunteer militia – in other words, they began to establish a private army within the United Kingdom. Initially, in January 1912, they began drilling in public, staying on the right side of the law by gaining licences from sympathetic magistrates. By the end of 1912, this loosely constituted militia was formalized into the Ulster Volunteer Force (UVF) and had enrolled an impressive 90,000 recruits. Craig, Carson and their colleagues within the unionist leadership realized that, if they were to be taken seriously by the British government, they would have to arm the UVF, despite the perverse situation this created, whereby unionists, who claimed to be British, were preparing for war against the United Kingdom. In April 1914, unionists smuggled over 25,000 rifles and 5 million rounds of ammunition into Ulster from Germany. The gun had arrived in Irish politics and was there to stay for the rest of the twentieth century.

By 1914, the government was in a difficult position. If it pushed through with home rule, it risked provoking a campaign of violence from the UVF, which had been preparing for such a fight for over two years. But if it backed away from the home rule policy, then moderate nationalism in Ireland would be destroyed and an even more widespread campaign of violence was likely from militant Irish republicans. Whichever way the government jumped, British policy was likely to spark violence between the armed unionists in Ulster and the nationalists in the rest of the Island. It was damned if it did, and damned if it didn't. The First World War intervened and served only to radicalize both sides even further. On Easter Monday 1916, a small group of revolutionary Irish nationalists occupied government buildings in Dublin and proclaimed an Irish Republic. Like the 1798 Rebellion, while the Easter Rising was a military failure, it sowed seeds of political activism that flowered for generations afterwards.

The 'solution' reached at the end of the war was to legislate for home rule but allow the mainly unionist counties of Ulster to opt out of the new arrangement by having their own parliament in Belfast. More accurately, six of Ulster's nine counties would be included in a new region of the United Kingdom, to be known as 'Northern Ireland'. The remaining twenty-six counties of Ireland were to be known as the 'Free State', which would have a devolved parliament in Dublin. Ireland was to be partitioned into two separate areas, the larger Free State with a 90 per cent Catholic nationalist majority, and the smaller Northern Ireland with a stable two-thirds Protestant unionist majority.

Unionists were unhappy and nationalists were unhappy, but neither group was so outraged that they were willing to pursue united and violent action. Carson regarded the partition of Ireland and the creation of Northern Ireland as a political and personal failure, and he retired from public life. James Craig was equally glum, but felt duty bound to lead the unionist majority of Northern Ireland into their new and uncertain future.

By 1920, therefore, the partition of Ireland was the 'least-worst option' for many people – hardly a ringing endorsement of the new political system in either part of Ireland, but just about sufficient – for just about enough people – to limp (if not stride) forward into the new political territory of Northern Ireland.

It is difficult to overstate the importance of the 'home rule' issue in the development of unionist and nationalist politics in Ireland. The 'death by a thousand cuts' nature of the policy saw British politicians vacillate between opposition and support over a fifty-year period, while from 1880 to 1914 it took three attempts to get legislation through parliament, only to have its enactment delayed for another six years by the outbreak of the First World War. Unionists were left embittered, scarred and split by the experience, while the delay in the granting of home rule breathed new life into militant republicanism. Frustrated at the delay in the implementation of home rule, the IRA stepped up its campaign of violence by shooting and killing two policemen in Co. Tipperary in January 1919. This was the beginning of the War of Independence, which lasted until 1921 and the signing of the Anglo-Irish Treaty.

## THE BIRTH OF NORTHERN IRELAND: FROM LABOUR PAINS TO PROBLEM CHILD

> We will be cautious in our legislation. We will be absolutely honest and fair in administering the law.
>
> James Craig, 1921

> I have always said I am an Orangeman first and a politician and Member of this Parliament afterwards ... The Hon. Member must remember that in the South they boasted of a Catholic State. They still boast of Southern Ireland being a Catholic State. All I boast is that we are a Protestant Parliament and Protestant State.
>
> James Craig, 1934

These two quotes from James Craig hint at the dysfunction of the political system in Northern Ireland after 1921. The note of conciliation within the first remark, made by Craig shortly after becoming the first prime minister of Northern Ireland in 1921, was swept away within a few short years through a combination of an insecure/arrogant unionist community, a disinterested/periodically hostile British government and an openly bitter/apathetic nationalist population.

The second remark has frequently been misused to paint Craig as a Protestant bigot; but rather than as the proclamation of a sectarian mission statement, it should be viewed as a somewhat artless attempt to ingratiate himself with his unionist followers. Craig remained prime minister until his death in 1940, but his political career shrivelled into political failure. Certainly, he played a vital role for unionism during the home rule crisis and he did indeed steer Northern Ireland through the difficult 1921–25 period, when its very existence was under threat. But in the end he presided over the creation of a one-party state, a parched and barren political land-scape with an unsustainable economy and a society that lurched between anger and apathy, to the long-term detriment of the whole population. Craig's legacy was a 'sad anti-climax' where 'Northern Ireland became not a half-way house sheltering a united and contented people, but a ramshackle lean-to rejected by one third of the population'.[18]

During the 1920s, the political culture within Northern Ireland was dominated by fear and uncertainty, seasoned with hearty pinches of bitter-ness and sectarianism. This insecurity about their political position has remained a key feature of unionists' psyche into modern times. Unionists, after all, had only managed to escape an all-Ireland home rule parliament by the narrowest of margins and had had to form a paramilitary militia – the UVF – and then threaten political violence against the state to which they declared allegiance.

Few marriages thrive when one partner holds the other at gunpoint, and right from the beginning unionists have felt they are in a loveless union, their callous and ungrateful partner periodically hinting at the attractions of divorce. Unrequited love can be a corrosive emotion, and this regular fear of abandonment has frequently combined with a sense of entitlement because of the loyalty unionists have displayed towards Britain. While it is easy to scoff at such sentiments, those who wish to understand unionism need to grasp this historical inheritance. The most lyrical and powerful demonstration of unionism's difficult relationship with Britain was written in 1912 by that great defender of British imperialism, Rudyard Kipling. His defence of unionist opposition to home rule in the poem 'Ulster 1912' remains as potent today as on the day of its publication in the *Morning Post* newspaper a century ago:

> The dark eleventh hour
> Draws on and sees us sold
> To every evil power
> We fought against of old.
> Rebellion, rapine, hate,
> Oppression, wrong and greed
> Are loosed to rule our fate,
> By England's act and deed.
>
> The faith in which we stand
> The laws we made and guard,
> Our honour lives and land
> Are given for reward
> To murder done by night,
> To treason taught by day,
> To folly sloth and spite,
> And we are thrust away.
>
> The blood our fathers spilt
> Our love, our toils our pains,
> Are counted us for guilt,
> And only bind our chains.

Before an Empire's eyes,
The traitor claims his price.
What need of further lies?
We are the sacrifice.[19]

. . .

Unionists clearly could not trust Britain; they certainly could not trust the Catholic nationalist community on either part of the island; and they were not even sure if they could trust each other. The sense of being besieged by hostile forces was certainly the mood of unionism during the 1920s, and it has never really left them. This culture of fear translated into a desire for political domination. Unionists were a majority in Northern Ireland, but were not so dominant that they could relax and view the Catholic population as unthreatening. Nationalists, on the other hand, were in the minority, but were not so few as to give up all political ambition. The nationalist community was too large for unionists to ignore, but its members could not be assimilated as fellow citizens either.

The predictable result was that unionists craved political control of Northern Ireland and inherited a system that allowed the majority party to exert control. Initial rules to protect the nationalist minority (such as proportional representation) were quickly eradicated by a unionist party that understood that electoral cohesion meant political control. Northern Ireland became a *de facto* one-party regime within the United Kingdom, with no rotation of power between the unionist and nationalist communities for over fifty years. The Unionist Party won every election between 1921 and 1969, while the Nationalist Party lost on every occasion. The legacy of this was huge apathy on both sides towards the political system, given that the outcome was such a foregone conclusion. The nationalist community became sullen and withdrawn due to decades of political exclusion and systemic discrimination. The inertia is demonstrated by the fact that, during this period (1921–69), over 37 per cent of all seats went unopposed, while in the fifty-two seat parliament at Stormont, unionists never won fewer than thirty-two seats.

From the outside (especially in London) Northern Ireland seemed to be a stable part of the United Kingdom. However, appearances can be deceptive, and nationalist resentment and anger eventually began to bubble to the surface. While the unionists and then also the British government tried to keep the lid on these frustrations, through various combinations of piecemeal political reform and harsh security policies, momentum grew during the 1960s to the point that it could not be contained. Politics went onto the streets; protests led to counter-protests; and the latent sectarianism that had been nurtured within the system for generations became manifest. By the time Britain and the rest of the world woke up to the fact that Northern Ireland had been incubating a serious political illness, it was too late to cure it – at least until a significant amount of self-harm had taken place.

# CHAPTER TWO

# WHY POLITICS FAILED AND VIOLENCE BEGAN, 1921–72

THE EMERGENCE OF political violence in Northern Ireland at the end of the 1960s was entirely predictable. The fact that it was not predicted by those who had the capacity to do something about it partly explains why it broke out in the first place. It was a product of political dysfunction on the one hand and, on the other, the grievances and frustrations of the nationalist community. This combined negatively with the fear and insecurity of the unionist population and the wilful neglect and ignorance of the British government. Politics failed because, from its formation in 1921 until its suspension in 1972, the political system was corrupt and corrupting. The Stormont government was dominated by the unionist majority and was focused on excluding the nationalist minority. As the formal political system was a practical irrelevance to most nationalists, as well as a hated symbol of their subservient status, they largely opposed and ignored it. The grievances smouldered and intensified during the 1920s, 1930s and 1940s and only required a spark to ignite them.

## RESISTANCE AND VIOLENCE

A tension has existed since the eighteenth century between reformist and radical types of Irish nationalism. One strand has sought 'constructive engagement' with Britain and attempted to use the political system to achieve change. This was the approach of the Irish Parliamentary Party and (eventually) the Nationalist Party led by Eddie McAteer at

Stormont – play by the rules, use the formal parliamentary system, build networks and trust among those with the power to deliver change.

The other strand of Irish nationalist opinion has adopted a more radical strategy – ignore the formal system, rigged by the powerful to maintain their interests come what may; break the rules; fight dirty if necessary; and build networks from the ground up – networks that will eventually become more powerful and relevant than the formal political system.

This was the preferred approach of the Irish Republican Brotherhood. It led to armed insurrections, such as the 1916 Easter Rising, and would eventually lead to the arrival of the Provisional IRA in 1969. It has also been the favoured strategy of dissident republicans in recent years, despite the establishment of new political structures in Northern Ireland that are acceptable to the vast majority of people there.

Back in the 1920s and the decades that followed, the record of the Nationalist Party at Stormont in 'playing by the rules' was less than impressive. In fifty years, the only legislation it managed to get through the Stormont parliament was the Wild Birds Act of 1932 – with such issues as unemployment, poor housing, electoral malpractice and the intimidatory nature of the state, this was hardly at the top of the political agenda. The legislative framework enshrined in the Special Powers Act (and policed through the newly formed *Royal* Ulster Constabulary and a wholly Protestant militia called the 'B Specials') made it abundantly clear that Northern Ireland was British, not Irish; and while reformist Irish nationalists attempted to use the formal political system to air grievances and highlight issues of concern, they achieved little of substance from the 1920s to the 1960s.

It is difficult to overstate the chaos, confusion and emotion that accompanied the creation of Northern Ireland in 1921. It was not a smooth transition. At the stroke of a political pen, a legal line was drawn across Ireland, separating six of Ulster's nine northern counties from the other twenty-six. These were not just any six counties, of course: they contained the majority of the Protestant and unionist population of Ireland and included the most industrialized and wealthy part of the country. Unionists were nervous and anxious, fearing that the new regime had been wrestled out of a reluctant British government, which might starve it of resources and make it politically unviable. The Boundary Commission that had been set up to decide on the final borders of Northern Ireland could have whittled the six counties down to four, which would have turned it into an enclave rather than a viable region of government with a recognizable political identity.

Nationalists in the northern counties were predictably furious, having been summarily cut off from their co-nationals on the rest of the island, transformed overnight from a majority into a minority, and delivered on a plate to their unionist foes within a political system that offered them second place in a two-horse race. Violence and sectarianism was the predictable result. By the end of 1920, more than 10,000 Catholics had been expelled from the Belfast shipyard, where they had previously found work during the First World War. They were driven out by force, pelted with ball bearings and bolts (which became known as 'Belfast confetti') while the police turned a blind eye. During 1921 and 1922, IRA violence was met with sharp reprisals by the police, and anti-Catholic violence rose sharply during the period. In one notorious case, police searching for members of Sinn Fein raided a house and shot dead five innocent people in their beds, including a seventy-year-old man and his seven-year-old grandson; another member of the family was bludgeoned to death with the sledgehammer the police had used to break their way into the house.[1] The gloves were off and the fight was on between the IRA and its supporters (a category interpreted liberally by the police) and the unionist government. Sectarian attacks were extreme, with bombs thrown at Catholic and Protestant schoolchildren, at people attending church and at people boarding public transport. Some 232 people were killed in 1922, the vast majority of whom were Catholic, as the unionist security forces 'cracked down' on what they regarded as an IRA threat to overthrow the new regime. In the two years before partition, 157 Protestants had been killed, but after the unionists got into power the death toll was noticeably higher within the Catholic community.

The Special Powers Act[2] was introduced in Northern Ireland in 1922 as an emergency measure to deal with the sectarian violence that accompanied partition. However, its sweeping powers proved extremely useful to the new police force and the unionist regime, so that the legislation remained in place long after the initial public order problems had subsided, and in fact it became the legal basis for policing and for the criminal justice system. Put bluntly, the Special Powers Act provided a structure for the legal use of violence by the police. It was just as important as any of the political actions taken thereafter, as it provided structural legitimacy for repressive policing and for the defence of unionist political control by force. The act provided the Royal Ulster Constabulary (RUC) with draconian powers, including the internment of suspects without trial; entry to a person's house without a warrant, for the purposes of interrogation; and a range of other measures designed to evade legal due process. Under its rules, there was no possibility of judicial review of RUC behaviour. It provided the police and the minister for home affairs with what amounted to a 'get out of jail free card' with its stipulation that both could 'take all such steps . . . as may be necessary for preserving peace and maintaining order'. In other words, so long as the police (and their unionist political masters at Stormont) could claim to be acting in good faith to protect public order, they were effectively provided with retrospective legal immunity for their actions, up to and including the use of lethal force. They could therefore kill people within the law, and they did so on numerous occasions, as the Special Powers Act appointed them judge, jury and executioner.

Nationalists hated the Special Powers Act. Their dislike stemmed not from the specific powers it gave the police, so much as from how it was used. It was targeted primarily at the nationalist community rather than at their unionist neighbours, and it added to their belief that they lived within a partial political system that was structurally designed to keep them down. The law (and the interpretation of the law) is not neutral in conflict situations: it takes sides.[3] The Special Powers Act took sides in Northern Ireland in helping the unionist government to cast itself as acting within the law and nationalist 'agitators' as being beyond it.

Moderate nationalists complained bitterly about the Special Powers Act and about the actions of the B Specials and the RUC, but from the 1920s until the 1960s they were unable to impact significantly on the formal political system. The Nationalist Party was sleepy at the best of times. It carped periodically from the sidelines, but was powerless to effect any real change, or even to challenge the abuses of power perpetrated by the unionist government. It pursued a form of political engagement that cast the nationalist community as hapless victims of circumstance, but it offered few solutions or strategies for action. The party lacked vigour and relevance for an increasingly restless Catholic population that wanted actions rather than words.

## THE SEEDS OF CHANGE

Ironically, the seeds of later political change were planted at the end of the Second World War, with the arrival in Britain of a new Labour government and the introduction of what is popularly known as the 'welfare state'. A key element of these reforms, in addition to a free health service, was the Butler Education Act of 1947. In the Northern Ireland context, this extended free secondary education to talented children, many of whom were young gifted Catholics who were irritated that, when they completed their studies, they were less able to get housing, less able to find a job and less able to get fair political representation within the Stormont regime than were their Protestant neighbours. For most of the 1940s and all of the 1950s, Northern Ireland was led by a curmudgeonly unionist by the name of Basil Brooke (later Lord Brookeborough), who made little secret of his sympathies or his priorities. On 20 March 1934, nine years before becoming prime minister, he addressed a meeting of the Derry Unionist Association, where he provided a blunt mission statement for unionist employers:

> I recommend those people who are Loyalists not to employ Roman Catholics, 99 per cent of whom are disloyal; I want you to remember one point in regard to the employment of people who are disloyal . . . You people who are employers have the ball at your feet. If you don't act properly now, before we know where we are we shall find ourselves in the minority instead of the majority. I want you to realise that, having done your bit, you have got your Prime Minister behind you.[4]

Judged by today's standards, this seems an outrageous remark. The political context of the period was that Brooke was 'playing to the gallery' of a unionist audience at a time of economic hardship and rising unemployment. Perhaps more shockingly, when Prime Minister James Craig was asked to repudiate Brooke's comment the following day at Stormont, he did the reverse: 'There is not one of my colleagues who does not entirely agree with him and I would not ask him to withdraw one word he said.'[5]

Brooke's was by no means an isolated voice; others were equally pugnacious in their view that unionists should receive preferential treatment in Northern Ireland over nationalists. Why? Ostensibly because the former were loyal to the British Crown and the latter were disloyal. At a more pragmatic and populist level, the unionist middle class was anxious to curry favour with its working-class supporters, who were also suffering from unemployment, poverty and poor housing. A young Stormont MP, Brian Faulkner (later to become the last prime minister of the 1921–72 Stormont administration), commented in 1955 that: 'the government must ask themselves whether it were safe to employ in government service people who openly advocated treason'.[6] Even as late as 1964, unionists were openly advocating discrimination against Catholics in employment policy: 'Charity begins at home. If we are going to employ people, we should give preference to unionists.'[7] The need for the middle-class leadership to placate a unionist working class in times of economic hardship goes some way towards explaining such outrageous remarks and attitudes. However, those on the receiving end did not have the luxury of taking such a holistic perspective and viewed them simply as evidence of malign unionist bigotry.

By this point, the cracks in the system were beginning to appear. Attempts to placate the unionist working class with sectarian rhetoric and scaremongering about the threat of Catholic domination were all very well, but did not put food on the table. One of the central planks of unionism throughout the 1930s and 1940s had been that Northern Ireland benefited economically from the Union, but the introduction of the welfare state in Britain highlighted problems that had always been there. Northern Ireland had never benefited from the Union *to the same extent* as people in 'mainland' cities, such as London, Manchester or Birmingham. Unemployment was nearly always higher than the UK national average, sometimes glaringly so: in 1961, unemployment in Northern Ireland stood at 7 per cent, compared with a UK average of 1.2 per cent. In the 1920s and 1930s, the unionist leadership had a degree of local control that allowed the middle-class leadership to placate the unionist working class by using language which emphasized that the government was targeting Protestant unemployment. The arrival of the welfare state and growing state intervention in the economy led to a slow but steady loss of local control. While unionists knew they were British, they were increasingly aware during the 1940s and 1950s that they were not as well-off as their counterparts in the rest of the UK. Attempts by the unionist government to target such unionist frustration through discriminatory housing and employment practices only served to highlight still further the sectarian nature of the region.

This negative spiral fuelled the fire of those Catholics who, having benefited from the Butler Education Act at the end of the 1940s, emerged blinking into Northern Ireland's gloomy daylight in the early 1960s. They did not demand an end to the partition of Ireland, and nor did they articulate the mantra of republican separatism. Rather more deftly, they sought to turn the Union against unionism by calling for 'British rights for British citizens' and demonstrating that the very principles of civil and religious liberty that were espoused by unionists as being at the core of their British identity were actually *being denied by them* in their administration of government in Northern Ireland.

## THE ARRIVAL OF O'NEILL: OLD WINE IN A NEW BOTTLE

By 1963, a new leader of the Unionist Party had arrived on the scene, younger and certainly more 'politically correct' than his predecessor, Lord Brookeborough. Terence O'Neill introduced a new tone into both his party and the government of Northern Ireland, with reformist rhetoric that would eventually lead to his political downfall. He did not differentiate (at least publicly) between the loyal and the disloyal, or claim that unionists should be favoured over nationalists in areas such as housing and employment. Instead, O'Neill preached the gospel of inclusiveness and reform, making it clear from the beginning that the status quo was unacceptable. He spoke of the need to 'build bridges' between the unionist and nationalist communities and to improve the overall economic performance of Northern Ireland, so that both sides of the community could prosper.

In other words, the mood music under O'Neill was up-beat and he seemed, initially at least, to be a breath of fresh air. Energetic, modern and technocratic, he looked outwards towards international investment and economic rejuvenation (which even the most ardent supporters of Brookeborough would admit was a step-change from his relatively part-time approach). This was captured by O'Neill himself in his later memoirs, when he delivered the following unflattering judgement on his predecessor:

> He [Brookeborough] was good company and a good raconteur, and those who met him imagined that he was relaxing away from his desk. What they didn't realize was that there was no desk. A man of limited intelligence, his strong suits were shooting and fishing in Fermanagh, and when he came up on Monday night or Tuesday morning it was difficult to shake him from some of his more idiotic ideas.[8]

The external atmosphere also played its part in the sense of change that pervaded unionism (and Northern Ireland more broadly) at the time. The early 1960s saw big political changes in the US and across Europe, with President Kennedy's arrival, the US civil rights movement led by Martin Luther King, student protests in Paris, the space race and so on.

Despite some initial signs of hope, however, few people across Northern Ireland's parched and withered political landscape felt compelled to turn on, tune in or drop out, and the public mood descended within a few short years from one of tolerance and conciliation into widespread sectarian violence.

The reasons for this are, of course, complex and are connected to both internal and external pressures, within Northern Ireland and beyond. In broad terms, however, O'Neill's rhetoric of reform failed to meet the nationalist population's rising expectation of change. At the same time, his grand political gestures and soothing public speeches unnerved the unionist community, many of whom felt that he was conceding too much ground and was jeopardizing the Stormont regime. A more specific explanation for O'Neill's inability to manage peaceful change in Northern Ireland is that he was unable to command sufficient support within his own party for reform and, more fundamentally, his analysis of the problem was woefully misconceived.

O'Neill believed that sectarianism in Northern Ireland was simply a matter of bad community relations and low Catholic self-esteem. In other words, he thought it was a *behavioural problem* caused by several generations of sullen opposition by nationalists to the Stormont system, accompanied by unionist arrogance and periodic bigotry. For him, therefore, the problem to be addressed was not the structural imbalances within the system over political representation, differential unemployment levels between Catholics and Protestants, the unequal distribution of housing, or even the existence of a partial and unrepresentative police force, but rather the behavioural relationships between unionists and nationalists. What was needed was a campaign to improve community relations, allied with an attempt to improve the Northern Ireland economy.

More critically, perhaps, this was to be a one-way street: he believed the problem to be that nationalists *perceived* themselves to be discriminated against and needed to be brought round from such a false consciousness. The fact that, even as late as May 1968, he was still holding the Northern Ireland political system up as a shining example for others to follow lends further weight to the argument that he wanted to preserve the system as far as possible, while co-opting the nationalist population into a permanent minority status: 'The fact of the matter is that in Ireland, North and South, we have a rather stable political situation, without the swings which are rather characteristic of politics in Britain. Stability may not be as exciting as change, but it is not necessarily any less democratic.'[9]

Anyone capable of making such a statement in 1968 was clearly not capable of reforming the system in such a way as to make it acceptable or relevant to the nationalist community who lived in Northern Ireland. Instead of actually tackling nationalist exclusion from the state (and community sectarianism more broadly), O'Neill embarked on a series of political stunts, such as inviting Irish Taoiseach (Prime Minister) Seán Lemass to Stormont for talks and visiting a number of Catholic schools. Beyond such photo-opportunities, little of substance was done to tackle the key grievances of the nationalist population. While a rising economic tide would 'lift all boats', by encouraging unionists to be nicer to nationalists the latter would become less sullen and more employable.

These two elements – a more prosperous economy and a nationalist community that managed to 'get its act together' – would provide a win-win scenario, where nationalists would benefit, but not at the expense of their unionist neighbours. They would, in short, start to live like Protestants, as he later admitted in an unguarded moment, when interviewed in America after leaving government in 1969: 'If you treat Roman Catholics with due consideration and kindness they will live like Protestants, in spite of the authoritative nature of their Church.'[10] The civil rights activist Austin Currie summed up the nationalist reaction to O'Neill's remarks, claiming that he took exception to the tone and arrogance of the suggestion: 'It is like a squire on his estate talking about the treatment of his cattle.' Gerry Fitt, a founding member and former leader of the nationalist SDLP, made the wry observation that 'while Craigavon and Brookeborough had walked over the Catholics with hob-nail boots, O'Neill walked over them with carpet slippers'.[11] In fact, despite the rhetoric of bridge-building and anti-sectarianism, O'Neill did very little in concrete terms to achieve such aims.

He was not helped by his personal manner: he came across to many local people as aloof and lacking the sort of gritty, blunt charm of some of his contemporaries. He spent his early years in Ethiopia and Australia, courtesy of his stepfather, who was a British diplomat. He was then educated at Eton, after which he received a commission in the Irish Guards. All of this provided him with an impeccable accent and enabled him to 'pass himself off' in polite English society; but such skills were of less obvious use within the gritty populism of Northern Ireland politics. A civil servant who acted as his right-hand man during much of his time in office said that he was a fundamentally shy individual, 'liable when presented with an awkward customer not well known to him, to throw up his head like a nervous and very highly-bred horse'.[12] Despite the dulcet tones, therefore, O'Neill's rhetoric of reform offended the ears of many of his colleagues within government and within the grass roots of the unionist community. Before long he was being castigated by radical pretenders to the unionist leadership in classic historical terms as the latest in a long line of traitors who had tried to undermine the unionist position.

One man above all others was to become his nemesis, waging a sustained and ultimately successful campaign to remove him from power. Rev. Ian Paisley, founder of the Free Presbyterian Church, was a firebrand preacher and political agitator who spent most of his political career attacking from the outside, rather than building from within political institutions. He ridiculed O'Neill's efforts to build bridges with the nationalist community, claiming that 'A traitor and a bridge are very much alike for they both go over to the other side.' Paisley's increasingly vitriolic attacks acted as a form of Chinese water torture on O'Neill's leadership.

Initially the combination of biblical references to Judas Iscariot and historical connections to unionist traitors such as Robert Lundy[13] were considered rather over the top by many mainstream unionists. However, over time and as the political situation deteriorated, Paisley found greater purchase for his unique brand of hard-core unionism within a scared and nervous electorate. O'Neill underestimated Paisley (and he would not be the last to do so), believing that he would be swept away by the first electoral breeze that came along. He was mistaken and he failed to appreciate that his response to growing nationalist dissent was frightening unionists as much as it was frustrating the new wave of Catholic activists who joined together under the collective banner known as the civil rights movement (CRM).

## CIVIL RIGHTS AND CIVIL WRONGS

It is fair to say that local government politics can be boring – the preserve of clubbable 'committee men' with an unhealthy interest in traffic-calming measures, road signage and the all-encompassing proto-fascism known as 'health and safety'. The micro aspect of local politics can seem peripheral to many of us, and this is sometimes reflected in poor – often lamentable – voter turnout when we periodically elect our local councillors. In Northern Ireland, by the mid-1960s, this could not have been further from the truth, for it was at the local level that sectarian friction between unionists and nationalists was at its most visible.

On Thursday, 20 June 1968, a young nationalist MP at Stormont called Austin Currie began a protest over housing discrimination by illegally squatting in a house in Caledon, Co. Tyrone. At a time when demand for housing was vociferous and many Catholic families with children had been languishing for years with little hope of being housed, the local unionist council had allocated the house to Emily Beattie, a nineteen-year-old unmarried Protestant, who happened to be the secretary of a local unionist politician. What possible grounds, Currie asked, could the council have for this decision? This was not an easy question to answer if you chose to avoid the patently obvious: namely, that Catholics were being discriminated against in favour of their Protestant neighbours. Currie was, inevitably, evicted and fined £5. But in the longer term his protest was an enormous success, catching the attention of the media and stimulating interest across Northern Ireland about the disparities in housing allocation by unionist-controlled councils. Currie later remarked of his fine: 'it was the best value for a fiver that I ever had!'

After the Caledon protest, Currie suggested to the recently formed Northern Ireland Civil Rights Association (NICRA) that a march should be held between the nearby towns of Coalisland and Dungannon to raise awareness about the iniquities of housing policy in Northern Ireland. A suitable vehicle for Catholics to vent their frustration at the unionist-dominated political system had been found: several thousand people marched between the two towns in a peaceful demonstration, singing 'We Shall Overcome' as the police looked on. Within a few months, the eyes of the world would be focused on Northern Ireland as peaceful civil rights protests descended into rioting and sectarian violence, and as the British army arrived on the streets in an attempt to restore order.

The CRM began gradually and grew from a small and rather sedate middle-class grouping into a mass protest, which took an increasingly confrontational approach to the police and the Stormont government. The new wave of politically literate, young and intelligent Catholics (along with some liberal Protestants) came together under the umbrella of NICRA. They highlighted inequalities to devastating effect, embarrassing the unionist government and attracting the attention of the international media. Matters intensified once the protests came into direct confrontation with the police and street disturbances descended into violence. In this sense, the British welfare state had, however inadvertently, created the motor for political change. The bright, young, confident (and now educated) Catholic population began to organize and devise tactics for confronting unionist control. By 1968, a new young leadership had emerged to breathe life into nationalist politics, as talented organizers and propagandists came forward – Eamonn McCann, Michael Farrell, Austin Currie, John Hume and – most vivid of all – Bernadette Devlin.

Even by Irish standards, Devlin's biography was dramatic. In 1969 she became the youngest ever MP at Westminster, standing in a Mid Ulster by-election as a 'united anti-unionist' candidate while studying for a degree in psychology at Queen's University Belfast. (Devlin was excluded from Queen's before graduating, and was jailed for affray during the aftermath of a civil rights protest in Derry.) A young ruddy-faced American student visiting Oxford as a Rhodes Scholar heard her 'electrifying' maiden speech in the House of Commons on the radio. His name was William Jefferson Clinton, and some trace his later commitment to the Northern Ireland peace process in the 1990s to that moment.

Bernadette Devlin (later McAliskey) was a fierce orator, her sharp, incisive 'no-holds-barred' manner quickly making her a cult figure within nationalism and a hate figure across unionism. 'Castro in a miniskirt' was the attempted put-down from her detractors as she carved a swathe through the British parliamentary elite and spat verbal bullets at the police and those she deemed responsible for discrimination in Northern Ireland. Physically she cut a slight figure, which was totally at odds with the power of her rhetoric as she tore strips off her chosen quarry. She famously crossed the floor of the House of Commons and slapped British Home Secretary Reginald Maudling in the face when he was in the middle of making a statement in the wake of Bloody Sunday in 1972 (she was denied a voice due to House of Commons protocol). The petty formalities of British parliamentary procedure were not for her, and this did her no harm in the minds of the Catholic community in Northern Ireland. A later republican mural at 'Stroke City's' Free Derry Corner immortalized her public image as a lank-haired, denim-clad waif, shouting through a loud hailer amidst scenes of stone-throwing and CS gas. The mural was to become a tourist destination, as the political conflict morphed seamlessly into the heritage industry.

Though born a Catholic, this feminist and revolutionary socialist was certainly no lackey of the Church, and nor was she bound by its catechism. She had a child (Roisín) out of wedlock in 1971 and, though she later married the father, Michael McAliskey, this cost her some support from more conservative Catholics in Northern Ireland. In 1981 she and her husband survived an assassination attempt at their home in Co. Tyrone, in which she was shot seven times by loyalist gunmen. This episode added somewhat to her mystique and posed some awkward questions for the British army, which had had her house under surveillance but had done nothing to stop the attack. In a supreme twist of irony (in light of the events of Bloody Sunday – detailed below), troops from the Parachute Regiment who heard the shots administered first aid to the victims and one soldier flagged down a car and drove to a neighbouring house to ring for an ambulance.

Devlin subsequently retired from the spotlight but she continues as a community worker in Tyrone, hitting the headlines periodically when her past collides with political sensitivities of the present. In August 1994, following the 'cessation of military operations' by the Provisional IRA, her caustic rejoinder was pithy and ominous in equal measure: 'The war is over – and the good guys lost!'[14] In 2003, she was detained at O'Hare airport in Chicago on her way to a family christening. US immigration officials denied her entry to the US and forcibly deported her back to Ireland on the grounds that she represented a 'serious threat to the security of the United States'.

Returning to the late 1960s, many of the civil rights leaders disagreed with each other politically, with some taking an Irish republican perspective and others an international Marxist position (there were also some unionists and non-aligned Protestants involved). In the initial stages they were all able to unite around the fact that Northern Ireland's system of government was undemocratic by any reasonable standards, and that reforms had to be introduced. As with many popular social movements, once the pace of change quickened not everyone could agree on what speed to go at or in which direction to travel. As the atmosphere became more violent, so the agenda radicalized, to the point where a peaceful popular protest movement was overtaken by sectarian violence and a confrontation between the police and more militant rioters, some of whom eventually defected to the emerging paramilitary organizations.

While tactical and philosophical disagreements would develop over time, in its early stages NICRA provided an umbrella that was broad enough for most to shelter under. Five key demands emerged. None of these was concerned with Irish nationalist ideology, and all were focused on economic and political grievances. The central issues concerned discrimination in the areas of housing allocation and employment, plus electoral malpractice. Derry became the focus for much of the protest, as it was there that the issues were most acute. In February 1967, for example, unemployment in the city stood at an eye-watering 20 per cent, compared with a UK average of under 3 per cent and a Northern Ireland average of 8 per cent. While the Stormont government was ultimately responsible for many of these issues, it was actually at the local level that the friction was most obvious, as district councils were responsible for housing allocation. This made local political control important and, in some cases (most notably in Derry/Londonderry), unionists had 'gerrymandered' electoral boundaries to ensure that they held onto their dominant position. They did this by making sure that unionist areas produced narrow but secure victories, while nationalist areas produced huge majorities for those elected – in other words, wasting as few unionist votes as possible and as many nationalist votes as possible. The net result was that, though in a minority in the area, unionists ended up having a majority control of Londonderry Corporation, to the obvious annoyance of the nationalist electorate. Such gerrymandering was in evidence elsewhere across Northern Ireland, in towns such as Armagh, Omagh and Dungannon.

Crucially, there was a connection in Northern Ireland between local elections and housing, in that the voting franchise was dependent on the payment of rates. Thus, to give a nationalist a council house was to give them (and their qualifying dependants) a vote at the local level. This was less problematic in areas where nationalists were in a majority, or even in those areas with large unionist majorities. However, in places such as Derry, where the unionist majorities were deliberately slim in order to maximize their political representation, providing nationalists with houses could potentially tip the balance and risk the unionists losing political control of the area.

Unionist councils were thus often very reluctant to give houses to Catholics. This is the political context that explains the apparently odd behaviour in Caledon. It was not simple bigotry, so much as a political necessity for unionists at the local government level. There were some bizarre and unfortunate situations where houses were given to Protestants instead of Catholics, irrespective of need. Some of the statistics make for embarrassing reading: in Fermanagh, between 1945 and 1967, 82 per cent of the 1,048 houses built were given to Protestants, even though Catholics made up the majority of the local population. While this was an egregious example, it was far from being an isolated one. Austin Currie's Caledon squat was informed by the fact that in 1965, across the whole of Dungannon, *every single one* of the 194 new homes built was allocated to a Protestant, regardless of need. The rest of the United Kingdom operated a 'points system' for housing allocation (based on means-tested factors such as income, family size and so on), but this was one area where the unionist government was reluctant to do as they did on the 'mainland'. Such glaring anomalies made housing allocation a central plank of the civil rights movement, and the adoption of a fair points system one of their key demands. The other central issues were an end to gerrymandering; the adoption of 'one man one vote' in local elections; disbandment of the exclusively Protestant B Special auxiliary force; the provision of a complaints system at local government level; and abolition of the Special Powers Act.

While legal frameworks can seem dry and perhaps a little dull in comparison to some of the more vivid events of the civil rights period, understanding their political function is crucial. They are the structure within which political behaviour takes place and they play a key role in defining what is legal and what is illegal – and, by extension, what is legitimate and what is illegitimate. When one of the sides in a conflict has control of the legal apparatus, as unionists had in Northern Ireland, the law can be used as a means of political control and self-preservation. Thus, while subsequent civil rights marches were declared to be unlawful by the unionist government, the underpinning legal structures had little legitimacy in the eyes of nationalists.

## CIVIL RIGHTS OR NATIONAL RIGHTS?

While civil rights campaigners, the wider nationalist community and many external onlookers believed that the protests were about achieving a degree of fairness within the political system, there was a strong feeling within unionism that they just provided a cover for more traditional opposition to the existence of the Northern Ireland state. Despite the growing body of evidence, many unionists denied the existence of systemic discrimination or anything beyond localized and disconnected instances of disparity. They regarded the civil rights movement as a carefully orchestrated front, a 'Trojan horse' for a political attack by Irish republicans on the Northern Ireland system of democracy and an attempt to undermine its credibility in Britain and elsewhere.

While some denied that any discrimination existed, others pointed to republican 'puppet masters' pulling the strings of NICRA and other groups. Rev. Ian Paisley went so far as to claim that it was all a Popish plot by the Vatican to undermine, colonize and eventually punish Protestant Northern Ireland. Following the 5 October 1968 civil rights march (see below), Paisley wrote in the *Protestant Telegraph* that the hand of Rome could be clearly seen:[15]

> Rome has come to believe that she is on the plane of equality in Ulster, and this has been brought to pass by the encouragement of those hireling prophets occupying professed Protestant pulpits, the ecumenists – the World Council [of Churches] fifth column in our midst. These men have helped to swell the bloated head of the monster of Romanism. The bared teeth of the fox of Romanism have been seen at the weekend in the city of Londonderry, and remember this, when Rome comes from a place of minority to equality and then to a place of majority, she is like a tiger ready to tear her prey to pieces.[16]

While Paisley's rambunctious conspiracy theories appealed more to his core Free Presbyterian audience than to the Protestant mainstream, a more secular branch of unionist opinion also believed that the CRM was a front for more militant factions – republican, communist, or a mixture of the two. The uncompromising minister for home affairs, Bill Craig, and the minister for agriculture, Brian Faulkner, both condemned NICRA publicly as an IRA front organization, a belief that still persists in quite mainstream unionist quarters. Former Ulster Unionist Party (UUP) leader David Trimble commented in the mid-1990s, for example, that the behaviour and tactics of the CRM showed that it was 'really just the Republican movement in a different guise'.[17]

It is true that there was some republican and communist involvement in the CRM and that it did eventually succeed in destroying the Stormont regime and in creating the conditions for the birth of the Provisional IRA. These events only came to pass, however, because unionist reaction to the CRM facilitated it – the thought was the parent of the deed. However unwittingly, unionists provoked the very outcome they feared the most: the loss of political control and the destruction of unionist hegemony in Northern Ireland. In the end, the moderate elements melted away and left the stage free for militant republicanism. In its early days, however, the CRM brought people together from a wide variety of backgrounds. They focused on a limited range of demands with, it seemed, the realistic possibility that a new, young, reforming leader of the Unionist Party would listen to them. O'Neill was indeed listening to the civil rights movement, but he misheard it and also misjudged his ability to contain the new energy within both nationalist and unionist politics.

By the middle of 1968, many nationalists had grown tired of waiting for O'Neill to deliver on his rhetoric. The removal of Austin Currie from his squat in Caledon triggered a chain of events which connected long-held grievance to short-term opportunism in the form of the protest march from Coalisland to Dungannon (see above). Though attended by only a few thousand people, it struck a spark that soon became an inferno, engulfing not only Northern Ireland but the British government, too.

A subsequent protest march, scheduled to take place in Derry on 5 October 1968, was to be a defining moment for Northern Ireland. If any day can be said to mark the beginning of the period popularly known as 'the Troubles', this has a better claim than most.

## 'NOTHING WILL EVER BE THE SAME AGAIN'

It was on 5 October 1968 that the civil rights campaign moved from being a rather quiet and disconnected protest to become a mass movement that shook the unionist government to its foundations. It also began the process by which the British government came to realize that Terence O'Neill was not capable of managing the deteriorating situation and that London would have to intervene directly in Northern Ireland once again.

While held under the auspices of the relatively moderate NICRA, the idea for the march came from the more radical Derry Housing Action Committee, which wanted to confront the unionist authorities and knew that the proposed route possessed the sort of historical symbolism that would generate a reaction from the Stormont government. The walled city of Derry had withstood a hundred-day siege by James II in 1689 and held a special place in unionist folklore. To many unionists, the idea that nationalist demonstrators would parade through the city and breach those walls that had been so stoutly defended by their ancestors was proof that the march had more to do with republican disruption and provocation than with civil rights. When Northern Ireland Minister for Home Affairs Bill Craig banned the march from its proposed route, a clash was inevitable; but just to be on the safe side, the loyalist Apprentice Boys[18] announced a counter-march – same day, same time, same route.

RUC officers warned the marchers that theirs was an illegal gathering. Initially the atmosphere was calm and peaceful, but a violent confrontation between the marchers and the police was literally just around the corner: when the civil rights marchers turned into Duke Street they were met by a wall of RUC officers with batons drawn, determined that the protestors would go no further and that the 'rule of law' would be enforced. Through loudspeakers the police called on people to disperse. They did not, and the atmosphere quickly became darker, with name-calling and jostling followed by violent skirmishes between the RUC and the marchers. The police used water cannon in an attempt to dampen the spirits of the marchers, but this served only to inflame matters further. The RUC ominously warned women and children to leave the area and then blocked off the top of Duke Street and the escape route behind the march. The civil rights protestors were trapped, sealed between two lines of police in a version of what would today be referred to as 'kettling'. The space between the opposing factions slowly reduced until the two were literally within arm's reach of one another. Suddenly the RUC launched an unprovoked attack on the marchers, clubbing them with their batons and indiscriminately attacking men, women and children.

Some officers were clearly out of control. Gerry Fitt, the Westminster MP for West Belfast, was struck down by a police baton and was shown on the evening news being helped into a police car with blood pouring from his head. He was taken to hospital, where he received several stitches. He later remarked of the RUC handling of the march that 'these were stormtrooper tactics at their worst'. Fitt was well regarded in London, especially within the British Labour Party: they knew him and liked him, and some wanted answers about why their colleague had had his head split open by the police.

The RUC officers lost their discipline in the melee, allowing the marchers to disperse, though many were beaten as they retreated or were knocked to the ground by water cannon (as were several bystanders and Saturday afternoon shoppers).

The television pictures were dramatic (even in grainy black and white) and they shocked many of those who watched them in Britain and around the world. They showed not just that Northern Ireland was descending into violence, but also that there was real surprise – even fear – on the faces of some RUC officers at their inability to contain the protests. In response to what nationalists perceived to be naked brutality by the RUC, petrol bombs were thrown at the police and rioting spread across the city, leaving over eighty people injured.

It was a massive embarrassment for the RUC, for the unionist government and internationally for the British government, as pictures sped around the world – first of the police attacking unarmed civil rights marchers, and then of a general breakdown in law and order within the

United Kingdom. The degree of force used by the police was considered by many (including the Cameron Commission, appointed by the British government to look into the disturbances) to be excessive, although many unionists felt that the police were simply doing their job and upholding the law.

The political impact of the 5 October 1968 civil rights march was profound. The marchers may have lost the battle on the streets of Derry but they certainly won the propaganda war: peaceful demonstrators in tweed suits and dufflecoats calling for civil rights and being bludgeoned to the ground by the police – all of it broadcast on television and viewed in every living room in Britain. One of those living rooms was in 10 Downing Street, where the British prime minister was able to watch the failure of the unionist government to maintain order at first hand. As one of the organizers of the parade later remarked, 'nothing will ever be the same again'.

The reformist rhetoric of Prime Minister Terence O'Neill was laid bare for all to see; it left him mortally wounded. The onset of street rioting meanwhile presented an opportunity for militant republican activists to enter the fray, which they did with gusto the following year. The 5 October march moved the civil rights campaign into the international spotlight, and the violent reaction of the RUC strengthened NICRA and weakened the unionist government. A month after the incident, O'Neill was summoned to London and forced to accept a reform programme that conceded many of the civil rights demands over unfair housing and electoral malpractice. As is so often the case, too little was done too late, and while these reforms might have been welcomed in 1967, by the beginning of 1969 the appetite for change was stronger. The unionist government at Stormont was on the run and the nationalists knew it.

## THE CROSSROADS: REFORM OR REVOLUTION?

From here, there were two directions in which the people of Northern Ireland could go. The CRM could wait and see if the proposed reforms were delivered to its satisfaction. Alternatively, the reforms could be viewed as being yet another piecemeal effort from a discredited regime that could be toppled through continued pressure. In the end, both of these options were taken, as NICRA held back and called for a moratorium on marches until the reforms were brought in, while the radical student movement People's Democracy (PD) pushed on.

In January 1969, the PD planned a four-day walk from Belfast to Derry, modelled on the US civil rights march from Selma to Montgomery. This time a loyalist counter-demonstration was ready for them and on the final day the march was attacked at Burntollet Bridge, just outside Derry. Predictably a riot ensued. The RUC was accused of collusion by the parade organizers, and the violence was covered comprehensively by the broadcast media.

From this point on, the civil rights movement became a focus for sectarian violence between nationalist demonstrators and loyalist counter-demonstrators, with the police largely malevolent and the Northern Ireland government largely irrelevant. While successive unionist governments since 1921 had promoted the idea that Northern Ireland and its parliament were 'sovereign', it was not – a fact that was made painfully clear when the British government eventually suspended the regional government in 1972.

But before this denouement, O'Neill called an election in 1969 and declared in a direct television address to the people of Northern Ireland that the people held the key to the future:

> Ulster stands at the crossroads. What kind of Ulster do you want? A happy and respected province in good standing with the rest of the United Kingdom? Or a place continually torn apart by riots and demonstrations and regarded by the rest of Britain as a political outcast? As always in a democracy, the choice is yours.[19]

While this was welcomed by many moderate unionists (and by some nationalists who were prepared to wait and see if his promised reforms materialized), the implied suggestion that the by now calamitous situation had nothing to do with him was typical of his rather Olympian attitude that he was somehow above the fray. In any event, by this stage it was too late for O'Neill. In footballing parlance he had 'lost the dressing room' and he resigned shortly afterwards, to be replaced by his cousin, James Chichester-Clark. He later admitted in his memoirs that the civil rights movement 'brought about reforms that would otherwise have taken years to wring from a reluctant government'.[20]

By now politics was being conducted on the streets, not by politicians at Stormont. The rhetoric of conciliation and reform was overtaken by the juggernaut of civil rights protests, street rioting by nationalists and unionists, and a violent response by the security apparatus in Northern Ireland.

While a paltry 400 people had taken part in the 5 October parade in Derry an estimated 16,000 people took part in a march on 16 October, as nationalists were energized rather than cowed by this new form of political activism and the unionist government's efforts to quell it.

## BATTLE OF THE BOGSIDE

By 1969, a familiar pattern had emerged of nationalist confrontations with loyalists on the one hand and with the RUC on the other. That summer a three-day riot took place in Derry between nationalist residents of the Bogside area and the RUC. It was sparked by violence between nationalists and a loyalist Apprentice Boys parade, which takes place annually on 12 August to commemorate the Siege of Derry in 1689. It is often a flashpoint in Northern Ireland's sectarian calendar, though August 1969 proved especially combustible. When the Apprentice Boys reached the junction between Waterloo Place and William Street, taunts and missiles began to fly between the opposing sides. The RUC pushed the nationalists back into Rossville Street and the Bogside area in an attempt to contain them. But unlike 5 October 1968, this time the nationalists were prepared for a fight. Large groups of youths pelted the police with stones, dropped petrol bombs onto them from the roof of Rossville flats, and used whatever they could lay their hands on – including concrete slabs from the broken-up pavement – as impromptu weapons. The police had walked into an ambush. Pre-prepared barricades were erected in the street to hinder the police from moving vehicles and reinforcements around, and dozens of police officers were injured before they withdrew. The Battle of the Bogside had begun. The police were ill prepared (not having flame-resistant uniforms, for instance) and were subjected to over two days of continuous rioting from the local nationalist population, led by the more radical voices within the civil rights movement, such as Bernadette Devlin and Eamonn McCann. The nationalists were able to demonstrate that the police could not control Derry, or at least the Bogside part of it. This led to the wall mural 'You Are Now Entering Free Derry', which has been a local landmark ever since and is now an essential part of local tours of the city.

The RUC drafted in reinforcements from across Northern Ireland to relieve the exhausted local forces and responded by firing over 1,000 CS gas canisters into the area. This made the region look even more like a war zone and prompted Irish Prime Minister Jack Lynch to announce that he could not stand by and watch innocent people be maimed or killed by the police and that his government intended to use the Irish army to set up ad hoc field hospitals on the Irish border to deal with those wounded in the violence. To both nationalists and unionists in Northern Ireland this sounded as if the Irish army was going to intervene directly in the situation. This was not the case, as that would have meant an incursion into British sovereign territory. But the Irish did set up hospitals at the border – a dramatic enough image of a region that was teetering on the brink of civil war. By 14 August it had become too much for the police and the unionist government to handle, and the Chichester-Clark government asked the British government to send in the army to help restore order.

By the end of 1969, both republican and loyalist paramilitary factions had crystallized into cohesive groupings with militant agendas and active support from increasingly frightened and angry communities. It was time for the hard men to come forward, and they were not backward in doing so, their emergence wiping out any realistic prospect of peaceful civil rights activism.

## THE BIRTH OF THE PARAMILITARIES

Paramilitary violence had existed in Ireland for many centuries, from the days of Gaelic clan resistance to the English Crown, through to the organization of the Irish Republican Brotherhood and the Ulster Volunteer Force at the beginning of the twentieth century. The original UVF was revived in 1966 in response to what some radical unionists felt was a weak response by O'Neill's government to the civil rights agitation and their belief that the republican goal was to destroy Northern Ireland. The IRA had been largely dormant from the 1930s until the mid-1950s, when it conducted a half-hearted border campaign. This amounted to a low-level campaign of violence against economic targets and petered out due to the organization's incompetence and a lack of support from within the nationalist community. The IRA had become as irrelevant to the majority of nationalists in Northern Ireland as the moribund Nationalist Party.

Government was remote from the nationalist community, if not downright hostile towards it; but militant republicanism was scarcely any more relevant. By early 1969, the IRA was dominated by Southern Marxists, such as Cathal Goulding, who were less focused on militant action than on developing a socialist alternative to the political status quo. Perhaps ironically, given their 'core business' of Irish republicanism, they were not terribly exercised by partition, nor by the seismic events taking place north of the border. In truth, Goulding and his Southern colleagues were more concerned with developing an Irish republican alternative in their part of Ireland (i.e. what used to be called the Free State and was now the Republic of Ireland) than with the events unfolding in Belfast or Derry.

These were 'thinkers' rather than 'doers', and matters began to veer alarmingly close to Pythonesque satire in 1969, when Ireland's main anti-partition movement took a partitionist stance itself, determining that '*the 26 counties* is the area in which the greatest anti-imperialist unity is possible'.[21] This understandably irked IRA members in Northern Ireland, who felt that there were more pressing concerns than refining the Marxist dialectic –the arrival of British troops on the streets, for instance, or the attacks on Catholics by the police, Protestant mobs, or both.

A split between Southern Marxist ideologues and Northern republican militants was inevitable. It came in January 1970, at the Sinn Fein *Ard Fheis* (party conference), when, by a narrow majority, it was decided to end the policy of abstention in the Irish parliament, in order to move republicanism into the democratic mainstream and away from its militant tradition. The Irish Parliament (Dail Eireann) had previously been regarded as an illegitimate partitionist structure, which was why republicans had refused to recognize its authority. This decision by Sinn Fein was too much for the large militant faction, which walked out of the *Ard Fheis*, mirroring a split in the IRA in December 1969 into 'Provisional' and 'Official' wings.

Unencumbered by Marxist dreamscapes about uniting the Catholic and Protestant working class in an anti-imperialist struggle, the Provisionals (or Provos as they became known) could get back to their main priority of 'armed struggle' against the British presence in Ireland. This was to become much easier when the British military arrived in numbers to deal with the rioting that now accompanied most civil rights protests. A brief power struggle between the Provisional and the Official IRA was quickly won by the former, while the latter declared a ceasefire in 1972 and 'went political', though not before carrying out several significant attacks on the British army and killing a number of civilians in 1971.

These disputes over abstentionism, the conditions of ceasefires and whether it was right to adopt a political rather than a militant strategy would become a feature of internal debate within the Provisional republican movement a generation later. Up to that point, the Provisionals were able to present a simple and uncompromising message to the effect that they were defenders of the nationalist community against loyalist attack and were the front line of resistance to the British occupation of Ireland.

The Battle of the Bogside had stretched the police to breaking point, not only in Derry but also in Belfast, where the heightened sectarianism of the time had similarly led to rioting. The unionist government had little option but to ask the British government for military support to help restore order. And so it was that on 14 August 1969 the British army arrived on the streets of Belfast and Derry in an attempt to reduce sectarian attacks.

At the time, their presence was seen as a temporary emergency measure, and their role was defined as a 'limited operation'. However, they were to remain in Northern Ireland for a generation. Initially brought in as peace-keepers, the troops soon came to be regarded within the nationalist community as an army of occupation – and, of course, as a convenient target for the resurgent Provisional IRA. 'Operation Banner' (as the military deployment was formally termed) would last until July 2007.

## OPERATION BANNER BEGINS

The descent of Northern Ireland from a place with a stable (if idiosyn-cratic) regional government into one wracked by civil rights protests, sectarian rioting and the emergence of nascent paramilitary groups shocked and horrified the British government. While British politicians had frequently sought to portray themselves as being above the fray, here the sins of omission were little better than those of commission – perhaps worse, as those politicians had ultimate responsibility and authority for the governance of the region.

It was convenient for successive British administrations to allow the unionist government to believe itself to be sovereign, and a convention was even established to further enhance this illusion: namely, that Northern Ireland affairs were not to be discussed in the House of Commons, as all such matters should be dealt with by the Stormont parliament. This aspect of devolution had the beneficial side-effect of allowing Britain to forget about Northern Ireland in any meaningful way, lodged as it was, like a dark secret, in the recesses of the political psyche. Such political negligence does not allow Britain to evade responsibility for the democratic short-comings of the post-1921 period, or the generation of sectarian violence that was about to unfold.

The British government supplied soldiers to the unionist government in August 1969 in order to keep the lid on sectarian violence, which by this stage was spreading across Belfast and Derry. By summer 1969, paramilitaries on both sides were cordoning off urban areas, setting up impromptu roadblocks and armed checkpoints, with masked men scrutinizing people's driving licences, carrying out vigilante attacks and ignoring what might theoretically be called 'the rule of law'. Street rioting was a nightly occurrence between rival mobs of petrol bombers, and by August 1969 the police were unable to cope with the level of street disturbances.

In the major urban centres, Catholics and Protestants existed in a tightly packed sectarian apartheid – often living side by side in the lattice of streets and alleyways, but their paths rarely crossing. The incendiary atmosphere of August 1969 made life intolerable for anyone living at such an 'interface' between the two communities, and attempts were made to 'remove' people physically or by simply burning them out of their homes. After one riot in mid-August, which lasted for several days in the network of streets between the mainly Protestant Shankill Road and the largely Catholic Falls Road in Belfast, eight people lay dead and over 700 were injured. Whole streets became iconic emblems of sectarian hatred, as people were filmed being burned out of their homes in Bombay Street and in surrounding areas. Many of those who were not burned out fled to safer areas and became refugees in their own country. British and international camera crews filmed homes being gutted and recorded the pitiful images of people loading their furniture and possessions onto trucks and vans before their homes were torched by their neighbours. In scenes reminiscent of wartime, large numbers of people in Belfast were becoming evacuees within the United Kingdom.

By the end of August 1969, over 170 homes had been burnt down and nearly 500 more had been damaged by arson, most of them owned by Catholics. The Scarman Tribunal, which was subsequently established to investigate the violent events of that summer, estimated that, in Belfast itself, over 1,800 families had fled their homes, 1,500 of them Catholic.[22] Nationalist mythology contends that the British stood back and watched Bombay Street burn, thus facilitating an anti-Catholic pogrom. The reality was more mundane and owes more to cock-up than conspiracy.

When they arrived on the streets of Belfast that August, the British army was ill-prepared for its mission. This point was encapsulated by the fact that the commanding officer, General Ian Freeland, only found out about the decision to deploy his troops when he tuned into the BBC's *World at One* radio programme on 14 August: Home Secretary (and future Prime Minister) James Callaghan had unveiled the decision in an off-the-cuff remark at a noon press conference, and his junior Home Office minister,

Roy Hattersley, had to be called out of a restaurant where he was having lunch to be told what was happening.[23] By 3 p.m. that same day, General Freeland found himself on the streets of Belfast trying to get between rival Catholic and Protestant communities, which had by this point been in a pitched battle for several days.

British troops cut an unusual sight in the built-up streets of Belfast and Derry, their light khaki camouflage gear standing out like a beacon against the dull grey of the local area. It was like a moon-landing – as much for the troops themselves as for the Northern Ireland locals they had been sent to deal with. In truth, the British army was deployed in Belfast with no idea of its mission (beyond quelling the immediate violence), no understanding of the politics of the region, and no strategic political leadership from the British government.

While the decision to deploy British troops onto the streets of Northern Ireland might seem at first glance like a reasonable response to a crisis situation (and it did save lives in the immediate term), it was yet another example of Britain's failure to seriously re-engage with the region politically. It demonstrated that Britain's tactical approach to Northern Ireland was to move reluctantly and incrementally, muddling through and never quite dealing with problems at an early enough stage.

In some ways, despite the violence, August 1969 presented an opportunity and is frequently cited as a point in time when Britain could have taken back political control and prevented a further escalation of violence. Had the British government suspended the Stormont government in 1969, instead of waiting until 1972, things may have turned out differently. Instead, it subcontracted the British army to an unstable and increasingly discredited unionist regime, which used it to shore up a dwindling authority.

During 1970, two factors changed the role of the army and made it difficult for it to continue in the guise of being an impartial peace-keeping force. First, because it was under the political direction of the Stormont government, rather than London, it became squeezed between the conflicting narratives of the unionists on the one hand and the nationalists on the other. Operational techniques such as house raids and curfews in Belfast were directed mainly at the nationalist community, which only added to the belief that the army was trying to shore up unionist power. Army tactics were insensitive and became increasingly more brutal, which infuriated the nationalist community and contributed to the recruitment of new members by the Provisional IRA.

The 'Falls Curfew' was a turning point in relations between the nationalist community and the army. In the space of a single weekend, the army, whose reputation was already severely dented in nationalist eyes, was confirmed for many as being there to shore up unionist power. In a direct response to a confrontation between nationalist youths and the army, followed by sporadic gun battles between both the Official and Provisional IRA and British soldiers (several of whom were badly injured), the army imposed a curfew on sections of the Belfast's Falls Road for thirty-six hours, beginning on Friday, 3 July 1970. The movement of people was severely restricted in around fifty streets in the Lower Falls area; the army cordoned the roads off with barbed wire to enable it to conduct house searches in the hope of finding weapons and explosives that were believed to be in the area. Helicopters hovered constantly over the area, using loudspeakers to warn residents to remain indoors.

During the mayhem that ensued between the republican paramilitaries and the army, hundreds of bullets were fired by both sides, though the army subsequently insisted (rather ludicrously) that the troops had discharged only fifteen bullets during the whole episode. Any journalists found within the curfew zone were immediately arrested, and over 1,500 canisters of CS gas were fired into the residential area and into people's homes, choking men, women and children. The army displayed a new degree of harshness: doors were kicked down, property was destroyed, floorboards were ripped up, and Catholic religious icons and statues were deliberately targeted in a display of thuggish behaviour. After twenty-four hours of this, the army announced (through its loudhailers) that residents would be allowed out for one hour in order to get vital supplies. The imagery of British oppression was classic and could hardly have been improved upon, even if the newly created Provisional IRA had had a marketing department.

The curfew was eventually broken on Sunday, 5 July, when 3,000 women from nearby Andersonstown arrived with food and other supplies for the beleaguered residents of the Lower Falls. While the British troops were trained in how to deal with the threat from the Provisional IRA, they were less equipped to respond to the anger of these formidable women; after a brief stand-off they were allowed through the barricades. When it later emerged that the army had driven two unionist ministers through the curfew in their Saracen armoured personnel carriers during the lockdown, that was it: from the nationalist perspective, the troops were merely doing the bidding of the unionist regime and had become its cutting edge.

While the Falls Curfew unearthed around a hundred guns and a substantial amount of bomb-making material, the army's success came at the expense of the destruction of property and of any remaining goodwill within the area and across the wider nationalist community. The fact that the curfew is also sometimes referred to as the 'Rape of the Lower Falls' indicates the emotions involved. In a final ironic/tragic twist, local Catholic man Charles O'Neill was knocked down on the Falls Road by an army Saracen, with many eye-witnesses claiming that he was deliberately run over. It turned out that O'Neill was an invalided British ex-serviceman.

The second reason why the relationship between the nationalist population and the army changed was simply that the troops did not protect Catholics from loyalist attacks. As an ineffectual army presence saw nationalists and unionists alike burned out of their homes, rival paramilitary groups, such as the Ulster Defence Association (UDA) and the Provisional IRA (PIRA), gained new members and supporters, since they could claim to be relevant to those communities.

From 1971 onwards, a vicious circle of relationships was established between republican and loyalist paramilitaries and the British army, which attempted to work towards what was euphemistically referred to as 'an acceptable level of violence' – a phrase coined by the (rather unsympathetic) home secretary, Reginald Maudling. While the 'security forces' sought to portray themselves as reluctant referees between two sides intent on violence, in reality they were also protagonists in what soon became an undeclared war. It was undeclared, because the British government wanted to depict the emerging conflict as domestic terrorism and criminality, and not as a political struggle (as the Provisional IRA preferred to cast it). This struggle for legitimacy was to become a critical element of attempts to internationalize the conflict over the next thirty years, as all sides settled in for the 'long war'.

## OPERATION DEMETRIUS: INTERNMENT BEGINS

The folly of British policy in Northern Ireland in the early 1970s was laid bare in the summer of 1971 when, caught between its desire for non-involvement and its responsibility to govern, the British government agreed to a harder security policy by an increasingly beleaguered unionist government. Brian Faulkner had by this stage replaced Chichester-Clark as prime minister of Northern Ireland. Faulkner was a physically slight man, and this belied his energy, tenacity and political ambition. He began his career as a hardliner and ended it a political moderate, a journey that other unionist leaders would make in subsequent generations.[24] By summer 1971, Faulkner had convinced British Prime Minister Edward Heath and Home Secretary Maudling that to pursue the path of political reform he needed to control the security situation. To do that, he had to get the 'men of violence' off the streets as quickly as possible by introducing a policy of internment (i.e. detention without trial). Heath reluctantly agreed, despite opposition from the army, because the bottom line of British policy on Northern Ireland was (and since 1921 always had been) one of non-involvement. This proved to be a fatal calculation for all concerned.

Internment was formally known as Operation Demetrius and it refers to the practice of arresting and detaining without trial people suspected of being members of illegal paramilitary groups. The legal basis was, of course, the Special Powers Act, which allowed for the indefinite detention of anyone considered to be a threat to public order. Suspects were 'lifted' for interrogation and either charged or simply detained without legal representation after questioning for as long as was thought necessary.

Internment was introduced on 9 August 1971 and continued in use until 5 December 1975. During this period, a total of 1,981 people were detained: 1,874 were Catholics, and only 107 were Protestants. It was heralded by dawn raids by the army on republican areas of Belfast; these resulted in fierce gun battles, in which twelve people were killed. The raids were conducted in brutal fashion by the army, which by this stage was clear in its own mind that the troops were there as peace-enforcers rather than peace-keepers. The British Independent Labour Party produced a well-documented account of events at the request of the SDLP; the following excerpt provides a flavour of the mayhem that was unleashed as internment commenced in the early hours of 9 August:

> Mrs C of Glenalena Road, who is four months pregnant, told us how she had been awakened during the early hours of the morning by the noise of breaking glass. When the soldiers entered the house she and her husband were upstairs. Her husband, partly dressed by now, was holding their ten-month-old baby. The troops smashed their way in shouting something about 'Fenian bastards'. They came up the steps shouting and creating a general commotion – the child was knocked out of the husband's arms and when Mrs C attempted to go towards him, she was knocked through a bedroom door and fell over her nine-year-old daughter. The husband was told to get outside and when he

asked if he could put his shoes on a soldier replied 'can you fucking hell'. He was then hit on the head with a rifle butt, which caused him to fall downstairs. At the foot of the stairs he was made to walk through the broken glass in his bare feet ... The husband was then taken away and charged, along with fifty-four others similarly arrested, with riotous behaviour. The case was later dismissed.[25]

The treatment of Noel Maguire, a twenty-year-old student who was interned and interrogated under the Special Powers Act on 12 August 1971, was not unusual for those who were lifted for questioning in Belfast and across other areas of Northern Ireland at the time:

I was then taken to Girdwood Barracks and thrown from one person to another until I reached the gymnasium. In the gymnasium I had to stand against a steel door with my hands and legs outstretched. Only my fingertips were to touch the door. I began to shake with nerves and caused the door to rattle. One soldier said that this was making him nervous and that when he became nervous he did things that he wasn't responsible for. Another soldier pressed the barrel of a gun into my face and threatened to blow my head off – this happened twice.[26]

These accounts are typical of hundreds of others and do not overplay the level of army hostility or the petty cruelty the troops exhibited towards the nationalist community. Suspects were subjected to casual beatings and petty humiliations, and were disoriented by being denied sleep for long periods. Any notion of the troops acting as peace-keepers had long since evaporated, and nationalists had learned to fear and hate the army and to mistrust the wider criminal justice system within which it operated.

Internment was a disaster in both military and political terms. It failed to catch the main paramilitary actors due to the poor intelligence available to an army that was still trying to understand the region and that had advised against the use of internment in the first place.

The selection of targets for internment was based on old RUC Special Branch intelligence on around 450 republican activists and their last known addresses. In practice, these lists were hopelessly out of date – in one case, the army spent some time in Armagh trying to find and detain a man who had been dead for four years! The hardline republicans that the army were after had received their own intelligence that raids were planned and had already made their escape and gone 'on the run'.

Approximately two thousand people were forcibly interned between 1971 and 1975, 95 per cent of them Catholics; no Protestants at all were interned until February 1973.Two-thirds of these people were released within six months of arrest, once it became clear that they had no connections with violence. The policy also overwhelmingly targeted the nationalist community, making the army appear complicit in an attempt to subjugate the nationalist population and shore up a failing unionist government. The main outcome of the policy was to provide recruits for the IRA, which did not have to try too hard to connect the actions of British troops in 1971 to those of their predecessors in generations past. A subsequent inquiry (the Compton Report) found that, while ill-treatment of prisoners had occurred, systemic abuse was not apparent. Those innocent nationalists who were arrested and detained without good reason did not spend too much time drawing such legalistic distinctions. For them, internment provided a role for the British army (and by extension the British government) that had been written for them long ago – and during the 1970s they took to it with gusto.

The IRA capitalized on the resultant nationalist anger by stepping up its campaign of violence against the British army in 1971 and 1972, which exasperated the British government and put more pressure on Faulkner and the Stormont administration to deliver reforms that would calm the situation. The nationalist MPs at Stormont walked out, claiming that their presence was lending a vestige of credibility to a system that had none remaining, and that the British government needed to step in to introduce fundamental political reform.

## BLOODY SUNDAY AND THE DEATH THROES OF UNIONIST POWER

The final nail in the coffin of the Stormont administration (an appropriate metaphor for the times) was driven home in Derry on 30 January 1972, a day that would henceforth be referred to as 'Bloody Sunday'. By now, the civil rights movement had become an anti-internment protest, and a march planned for that day was to provide the tipping point for an escalation of political violence.

For a number of weeks, anti-internment protesters and the wider nationalist community had been shaping up for a fight with the British army and Stormont government, and on that cold, crisp Sunday afternoon in Derry the latent tensions came pouring out. Nationalists had become increasingly angry at the tactics of the government, which hid behind the police and a bogus public order agenda. They were also emboldened at this stage by recent PR victories and were aware of the global media interest they had helped to stimulate.

For their part, many unionists were becoming alarmed at the breakdown of law and order and some felt motivated to get behind Paisley, who was organizing a counter-demonstration. The British government was becoming increasingly agitated by the embarrassing scenes of lawlessness taking place and by its humiliating inability to govern the region effectively. The police and army were embattled, exhausted, ill-prepared to act as peace-keepers in the region and angered by the increasing violence being directed at them by the Provisional IRA.

Some 12,000 nationalist demonstrators gathered at 3 p.m. in the Creggan housing estate in Derry for the march, which had been declared illegal by the Stormont government. Paisley had just called off his counter-demonstration, which had also been banned. The organizers of the anti-internment march had been careful to hold several meetings the previous week that had emphasized the need to maintain discipline and ensure non-violence. They were aware that the security response was likely to be heavy-handed and that, with the international media coverage, this would maximize the propaganda value of the event. Had they known just how heavy-handed it would be, they might have reconsidered their decision to proceed.

The banners of the marchers displayed familiar slogans: 'End Internment', 'Civil Rights for All', 'End the Special Powers Act'. Thousands of people marched from the Creggan down to the Brandywell and then into the Bogside area, their ranks swelling at every street corner. By the time they reached the Bogside, their numbers were estimated at over 20,000. Shortly after 3.30 p.m. the predictable confrontation took place as CS gas and rubber bullets were fired at the demonstrators by the police and general mayhem broke out on the streets. In the context of the times – in the dog-days of the civil rights movement – it seemed an unremarkable Sunday afternoon. But that day was different: through the gagging smell of CS gas and the characteristic thud of rubber bullets came a different sound – louder, sharper, piercing the air periodically. It was the sound of high-velocity British army rifles, as snipers from the elite Parachute Regiment who had taken up elevated positions in nearby flats opened fire indiscriminately on the marchers. Among the many eye-witnesses was an Italian journalist:

> I saw a young fellow who had been wounded, crouching against the wall. He was shouting 'don't shoot, don't shoot'. A paratrooper approached and shot him from about one yard. I saw a young boy of 15 protecting his girl friend against the wall and then proceeding to try and rescue her by going out with a handkerchief and with the other hand on his hat. A paratrooper approached, shot him from about one yard into the stomach, and shot the girl into the arm.[27]

The Parachute Regiment killed thirteen people that afternoon (a fourteenth later died from his wounds in hospital). The youngest was sixteen years of age. None of those killed was carrying any weapon and none of them posed a threat to the lives of the soldiers who shot them. While the British army defended its actions by claiming that it had been fired on, it was not able to provide any evidence of this, and nor was it able to disguise the fact that none of those killed – some of whom had been shot in the back or while lying prostrate on the ground – had fired weapons at army positions. To the nationalist community, this was murder, pure and simple, of unarmed Catholics by a ruthless and callous British military presence. The Provisional IRA subsequently welcomed hundreds of new 'volunteers' and prepared for a sustained campaign of violence against the 'British presence' in Ireland. This was fuelled by the fact that the British government held no one to account for Bloody Sunday, appointing a toothless inquiry led by Lord Chief Justice Widgery that exonerated those responsible. Widgery's conclusion that there had been large numbers of armed civilians in the area who had fired at the army merely added insult to the considerable injury of the victims.[28] The nationalist feeling that the British were shedding crocodile tears was heightened by a leaked letter to Col. Derek Wilford (the regiment's commanding officer) from a former colleague in the Paras, which was printed in the *Sunday Press* newspaper the week after Bloody Sunday:

> Dear Wilford,
>     As an ex-parachute Brigade Commander I write just to say how proud it made one feel to see the way, on TV, on which your lads went into action against those blighters last Sunday. They looked splendid and, as usual, bang on the ball. It seems to me and many others that

prompt retaliatory action such as this is long overdue. It will have, I've little doubt, a most salutory effect. Should have happened long since . . .[29]

The unionist government tried to pin the blame on the organizers of the parade, and Prime Minister Brian Faulkner rather lamely cited the IRA as the cause of the deaths: 'Those who organised this march must bear a terrible responsibility for urging people to lawlessness and for providing the IRA with the opportunity to again bring death on our streets.'[30] The Derry coroner, Hubert O'Neill, who examined the dead, noted that many of them had been shot in the back and he laid the blame squarely at the door of the Parachute Regiment: 'It strikes me that the army ran amok that day and shot without thinking. They were shooting innocent people . . . I say it without reservation – it was sheer, unadulterated murder.'[31] Others detected a more sinister agenda, arguing that the most disciplined regiment in the British army was trained not to 'run amok' or lose its cool, regardless of the pressure:

It is stretching credulity very far to assert that in the presence of the Commander of Northern Ireland Ground Forces – who was in Derry that day – they collectively lost their cool and breached orders. It can safely be taken for granted that they took up the positions they were instructed to take up, laid down the lines of fire they were instructed to lay down and aimed at targets which they had been told to aim at.[32]

The long-term implications of Bloody Sunday were profound. It internationalized the conflict in Northern Ireland and shone a powerful beam on the failures of government in both London and Belfast. The Irish government, despite its lack of any practical control over events, felt obliged to at least make some noise about the breakdown of law and order in Northern Ireland. Internal public opinion in the Irish Republic demanded that the government should call Britain to account, and a large protest in Dublin of around 30,000 people burned down the British embassy, with other attacks being carried out in Cork and Limerick. International outrage was widespread, and Britain was embarrassed and humiliated in the court of international opinion. By this point it was clear that Northern Ireland was ungovernable, that Faulkner's unionist government was incapable of restoring law and order and that the British had no alternative but to politically re-engage with Northern Ireland after fifty years of neglect.

## CONCLUSION: THE LAST DAYS OF STORMONT

For God's sake bring me a large Scotch – what a bloody awful country.[33]

This remark was uttered by Conservative politician Reginald Maudling in July 1970, following his first visit to Northern Ireland as Home Secretary. The outburst epitomized two emerging trends. First, the slow and reluctant re-entry of Northern Ireland onto the domestic agenda of British politics in the wake of the rising levels of sectarian violence and destruction in the region. Second, the complete lack of understanding or empathy that the British political elite had for people in Northern Ireland, irrespective of their political allegiance. This was frequently displayed as frustration within British political circles, but it stemmed from an abiding fear that they were being sucked inexorably back into the quicksand of Irish politics that had sunk so many British politicians in the past. These brooding worries were not misplaced, as Northern Ireland lurched from crisis to disaster in the early months of 1972. Community sectarianism and rioting evolved into more targeted violence against individuals and families, many of whom were burned out of their homes as the urban landscape crystallized along sectarian lines. This grim litany reached a tipping point in 1972, following Bloody Sunday. The British government realized that its attempt to govern Northern Ireland at arm's length, through the beleaguered proxy of the unionist regime at Stormont, was failing. Following the international condemnation that was heaped on Britain in the aftermath of Bloody Sunday, it was clear that a more hands-on attitude was required and that security policy in particular needed to be taken away from the unionist government. When British Prime Minister Edward Heath summoned Brian Faulkner to Downing Street to inform him of this more strident approach, the unionist delegation walked out. At a subsequent strategy meeting in Belfast, the Northern Ireland government resigned *en masse*, incensed at how much authority had been stripped away from Stormont.

Direct rule had been born, and it signalled the end of unionist political domination and the arrival of a much more remote form of governance, with most policy decisions being taken in London by unaccountable British cabinet ministers and civil service mandarins. This was, of course, a 'make do and mend' response, rather than the fulfilment of a carefully thought-out strategy. It was also regarded as a temporary arrangement until such time as the local political system could be patched together again, though this would take another generation to achieve.

On 1 April 1972, fifty years of devolved government at Stormont was brought to an end when 'direct rule' from Westminster was introduced and William Whitelaw was appointed the first secretary of state for Northern Ireland. A new phase in the political history of Northern Ireland was about to begin.

# CHAPTER THREE

# THE RATIONALITY OF WAR, 1972–74

## FIRST PRINCIPLES OF SECTARIAN GEOGRAPHY

I GREW UP in East Belfast during the 1970s and, as a young Catholic living in a predominantly Protestant area of the city, my childhood memories are laced with incidents of sectarian conflict. This reality required a particular 'working logic', which seemed normal at the time when viewed through the prism of community-based violence. As I lived in a relatively mixed area, I had both Catholic and Protestant friends, but when I met the friends of my Protestant friends, an unspoken charade frequently ensued. I would acquire a different Christian name to avoid trouble – for their part, they were anxious not to endanger me, while I wanted to be careful not to implicate them in knowing a 'Fenian'. The same would happen to them in reverse when they met some of my Catholic friends (so long as they were not wearing their school uniforms, which functioned as a sectarian branding-iron, due to the religious segregation of education).

From a very early age, therefore, it became clear that danger lurked beyond the safety of the local street corner, and we all adapted to that reality by being aware of our political geography and by being cautious about what we said, where we went, and whom we spoke to.

We learned to fear the 'Tartan gangs', young Protestant hooligans who periodically roamed the streets, looking for Catholics to beat up. This was a curious sub-culture of early 1970s Belfast, linked, in part, to the popular culture of the time. The tartan was essentially a gang symbol, spuriously linked to the Scottish heritage of Ulster Protestantism, but owing just as much to the availability of tartan edging on shirts and trousers facilitated by the popularity of the Scottish bubble-gum pop band of the time, the Bay City Rollers. The 'Rollers' were more Osmonds than Sex Pistols, but the heavily merchandised cheap nylon clothing spawned by 'Rollermania' in the mid-1970s was a boon to proto-paramilitaries in the Tartan gangs, many of whom later graduated into the more hard-core activities of the Ulster Defence Association.

My secondary school in East Belfast was bombed by loyalist paramilitaries, as it provided an easy target and a symbol of hated 'otherness'. During one English literature lesson, one of the men working on the school building etched the letters 'UVF' – Ulster Volunteer Force – into the encrusted dust on the window pane, while the unfortunate teacher tried to instil an interest in the novels of Thomas Hardy in her unwilling and unruly pupils. It was a hopeless task. Given this wider context, perhaps it is no surprise that she found more purchase with *Lord of the Flies*. Our school and the neighbouring Protestant college would 'stagger' the end of the school day: the students from the two schools were released fifteen minutes apart, in order to avoid large-scale violence and street disorder. They stoned our school bus; we stoned theirs.[1] This was my normality, though, as a child, I was more afraid of the casual brutality, sadism and psychological dysfunction that came from my teachers, than I was about the prospects of being attacked by those beyond its gates.

My local Catholic church, which was situated in a working-class Protestant area, was also bombed by loyalist paramilitaries in 1973 (thankfully at night, when no one was there, though the explosion reduced the small chapel to a mangled pile of bricks and debris). The ironic result was that a high metal fence (topped off by a fetching display of looping barbed wire) was built around the perimeter of the church, and a platoon of British soldiers kept guard over the parishioners every Sunday until Mass had ended. One Christmas, at Midnight Mass (in the days when it used actually to be held at midnight, rather than at 6 p.m.), the usual painfully dull sermon was livened up considerably by a loyalist mob, which threw stones through the stained-glass windows and vandalized all the vehicles in the car park, as the parishioners huddled inside. Through a child's eyes, this was all massively exciting and a blessed relief from the aching boredom of Mass, but the adults were not laughing and the church eventually closed down in the early 1990s following a steady decline in the Catholic population and concern about further sectarian attacks.

There is an ironic twist to all this: many years later, when I was preparing to get married in Lancaster, I attended the obligatory (and inordinately lengthy) Catholic marriage classes. Once the local priest had finished tut-tutting to himself (not quite *sotto voce*) over the fact that my fiancée and I lived 'in sin', it became clear that he knew the geography and the detailed history of this tiny chapel. This seemed unusual, even allowing for the tight network and peripatetic nature of the clergy, but gradually other elements started falling into place. During the short breaks between his unanswerable questions ('What do you think marriage means in the context of the Catholic faith?'; 'What did Jesus teach us about love?'), he spoke of his skiing holidays in Germany, his camping trips and his concern about the *ethics* of war. As I danced around the moral landmines he planted in my way, it slowly dawned on me – he was a 'Brit'! He turned out to have been an army chaplain to the Parachute Regiment in Northern Ireland during the 1970s and knew intimately the area that I was from. While I counted to ten and bit my lip into bloody shreds, he mused about how he used to counsel 'his boys' about when it was morally right to 'shoot to kill' on the streets of Belfast. My fiancée and I eventually decided that we needed to be married by someone else, though it did make me think that God had a devilish sense of humour.[2]

Back in Belfast in the 1970s, a culture of sectarian division was therefore etched into everyday life, to the point that it was normal and unremarkable. The daily routine was fractured by army checkpoints, bomb scares and the drip-feed of fatalities reported on the media. In terms of its physical geography, Belfast became grotesque – a mangled sprawl of wire-mesh fortified police stations, damaged buildings, closed streets, army lookout posts and barriers laughingly referred to as 'peace walls' (whereas in fact they were anything but). As for nightlife in Belfast, there was none to speak of in the centre of the city, which shut down after the shops closed at 5 p.m., when people retreated to their respective enclaves.

On the streets, the British army presence was palpable, as the soldiers cruised around in armour-plated Saracens (locally referred to as 'pigs') and mounted heavily armed foot patrols, which were frequently undertaken by (understandably) nervous teenage boys. The drone of army helicopters hovering constantly over West Belfast and of Chinook troop carriers lumbering across the skyline became part of the region's daily soundtrack during these decades.

To get into the centre of town you had to pass through security barricades and turnstiles that had been set up by the army in an effort to stop the IRA from bombing commercial premises in the city. 'Would the key-holder please return to their premises' became an unwelcome catch-phrase on the radio news, usually indicating that a bomb had been planted in a shop and that the army bomb-disposal specialists needed access to deal with it. 'Suspect device' became part of the local language, to the point that the glorious Belfast punk band Stiff Little Fingers immortalized it in their 1978 punk classic of the same name.

The army would stop you and ask: 'Who are you? Where are you coming from? What are you doing here? Where are you going to?' – what Irish poet Ciaran Carson termed 'a fusillade of question marks'.[3] In truth, these enquiries were not always so polite, and dawn raids by the army on Catholic homes in republican areas of Belfast and Derry were a common occurrence in the 1970s. A school friend once told me of how, on his way to a music lesson, he had been stopped by a soldier. Asked what was in the long, cylindrical case on his shoulder, he (truthfully) replied 'my bouzouki'. Predictably he was put up against the nearest wall and robustly searched, the soldier unaware that this Greek stringed instrument (with a name uncomfortably similar to 'bazooka') had been adapted into the Irish folk-music tradition.

## JAW-JAW AND WAR-WAR

By the middle of 1972, Northern Ireland had settled into its new, ugly reality. The Catholic and Protestant communities had fractured physically, with barbed-wire fences and walls being erected in interface areas to keep them from attacking each other. There was violent mayhem on the streets on a regular basis, as the paramilitary groups on both sides had crystallized, gained recruits and resources from their frightened and angry communities, and devised their basic tactics. Northern Ireland was engulfed in violence in the early 1970s. In 1970, there were 25 deaths, 213 shooting incidents and 170 bombs planted; in 1971 this rose to 174 deaths, over 1,700 shootings and over 1,500 bombings; by 1972 the figures had risen again, with 467 people killed, over 10,500 shooting incidents and over 1,800 bombs planted.

Both republican and loyalist paramilitaries had evolved organically and haphazardly in response to violent sectarian events that surrounded their communities, in a context where the state seemed powerless to exert control. The Ulster *Defence* Association was called that for a reason; while the Provisional IRA also emerged initially with a remit to defend nation-alist areas from sectarian attacks by Protestants.

The UDA began as a local militia in the early 1970s, recruiting large numbers of working-class Protestants in Belfast. By 1972 the UDA could boast a membership of over 20,000. Its rudimentary uniform of black berets, sunglasses and combat jackets, together with its quasi-military drilling in the streets, was intended to demonstrate that it had significant numbers, was well organized and was prepared to defend its areas from attack by militant republicans. The UDA did its killing under other organizational names, mainly the Ulster Freedom Fighters (UFF), though the two groups' membership overlapped significantly.

The loyalists were able to demonstrate through the public parading of masked UDA men through the streets that they could mobilize the Protestant working class into a disciplined militia and that they had the stomach for a fight. They had done this before – and it showed: rather judiciously, the leaders of the main loyalist paramilitary factions built alliances with the mainstream unionist political establishment, so that a united front could be presented to their common enemies. It was always an uneasy alliance (for both sides), but Ian Paisley and Bill Craig, the former Stormont home affairs minister (and *bête noire* of the civil rights movement), were not slow in coming forward to provide a bridge with loyalist militants. The two men hated each other, of course, as they jostled to be seen as the spokesman for Protestant Ulster; but their need for co-operation was greater than their personal antipathy.

By 1972, Paisley had one of the highest political profiles in Northern Ireland. The ruddy-cheeked preacher was charismatic, a master orator and rabble-rouser, and he had a shrewd political intelligence, which he exploited to great effect. He frequently sailed close to the wind in terms of his connections to actual violence, but he usually managed to stay on the right side of the law – or at least to convince those interpreting it that he should not be prosecuted. Though he was arrested on several occasions, and was even jailed for a short time in 1966, for the most part those arrests were linked to minor public order offences, rather than to more serious allegations of terrorist-related activities. While Paisley dallied with militant loyalists, he made sure that he had 'plausible deniability' for their violent actions. This made the loyalist paramilitaries and some of his more militant colleagues in the Democratic Unionist Party (DUP) mistrustful of him. Some compared him to the Grand Old Duke of York, famed for leading his troops up to the top of the hill to do battle, but not joining them in the fight:

> What strikes you about Ian is that . . . there's a point at which he will always retreat. He'll huff and puff to bring about a situation and then he'll come back from the edge. People are in jail for going over the top because they thought he was leading them there.[4]

For many unionists, frightened by the meltdown of law and order taking place around them, 'Big Ian' was a breath of fresh air in comparison to the bloodless and toothless politicians that unionists were used to. He was part medicine-man, part illusionist, a whirling dervish who thundered and raged against the establishment and at the 'enemies of Ulster'.

Shortly before Stormont fell in March 1972, Bill Craig founded Ulster Vanguard, a pressure group that evolved into a political party. It became both a platform for Craig to display leadership and an umbrella for unionist politicians and loyalist paramilitaries to shelter beneath. While Paisley was a rambunctious orator, his hatred and threats laced with laughter and devilment, Craig was a cold fish, his speeches delivered in a sullen, nasal drone and in a manner that increasingly came to resemble that of Oswald Mosley, the British fascist leader of the 1930s. Vanguard instinctively looked inwards to Northern Ireland, rather than outwards at its allegiance to Britain, and it focused on the failures of British security policy, as well as on its malign political interference. If the British government was unable to protect the Protestants of Ulster, then Vanguard demonstrated that it was willing to step up to the plate. Craig gathered supporters quickly, and an estimated 70,000 people attended a Vanguard rally in Belfast's Ormeau Park on 18 March 1972 to listen to Craig's spine-chilling call to arms:

> We must build up a dossier of the men and women who are a menace to this country, because one day, ladies and gentlemen, if and when the politicians fail us, it may be our job, to liquidate the enemy.[5]

He meant Catholics, of course – and everyone knew it. Six days later, British Prime Minister Edward Heath prorogued Stormont. Unionists were incensed at the British government for (as they saw it) sacrificing their parliament on the altar of IRA violence. By contrast, nationalists were predictably triumphant, as the hated symbol of political, economic and cultural domination had been brought down. A bitter valedictory statement released by Faulkner and his Cabinet colleagues in March 1972, following the resignation of the Stormont government, emphasized their view that the sword was actually mightier than the pen in Northern Ireland:

I fear . . . that many people will draw a sinister and depressing message from these events: that violence *can* pay; that violence *does* pay; that those who shout, lie, denigrate and even destroy earn for themselves an attention that responsible conduct and honourable behaviour do not.[6]

However, in spite of the stamping of unionist feet and sinister hints about possible disorder from radical voices such as Ian Paisley and Bill Craig, silence finally fell over the Stormont parliament after the last session ended on 28 March 1972. The following day there was no unionist government in Northern Ireland. Fifty years of unionist power had come to an end, and there was an eerie silence at Stormont in the days that followed, punctuated only by the sound of bombs exploding across Belfast as the Provisional IRA and loyalist paramilitaries sought to provide a military answer to the political problem.

Violence escalated from the IRA and loyalist murder gangs in response to this political tumult, while Vanguard continued to build alliances between mainstream unionist politics and more militant factions. Following a speech to the British Conservative Party's right-wing Monday Club in the wake of Stormont's suspension, Craig demonstrated that Vanguard had closed the gap between the political and paramilitary aspects of Ulster loyalism: 'We are prepared to come out and shoot and kill. I am prepared to come out and shoot and kill. Let us put the bluff aside.'[7] Neither Craig nor Paisley was a killer in any direct sense, but both men did seem to have a soft spot for paramilitary chic and for the power that such alliances gave them in the eyes of others – not least the British government, which was trying to look out for who spoke for the Ulster Protestants.

In February 1973, Craig called a one-day general strike as a show of strength against the British government and to prove that he had the backing of the loyalist hard men. This resulted in electricity blackouts, a number of explosions, multiple arson attacks and two fatalities. While this episode was too much for some unionists and damaged Craig politically, it was a sign of things to come, as an angry and frightened unionist community looked for answers.[8] Their beloved parliament had been ripped from them, the Provisional IRA was wreaking havoc on the streets, and the British seemed helpless to do anything to arrest the decline.

Most of the paramilitary activity had a certain logic and was not 'mindless' violence. It was targeted, strategic and designed to apply political pressure on the British government. The IRA believed that it could sap the will of the government and its 'domestic' population in Britain and force it to withdraw from Northern Ireland, thus precipitating the nationalist goal of a 'united Ireland'. The loyalists used violence both to destabilize political initiatives they felt were dangerous to unionist political interests and to demonstrate to the British government that they were organized, powerful and could become just as big a problem as their republican counterparts if their voice was ignored.

There was also a great degree of confusion within British political and military circles, as they struggled to cope with the carnage that was unfolding. Who were these people behind the alphabet soup of the IRA/ UDA/UVF/UFF (to say nothing of the Irish National Liberation Army (INLA) or the Red Hand Commando (RHC))? What did they want, and crucially, what would it take to stop them?

The Provisional IRA developed its strategy gradually over time, and it emerged quite pragmatically rather than being driven by any ideological imperatives. The initial instincts, according to its first chief of staff, Seán MacStiofáin, were defensive rather than offensive. The Provisional leadership, represented by its 'army council', took the view that the unionist state was unravelling and that the British government would be unable to control the anger as the unionist position continued to unwind. The first priority, therefore, was to build a defensive capability to protect nationalist areas from attack by loyalist mobs. This led to a second objective, which was to complement this defensive action with targeted reprisals against British troops who killed or intimidated civilians within nationalist areas. The third objective was to take proactive offensive action against British Crown Forces in Ireland and Britain. Initially, this focused on British troops and bomb attacks in Northern Ireland, but the bombing campaign was soon exported to Britain itself and its large urban centres.[9] The strategic objectives were threefold. First, the campaign of violence aimed to disorientate the British army and police response and to make clear that a war situation existed (rather than mere acts of criminal terrorism, as the British tried to allege). Second, the Provisionals wanted to demonstrate to the nationalist community that they were a disciplined and professional guerrilla movement with a cutting edge that would achieve change in a way that democratic politics had so spectacularly failed to do. Third, the sustained campaign of violence aimed at sapping the political will of the British government and of wider public opinion to remain in Ireland.

From the British side, a range of contradictory responses emerged: internment and curfews on the one hand, and negotiations on the other. Initially there was an understanding within government circles that paramilitary violence was both rational and strategic on the part of both republican and loyalist militants. There was at least a basic understanding that the bombings and shootings taking place were linked to the wider political context and directed at particular targets (e.g. to damage political leaders, to destabilize talks, or, in the case of the IRA, to force a response from the British army that would damage its image within the nationalist community and thus increase support for the Provisionals).

As the intensity and ferocity of the IRA campaign accelerated, however, this perception altered and the actions of the 'men of violence' were cast as being 'mindless', 'cowardly' and even psychotic. For the most part, this is a misunderstanding of the dynamics of paramilitary violence; in the main it was driven (on both republican and loyalist sides) by a particular type of rationality and logic, however warped it might have seemed to outsiders. Ultimately what perpetuated the violence was a belief that violence *worked* and could achieve changes that democratic peaceful methods could not. The Provisional IRA did periodically engage in dialogue with Britain and on occasions it observed ceasefires to facilitate this. However, rather than the ballot box, for most of the period the Armalite was seen as the catalyst for change by paramilitary groups on both sides.

While the ongoing violence was an immediate security problem for the British government, controlling it also became a political necessity, especially when the Provisional IRA extended its bombing campaign to mainland Britain. On 22 February 1972, in retaliation for the previous month's Bloody Sunday (see chapter 2), the Official IRA exploded a bomb at Aldershot army barracks, the headquarters of the Parachute Regiment, killing five women in the kitchens and an army chaplain. On 14 November 1973, an IRA bomb squad detonated car bombs at the Old Bailey courthouse and Scotland Yard police station in London, killing one and injuring 200.

In July 1972, shortly after the Stormont parliament was prorogued, the new secretary of state for Northern Ireland, William (Willie) Whitelaw, flew a delegation of Provisional IRA leaders to London for talks. This unlikely event was most definitely not a meeting of minds, as Whitelaw's attempts at cordial bonhomie fell flat with his stony-faced and uncompromising guests, one of whom was Martin McGuinness. Whitelaw was a consummate British politician and the epitome of bluff English charm, but his affable manner sat uneasily with his Irish guests, who saw him as the quintessential English squire (though by birth he was actually Scottish). The IRA leaders saw past his 'splendid, dear boy' politeness and correctly assessed that he was not as stupid as he appeared.[10] After the IRA delegation had refused Whitelaw's offer of a drink to 'take the edge off', Seán MacStiofáin, the chief of staff of the Provisional IRA (and enthusiastic teetotaller), was told to speak freely. Ironically MacStiofáin was born in London as the slightly less exotic John Stephenson and never quite managed to eradicate his cockney accent, which must have been intensely irritating for him, given his reinvention as an Irish republican revolutionary. Whitelaw later claimed to be unnerved by this tightly wound former member of the RAF and considered him to be 'mad'. The zeal of the convert is frequently unconvincing and MacStiofáin gave the impression of wanting to be more Irish than the Irish themselves. He learned to speak fluent Gaelic and was a devout Catholic. Despite his grisly sobriquet (Mac-the knife), he was a clean-living type, often irritated by some of his hard-drinking and politically incorrect colleagues.

The two sides came to the London meeting poles apart, and they left it no closer. MacStiofáin reeled off the usual bullet-point list of demands, the main one being that the British must indicate a timetable for withdrawal (before 1 January 1975) if the IRA ceasefire that had been called to facilitate their get-together was to continue. The meeting was an unmitigated disaster in immediate terms: while the IRA was naive and inflexible, the British were hopelessly misinformed about the mood and aspirations of Irish republicans at the time. Taking the longer view, however, the failure of this meeting did inform later attempts to open dialogue between the two sides, and from that perspective it might be judged to have been not an entire waste of time.

Alongside this jaw-jaw between the IRA and British security forces came war-war. The conflict was always an 'undeclared' one in British eyes, to avoid elevating the violence above the level of domestic criminality and giving it the political legitimacy and international credibility that Irish republicans craved. This struggle for legitimacy over the narrative of the conflict was integral to the political strategies of both sides and became a key part of the propaganda war over the next three decades. Winning the propaganda battle drove the political logic of the Provisional IRA and the British government, despite the brutal activities that this necessitated on both sides.

## BLOODY FRIDAY

Less than two weeks after the disastrous meeting with Whitelaw, the Provisional IRA committed one of the worst acts of violence in the history of the Northern Ireland conflict. The word 'atrocity' has been so overused by the media in their coverage of the Northern Ireland conflict that its impact has become diluted. The word should have been reserved for days like this: in the space of an hour, on the afternoon of Friday, 21 July 1972, nineteen bombs exploded in various parts of Belfast city centre. There were no effective warnings given by the IRA to prevent the mayhem and carnage that followed from the series of car bombs and explosions at bus and railway stations, hotels, shops and offices. The bombs were planted with the intention of killing as many people as possible, and in this they succeeded: men, women and children were literally blown to pieces on the streets of the city. Among the dead was fourteen-year-old Stephen Parker, a student at the City of Belfast School of Music, which later established the 'Stephen Parker Award' in his honour. In scenes reminiscent of the Belfast Blitz of the Second World War, plumes of smoke could be seen rising all over the city, accompanied by a cacophony of sirens from the emergency services and fire alarms from burning commercial premises. Deafened by the noise, dazed and frightened, Friday-afternoon shoppers wandered around looking for a route out of the chaos.

The footage of the clean-up operation at Oxford Street bus station, where six people died, is still too graphic to be shown on mainstream television. The grainy pictures of firemen shovelling the charred remains of bodies into plastic bags and lifting severed limbs and other unrecognizable parts of the victims off the pavement are difficult to stomach. These are among the most shocking visual images of the conflict, and I show them to my undergraduate students every year to remind them of the reality behind the statistics of violence, as they sit in awkward silence watching the footage of what became known as 'Bloody Friday'.

Peter Taylor, a British journalist whose first story in Northern Ireland was Bloody Sunday, related the recollections of a police officer a quarter of a century after he witnessed the event:

> One of the most horrendous memories for me was seeing a head stuck to the wall. A couple of days later, we found vertebrae and a rib cage on the roof of a nearby building. The reason we found it was because the seagulls were diving onto it. I've tried to put it at the back of my mind for twenty-five years.[11]

Miraculously, given the number and force of the explosions, only nine people died, though over seventy women and girls and over fifty men and boys were injured. In Britain and across the world, the reaction to Bloody

Friday was one of revulsion. In Ireland as a whole it was condemned by the vast majority, including many nationalists and republicans who were shocked at the scale and severity of the attacks. The highly respected *Irish Times* newspaper compared the IRA to Nazis and questioned the moral compass of a nation that could harbour such violent intent:

> Throughout the 32 counties Irish men and women should ponder how a virulent Nazi-style disregard for life can lodge in the hearts of our fellow countrymen; all the more virulent in that once again the Innocent have been the main sufferers. Hitler in his Berlin bunker decided that the German people were no longer worthy of him and deserved not to survive. Yesterday's dead and injured are testimony to something similarly rotten in our philosophy of life.[12]

The Provisional IRA admitted operational responsibility for the attacks, but accepted no moral or political culpability. MacStiofáin looked metaphorically through the debris to find that five of those who died were 'innocent civilians' and found it in his heart to admit that 'our attitude was that it was five too many'. But of course, for MacStiofáin and his colleagues in the IRA, the underlying cause was the continued British presence in Ireland and the failure of the British Crown Forces to pass on the warnings that had been given to them.[13] Such qualified regret cut little ice with anyone beyond the hard core of the Provisional movement. It would not be the last time that the Provisionals (and their loyalist counterparts) would view the aftermath of their activities as if the suffering they had inflicted was somehow disconnected from them – a force of nature, like a flood or an earthquake, rather than an act of human agency. As the political development of Sinn Fein gathered pace during the 1980s, the declarations of 'regret' for 'mistakes' made became as convincing as Bill Clinton's admission during his presidency that, while he may have taken illegal drugs in his youth, he 'didn't inhale'. In political terms, Bloody Friday was as much an own goal for the IRA as Bloody Sunday was for the British army. It was a propaganda disaster, and the IRA knew it.

Bloody Friday presented Whitelaw with an opportunity, albeit an unwelcome one. The public reaction to the violence had increased the political space available to him to pursue a more robust security strategy. British public opinion demanded it and Irish opinion accepted it – in the short term at least. Whitelaw's parliamentary statement in the aftermath of Bloody Friday was a declaration of intent to take a harsher security line in relation to the Provisional IRA:

No one can deny ... that Her Majesty's Government have now an absolutely unchallengeable right to ask the House, the country and, indeed the whole world for their support in an absolute determination to destroy the capacity of the Provisional IRA for further acts of inhumanity. It has degraded the human race, and it must now be clear to all that its sole objective is to promote its aims by violence and by violence alone.[14]

Whitelaw now had the pretext he needed to send the army into the 'no-go' areas of Belfast and Derry. Here, semi-permanent barricades had been set up by the IRA (and to a lesser extent by the UDA) and the British rule of law scarcely existed, as armed paramilitaries stood around openly checking cars and people's driving licences while the police and army looked on helplessly. The British government had effectively ceded *de facto* control of these parts of the United Kingdom to armed republican and loyalist militias. Despite unionist objections to this abdication of responsibility, the British had felt it expedient to ignore the challenge to its sovereign authority, out of fear that taking it on would inflame an already tense relationship between the army and the nationalist population. Bloody Friday changed that. The following weekend, seven more battalions of British soldiers arrived in Northern Ireland, raising troop levels to 22,000, the highest since 1922.

## OPERATION MOTORMAN

The largest British military exercise since Suez in 1956 was launched by the army at dawn on Monday, 31 July 1972.[15] On the preceding Saturday and Sunday, large military transport planes had landed at the local airport every five minutes, bringing tens of thousands of extra troops into Northern Ireland for what was seen as a make or break effort to reassert British control. Serious military hardware accompanied the arrival of the troops, including a plane-load of riot shields, a hundred armoured personnel carriers and tanks.[16] There was plenty of warning that the British army was being 'tooled up' to go on the offensive and reassert its authority (and that of the government) over urban areas that had effectively made a mockery of the idea that Britain was in control.

Operation Motorman targeted the no-go areas of Belfast and Derry that were effectively run by the IRA and were beyond the reach of the British army or police. Thirty-eight army battalions were involved, as 30,000 British troops saturated the no-go areas and used tanks and bulldozers to smash through the paramilitary barricades that had been set up to keep them out.

Though Prime Minister Edward Heath had been bracing himself for up to 1,000 casualties, the operation in fact met with little resistance.[17] Unlike the disastrous internment policy, Operation Motorman was well planned, properly resourced and effectively led by the army, in close harmony with Whitelaw and Heath. Just as importantly, the timing of this military initiative was unusually deft, coming at a point when all but the most ardent supporters of the republican 'armed struggle' accepted that there was a need for some restoration of law and order, in order to try and ensure that the events of Bloody Friday were not repeated. It was an open secret that a major military initiative was being planned, and this allowed many IRA leaders to evade capture. However, the operation was carried out very swiftly: it began at 4 a.m. and the troops had control of all their major targets before most people living there had finished breakfast. Whitelaw later made a public statement explaining that Operation Motorman was designed to 'remove the capacity of the IRA to create terror and violence'.[18] While this would remain more of an aspiration than a reality, it was a rare example of a clearly thought-through and well-timed military move that regained the political initiative from the IRA.

Notwithstanding this assertion of control, British policy in Northern Ireland during the early 1970s was highly inconsistent. On the one hand, security initiatives such as internment and Operation Motorman attempted to get the Provisional IRA under military control, to arrest and detain the main paramilitary leaders and to prevent them from operating effectively. On the other hand, political expediency and short-term pragmatism were the main drivers in determining what could be done to encourage the paramilitaries to stop their violence. This could be viewed either as a sensible attempt by the British government to explore creative political alternatives in order to neutralize the paramilitary factions, or as a grubby attempt to pacify the IRA and buy it off.

Not for the last time, the British risked being accused of double-dealing: they were talking (and acting) tough in an attempt to 'root out the terrorists' and to establish a clear moral divide between the democratic process and the gunmen, but at the same time they were speaking to the very people who were carrying out the acts of violence and were apparently caving in to their demands: in 1972, following an IRA hunger strike in prison (but before Bloody Friday), Whitelaw conceded the principle of 'special category status' to prisoners convicted of paramilitary offences.

## WEAPONS OF THE WEAK

The tactic of the hunger strike contains a powerful mythology within Irish history, and it plugs into a logic of resistance and redemption that can transform apparent political impotence into more dynamic forms of power. In simple terms, the hunger strike turns the tables on the seemingly powerful and strengthens those who may, at first glance, appear to be the weaker party. It is the very vulnerability and physical decline of the hunger striker that throws the power of the state into such sharp relief. It also demonstrates the intense level of commitment of the hunger striker and those who support him/her to their political cause.

The hunger strike is not, of course, a particularly Irish form of resistance: it has been used as an act of political protest in over fifty-two countries, by groups and individuals. In 1932, Mahatma Gandhi engaged in a twenty-one-day hunger strike in protest against the British authorities in India, and there are numerous other examples of this form of civil disobedience being used to achieve political change. In Ireland, the tactic of the hunger strike has been used as a means of political protest and as a way of emphasizing to potential supporters the moral and ethical gap between British occupation/oppression and Irish victimhood/resistance. Within the Irish context, the tactic of the hunger strike also connects into the Catholic psyche of redemption that comes through suffering and self-denial. From this perspective, temporal death was merely a staging post to spiritual salvation; and just as Christ laid down his life for mankind, so the republican hunger striker would give up his (or her) life for others, in an ultimate act of self-sacrifice.

The hunger strike as a form of political protest gained in popularity in Ireland following the 1916 Easter Rising. In 1917, Thomas Ashe, jailed for the part he played in the Rising, went on hunger strike and refused to do prison work or wear a prison uniform. He died while being force-fed in hospital in Dublin and was immediately hailed as an Irish martyr. An estimated 40,000 people attended his funeral procession in Dublin, which became a rallying point for increasing nationalist sentiment in Ireland. In 1920, Terence MacSwiney died after spending seventy-four days on hunger strike in Brixton jail in England. This was a highly publicized protest within and beyond Ireland, as MacSwiney had been elected to Dail Eireann in 1918 and had become lord mayor of Cork earlier in 1920. Eleven other republican prisoners in Cork went on hunger strike at the same time in solidarity, and MacSwiney's death attracted worldwide attention. He became a symbol for the integrity and durability of the republican cause in

Ireland, as he played David to the British Goliath. His comment during his inauguration as mayor of Cork in March 1920 – 'it is not those who can inflict the most, but those who can endure the most who will prevail' – was to resonate down through generations of Irish republicans.

Billy McKee was a founding member of the Provisional IRA. In 1972, he led forty other republicans in Crumlin Road prison on hunger strike, demanding that they be treated as prisoners of war rather than as common criminals. Fearing that McKee's death would spark greater support for the IRA and an intensified campaign of violence, the new secretary of state, Willie Whitelaw, acceded to their demands and granted special category status. While this did not explicitly define paramilitaries as prisoners of war, it did treat them as a special case and allowed the IRA to argue that they were political dissidents rather than common criminals.

In 1972, the British government was oblivious to the wider context of the hunger-strike tactic and its role in Irish history, and did not initially appreciate the important connection between the hunger strike and the wider attempt by the IRA to define its armed struggle as political and legitimate. Whitelaw later regretted his decision to grant special category status in return for the prisoners ending their hunger strike, and he came to regard it as one of his biggest political mistakes. While it was an act of short-term expediency it had long-term implications, allowing the Provisional IRA (and their loyalist counterparts, who also benefited from it) to claim that they were 'political prisoners'. This was again critical in the propaganda war and would later come back to haunt both the British government and the republican movement.

Mixed messages rarely clarify political problems, and it seemed clear that the paramilitaries on both sides were out-thinking and out-flanking the politicians, within and beyond Northern Ireland. From the British government perspective, the need to reduce the attacks in Britain and Northern Ireland became an over-riding political priority. Aside from efforts to restrict paramilitary activities to 'an acceptable level of violence', the key security objective in this period was to 'criminalize' the 'terrorists'. To do so, the police/army had to delegitimize the paramilitary factions and cast them as murderous thugs. If the military goal was to contain civil unrest and paramilitary violence, the political objective was to isolate the 'men of violence' from the wider communities, whose active and passive support they required to continue their armed campaign.

Accurate intelligence came to be of paramount importance for the British, and their security strategy quickly revolved around the use of emergency law, surveillance operations and efforts to undermine the legit-imacy of the paramilitaries within their own communities. Perhaps most controversially, the drive for better intelligence, allied with the permissive legal apparatus, led to a lengthy detention of suspects, coercive and abusive questioning, and a perilous lack of accountability or political oversight of the security agencies.

The legal apparatus was the bedrock for security policies in Northern Ireland during this period. The Special Powers Act of 1922 and its successor, the 1973 Emergency Provisions Act (EPA), provided the legal basis for many of the counter-insurgency activities of the 1970s and 1980s. The 'emergency' powers were made permanent in 1933, until the 1973 EPA replaced this legislation with the introduction of Diplock courts (trial without jury) for a range of 'scheduled' offences. This 'scheduling' packaged together certain offences that carried a mandatory prison sentence, such as membership of a paramilitary organization or possession of firearms. The Diplock courts required a low burden of proof (e.g. uncorroborated confessions obtained from prisoners in custody) and the cases came before individual judges in non-jury trials. This led to fast and efficient prosecutions, but also to allegations of injustice and maltreat-ment. The Prevention of Terrorism Act (PTA) was introduced in Great Britain in 1974, following the Birmingham bombings, and was similar in nature to the EPA in Northern Ireland: both the EPA and the PTA were defined as unfortunate but necessary temporary legal arrangements, required to cope with an extraordinary situation. However, when an emer-gency becomes normality, the consequence is that the criminal justice system inevitably becomes politicized.

While the legal framework served to provide a cloak of respectability for all of this, the security techniques that were enabled by such legislation only served to alienate the nationalist community still further, and thus to perpetuate the existence of republican violence. The phrase 'extraordi-nary rendition' became a notorious aspect of American efforts to improve intelligence following the attacks on New York and Washington on 11 September 2001. This has also been referred to as the 'outsourcing of torture', whereby the US government, with the tacit approval of its allies (including the Irish, British and other European governments), forcibly apprehended suspects abroad and flew them to countries such as Yemen, Jordan, Morocco and Uzbekistan for interrogation. Coercive questioning up to and including torture was, however, a feature of counter-insurgency policies long before the 'war on terror' commenced. In the case of

Northern Ireland, it was not necessary to transport suspects out of the country in order to participate in this form of intelligence gathering:

> A hood was pulled over my head and I was handcuffed and subjected to verbal and personal abuse, which included the threat of being dropped from a helicopter which was in the air, being kicked and struck about the body with batons on the way ... After this all my clothes were taken from me and I was given a boiler suit to wear which had no buttons and which was several sizes too big for me. During all this time the hood was still over my head and the handcuffs were removed only at the time of the 'medical examination'. I was then taken into what I can only guess was another room and was made to stand with my feet wide apart and my hands pressed against a wall. During all this time I could hear a low droning noise, which sounded to me like an electric saw or something of that nature. This continued for what I can only describe as an indefinite period of time ... My brain seemed ready to burst. What was going to happen to me? Was I alone? Are they coming to kill me?[19]

This quote refers to the treatment not of an inmate at Abu Ghraib jail in Iraq or at the Guantanamo Bay detention centre, but of a suspect held without charge at Magilligan army base near Belfast in 1972. Paddy Joe McClean, a schoolteacher from Co. Tyrone (who subsequently turned out to have no paramilitary connections), was one of a group of fourteen detainees, since referred to as the 'guinea pigs', who were subjected to the 'five techniques' of sensory deprivation during coercive questioning in 1972. These techniques involved a typical pattern of physical and mental ill-treatment, combined with attempts to confuse and disorient suspects to make them more suggestible, through hooding, sleep and food deprivation, repetitive questioning, subjugation to white noise and a range of more petty harassments over a period of days. Such questioning was carried out by the British army's Force Research Unit (FRU) and the RUC Special Branch at a number of army centres, chiefly Palace Barracks on the Old Holywood Road, and Magilligan and Ballykinler army camps.

The European Court of Human Rights judged that substantial ill-treatment of prisoners had taken place during this period:

> Quite a large number of those held in custody at Palace Barracks were subjected to violence by members of the RUC. It also led to intense

suffering and to physical injury which on occasions was substantial
. . . Those in command at Palace Barracks at the relevant time could
not have been ignorant of the acts involved.[20]

The British found themselves in the position of having to stretch a legal
canopy across the conflict without allowing it to be defined as a state of
war, which would have required the treatment of suspects as politically
motivated prisoners. During the 1970s and 1980s, the aggressive policing
of nationalist areas was accompanied by more sinister techniques directed
at gathering intelligence from suspects in custody and alleged extra-judicial
killings by elements within the security agencies. Allegations of collusion
between the security forces and loyalist paramilitaries further reduced
nationalist confidence in the rule of law and remain sensitive issues to the
present day.[21]

## FROM THE ARMALITE TO THE BALLOT BOX

During the early 1970s, the logic of paramilitary violence was relatively
straightforward. The Provisional IRA believed in the transformative power
of 'armed struggle'. In very simple terms, the view was that the British had
a colonial commitment to remaining in Northern Ireland and geopolitical
security interests in staying there. They could not be persuaded to leave
through the power of argument, but could be shifted by physical force, if
republicans made it too uncomfortable for them to remain. Allied to this,
they believed that a 'long war' would eventually wear the British resolve
down and achieve what democratic methods could not.

The loyalist paramilitaries were also working – for the most part – to a
rational agenda. They used the threat of violence to persuade the British
government not to concede ground to the republicans, and violence itself
as a means of retaliation. By the early 1990s, in a deliberate attempt to
increase the pain felt within the nationalist community, loyalist paramilitaries were responsible for more deaths than the republicans. The hope
was that the republican grass roots would question whether the goals of
the Provisional IRA were worth it.

The British government consistently argued that the 'men of violence'
would never succeed and that Northern Ireland policy would never be
swayed by their actions. Such protestations did little to alter the determination of militants on either side. For one thing, recent history had made it
clear that British policy could be affected by violence: republicans were

mindful of the fact that this had produced talks with Whitelaw in 1972. Despite the 'collateral damage' caused by their 'mistakes', Northern Ireland was firmly on the international political agenda because of the violence of the Provisional IRA. Loyalists were conscious that the threat of violence by the UVF in 1914 had led to the creation of Northern Ireland in the first instance and to their exclusion from the 'home rule' arrangements made for the Irish Free State in 1920 (see chapter 1). Both sets of paramilitaries were also well aware of Britain's colonial history and of its habit of calling people criminal 'terrorists' one day and responsible 'statesmen' the next. So short-term condemnations from British politicians counted for little as the paramilitaries fought to win the wider propaganda war.

## A NEW INITIATIVE EMERGES

By 1973, a new political plan was desperately required – one that would provide a democratic alternative to violent militancy. In an effort to wrest the initiative from the paramilitary gangs, William Whitelaw published a White Paper outlining a scheme to restore devolved government to Northern Ireland (which unionists wanted), but only on the basis of power-sharing with nationalists (which they did not want). The White Paper also outlined a plan for a Council of Ireland, which would provide an institutional role for the Republic of Ireland, and this left many unionists fearing that the constitutional position of Northern Ireland was at risk. The predictable result was a further radicalization of the unionist electorate, as illustrated by elections in June 1973. At this poll the political centre was squeezed, as the DUP and the newly formed Ulster Vanguard won more seats than Faulkner's Official Unionists. Even within this group of moderates, Faulkner's authority looked extremely shaky. Right from the beginning, the political arithmetic barely added up for Whitelaw, as unionists who might be prepared to give his White Paper their lukewarm support were outnumbered by those who were implacably opposed to it.

The Social Democratic and Labour Party had emerged in this election as the clear voice of moderate nationalism, but it was no friend of Faulkner's unionists either. What resulted was a very unstable three-legged stool. Moderate and radical unionists were at loggerheads with one another, while Faulkner's rag-bag of lukewarm 'official unionists' eyed the SDLP with a mixture of distaste and desperation. For its part, while the SDLP had the political stage to itself as the only significant electoral representatives of the nationalist community, its members were constantly looking over their shoulders at militant republicans. Whether orange or green, politicians of all colours were constantly strung out by the continuing paramilitary violence, which persisted like a poisonous drip-feed into the body politic.

In many ways, Whitelaw's plan, as outlined in his 1973 White Paper, was a political lowest common denominator. It emerged because its basic political geometry – 'power-sharing with an Irish dimension' – was the price the SDLP felt it needed if it was to avoid being vilified by republicans for participating in a 'partitionist' institution. While the SDLP was committed to non-violent political change, it was, at times, a loose and incoherent coalition of interests, with some socialists favouring alliances with the Protestant community, but its republican members wanting progress towards a 'united Ireland'. Whitelaw championed the White Paper because he was keen to support the fledging SDLP and to send a message to the wider Catholic community that the democratic process was capable of producing peaceful change without the need for armed insurrection.

Faulkner and his allies supported Whitelaw's initiative on account of their innate political weakness. They had nowhere else to go and Faulkner was desperate for a political success that would send a message to moderate unionists that cross-community co-operation with nationalists was a viable alternative to the bellicose rhetoric of Vanguard and the DUP (and the murder gangs of the UDA and UVF). In summer 1973, when the SDLP, with the support of the Irish government, increased its demands for the scale of the Council of Ireland, Whitelaw held his nose and reluctantly agreed, since he needed the SDLP on board. Faulkner, forced to stick or twist on the deal, hoped to water down the remit of the Council of Ireland in negotiations, but was largely unsuccessful in doing so in the eyes of the wider unionist electorate.

In spite of these unpromising beginnings, by November 1973 an agreement had been reached in principle for a new form of devolved government in Northern Ireland. Faulkner's unionists agreed to share power with the SDLP in a cabinet-style government, with Faulkner as leader and the SDLP's Gerry Fitt as his deputy.

In contrast to the straight-laced, buttoned-down Faulkner, Fitt was a straight-talking, gravel-voiced socialist, whose commitment to non-violent social change was greater than his desire to pursue Irish nationalist goals against unionist wishes. He was to become a controversial political figure within Northern Ireland, as many unionists were affronted by his pugnacious style and his ability to convince politicians in London that serious political reform was necessary in Northern Ireland. Unionists disliked Fitt because he stood up to them effectively. As his political career wore on through the 1970s and 1980s, nationalists and republicans came to dislike him for being too quick to take the unionist side of the argument. In the 1970s, he seemed far too friendly with Faulkner for some; to the dismay of many nationalists, he also denounced IRA violence and, later, the 1981 hunger strike. 'Fitt the Brit' was the antagonistic graffiti daubed on walls in West Belfast, and when he took a seat in the British House of Lords in 1983 (as Lord Fitt of Bell's Hill) his critics accused the lifelong socialist of political hypocrisy. This went further than just name-calling or verbal sparring: on several occasions his home in Belfast was attacked by militant republicans, causing him to relocate his family to London. Like many others before and since, Fitt eventually found it impossible to pursue socialist ideals within the sectarian structures of Northern Ireland politics.

Back in 1973, a new form of government was in the process of being born. While perhaps an ugly child, it was at least a live birth. Whitelaw was delighted, and not without cause: while the finer detail still had to be ironed out between the various parties at a four-day conference the following month at Sunningdale in Berkshire, the basic building blocks had been agreed. The new institutions would be based on powers shared between unionist and nationalist elected representatives, along with an Irish dimension to reflect the identity of the nationalist community.

Few people would have imagined a year earlier that Brian Faulkner – the man who had castigated the reformist policies of his predecessor Terence O'Neill, who had publicly opposed the concept of power-sharing and who had so zealously prosecuted internment against the nationalist community – would be sitting down so soon with his erstwhile enemies. The supporters of this devolved government hoped that finally a new dawn had broken and that the dark days of violence would be replaced by this power-sharing initiative between moderate unionists and moderate nationalists. At last it looked as though the democratic process had worked and that the politicians had come through and delivered a settlement.

# CHAPTER FOUR

# DIRECT RULE AND THE GROWTH OF INFORMAL POLITICS, 1974–90

UNFORTUNATELY, THE OPTIMISM that accompanied the arrival of the 'power-sharing executive' was misplaced. The smiles and back-slapping soon faded as the initiative came under sustained attack by militants on both sides and as the British government displayed crass mismanagement. The IRA predictably accused the SDLP of collaborating with the British, while the DUP and Vanguard accused Faulkner of treachery against the unionist community.

From the outset, Faulkner had a questionable mandate for the enterprise. Within days of his official installation as head of the power-sharing government in January 1974, a meeting of his party's ruling body (the Ulster Unionist Council) voted to reject the Council of Ireland and forced his resignation as party leader. The meetings of the Executive were accompanied by public protests and demonstrations co-ordinated by the DUP and Vanguard, and by increased violence from loyalist paramilitaries in a calculated attempt to squeeze the life out of the devolved government. Media attention focused on the antics of Paisley (memorably dubbed 'the demon doctor' by a clearly exasperated and beleaguered Faulkner), rather than on the less colourful administrative details of the new venture. 'If it bleeds, it leads' has often been the guiding principle of the media, and this occasion was no different. Unionists opposed to the Executive seized the initiative and provided better photo-opportunities and sound bites than those on the inside.

The Executive was also undermined by the wider political context in the UK. By the end of 1973, Prime Minister Edward Heath had become more concerned with economic problems and industrial relations disputes in Britain than with events in Northern Ireland. As a result, in December 1973 Whitelaw was moved from his job as secretary of state for Northern Ireland to trouble-shoot threatened strike action in Britain from the National Union of Mineworkers (NUM). Eventually Heath called a general election in February 1974, campaigning under the slogan 'Who governs Britain?' He soon discovered that it would not be him, as he narrowly lost the election to the Labour Party, which came to power under the leadership of the pipe-smoking 'everyman', Harold Wilson. This was, of course, a carefully constructed image designed to portray Wilson as an ordinary – if highly intelligent – chap, who could empathize with and remedy the problems of the 'man in the street'.[1] The loquacious but largely ineffectual Welshman Merlyn Rees took over as secretary of state for Northern Ireland in February 1974, arriving in time to administer the last rites to the power-sharing agreement. Rees was rapidly to learn the painful lesson that the formal political process which produced democratically elected institutions could be overtaken by more powerful informal community-based activism. Within a few short months of Rees's arrival, the political process had disintegrated, the unionist leadership had fragmented and the paramilitary factions had been further strengthened. Ironically, the formal democratic process actually played a part in the cataclysmic events of 1974, opening space for more ad hoc forms of community activism spearheaded by paramilitary leaderships on both sides. The general election of February 1974 hit Faulkner and his rump of unionist allies hard, as Protestant voters flocked to support more radical alternatives, such as Vanguard, the DUP and the 'Official' Unionists who had recently dumped Faulkner. These opposition groups came together under the alliterative banner of the United Ulster Unionist Council (UUUC) and won eleven of the twelve Westminster seats available. This was a political disaster for Faulkner, and the lack of a mandate within unionism for the Sunningdale Agreement was now laid painfully bare. The survival of the power-sharing executive looked bleak, even before the hard men got involved to ensure its demise.

Loyalist militants knew that this hated political experiment was now teetering on the brink of collapse, and a coalition crystallized around a new group calling itself the Ulster Workers' Council (UWC) to help push it over the edge. This brought together Paisley's DUP, Craig's Vanguard movement, radical Protestant trade-union and business leaders, the Orange Order and, of course, loyalist paramilitaries in the shape of the

UDA. The commander of the UDA at this point was Andy Tyrie, a small rotund man with big glasses and an even larger moustache. Tyrie was initially excluded from the UWC, as the politicians worried about guilt by association; but they needed him to provide a cutting edge to their protest. Tyrie skilfully deployed the UDA across Northern Ireland to cajole, intimidate and attack people who failed to comply with UWC directives.

The UWC called for a 'workers' strike' against the power-sharing executive in May 1974, casting this as a 'constitutional stoppage'. This was 'people power' Northern Ireland style, in that it was a demonstration of power from only *one* section of society. It offers an example of the way in which the introduction of direct rule in 1972 had altered the political dynamics of the region and opened up space that more informal coalitions could inhabit. Before direct rule was brought in, political activity (leaving aside the civil rights movement) was relatively formalized. There was an established set of political institutions at Stormont and a Northern Ireland government that, however problematic, was responsible for setting policy and administering services in the region. Direct rule had muddied these waters considerably, as there was no longer a local tier of government, while there was a cacophony of political voices clamouring to be heard and wider coalitions coming together to exert an influence on events. The UWC provides an excellent illustration of this informal political activity, as it brought together relatively moderate unionist politicians at one end of the spectrum and loyalist paramilitaries at the other, with a number of trade unionists and businessmen also in the mix.

The UWC was going to show the Wilson government that it (and not the British government) controlled Northern Ireland at a *de facto* level. The leadership of the UWC announced that electricity production would be reduced from 14 May onwards and that there would be an indefinite shutdown of economic life across Northern Ireland. As the leaders wanted to indicate that they were taking this action reluctantly and in a responsible manner, they announced that essential services would be maintained. Initially this looked like a failure, as the following day many businesses reported staffing levels at around 90 per cent. Worried that their bluff had been called, the UWC deployed Tyrie and the UDA, which roamed parts of Belfast and other major towns armed with clubs and other impromptu weapons, threatening shopkeepers with violence if they did not close down. Workers at the Harland and Wolff shipyard in Belfast were warned on the first day of the strike that any vehicles remaining in the staff car park after 2 p.m. would be set on fire.[2] Buses and cars were hijacked and set alight, and barricades were set up across major arterial roads to prevent traffic from flowing (unless the UWC allowed it), to control the fuel supplies at petrol stations and to demonstrate that the UWC was in charge. In effect, the UWC was in government – not Brian Faulkner or his power-sharing colleagues at Stormont. It was plain to see that informal rather than formal political processes were what mattered in Northern Ireland – a fact brought home when senior civil servants were seen queuing up for travel passes and petrol coupons that were being issued at the UWC offices in Belfast![3] By mid-May, there were power cuts across Northern Ireland, as electricity was rationed by the power stations – the result of a deliberate reduction in supply by the UWC, which controlled them. By the end of the month, the postal service and the telephone system had all but collapsed; food provision was at a critical level as bakeries had closed, farms were unable to function properly or to feed their livestock, and panic buying had left little food in the shops. The UWC was in control and was maintaining its stranglehold on Northern Ireland through a combination of having committed supporters in key sectors of the workforce and UDA intimidation of anyone who tried to break the strike.

At an anecdotal level, I remember a large barricade being erected at the bottom of the Holywood Road, where I lived. When, as a rather nosy eight-year-old, I pitched up to the masked men on my bicycle one evening to ask what they were up to, their response was both informative and memorable: 'Clear off, wee lad, unless you want your bike to go on our barricade!' My curiosity satisfied, I obeyed their instructions and rode off swiftly into the Belfast sunset, anxious to hang onto my 'wheels', but content in my own imagination that I had forced them to account for themselves.

Thanks to the UDA and sympathetic trade union leaders in the power stations, the UWC was in charge and began to micro-manage the 'constitutional stoppage' at street level in East Belfast and across other parts of Northern Ireland, where they exerted control. This reached the point of deciding how much electricity would be produced, how much drinking water would flow through the system and who would be allowed fuel at the petrol stations. At a personal level, I vividly remember my mother trying to get fuel for the car, so that she could take me, my brother and some friends on a trip to the swimming baths to get away from the sinister atmosphere on the streets. When she pulled into the local petrol station, a masked youth loitering by the pumps wanted a word before she could fill up. 'What do you work at, love – are you part of an essential service?' 'Yes,

I'm a nurse', my mother replied, as we sat in the back whispering 'No you're not, mum, you're a teacher!' Whether or not this local 'hood' heard us, the point is that people adapted to this latest irritation pragmatically and tried to get on with their lives as best they could.

During all of this disruption, the police and the army stood back and let it happen. They were instinctively on the unionist side of the argument and they received little encouragement from their political masters to do anything other than stand around and let the loyalist militants take control. At a pragmatic level, they were willing to allow the loyalists to let off steam, rather than intervene and potentially inflame the situation further. By the time they did become more interventionist, the UWC had gained traction and was able to demonstrate that the army could not run all of Northern Ireland's power stations, milk all of its cows, and drive all of its oil tankers without the consent of the unionist population. From the nationalist viewpoint, it looked like the police and army were doing the unionist bidding yet again, and that the Labour government was afraid to take on its own security agencies.

The UWC had effectively brought Northern Ireland to a standstill, and Faulkner's power-sharing executive sitting up on the hill at Stormont had become a meaningless political decoration. As with the civil rights period at the end of the 1960s, politics was happening at the informal level, not in parliamentary chambers or committee rooms, and it was on the streets that people could see cause and effect within the political process. What the UWC leaders said during their sinister, dimly lit and rather self-important press conferences mattered to people, because it was going to affect their lives directly. Would they have power? Could they flush the toilet or have a bath? Would they be able to travel to work or school in the morning? The statements being made by Faulkner and his Executive, on the other hand, were increasingly irrelevant and disconnected from day-to-day realities, as this sectarian version of people power took hold.

Ten days into the UWC stoppage, Harold Wilson managed to pour petrol on the flames with a television broadcast that, once again, misread events and London's ability to control them. In an effort to marginalize the UWC and its strike action, Wilson enraged the unionist community and increased support for the strikers. He referred to the UWC as 'thugs and bullies' – fair comment, perhaps, but he then went on to accuse the unionist community more generally of being a parasite on the rest of the United Kingdom:

People on this side of the water, British parents, British taxpayers, have seen their sons vilified and spat upon and murdered ... They see property destroyed by evil violence and are asked to pick up the bill for rebuilding it. Yet people who benefit from this now viciously defy Westminster, purporting to act as though they were an elected government, spend ... their lives sponging on Westminster and British democracy and then systematically assault democratic methods. *Who do these people think they are?*[4]

This speech lacked any nuanced understanding of how it would be received in Northern Ireland and suggested that Wilson was more interested in the public reaction in Great Britain, where people were becoming increasingly exasperated by events, than in reducing support for the UWC in Northern Ireland. Sir Kenneth Bloomfield, the leading civil servant during the period, recalled in his memoirs that the speech was 'catastrophically unhelpful':

Listeners in Northern Ireland who had been risking their very lives day and daily in the face of an appalling terrorist threat, and who had continued to work in the face of great difficulties or been turned back from work when the forces of the state had failed utterly to support them, listened with indignation as the prime minister of the United Kingdom classified them, alongside the thugs and hooligans of the UDA and UVF and the demi-constitutional politicians of the UUUC, as 'spongers'. I myself bitterly resented it.[5]

The answer to the prime minister's rhetorical question – 'who do these people think they are?' – was that they thought they were in charge, and they believed that the muscle of the loyalist paramilitaries, combined with an alliance of anti-Faulkner unionists, would bring down the power-sharing executive. And they were proved correct, as once again the message was sent out that violence and intimidation could achieve what democratic politics could not. In the middle of the strike, car bombs went off in the Irish Republic, killing twenty-two people in Dublin and another five in Monaghan. Responsibility for these attacks was quickly laid at the door of the UVF, but the stench of collusion with aspects of British covert intelligence hung over these bombings, and continues to do so. The reaction of the UWC to the carnage ranged from indifference by some to gloating by others. UWC member Sammy Smyth demonstrated how some loyalists saw this violence as part of a wider political battle: 'I am very happy about the bombings in Dublin ... There is a war with the Free State [Irish Republic] and now we are laughing at them.'[6]

The lights literally went out on the power-sharing executive on 28 May, when Faulkner, unable to cope with the power cuts, water shortages, petrol rationing and closure of sewage plants, bowed to the inevitable and resigned from the Executive, precipitating its total collapse – amidst much mutual recrimination. Unionists had performed their biggest act of resistance to an unwanted British government policy since the Home Rule crisis of 1912, and it had been achieved by the mobilization of the Protestant working class in a demonstration of community solidarity.

There was plenty of blame to be apportioned for this political failure. Allegations that unionists just could not stomach sharing power with Catholics, and that the nationalists were using power-sharing as a Trojan horse to damage the constitutional integrity of Northern Ireland, pinged across the media. Ultimately, the power-sharing executive fell due to a lack of sufficient internal consensus within Northern Ireland, so brutally exposed by the destruction of Faulkner and his unionist allies at the ballot box. The SDLP and the Irish government pursued the Council of Ireland dimension too stubbornly, without sufficient understanding of how this would damage Faulkner and his dwindling support base within the unionist community. The UWC ruthlessly exposed the Executive's lack of support and used its paramilitary muscle to hold Northern Ireland and the British government to ransom. However, the vacillating attitude of Merlyn Rees, Harold Wilson's ill-judged playing to the gallery in Britain and his predecessor Edward Heath's cynical decision to put the life of his government ahead of the lives of people in Northern Ireland also all played crucial roles in the debacle.

It was not that Rees and Wilson were opposed to the Executive at any ideological level, but that they had little political capital invested in it, and consequently left it to wither and die. While Rees subsequently tried to pass this off in his memoirs as well-judged statesmanship (on the basis that he would have done more damage had he intervened to save it), this is little more than self-serving hubris. He came to bury the power-sharing executive, not to praise it, and that had been his intention from an early stage, as he sniffed the political wind in Northern Ireland and prepared to back the likely winners.

Rees and Wilson displayed both political ineptitude and an abrogation of responsibility in their failure to confront hardline loyalists and support the power-sharing executive. However, there are rarely votes in Northern Ireland for British politicians and Wilson's priorities lay elsewhere. He played to the gallery of 'mainland' British public opinion from time to time, but did little to actually assist the Executive and in fact made matters worse on a number of occasions. As a result, Northern Ireland was left to pick at its bloody scabs (and create new wounds) for another twenty-five years as, once again, the British government displayed its reluctance to govern.

## DIRECT RULE AND THE UTILITY OF VIOLENCE

By summer 1974, the lack of any credible political process helped the various paramilitary groups to argue that political power flowed out of the barrel of the gun. While nature may abhor a vacuum, the paramilitary groups in Northern Ireland were emboldened by its political equivalent. When the latest attempt to restore devolved government to Northern Ireland failed in 1974, the British attempted to administer the region via remote control from London, through the secretary of state and civil servants in the Northern Ireland Office (NIO). The formal political system became externalized and largely invisible to those who lived in Northern Ireland; decisions were taken in London, while local politicians carped from the sidelines but were generally unable to influence events.

Violence became institutionalized in a vicious downward spiral involving the Provisional IRA, the British army and other 'Crown Forces', such as the police. Loyalist paramilitary groups such as the Ulster Freedom Fighters and the UVF killed Catholics on a regular basis: if they could not get a member of the IRA, then the maxim 'any Taig will do'[7] was followed by such groups.

For its part, by 1974 the Provisional IRA had expanded its activities to mainland Britain with a number of high-profile bomb attacks. The logic was brutally simple: they concluded (quite correctly) that killing people in Britain would get them more attention and would put greater pressure on the British government than could be achieved by continuing to kill people in Northern Ireland. This realization did not dent their enthusiasm for continuing their campaign of violence in Northern Ireland, but extending it into Britain became a crucial part of republican strategy. No-warning bomb attacks took place in public bars in Guildford, Woolwich and Birmingham in 1974, killing five, two and twenty-one people, respectively. This incursion into the domestic life of mainland Britain placed the

Northern Ireland conflict on a new level and increased pressure on the government and the police to take effective steps to catch those responsible and prevent further attacks.

The Guildford bomb was left in the Horse and Groom pub, which was known to be popular with British soldiers serving in Northern Ireland.[8] Conservative MP David Howell, who had been a minister at the Northern Ireland Office, emphasized the sense of urgency in apprehending those responsible: 'I'm afraid I thought I'd seen the last of this in Belfast. It's quite clear that we must hunt down the maniacs and the animals who would do this kind of thing.'[9]

Following the bombings, a number of people were arrested and forced to confess under coercive interrogation by the police. The convictions of the 'Guildford Four' and the 'Birmingham Six' were made on the basis of flawed forensic evidence and uncorroborated confessions that were beaten out of the suspects. The convictions were all eventually quashed, but not before the innocent victims had spent over sixteen years in jail. Eighteen years after his release, Paddy Hill, one of those convicted of the Birmingham bombings, vividly recollected his experience in custody:

> They jammed a pistol in my mouth and smashed it around, breaking my teeth so badly it was agony to even have a sip of water until I finally saw a dentist, two weeks later. They told me they knew I was innocent but that they didn't care: they had been told to get a conviction and that if I didn't admit to the bombing, they would shoot me in the mouth. They slowly counted to three, then pulled the trigger. They did that three times. Each time, I thought I was going to die.[10]

During the Birmingham Six's first appeal against wrongful conviction, they came up against Lord Widgery (the same man who had presided over the now discredited tribunal into the events of Bloody Sunday in 1972). Widgery's conclusion that their experience during questioning amounted to 'no ill treatment beyond the normal'[11] was hardly a ringing endorsement of the West Midlands Serious Crime Squad, which was eventually disbanded after persistent allegations of abuse and corruption.

By the mid-1970s, bomb attacks in Britain and Northern Ireland had become a regular and grisly feature of news bulletins, while the police and criminal justice system struggled to keep pace with the level of violence, and at times compromised themselves in the effort to gather intelligence on paramilitary activities.

## THE NIGHT THE MUSIC DIED

In the small hours of the morning of 31 July 1975, a minibus was stopped at an army checkpoint just outside Newry in Co. Down. Army checkpoints were by this stage very common in Northern Ireland, as the security services attempted to intercept paramilitary bomb squads and murder gangs. Unusually, however, the occupants of the van were ordered to get out and line up by the roadside while the van was 'checked'.

While several of those manning the checkpoint were serving British soldiers in the locally recruited Ulster Defence Regiment (UDR), all were also members of the Ulster Volunteer Force: it was a loyalist paramilitary ambush, not a British army checkpoint. The men in the van were musicians from the Miami Showband, a popular Dublin-based act, whose members came from both sides of the border and were a mix of Catholics and Protestants.

While ostensibly checking the van, two of the bogus soldiers tried to plant a bomb in the rear of the vehicle, but the device went off prematurely, killing them both instantly. The remainder of the UVF unit then opened fire on the musicians with machine guns in a bid to eradicate witnesses. Three musicians were shot in the back. Two of the band members had been blown into thick vegetation by the force of the explosion and only survived by pretending to be dead.

The scene was one of utter devastation. Two decapitated and badly charred bodies of fake British soldiers lay near the van. A grisly detail that emerged later was that the severed arm of one of the bombers, complete with its 'UVF Portadown' tattoo, was found 100 yards up the road, blown there by the force of the blast. The three dead band members had been shot in the back with bullets, some of which were 'dum-dums',[12] which cause particularly disfiguring exit wounds.

This episode became known as the 'Miami Showband massacre'.

Three members of the UVF gang were eventually convicted and, in a symbol of public revulsion at the attacks, were sentenced to thirty-five years in jail, the longest life sentences ever handed down in Northern Ireland.[13] This seemed like a new low – even by Northern Ireland's violent standards – as entertainers in glam-rock outfits were targeted by those who claimed to be fighting to protect their British heritage and citizenship.

Sadly, such lows were all too common in Northern Ireland. Place names once defined by beauty and local history were to become a map of destruction and a roll call of the dead. To pick just two of the worst cases in the 1970s is in no way to diminish the many others.

On 31 July 1972, nine people were killed and dozens wounded when three car bombs exploded in Claudy, a small village in Co. Derry. The youngest victim was nine years old. While the Provisional IRA denied responsibility, it was widely believed to have carried out the attack. It was also believed that a local priest, Fr Jim Chesney, had masterminded the attack; Chesney was suspected of involvement by the police but was never questioned.

On 17 February 1978, the Provisional IRA exploded a fire bomb at the La Mon hotel, on the outskirts of Belfast, in one of the grisliest attacks of the whole conflict. It was a crude but deadly device, with a bomb attached to canisters of petrol and sugar and hung on meat-hooks outside the window of the hotel. The sugar was intended to provide adhesion, so that the fire would stick to anything it hit. Unfortunately for the 400 or more people who were attending a dinner dance, the IRA's efforts to phone through a warning message came too late. When the deadly cocktail exploded, a fireball engulfed the function room and literally burned the victims alive. The heat was so intense that it caused some bodies to shrivel to the point that initially adults were mistaken for children. Many of the injured fled the building with their hair on fire and with burns that disfigured them for life. It was an embarrassment for the IRA, which later admitted responsibility and apologized for the inadequate warning that was given.

The Miami Showband massacre connects into the litany of horror that came before and after. One reading of the attack was that loyalist gunmen stopped a van en route to Dublin and, assuming the occupants were all Catholics (which they were not), saw this as a convenient opportunity to 'get a few Fenians'. In other words, the attack was motivated by blind religious hatred and opportunism. Another reading of events is more plausible: this UVF unit had more strategic political objectives, as well as purely bloodthirsty ones. It could, after all, have just shot the band members at the outset, without going to the trouble of planting a time bomb in the van. This took more logistical effort, more technical know-how (notwithstanding the bomb's premature detonation), and it was very unusual for loyalist paramilitaries to use car bombs in the 1970s in any case. So why go to the trouble? The wider political context of the time was that loyalists were becoming increasingly worried about what they saw as the Republic of Ireland's interference in the political affairs of Northern Ireland and the lack of zeal with which the Republic's government pursued the Provisional IRA, whose members frequently crossed the border to escape capture by the security forces in Northern Ireland. A political initiative involving power-sharing between unionists and nationalists, and which included an unprecedented role for the government of the Irish Republic, had recently been brought down by loyalists, through a combination of political and paramilitary resistance. The Provisional IRA had declared a Christmas ceasefire at the end of 1974 and the British had already held covert discussions with the IRA on several occasions. It seemed that the British and Irish governments were drawing closer together in their policies towards Northern Ireland, and this represented an obvious threat to some loyalists who defined the Republic of Ireland as being sympathetic to the Provisional IRA.

Looks can be deceptive, of course, and the loyalists misread and exaggerated the position of the Republic of Ireland. While from time to time there was a rhetorical nod in the direction of Irish reunification by Southern Irish politicians, this was nearly always expressed as a future aspiration rather than as an immediate political priority. Like the desire for world peace and a hope for better weather, such musings rarely held any specific policy implications. In reality, Republic of Ireland politicians were mainly concerned about how the violence in Northern Ireland was going to impact on their state, both in direct security terms and through knock-on effects on tourism and economic investment. In general terms, successive Irish governments wanted the British to maintain order in Northern Ireland in a manner consistent with international human rights standards. While they would have liked greater consultation at times over security matters (especially those that affected the treatment of the nationalist community), they were not seeking fundamental political reform. Despite the wording of the Irish constitution, few Irish governments during the direct rule period were at all interested in pursuing a policy of Irish reunification. In reality, loyalist paramilitaries had little to fear from Dublin, as the last thing any Irish government wanted to do was to absorb 700,000 reluctant unionists, or to assume political responsibility for the warring factions in the North.

As is often the case, of course, periodic posturing by some politicians in the Republic, together with a fear that the Irish government's relatively minor involvement in Northern Ireland could escalate into something more significant, led to a degree of paranoia within some sections of loyalist thinking. All of the mood music in the mid-1970s worried the UVF and other loyalists. Their default setting was that, given the opportunity, British governments would 'sell them out' and it was up to loyalists to thwart such political malfeasance.

It is within this wider context that attacks such as the Miami Showband massacre of 1975 should be understood. It was an act of brutal paramilitary logic, not 'mindless' opportunist violence. The UVF planted a bomb that was timed to go off when the vehicle had crossed the border into the Irish Republic. In addition to killing everyone in the van, this would have allowed loyalists to claim that the band (and by extension the wider Catholic population who might be defined as non-combatants) were IRA sympathizers. In propaganda terms, this would have allowed the band to be seen as part of the wider republican infrastructure, transporting explosives on behalf of the Provisionals, under the indulgent gaze of the Irish government. The UVF hope was that, as well as casting the wider Catholic community as 'terrorist sympathizers', this would have embarrassed the Irish government, damaged Anglo-Irish relations and forced Dublin to take a more aggressive approach to apprehending the IRA and co-operating with the security forces in Northern Ireland.

None of this seeks to disguise in any way the cold-blooded nature of the murder that took place; but it is important to understand that the motivation of the paramilitaries on both sides was frequently more complex than simple sectarian hatred. There was often a political logic (however warped) that drove the actions of such people, and by dismissing them simply as 'men of violence' or 'evil psychopaths', as the popular media frequently did, the opportunity was often missed to question the underlying rationality and political analysis which they espoused.

A more dismal perspective pervades the period, which is the frightening reality that violence was the active currency because violence worked, in the immediate sense at least. Violence (or more precisely the threat of violence) could achieve direct political change in a way that political dialogue could not. Gerry Adams made this point himself, in a book written in the mid-1980s, when he was already searching for a bridge between violent militancy and political dialogue: 'The tactic of armed struggle is of primary importance because it provides a vital cutting edge. Without it, the issue of Ireland would not even be an issue ... armed struggle has become an agent of bringing about change.'[14] Loyalist and

republican paramilitaries and their wider support networks both understood this, and while church leaders – and, to a more ambivalent extent,
politicians – preached on the evils of violence, their words often fell on
deaf ears.

## DIRECT RULE AND THE EMERGENCE OF
## A DEMOCRATIC DEFICIT

> Direct rule makes our rulers arrogant, deters the best brains from
> going into politics, breeds servility in the population and absolves
> voters from responsibility for their actions.[15]

The decision to run Northern Ireland's political and economic affairs from
London via a secretary of state was a short-term emergency measure,
forced on the British government by the paramilitary violence in the
region and the failure of local actors to reach any political agreement.
However, the implications of direct rule were profound for both Britain
and Ireland. Its implementation in 1972 shattered the political logic that
had held sway since 1921. It made the British government (and the secretary of state for Northern Ireland) immediately and directly responsible
for the region. While it was seen as a temporary measure, it endured for a
generation, and the transparency of administrative responsibility made
Northern Ireland a day-to-day domestic priority for the British government, whereas in the past it had been able to use the unionist regime at
Stormont as an institutional shield to protect it from criticism. Local actors
(both political and paramilitary) would continue to be blamed for their
extremism and stubborn failure to compromise, but direct rule made it
clear that the British government in London exerted ultimate power,
control and responsibility in the region.

Direct rule also led to new forms of politics emerging in Northern
Ireland. Local politicians were effectively excluded from the policy process,
which was determined and implemented by the secretary of state in
conjunction with a small coterie of ministers. This led to the growth of
what subsequently became known as the 'democratic deficit' in Northern
Ireland, a phrase used to describe the fact that decisions were taken by
ministerial decree from British-based politicians, while local people and
their political representatives had very little means of influencing the
political process. This form of politics 'by remote control' saw power

being exercised over Northern Ireland by politicians and civil servants in London and the marginalization (at times self-inflicted) of the local political parties. The secretary of state functioned as a modern colonial governor, while legislation relating to Northern Ireland was passed through a mechanism known as 'Orders in Council'. These effectively cut the local political parties out of any serious debate over government policy, as amendments could not be made to these orders, which had to be passed in their entirety or rejected by parliament altogether. Thus, from 1972 until 1999, Northern Ireland legislation was imposed from London, regardless of local opposition or wishes. This contributed further to the political malaise in the region, reduced the practical relevance of the main parties and increased the gap between the formal political process in Northern Ireland and the experiences of the people who lived there.

To add insult to injury, the main political parties in Britain (Conservative, Labour and Liberal) did not organize in Northern Ireland, with the result that people were unable to vote for those who governed them. This did further damage to the political fabric of the region, as 'national' politics within both the UK and the Republic of Ireland were out of reach of the people who lived in Northern Ireland, while the internal political parties were consigned to local government functions. Like many other policy decisions made by Britain, direct rule was an emergency short-term measure that became part of the longer-term fabric of governance in the region. In short, it was an unaccountable and undemocratic political system, and while perhaps not as corrosive as the unionist regime at Stormont which preceded it, direct rule infantalized politics in the region. The centralization of political authority within the NIO and the secretary of state removed responsibility from local politicians and treated them (and by extension their constituents) as irresponsible children who were incapable of managing their own affairs. Unburdened by the need to balance budgets, manage the economy or deliver services (all of which was done for them), local politicians contented themselves with snarling at each other across the sectarian barricades and complaining about the injustices or inefficiencies of British policy. This tended to be quite popular in terms of building rapport within their respective support groups, but it did very little to move the political debate forwards or to actually tackle any of the political problems linked to poor housing, poverty or unemployment that were facing people at the time.

After 1972, therefore, politics became disconnected from the process of day-to-day government, which had an obvious knock-on effect on the relevance of the formal political system for the people who lived in Northern Ireland. As power and responsibility transferred from the local political class to unelected quasi non-governmental organizations (quangos) and civil servants in the Northern Ireland Office, many talented and motivated people chose to put their energies into the voluntary and community sector, rather than into the formal political process. The reason for this was entirely logical, as it was at this micro level that they could exert some control over their lives and have some influence over what was happening within their communities. This 'democratic deficit' was recognized by the report of the Opsahl Commission in 1993, which was a non-official attempt to take the political temperature of 'ordinary people' in Northern Ireland and, instead of the moribund formal political process, to seek alternative ways forward: 'The people of Northern Ireland have no say whatsoever in the government that "rules" them. They cannot vote for either the Labour Party, the Conservative Party or the Liberal Democrats . . . Government is remote, imperial and non-accountable to the electorate, which did not elect it in the first place.'[16]

The rise in political violence during the early 1970s caused a level of suffering and human trauma that led many people to draw on their own resources and those of their local community, rather than seek assistance from the state or their elected political representatives. Following the community dislocations of the 1970s and 1980s, many people did not wait for leadership from the formal political process, but became activists themselves and looked for ways of dealing with grievances or needs within their own communities. Political activism therefore developed in spite of, rather than because of, the formal political system.

By the mid-1970s, the political debate between unionist and nationalist parties had become totally dominated by the 'constitutional question' – namely the issue of whether Northern Ireland would remain within the United Kingdom or become part of a 'united Ireland'. While this was a crucial issue for many, it became an increasingly shrill and circular debate with limited bearing on the everyday lives of the people who lived in Northern Ireland. Direct rule had severed the link between political decision-making and what actually happened in Northern Ireland. Before 1972 there was at least a rational cause and effect within the policy process; but after direct rule was introduced, local politicians became bit-players within the political arena, rather than central to the decision-making process. Ironically, therefore, while the political system arguably became fairer after 1972, with less overt discrimination against the nationalist community, at the same time it became less accountable. As power transferred across from the political parties to British ministers and unelected civil servants, it became increasingly difficult for political organizations to recruit members. This trend was recognized by the Opsahl Commission, which concluded that direct rule had caused a brain drain in the political culture, and that this had inhibited the region's subsequent development and had led motivated and talented people to engage with politics at an informal level: 'In the absence of democratic structures, the powers and influence of the civil service have increased substantially: Many people, who otherwise might join a political party choose instead to join a community organisation or voluntary one.'[17]

## THE RISE OF CIVIL SOCIETY IN NORTHERN IRELAND

Civil society played a more advanced role in the governance of Northern Ireland than I think would be the case in other areas. I think it really did fill for a long time that democratic deficit whereby Northern Ireland most of the way through direct rule has really been a technocracy – basically run by civil servants with some oversight from British ministers.[18]

For the remainder of the 1970s, it appeared that politics had died and that violent political conflict had become intractable, unresolvable and never-ending. After the UWC strike had brought down the power-sharing executive, the Labour government focused on running an effective security policy and keeping a lid on the paramilitary violence. Merlyn Rees's successor as secretary of state was Roy Mason, a pugnacious Yorkshireman who could barely conceal his antipathy towards the region's political class: '"County councillors" he called them – bad county councillors. Mushrooms that grew and died in the frost.'[19] Mason was a short, portly man, fond of wearing an unflattering tweed safari suit (unusual even given the sartorial standards of the time) for his tours of the province. During these 'see and be seen' events, he would buzz around local factories with the local media in tow, explaining how he was going to improve law and order and the economy. It would be fair to say that Mason was a broadcaster rather than a receiver, and that his focus was unambiguously on the security situation, rather than on any ambitious new political initiatives. Mason did indeed 'crack down' on the Provisional IRA during his term as secretary of state, and took the war to republican paramilitaries by deploying units of the SAS, especially in rural parts of Northern Ireland. This endeared him to unionists for a time, while it drew antipathy from the nationalist community. Martin McGuinness later offered a back-handed compliment of sorts with his admission that 'Mason beat the shit out of us'.[20] He even earned the dubious honour (for a Labour politician) of being feted on his eightieth birthday by the right-wing *Daily Telegraph* newspaper as the best secretary of state Northern Ireland had ever had: 'He belongs to a type [of Labour Party politician] that has almost disappeared, from the days when the Labour Party hadn't been taken over by sociology lecturers and focus groups and was still what its name said, the political voice of the working class.'[21]

While Mason was not offering any new political initiatives in the late 1970s, the local political parties showed little appetite for compromise in any case, as unionists struggled to come to terms with the idea of sharing power with Catholics, and as the nationalist SDLP sought in vain to reheat the Sunningdale agreement.

At an immediate level, the political situation was deadlocked and sectarian violence continued unabated. With the benefit of hindsight, however, the drift of people into grass-roots activism sowed seeds that would later flower as the peace process evolved in the 1990s. Equally importantly, perhaps, it allowed some in Northern Ireland to behave as proactive citizens, despite the gridlock at the formal political level and the street violence taking place around them. This activity was driven frequently by anger and frustration at the sectarian violence that surrounded the people, but there were more constructive motivations as well. One was the philosophical belief in social capital and a sense of community cohesion in Northern Ireland. For all its faults and problems, the political fabric of Northern Ireland has been defined much more obviously by a sense of community and group solidarity than it has by individualism. The concept of social capital, popularized in recent years by social scientists such as Robert Putnam, was very evident in Northern Ireland during the conflict, with an almost limitless array of interconnecting cultural, social, religious and political networks. Many of the people who live there have a very well-defined sense of community, care about that community deeply, and are willing to volunteer to help it, without expectation of immediate personal reward. The problem with this is, of course, that there is more than one community in Northern Ireland. There have traditionally been two communities held in an antagonistic embrace, and the definition of mutually exclusive interests by either community has resulted in human destruction across both.

During the height of the conflict, people were not slow to join groups or to 'volunteer' their unpaid services; but more often than not these energies were directed towards paramilitary groupings or exclusivist cultural organizations such as the Orange Order, rather than into the bowling leagues or parent–teacher associations that Putnam envisaged. To those on the outside, this might seem like the antithesis of social capital or civil society activism; but the motivations of such individuals were very similar to those identified by scholars and policy makers such as Putnam, who identified 'associationalism' as a crucial aspect of a healthy and functioning democracy. They wanted to make a positive contribution to their community and to defend the cultural, political and civil rights of those within it; but some came to the conclusion during the 1970s that the best way of doing this was to kill people in the other community, which they regarded as threatening their interests. The point here is that the dynamics of informal political activism produced violent as well as peaceful outcomes; and while it led to the establishment of numerous NGOs (non-governmental organizations) and a vibrant civil society, it had a darker side, too. In truth, there are positive and negative sides to civil society activism, which 'is as divided as the society within which it is embedded'.[22]

The other driver for informal political activism was a belief in the power of collective group activism. This was partly a lesson learned from the civil rights activism of the 1960s, but was also an attitude of mind among some people who believed they could change their political environment through collective action. As energy drained away from political activism, it began to seep into a new wave of NGOs, many of which were a direct product of sectarian violence. Some of those who felt disenchanted with politics at a formal level moved into other spheres of activity, such as the trade union movement, community groups and more focused NGOs committed to non-violence.

The activities of these groups varied enormously, ranging from immediate self-help for people in distress to more generalized consciousness-raising activities, focusing on the human costs of violence. This resulted in the provision of counselling services to the bereaved victims of violence, or advice on rehousing to those who had been forced to leave their homes, as well as large demonstrations and rallies to provide physical evidence that a large section of the population was opposed to paramilitary violence. As one activist within the Derry-based community group Dove House explained:

> I think one of the earliest things was getting people to be aware of their position and what sort of rights they basically had. That would include everything from rights in terms of people's situation [vis-à-vis] the conflict. [For example] if they had a son or daughter arrested, or if the house was raided [we would inform them of] what their rights were. Also then [in terms of] welfare rights, if someone had a sick or invalid relative [we would inform them] of what rights were available to them.[23]

The proliferation of these networks and organizations illustrated that day-to-day political concerns relating to social and economic problems had filtered down into this informal sector of society from the main parties, which were much more focused on the 'constitutional question' and the security situation. They demonstrated that while Northern Ireland remained politically deadlocked at the formal level, grass-roots organizations were harnessing and providing outlets for the informal political energies of the society. Such groups often emerged quite organically in the wake of surrounding events, sparked off and driven forwards by motivated individuals, gradually evolving into larger groups with more rigid managerial structures and financial systems. Put crudely, many of these networks emerged out of the pain and suffering being experienced at the time, and out of the grievances that the violence produced.

Some NGOs, such as the Peace People in the 1970s or Families Against Intimidation and Terror (FAIT) in the 1990s, were created out of the brutality of violence. FAIT was founded in 1990 by Nancy Gracey after her son was 'kneecapped' by members of the Provisional IRA for alleged 'anti-social behaviour'. These were also referred to as 'punishment shootings' and were a brutal form of summary justice employed by paramilitary groups as a means of exerting control in urban working-class areas and providing a rationale for the continued exclusion of the police from nationalist areas. FAIT's *raison d'être* was focused, therefore, on the human cost of the conflict, rather than on any broader political manifesto. It campaigned for an end to what it called 'mutilation attacks', and confronted those it held to be chiefly responsible for them, eschewing more analytical positions on the causes of the political conflict.

The origins of the Peace People were even more traumatic. On 10 August 1976 there was a chase in West Belfast involving a car being driven by a member of the Provisional IRA and a British army Land Rover. Along the road, Anne Maguire was wheeling a pram containing her six-week-old baby and with her three other children (aged from two to eight years) in close attendance. The soldiers shot the car driver, killing him instantly but causing the vehicle to career off the road and into the Maguire family, killing the baby and two of the other children and severely injuring the mother. Though she recovered from her physical injuries, Anne Maguire never got over the mental trauma of losing her three children and took her own life several years later.

Even by the standards of the time, this tragedy shocked the community. In solidarity, some women set up a shrine at the scene of the incident and held a walk through the housing estate where it had occurred. Anne's sister, Mairead Corrigan, went on television to appeal for an end to the violence, and women across Northern Ireland started a door-to-door petition calling for paramilitary ceasefires. This spontaneous activism, sparked by the human cost of the conflict, was typical of many of the NGOs that emerged at the time. It was also the type of story that the media found it easy to cover, as it focused on the anguish caused by violence without the need for any further context or complex political analysis.

Who was responsible? The IRA driver for hijacking a car and robbing a bank, or the British soldiers for recklessly shooting the driver dead? For most of those caught up in the human tragedy, the answer did not matter very much. As the British and international media interest in the 'human angle' grew, more energy flowed into the wider community and the parades and vigils increased, until Mairead Corrigan joined with two other activists (Betty Williams and Ciaran McKeown) to form the Peace People. Over the next twelve months this grew into a mass movement, with peace rallies across the island of Ireland, as well as in the United States and Britain, where a vigil in Trafalgar Square drew a crowd of over 10,000 people. The three leaders of the Peace People were awarded the Nobel Peace Prize in 1976, but gradually faded into the background as public enthusiasm waned and as paramilitary violence continued unabated into the 1980s. The Peace People movement was also viewed with suspicion by the republican community, many of whom saw it as part of the British propaganda machine, while the simplistic emotional demands for an end to violence offered little to those who believed themselves to be victims of British injustice.

While the wider impacts of this activity on the political fabric of Northern Ireland are difficult to quantify, the public rallies organized by the Peace People in the 1970s did, at the very least, provide a safety valve for society and a clear demonstration that progressive non-violent and anti-sectarian thinking was taking place in the region, despite the lack of progress at the formal political level.

These NGOs proliferated during the 1970s and throughout the 1980s, encouraged by the British government, which saw the voluntary and community sector as a potential centre for community leadership and as a useful partner agency in the delivery of economic and social policy. The British government was keen to provide financial support to a lot of these NGOs, and this money was subsequently boosted by other funding sources within the US and the EU, all of which were keen to encourage the sorts of cross-community initiatives that were taking place at a local level.

On an individual basis, very little of this activism had any discernible impact on political violence, or on the attitudes of the main political actors in Northern Ireland or in Britain. Those involved were often derided for being naive or dangerous pawns, easily manipulated as tools of British propaganda, or for being part of the middle-class community relations 'industry', whose philanthropic efforts misunderstood the structural needs of the urban working class.

Looked at cumulatively over time, however, a more positive assessment can be made. The voluntary and community sector did a lot of the 'heavy lifting', in terms of helping to reconnect social and economic issues linked to poverty and social deprivation with the formal political debate. The democratic deficit that accompanied the introduction of direct rule in 1972 produced a swathe of informal political engagement throughout the 1970s and on through the 1980s. This informal sector helped to connect the political elites to grass-roots communities, and at times to encourage and cajole them into exploring the opportunities for dialogue.

## POLITICS, PRISON AND THE PROPAGANDA WAR

While informal political activism was coming from civil society groups in the mid-1970s, the paramilitaries and the British government were also becoming more innovative and nimble in pursuing their objectives outside the formal political process. In the absence of political institutions during the direct rule period, other avenues were explored in an attempt to gain the political advantage. Chief among these informal political fronts was the struggle for legitimacy between the British government and the Provisional IRA. By the mid-1970s, winning the propaganda war had become just as important for both sides as achieving military victory. The British were intent on painting the paramilitaries as terrorists and criminals, while militant republicans were desperate to define themselves as reluctant freedom fighters, whose only path to reform was armed struggle.

From the IRA's perspective, the narrative that they were political prisoners was key. This elevated them above baser criminal activity and connected them into the rich history of Irish patriotism. It also helped them to cross over into international legitimacy, as the Provisional IRA sought to ally itself with other liberation movements, such as the African National Congress in South Africa and the Palestine Liberation Organization (PLO) in the Middle East. This helped the IRA to maintain political support for its actions both internally and among international sympathizers in America and elsewhere. It also helped it to finance the 'armed struggle' and procure the necessary weapons and explosives.

The struggle over whether the paramilitaries were politically motivated 'volunteers' or common criminals dominated the thinking of both sides from the mid-1970s onwards and eventually led to a major strategic readjustment within Irish republicanism. As the 1970s wore on, all sides began to understand the importance of building political support for their military and paramilitary activities. While violence continued and became entrenched, the context within which it took place became more nuanced and contested. By 1976, Northern Ireland's prisons had become the crucible within which this struggle for political control took place.

When Merlyn Rees took over from Whitelaw as secretary of state for Northern Ireland in 1974, he decided to withdraw 'special category status' in order to criminalize the paramilitaries: 'To treat the perpetrators of such crimes as special, politically motivated people was morally and legally wrong; they were plain murderers.'[24] As part of this policy shift, Rees built new prison accommodation in Long Kesh that became known as the H-Blocks (due to their shape) and renamed the jail the Maze prison (after the local area). Special category status was removed on 1 March 1976, and this sparked a new phase in the conflict.

Previously, those granted special category status were not treated like other prisoners. They wore their own clothes, organized their own activities and formed their own hierarchies, all of which suited the prison authorities, as (aside from periodic escape attempts) life was relatively orderly within the jail. Prisoners were allowed to associate freely and to set up a structure that included regular lectures and debates on Irish history – as well as weapons training and bomb-making classes. During exercise periods, both sets of paramilitaries would drill and parade in quasi-military fashion in the exercise yard, while the loyalists even had an Orange band (though its parades were rather 'geographically challenged', given the proximity of the barbed-wire fencing).

While Long Kesh looked secure, it was actually extremely porous and the lax regime made smuggling a relatively straightforward process. Messages and materials (including weapons and radios) were often broken down into their component parts and brought into the prison. As the authorities tightened up and began to strip-search visitors and prisoners, other means were found of getting materials in and out of the jail, including secreting items in obvious bodily locations to evade detection. One IRA prisoner, Patsy Quinn, later recalled how, following a visit, he had smuggled a radio back into his cell via this method: 'Getting it up there was hard enough, but getting it out again – was excruciating!'

Once special category status ended, a power struggle over the issue of political legitimacy began to take shape between the British government and prison authorities on the one hand, and republican prisoners on the other. The first person to be imprisoned under the new regime in September 1976 was Ciaran Nugent, who had been given a three-year sentence for possessing weapons and hijacking a car. When Nugent was ordered to wear standard prison clothes, he refused to do so and thereby to recognize the new regime. The following day he was given a blanket and wore this to take exercise – the 'blanketmen' had been born, as subsequent prisoners arrived in the H-Blocks and also refused to wear prison clothes. By the end of the 1970s, more than 200 republicans had gone 'on the blanket', and the issue became a rallying point for support outside the jail. Relations between prisoners and warders worsened and a grisly battle of wills ensued between the two sides. There were regular beatings by prison officers angered at the IRA's assassination of their colleagues. By 1978 the blanket protest had degenerated further, as some prisoners refused to leave their cells to defecate, on account of the beatings that frequently accompanied the journey. When warders refused to clear this up, the prisoners began pushing it under the doors and out the windows of their cells. When these were sealed, they spread it over the walls of their cells to reduce the smell. By the end of 1978, some 300 republican prisoners were on 'the dirty protest' and this did succeed for a short time in bringing international media attention to the issue of political status, especially across Irish-America. The leading Catholic cleric in Ireland, Cardinal Tomas O'Fiaich was allowed to visit the prisoners in the H-Blocks, and his subsequent statement gained international publicity:

> One would hardly allow an animal to remain in such conditions, let alone a human being . . . The stench and filth in some of the cells, with the remains of rotten food and human excreta scattered around the walls was almost unbearable.[25]

Perhaps surprisingly, television crews were given access to the prison, and the images of lank-haired men wrapped in blankets, the walls of their cells covered in human faeces, shocked the world. While this caused some embarrassment to the British government, it was considered worthwhile, given the larger priority of criminalizing the paramilitary organizations.

Despite the international headlines that this degradation generated, in time interest in the dirty protest began to wane, partly because it seemed that the prisoners were inflicting the conditions on themselves. By 1980, the 'blanket' and 'dirty' protests had been going on for four years and the prisoners were becoming demoralized as the British government showed no sign of budging. Margaret Thatcher had become prime minister the previous year and she had a reputation for strong leadership. The blanketmen were stuck, as to back down and lose face would be a huge propaganda defeat – not just for the prisoners themselves, but also for the wider republican movement outside the jail. But it was quite clear by 1980 that they needed a new direction to reinvigorate the campaign for political status. Discussions began inside the jail about the possibility of using a hunger strike, as this had been the tactic used to get special category status in the first place in 1972. Enthusiasm for the hunger-strike idea was initially high within the prison, but it was born more of desperation than anything. On 27 October 1980, seven republicans (six IRA and one from INLA) led by Brendan 'Darkie' Hughes refused breakfast. This act of defiance lit the fuse that eventually led to the political emergence of Sinn Fein and ultimately to the peace process itself.

The initial hunger strike lasted for fifty-three days, causing upheaval within Northern Ireland and generating worldwide media attention. While the British said there would be no concessions to the hunger strikers, a number of discussions were held to determine if a solution could be found. Eventually a document was produced that seemed to indicate movement on the crucial issue of prison clothing, and the strike was called off with one of the prisoners, Sean McKenna, close to death. However, when the prisoners looked more closely at the details, it transpired that they were to wear 'civilian-type' clothing issued by the prison, rather than their own clothes. This was more than a semantic point, as in essence it involved simply a different type of prison uniform, rather than recognition that they were political prisoners. The enduring narrative of the period was that the 1980 hunger strikers were tricked into giving up their fast by a British government that reneged on a previous agreement. However, it has recently been alleged that Hughes conceded defeat unilaterally, without any promises being made. Danny Morrison, Sinn Fein's former 'director of communications', admitted thirty years later that the claim of British duplicity was invented by Sinn Fein as a way of spinning the failure of the hunger strike:

> Brendan Hughes ended the hunger strike unilaterally ... we on the outside finessed the sequence of events for the sake of morale and, at a midnight Press conference, merged the secret arrival of a British Government document ... with the ending of the hunger strike ... it was either that or admit – which to the republican base was inconceivable – that Brendan [Hughes] had ended the strike without getting a thing.[26]

Many of those involved in the hunger strikes and who survived the period were to fall out with one another in subsequent years, as Sinn Fein's political strategy developed.

One thing clear at the time to Bobby Sands, the new IRA leader in the prison, was that a more nuanced form of hunger strike was required, and this would be a fight to the death for those involved. Sands led a new hunger strike in 1981. This was designed to extract maximum publicity and propaganda value by staggering the timing: the hunger strikers embarked on their fasts at one-week intervals. Initially Sinn Fein and the IRA outside the jail were against a second hunger strike, mainly because, after the first one, they were worried that it would fail and would also dominate the agenda when they were trying to develop a range of tactics in addition to violence. This opposition was admitted by Sinn Fein President Gerry Adams, when he recalled the period: 'We were well aware that a hunger strike such as was proposed would demand exclusive attention, would, in effect, hijack the struggle, and this conflicted with our sense of the political priorities of the moment.'[27]

The second hunger strike began on 1 March 1981 (the fifth anniversary of the ending of special category status), when Bobby Sands refused food. This fast went on from March to October 1981 and ended in the death of ten republican prisoners, two of whom – Bobby Sands and Kieran Doherty – were elected to Westminster and the Irish parliament, respectively. Over 100,000 people attended Sands' funeral, and the ripple effects were felt around the world. British embassies were attacked in Dublin and across Europe, while the French government made two gestures of solidarity to the Irish government, both of which were declined. One was an offer to boycott the forthcoming royal wedding of Prince Charles and Lady Diana Spencer, while the second was to have President Mitterrand attend Bobby Sands' funeral. A minute's silence was observed in the Indian parliament as a mark of respect for Sands, while a number of other commemorations were held across the world. Some countries used the event opportunistically as a means of tweaking the British imperial tail. The Iranian revolution of Ayatollah Khomeini was now in full swing, and his government took the chance to rename the Tehran street on which the British embassy was situated from Winston Churchill Boulevard to Bobby Sands Street! The embassy subsequently moved its main entrance to another side of the building, so as to avoid having to put 'Bobby Sands Street' on its letterheads. In a surreal twist, a local sandwich shop in Tehran changed its name to the Bobby Sands Snack Bar – perhaps a shade tasteless in view of the circumstances of his demise. Loyalist graffiti, meanwhile, used black humour to suggest that his death was a meaningless gesture that would soon be forgotten: 'We'll never forget you – Jimmy Sands'. This hope was a rather sanguine one, as his image in fact became an icon of the conflict.

In political terms, the 1981 hunger strike marked a sea change in republican politics and in the history of the Northern Ireland conflict. On the one hand, the hunger strikers demonstrated that they believed in their cause sufficiently to endure suffering themselves, rather than simply inflicting it on others. On the other, the deaths of the hunger strikers revitalized the political dynamism of republican politics and demonstrated – through the election of Sands and Doherty – that electoral gains could help broaden their struggle.

In more recent years, as republicans have fallen out over the course of the post-1998 peace process, a disagreement has emerged over the conduct of the strike, which mirrors wider political divisions. This relates to an allegation by former IRA prisoner Richard O'Rawe in 2005 that a deal was offered by the British Foreign Office that conceded the majority[28] of the five main demands of the hunger strike and that was accepted by the IRA leader in the prison, Brendan 'Bik' McFarlane, who had taken over command when Sands went on his fast. O'Rawe has alleged that this was subsequently over-ruled by senior republicans outside the prison, including Adams himself, who wanted to prolong the strike for political reasons. Bobby Sands' election agent, Owen Carron, was contesting the by-election caused by Sands' death and stood a better chance of winning if the strike was still going on; another six hunger strikers died in the intervening period. This allegation – which amounts to a suggestion that those on the outside caused the death of six of the hunger strikers through a combination of ineptitude and callous disregard for the welfare of those involved – has been flatly denied ever since by McFarlane himself and by other senior figures within Sinn Fein.

Back in 1982, Sinn Fein contested local assembly elections on an abstentionist platform and won five seats. In 1983, Gerry Adams was elected to the Westminster parliament, winning the former safe SDLP seat of West Belfast, again on an abstentionist ticket. In 1985, Sinn Fein won fifty-nine seats in local government elections and had by this stage established a firm electoral platform.

Militant republicanism had discovered, through the hunger strikes, that political support was available to it and was a useful counterpoint to its armed struggle. It required an electoral strategy, however, which former Sinn Fein Director of Publicity Danny Morrison clumsily (but memorably) saw as being complementary to the IRA's military campaign. At Sinn Fein's *Ard Fheis* (conference) in 1981, Morrison tried to calm hardline elements within the movement by arguing that politics was not a replacement for violence, but could be used alongside it: 'Who here really believes we can win the war through the ballot box? But will anyone here object if, with a ballot paper in this hand and an Armalite in the other, we take power in Ireland?'[29]

The big problem with this was, of course, that for most of the period there were no political structures to tap into in Northern Ireland. Direct rule and the focus on political violence and the security situation had left a barren political legacy in the region. Northern Ireland was being governed from London by a quasi-colonial secretary of state and an array of faceless quangos and civil servants. Power lay in London, not in Belfast; and while Sinn Fein saw merit in an electoral strategy in the early 1980s, and while there was certainly no shortage of elections in the region, a more fundamental question presented itself: what was the point of politics in a place that had no structures (beyond those of local government) where it could be practised and no institutions that were anything other than the unacceptable face of partition? So, while Sinn Fein had become aware of its electoral potential by the early 1980s, it was not at all sure what to do with it, given the formal political context in which neither the British government nor the main unionist parties would engage with the party.

By the 1980s, the IRA and the British government had settled in for the 'long war', the formal political process was deeply polarized, and it was becoming clear to all sides that they were in a stalemate. The British had known for many years that they could not defeat the IRA militarily, and senior figures had admitted this publicly on a number of occasions. Despite its public bravado and periodic successes, the IRA also came to realize during the 1980s that it was unlikely to force the British to withdraw from Ireland through physical force alone. While both sides could maintain their positions, they could not make significant progress towards their objectives. If they could not fight their way through, then the obvious alternative was to explore the possibility of talking their way out of the military and political impasse.

This did not stop the killing, of course, and a number of infamous episodes were burned onto the public consciousness during the period under consideration. On 27 August 1979, eighteen members of the Parachute Regiment were killed in bomb attacks in the border town of Warrenpoint. That same day, Lord Mountbatten, a cousin of Queen Elizabeth II, was blown up by a bomb in his fishing boat, while on holiday in Co. Sligo in the Irish Republic, along with one of his grandchildren and a local boy working on the boat.

On 20 November 1983, worshipers at a small Pentecostal church in Darkley, a little town in Co. Armagh, were attacked by a new republican paramilitary group calling itself the Catholic Reaction Force. Three people were shot dead in the church and a number of others were wounded as the gunmen sprayed the room with bullets. The Catholic Reaction Force was connected to INLA.

Most famously, perhaps, just before 3 a.m. on 12 October 1984, the IRA came within a whisker of assassinating the British Prime Minister Margaret Thatcher and a number of leading members of her government when it bombed the Grand Hotel in Brighton, where senior figures were staying for the Conservative Party conference. The explosion ripped out the front of the building and the hotel appeared on breakfast television the next morning looking as though it had been hit by a missile. Two people were killed and many others were seriously injured, including the wife of high-profile right-wing Trade and Industry Secretary Norman Tebbit. She was permanently crippled, and Tebbit himself was pictured live on television being stretchered from the rubble of the hotel while still in his pyjamas. This became an enduring image of the IRA's bombing campaign in Britain, and the chilling IRA press release that followed had a direct political impact in the years that followed: 'Today we were unlucky, but remember, we only have to be lucky once; you will have to be lucky always. Give Ireland peace and there will be no war.'

The Brighton bombing was significant in that it marked the arrival of Semtex explosives in Britain. The bomb had been planted by IRA volunteer Patrick Magee weeks before the conference. This represented a new level of military sophistication for the IRA and a new level of threat to the security of everyone in the UK – up to and including the prime minister. This fear of what the IRA was *capable* of doing, rather than what it actually did on a day-to-day basis, partly explains Thatcher's most ambitious political initiative in Northern Ireland. The Anglo-Irish Agreement, signed on 15 November 1985 by the British and Irish prime ministers, was an attempt to curb the political rise of Sinn Fein and bolster the constitutional nationalism of the SDLP. The Brighton bomb was a catalyst for this initiative, as Thatcher desperately sought ways of improving security. The message that the IRA took from this was that its campaign of violence was capable of producing political movement from the British government.

On 8 November 1987, the IRA exploded a large bomb at the war memorial in Enniskillen, during a ceremony on Remembrance Sunday. Eleven people were killed by the initial blast and a twelfth died after spending thirteen years in a coma. Over sixty people were injured. The IRA said that the bombing had been a 'mistake' and its Fermanagh unit was permanently 'stood down'. This event is frequently seen as a turning point in the analysis of Sinn Fein, on account of the revulsion it caused across the community and internationally. Gerry Adams, president of Sinn Fein, apologized for the bombing in 1997.

Attacks such as these scarred not just the victims caught up in them, but also the very sinews of the land itself, converting little-known village names and 'townlands' into infamous indelible stains on the map of violent conflict. The Northern Ireland poet John Hewitt captured this rupture of place brilliantly in his poem 'Post Script, 1984', in which he amended a previous work, 'Ulster Names', that had been written thirty years before and that had lyrically extolled the earthy beauty of the landscape, community and people of Ulster. That poem revelled in the linguistic derivation of place names and showed his love and affection for the region, its history and its people:

> The names of a land show the heart of the race;
> they move on the tongue like the lilt of a song.
> You say the name and I see the place –
> Drumbo, Dungannon, Annalong.
> Barony, townland, we cannot go wrong.[30]

'Postscript, 1984' is worth recording here in full, as it emphasizes how violence had seeped through into the very fabric of the land itself, as well as into those who lived upon it – and clearly into the psyche of the poet himself:

> Those verses surfaced thirty years ago
> when the time seemed edging to a better time,
> most public voices tamed, those loud untamed
> as seasonal as tawdry pantomime,
> and over my companionable land
> placenames still lilted like a childhood rime.
>
> The years deceived; our unforgiving hearts,
> by myth and old antipathies betrayed,
> flared into sudden acts of violence
> in daily shocking bulletins relayed,
> and through our dark dream-clotted consciousness
> hosted like banners in some black parade.
>
> Now with compulsive resonance they toll:
> Banbridge, Ballykelly, Darkley, Crossmaglen,
> summoning pity, anger and despair,
> by grief of kin, by hate of murderous men
> till the whole tarnished map is stained and torn,
> not to be read as pastoral again.[31]

Poignant, haunting and certainly heart-breaking for those caught up in the events to which these place names allude. No academic analysis has come close to capturing the impact of sectarian violence in Northern Ireland as sympathetically as Hewitt's poem. Beyond all of this human tragedy it was becoming clear to the British government and the Provisional IRA that they had reached a stalemate. If they were unable to defeat the enemy, then the only other option was to talk to each other.

# CHAPTER FIVE

# TALKING TO THE ENEMY, 1993–95

Our position is clear, and it will never, never, never change. The war against British rule must continue until freedom is achieved.

Martin McGuinness, 1986

It is very hard for democratic governments to admit to talking to terrorist groups while those groups are still killing innocent people. But on the basis of my experience I think it is always right to talk to your enemy. Luckily for this process, the British government's back channel to the Provisional IRA had been in existence whenever required from 1973 onwards.

Jonathan Powell, 2008

IN 1993, THE Labour Party backbencher Dennis Skinner asked the then British prime minister, John Major, a pointed and tricky question in the House of Commons. Would his government be prepared to follow the example set in the Middle East by talking to the Provisional IRA, as the Israelis had done with the PLO? Major's response seemed clear and unequivocal: 'If the implication of his remarks is that we should sit down and talk with Mr Adams and the Provisional IRA, I can say only that that would turn my stomach and those of most Hon. Members; We will not do it . . . I will not talk to people who murder indiscriminately.'[1]

However, it became clear shortly afterwards that this was precisely what he had been doing for the previous three years, via a secret back channel between MI6 and intermediaries for the IRA. The yawning gap between his stated public position and his secret arm's-length dialogue with militant republicans was politically embarrassing for Major, but he would later conclude in his memoirs that 'Making peace is a tricky business.'[2]

## TAKING THE FIRST STEP

John Major's arrival as prime minister in 1990 signalled an opportunity. For one thing, he was not Margaret Thatcher and carried none of her associated baggage. Thatcher had been a *bête noire* within Irish nationalist circles since the 1981 republican hunger strikes, and her simplistic political fundamentalism made her wholly unsuited to pragmatic realignment. The idea that the 'Iron Lady' could (or would) explore the possibility of ending paramilitary violence through dialogue and compromise was unconscionable.

John Major was cut from a different cloth altogether and was the essence of a consensus politician. He later told a journalist that when he became prime minister in 1990, he sat down in the Cabinet Office in Downing Street and drew up a list of priority issues that he wanted to address in his administration: 'and Northern Ireland was on that list'.[3] When pressed as to where exactly it was on his list, he replied 'it was right at the top of the list'. What Major lacked in charisma or inspirational rhetoric he made up for in dogged determination and endurance, as he was to pursue this issue until he lost power to Labour at the 1997 general election.

At first, movement was secretive and imperceptible. Sinn Fein President Gerry Adams sent what he called a 'Dear John' letter to Major when he took over as prime minister, in which he stressed the need to secure an end to British rule in Ireland. Major had been in his new job for only two days when he received the letter. It was significant not so much because of *what* the letter said, so much as *why* it had been sent. As Major was to say:

> It was the Sinn Fein case in straightforward terms – that he [Adams] believes that the British should leave Ireland and there should be a united Ireland. But there just seemed a flavour about the letter: it might be possible that Sinn Fein were looking for a way out of the last 20 years, that they were looking for a way to end the violence.[4]

Adams' account of this letter combines revolutionary whimsy with the more pragmatic desire to open up dialogue with the new British leader:

It struck me, something I just read somewhere, that Ho Chi Minh or someone like that had, through all the decades for the liberation of Vietnam, continuously written to the colonial power. It just struck me that here we were, and we had never made any attempt to proactively engage with the British prime minister.[5]

His letter was (alarmingly) posted to the wrong address and arrived at 10 Downing Street, *Shankill Road, Belfast* (a staunchly loyalist part of the city). Mercifully, however, it was redirected to its intended recipient in London. Michael Oatley, an intelligence officer in MI6, subsequently met Martin McGuinness in Derry in January 1991 to gauge the mood of the IRA and determine what (if any) possibility existed for progress towards an IRA ceasefire. Whether these exchanges amounted to 'negotiations' perhaps depends on how broadly we define such terms. They were certainly fact-finding exercises for both sides, where they set out and informed the other of current thinking within their respective organizations. This would become important later on, as they tried to move forwards into more open dialogue with each other. Oatley's report on his meeting in Derry made it back to John Major's desk in Downing Street and the pace began to quicken a little.

British politicians had already started sending copies of relevant speeches to Sinn Fein, with important paragraphs highlighted to ensure that their significance was not overlooked. One such address by the secretary of state, Peter Brooke, was to become a cornerstone of the IRA ceasefire in 1994 and a foundation for the peace process that followed. If ever 'peace' began in modest circumstances, this was surely the occasion: addressing the Association of Canned Food Importers in London on 9 November 1990, Brooke announced that Britain had 'no selfish strategic or economic interest' in Northern Ireland and would legislate for a united Ireland when the majority of the people of Northern Ireland expressed such a wish.

This was, in a nutshell, the basis on which the peace process was constructed, and these words became a mantra of the political discourse from this point onwards. In retrospect (and with no disrespect to his hosts), it is not surprising that Brooke picked such a low-profile occasion to book-mark a significant change in the tone of British policy. The key audience here was Sinn Fein, and Brooke was signalling that the British government was 'neutral' with regard to the constitutional future of Northern Ireland. It was *de facto* rather than *de jure* British (its sovereign status a matter of internal preference, rather than legal ownership); while at one level this was a semantic point, the fact that the British were not saying this about any other region of the United Kingdom was not lost on either unionists or nationalists living in Northern Ireland. In terms of demystifying the language, the British were saying that Northern Ireland was different from the rest of the UK – it was 'special', and they were politically agnostic about its future.

Once again, it was the mood music that mattered rather than the details; and to many nationalists it sounded quite melodic, as Britain was at least holding out the theoretical prospect of Irish unity as a legitimate political objective. However, unionist ears heard the speech in a minor key, fearing that it once again demonstrated the British government's lack of commitment to the political Union of Great Britain and Northern Ireland. For them, Britain *should* have a selfish interest in Northern Ireland, given the latter's loyalty over numerous generations. While Brooke's speech, and future British iterations of the same position, did not signify any imminent change, few relationships are improved when one partner states that, while they recognize the existence of their marriage, they have no 'selfish interest' in it and would be happy to get a divorce as soon as the other partner wants one.

The Provisional IRA responded to Brooke's verbal semaphore by announcing a three-day ceasefire over Christmas 1990 (its first 'official' ceasefire of any kind since 1975), though it then followed this up with an audacious mortar attack on 10 Downing Street in February 1991. Ironically, Major was chairing a special Cabinet meeting on Iraq and the first Gulf War when Downing Street came under attack from rather more traditional adversaries. In the middle of a snowstorm, an IRA active service unit drove a transit van into the centre of London and parked it beside the Ministry of Defence – some 200 yards 'as the mortar flies' from the rear of 10 Downing Street. A few minutes later, three mortar shells were launched remotely through a hole that had been cut in the roof of the vehicle; then the van itself was blown up by an incendiary bomb to destroy any remaining forensic evidence that could be used to trace the bombers. Two of the mortar bombs landed in the grounds of the Foreign and Commonwealth Office but failed to detonate. The third exploded in the garden of 10 Downing Street, just yards from the room where the Cabinet was meeting. While not a particularly sophisticated attack, this was one of the boldest IRA operations mounted during the conflict and came within a whisker of wiping out the leadership of the British government. Peter Gurney, who led the explosives unit of the Anti-Terrorist Branch of the

Metropolitan Police in London and who defused one of the unexploded mortar shells with a spanner he had hurriedly picked up in the Downing Street boiler room, spoke in admiring terms of the chutzpah and technical skill of the attack:[6]

> It was a remarkably good aim if you consider that the bomb was fired 250 yards [across Whitehall] with no direct line of sight. Technically, it was quite brilliant and I'm sure that many army crews, if given a similar task, would be very pleased to drop a bomb that close. You've got to park the launch vehicle in an area which is guarded by armed men and you've got less than a minute to do it. I was very, very surprised at how good it was. If the angle of fire had been moved about five or ten degrees, then those bombs would actually have impacted on Number Ten.[7]

As the Cabinet and senior civil servants picked themselves up from their huddled position under the table, Major suggested, with more than a hint of understatement: 'I think we had better start again somewhere else.'

The message being sent by the IRA to Major throughout this period was that, while it was interested in the possibility of political dialogue, it was still capable of turning violence on as well as off, and there was no limit to the ambition in its choice of targets.[8] On the positive side, it demonstrated to the British government that the IRA could deliver on any agreements that it made and had the power to control republican violence.

The public mood in Britain and Ireland at the time was rather jaundiced, but most had come to accept the fact that military solutions were unlikely to succeed, even if dialogue and negotiation remained inconceivable. Everyone claimed to want peace, of course, but this was a little like hoping for better weather even if you knew that it was going to rain for the foreseeable future. So there was a *desire* for peace, but not a *demand* for it. Neither unionist nor nationalist political parties lost votes because they would not talk to their opponents. If anything, it was quite the reverse, especially on the unionist side. The sad truth is that no unionist leader since 1963 had lost power for being too hardline, and most lost popular support because they were seen as being too weak, too liberal or both. The painful fact was that many people in Northern Ireland had become used to the violence and even accepted it as part of their everyday reality. Those who could do so developed coping strategies, and some self-medicated their way through the harsh sectarian atmosphere with the help of prescription drugs and alcohol. Many others simply left Northern Ireland in search of a more secure future. Optimism about the potential of the formal political process to deliver peace was thin on the ground across both unionist and nationalist communities during the early 1990s.

Simply because many realized that they had fought one another to a standstill did not mean they could see a way out of the situation. The dead-lock produced a sense of resignation and cynicism about the capacity of the formal political process to make a positive difference. The Opsahl Report commented on this endemic sense of powerlessness and apathy as a result of repeated political failure:

> In our focus groups we asked participants whether they had expected the [Brooke/Mayhew] talks to fail.[9] They, for the most part, said that they had, and there was almost across-the-board agreement that, even if the talks were to start up again, they would be doomed to failure. A survey taken by the Shankill People of 202 residents of the Shankill found that 78 per cent wanted the parties to get around the negotiating table; a similar percentage, however, thought talks would not result in a settlement.[10]

From time to time there would be a public outcry over the latest atrocity committed by the paramilitaries or the British army, but very few people talked publicly about strategies for bringing the violence to an end. A generation of conflict had produced a pervasive pessimism within public opinion, and the vast majority of people saw the political process as little more than a talking-shop, while they got on with their lives as best they could.

While people were jaded and generally pessimistic about the chances of political progress during the early 1990s, movement was taking place under their feet – but only those with the most sensitive nerve endings could detect it. Feelers were now being put out by the IRA and the British government to determine if dialogue was possible. This was largely done, using smoke and mirrors, by the British intelligence community and the IRA, through a number of third parties.

The next chapter in the unfolding story of secret British contacts with the IRA remains contested. The British government claims that on 22 February 1991 it received a message from Martin McGuinness (on behalf of the IRA army council) which said that 'the conflict is over, but we need your advice on how to bring it to an end. We wish to have an unannounced ceasefire in order to hold a dialogue leading to peace.'[11] The message went on to state that the IRA could not commit itself to non-violence publicly, as that would be interpreted by republicans and others as surrender, but that private assurances would be provided. McGuinness denied ever sending such a message, alleging that it was a piece of black propaganda from British security sources, designed to undermine his reputation within the republican community. However, again cock-up rather than conspiracy seems the most plausible explanation, as an *aide-mémoire* (drafted by several different hands) following a meeting with McGuinness was confused with his own words.

This was perhaps *the* key moment in the whole of the peace process of the 1990s – and it was based on a critical misunderstanding. However, by the time this had become apparent, amid mutual recriminations, events had acquired their own momentum. Major thought that this message had genuinely come from the IRA (via McGuinness) and convened a special Cabinet meeting to discuss how to respond. A month later, he sent Sinn Fein a reply, saying that, in the event that the IRA called a ceasefire, the British government would be 'bold and imaginative' in its response. By this stage, both the British government and the Provisional IRA had scented a faint whiff of change in the air and both sides pushed further forwards (encouraged by the Irish and US governments) to determine whether meaningful progress could be achieved. The British pushed for the IRA to declare a permanent ceasefire in order to facilitate direct talks, while Sinn Fein demanded that the British provide a dynamic for change, by acting to persuade the unionists about Irish reunification.

The violence continued during the early 1990s, though it was usually aimed at economic disruption rather than human destruction. Bomb scares on the London underground became a frequent irritant to commuters during this period, while IRA spectaculars, such as the Bishopsgate bomb, sought to maximize damage to the UK economy rather than to take human life. In the early morning of Saturday, 24 April 1993, a truck was parked outside the Hong Kong and Shanghai Bank in the Bishopsgate area, in the financial heart of the City of London. It was carrying a one-tonne fertilizer bomb, which exploded ninety minutes after a warning had been sent to the police, causing damage estimated at around £1 billion. This was the largest and most expensive attack launched in Britain, with over 140,000 square feet of prime office space destroyed and iconic buildings such as the NatWest Tower suffering major blast damage. The historic St Ethelburga's church, which dates from around 1250 and which had survived the Great

Fire of London in 1666 and the London Blitz in the Second World War, collapsed due to the force of the explosion and was later rebuilt to incorporate a peace and reconciliation centre. One person was killed – a photographer from the tabloid *News of the World* who had ignored police warnings to stay at a safe distance. If the bomb had gone off during the working week, it is likely that many more people would have been killed; but a Saturday was chosen because the IRA wanted to target the high-profile banks and Britain's economic infrastructure, rather than kill those working inside these glass monuments to capitalist industry.

The IRA was not going soft. There was more propaganda value to be had in demonstrating its capacity to reach into and rip apart London's financial heart than there was in taking human life on a grand scale, as this would have increased the difficulty of entering dialogue with the government. It was now a question of when – not if – the British would talk directly to militant republicans.

## FOUNDATIONAL STEPS TOWARDS PEACE

By late 1993, Irish Taoiseach Albert Reynolds was trying to hammer out an agreed joint position on the peace process with John Major. This dialogue was often tense and fractious, and several times it bordered on total breakdown, as each government pulled in different directions. Reynolds wanted any joint statement to contain enough momentum for change to convince the IRA to announce a ceasefire. Major wanted to make sure that its wording would not scare unionists into public dissent. An angry (though eventually productive) Anglo-Irish summit took place in Dublin, where both leaders haggled over the terms of their joint statement in a number of ill-tempered exchanges. They shouted and swore at one another, Major banging his fist on the table and breaking his pencil in frustration; Reynolds threatening to walk out before lunch had even been served. However, their frank exchanges seemed to have a cathartic effect, as both sides eventually calmed down and came to the conclusion that they could move forward together. When asked afterwards for a summary of the meeting, Reynolds told a colleague: 'Well, he chewed the bollocks off me, but I took a few lumps out of him.'[12]

One of the curious aspects of this cloak-and-dagger dialogue was the extent to which the formal discussions between the political elites were supplemented (and at times subverted) by informal conversations taking place in secret. The result was a degree of political progress, but also a high level of confusion and paranoia for those inside and outside these concentric circles.

So, to summarize: in 1991–92, the British were trying to encourage public 'constitutional' talks between unionists and nationalists (though Sinn Fein was excluded because of the lack of an IRA ceasefire), as well as to build diplomatic relations with the Irish government. Privately, they were in contact with Sinn Fein and the IRA through a secret back channel managed for them by MI6, without the knowledge of the Irish government or the SDLP or the main unionist parties. SDLP leader John Hume and Adams, meanwhile, had been in secret (though periodic) dialogue for five years between 1988 and 1993, without the knowledge of either their own parties or the Irish and British governments. The Irish government, for its part, had also established a separate set of contacts with both republican and loyalist paramilitaries which they did not share with their British counterparts or even with the SDLP. Nobody really knew for sure who was talking to whom, or whether anybody was actually listening in any case.

This culture of secrecy pervaded the relationships of the formal political actors throughout the peace process, as politicians scuttled around having clandestine meetings with one another. It all resulted in progress of sorts, but also created bedroom-farce diplomacy, confusion over who knew what, and a profound mistrust among those involved. On one occasion (before the IRA ceasefire of August 1994), Sinn Fein's chief negotiator Martin McGuinness went to Dublin for secret discussions with the Irish Department of Foreign Affairs. He later recalled the unfortunate timing of his furtive arrival at the government offices, which coincided with an open-top bus full of American and Japanese tourists on a sightseeing trip around Dublin drawing up at the traffic lights outside the office. 'I was attempting to get into the building without being seen and suddenly I hear, through the loud speaker on the bus, the man saying: "And the Chief Negotiator for Sinn Fein, Martin McGuinness, is now entering the Department of Foreign Affairs." This was all over Stephen's Green [the nearby public park] – I couldn't believe it.'[13]

The result of all these Chinese whispers was a heightened unionist fear that beyond the formal political process being conducted by the political elites lay a labyrinth of secrets and lies between the British government and those the unionists had started referring to as the 'pan-nationalist front' (the IRA, Sinn Fein, the SDLP and the Irish government). Given Northern Ireland's highly charged political atmosphere at the best of times, the revelation in 1993 of the various layers of secrecy created a febrile atmosphere and a sense that significant movement was imminent. The suspicion of those not 'in the loop' was heightened by the fact that draft documents from these meetings (not all of which were identical) were apparently in existence, but their contents were either not released or were contested by the various parties concerned.

Nor was the political mood helped by the fact that the admission of secret talks came at a time when paramilitary violence had risen in October/ November 1993. On Saturday, 23 October 1993, two IRA bombers – Sean Kelly and Thomas Begley – left a bomb in Jimmy Frizzell's fish shop on the Shankill Road. It exploded prematurely and without warning, killing nine shoppers and one of the bombers (Begley).[14] A meeting of the commanders of the West Belfast UDA was believed to be scheduled for that morning above the fish shop, though the information was wrong. The IRA had being aiming to assassinate UFF leader Johnny 'Mad Dog' Adair, but they missed their target and killed Saturday shoppers instead. The building collapsed, trapping many people under the rubble. The television footage of the carnage, with passers-by and relatives of the dead and injured pulling the victims from the debris, had to be carefully edited. Two young girls, seven-year-old Michelle Baird and thirteen-year-old Leanne Murray, were among the dead. Leanne's mother gave an interview to journalists the following day that provides a stark reminder of the fragility of life in conflict and the impact of violence on its victims:

> Leanne had just left me to go in to the fish shop. Suddenly there was this huge bang. We ran screaming for Leanne. We couldn't find her. No-one had seen her. There were people lying in the street covered in blood. My little girl was underneath all that rubble. We started clawing at it with our bare hands. I was screaming her name. But it was no use. My little daughter was dead – just for a tub of whelks.[15]

Begley was given a full republican funeral and his coffin, draped in the trademark Irish flag and IRA standard-issue black beret and gloves, was carried by Sinn Fein President Gerry Adams amidst a storm of media criticism. The *Sun* newspaper was typically the most vivid and hyperbolic: 'Gerry Adams – the two most disgusting words in the English language'.[16]

The loyalist retaliation was not long in coming. On 30 October, the crowded Rising Sun pub in the village of Greysteel, Co. Derry, was attacked by three members of the UFF, who killed eight people. The gunmen yelled 'trick or treat' as they opened fire on patrons celebrating Halloween. Some of the victims pleaded for mercy as the killers reloaded their weapons and opened fire on them.[17] The UDA later claimed that the attack had been a reprisal for the previous weekend's Shankill Road bombing.

Over twenty people had been killed in the space of a week and the television news was filled with condemnations, funerals, grieving relatives and a pervading sense of dread and hopelessness across Northern Ireland that things were getting worse rather than better. One of the enduring images of the period was of SDLP leader John Hume breaking down in tears at the funeral of one of the victims of the Greysteel shootings. In part, this was the result of months of pressure over his dialogue with Gerry Adams, but it was triggered when the daughter of one of the victims approached him during the ceremony and said: 'Mr Hume, we prayed for you last night in our house, and we prayed that you would be successful in the work that you're doing, so that what happened to us will not happen to anybody else.'[18]

Ironically, perhaps, incidents such as these jump-started the formal political process and drove it forward, as politicians across Ireland and Britain recognized the weight of responsibility on their shoulders and the human cost that would result if they should fail. More deaths, more funerals, more tears, more grieving families, and no political answers.

The initial result of the official talking between the two governments came with the publication of the Downing Street Declaration on 15 December 1993. The document was unveiled, with much media hoopla, by two grinning prime ministers on the steps of Downing Street, but it said nothing about the British acting as 'persuaders' of the unionists, or about British intent to withdraw from Northern Ireland. However, it did underline two key principles that became foundation stones for the subsequent negotiations that led to the Good Friday Agreement in 1998. First, that Britain had no selfish interest in remaining in Northern Ireland against the wishes of a majority of the people living there. If and when the majority wanted to end the Union and integrate with the rest of the island of Ireland then Britain would commit itself to enacting the necessary legislation to facilitate this transfer of sovereignty. Second, the Irish government recognized that the consent of the people in Northern Ireland to any such change was a prerequisite for Irish unity, irrespective of Articles 2 and 3 of the constitution of the Irish state.

## SILENCING THE GUNS

The months that followed were among the most important in the history of modern republicanism. The militants had reached a crossroads and were running out of room for manoeuvre. To go in the direction of continued armed struggle looked increasingly like a strategic dead end to the IRA leadership and would have resulted in their political isolation and international condemnation. The other route, of moving to a ceasefire and political dialogue with the British government and unionist parties, was an equally precarious path. There were significant benefits to be gained from taking the latter course, but it was a big gamble: they knew that they might end up with no sizeable concessions to republican objectives and instead become destabilized and split. Which way they turned would be a pivotal moment in the history of Northern Ireland. There was a lot riding on the decision for republicans, unionists, the British and the Irish governments, as well as for the 'ordinary' people most likely to end up as the victims of paramilitary violence. The stakes were high for the republican leadership, whose members were putting not just their personal reputations on the line, but the whole struggle itself.

While the IRA was disappointed that neither government was prepared to advocate Irish unity, it was hopeful that this would at last be on the table for discussion in negotiations, and that Sinn Fein would have access to the talks thanks to an IRA ceasefire. The Downing Street Declaration was a masterpiece of ambiguity and was one of the cornerstones of the peace process, upon which everything else was subsequently built. The British and Irish governments presented themselves as facilitators (rather than advocates) of political change, and as neutral over the major constitutional fault-line that ran through the conflict: was Northern Ireland to remain within the United Kingdom or become united with the rest of Ireland? Well, that was for the people of Northern Ireland to determine, and both governments would abide by whatever majority view was expressed. It also made clear that the engine of political change was the democratic process, and that all those with a political mandate who committed themselves to exclusively peaceful methods had a right to participate in it.

Both Sinn Fein and the IRA were stung by what they regarded as the weakness of the Downing Street Declaration and provided a characteristically ambivalent response, claiming that some of its clauses required 'clarification', which would be followed by 'consultations' with the republican community. This was a stalling tactic while they worked out what to do next and took the internal temperature of the republican community to ensure that they did not move too far ahead of their core support. Adams knew that such lukewarm aspirational rhetoric demonstrated little commitment to change from the British side and provided no basis for an IRA ceasefire. At the same time, however, his strategic agenda by this point was based on getting Sinn Fein into negotiations with the government, and this, he knew, necessitated a ceasefire. Sinn Fein demanded clarification before committing itself, while Major publicly refused to provide it, paranoid about being sucked into negotiations with Sinn Fein before the prize of an IRA ceasefire had been won.

By this stage, both sides had learned the choreography of the dance, and while they struck verbal poses in public, their written interactions were more productive. In April 1994 Adams wrote again to Major, asking for twenty points of the Declaration to be clarified. The government eventually published answers to all the questions.

It was decision time for Sinn Fein and the Provisional IRA. They were under pressure from the British, the Americans and moderate nationalists in the SDLP to announce a ceasefire, in order to unblock the political process and allow a new phase of dialogue to begin. None of this made the IRA do anything it did not want to do or caused a strategic rethink within the IRA army council. However, it knew that time was running out. There were only two possible courses of action – to halt its campaign of violence or to burn its political bridges – and it was going to have to choose one of them. At a republican rally on 14 August, a speech by Gerry Adams hinted that a major shift within republicanism was imminent. Typically with Adams, there was nothing definitive, but the tone was upbeat, enigmatic and suggested that a new, more energetic and challenging phase for republican politics was about to begin:

> It will be difficult and dangerous, it will take time and as events unfold in the months ahead there will be the inevitable begrudgers, the doubters and the revisionists, those who were never for the peace process and who will tell us that it cannot succeed . . . I am especially confident that after twenty-five years of unparalleled courage and self-sacrifice, the nationalist people of this part of Ireland are prepared to show the way to a new future while at the same time reaching out the hand of friendship to unionists.[19]

Sinn Fein had used the consultation period following the Downing Street Declaration of December 1993 for intensive internal discussions about how to respond. The above remarks by Adams the following August made clear to most external observers the direction in which the republican leadership was turning. It was preparing the ground for a major announcement, and at the end of August it was evident that matters were coming to a head. The Irish-Americans arrived in Ireland, held positive meetings with the Irish government in Dublin and Sinn Fein in Belfast, and made optimistic statements about the potential for significant political progress. On Sunday, 28 August, SDLP leader John Hume and Sinn Fein President Gerry Adams issued a joint statement to the effect that the necessary criteria for the achievement of *'justice* and peace' in Ireland might now be available.[20] On 29 August, Gerry Adams issued a public statement, saying he had advised the IRA that he now believed the potential existed to break the political and military stalemate and that he would communicate its response when he received it. Speculation was now rife that the Provisional IRA was on the cusp of a major announcement.

On 31 August 1994, the political universe in Northern Ireland was tilted on its axis by four paragraphs of relatively plain prose issued by the IRA army council. The key phrase was: 'as of midnight, August 31, there will be a complete cessation of military operations'. Some people were delighted (notably John Hume, Bill Clinton and Albert Reynolds), but many others expressed disappointment. Bernadette Devlin invoked Canadian singer-songwriter Leonard Cohen: 'the war is over – and the good guys lost', meaning that the IRA had received no guarantee that political change would result from the end of its campaign.

## COMING IN FROM THE COLD

Two questions dominated people's minds at this point. First, would the ceasefire last and was the 'long war' finally over? Second, how long would it take for the British government to invite Sinn Fein into the formal political process to engage in negotiations with the other parties in Northern Ireland? Predictably, neither of these questions would have a straightforward answer.

The IRA announced its ceasefire in August 1994 because it had come to two conclusions. First, it had accepted that armed struggle alone would not lead to Irish unity. In fact, there were clear signs that the campaign of violence was inhibiting wider political development and that Britain could live with it both militarily and politically. Second, it was clear to the IRA by then that a dynamic for political change existed through dialogue, especially in the context of a joint Sinn Fein–SDLP–Irish government position, facilitated by the Clinton administration in the United States. While the British might not be prepared to act as 'persuaders' of the unionists to accept political change, the united Irish nationalist constituency could persuade the Americans to persuade the British to persuade the unionists of the need for reform. This stretched the fabric of everyone's patience, as many republicans worried about such a vague and indirect dynamic for change and about the lack of up-front promises about Irish unity.

Unionists and the British government were both concerned about the sincerity of the Provisional IRA and about whether they were being lulled into dialogue with the constant threat of a return to violence if concessions were not delivered to republicans. The spectre of negotiating peace with people who had 'guns under the table' became a major sticking point for unionists, especially those who were trying to assess whether the risk of sitting down with republicans was worth taking. Talking to 'terrorists' was not easy for the British government, but it was even harder for moderate unionists, many of whom had literally been in the firing line of the IRA for a generation.

From the IRA's point of view, it had stopped its campaign of violence to test the commitment of the British government and unionists to reform. The prospect that it maintained its capacity to return to violence was a necessary latent threat to motivate these unwilling brides into whatever shot-gun marriage could be arranged, unpleasant though that might be for all parties concerned.

Part of the problem relates to the language that was used in 1994, as the long-awaited IRA ceasefire was by no means unconditional. The word 'ceasefire' was not even used in its statement, the critical wording being that there would be a 'complete cessation of military operations' to facilitate direct and inclusive negotiations in the search for a lasting peace. This could be read in a number of ways and a long queue of differing opinion quickly formed. John Hume, the Irish government and the Clinton administration favoured an optimistic and pragmatic approach, believing this to be the signal that the war was over and that the momentum created needed to be quickly built upon by including Sinn Fein in the formal political process. In short-hand terms, the IRA had conceded political, if not military, defeat, and more was to be gained by seizing the moment and welcoming it into the democratic fold than by rubbing its noses in defeat and humiliating it. The US ambassador to Ireland, Jean Kennedy Smith, recalled the sense of jubilation and momentum that overtook the US side at the time: 'I was with two friends and we heard it and we all screamed and yelled. Then I talked to Gerry Adams and I congratulated him. Then the President [Clinton] called and he congratulated me and I congratulated him, and he said we had to make the peace work. That night we had some people for dinner and we all sang and drank toasts and all that.'[21]

Many others took a different view. The IRA had clearly not surrendered or even said that its armed campaign of violence was at an end. Nor was there any trace of remorse or regret about the past or about those who had died at its hands. Its statement was linguistically dextrous and provided no clue as to the future, or even as to whether the 'cessation of military operations' extended to other areas of militant activity, such as intelligence gathering, targeting or the procurement of weapons. Some unionists were a little alarmed by the exuberant celebrations in West Belfast that accompanied the IRA statement. A cavalcade of black taxis blared their horns on the Falls Road, while people waved Irish flags and Sinn Fein posters from their cars and gathered in the streets in a spontaneous mixture of relief, confusion and excitement. One local teenager summed up the general mood: 'I've waited all my life for this. It's like winning the World Cup.'[22]

\*\*\*

That morning I was driving back from a job interview in the Irish Republic, my ear glued to the radio. It was a beautiful, sunny, late August morning with just a hint of autumn chill, and it was difficult not to get caught up in the euphoria of the occasion. I found my mind drifting to a quiet part of rural Co. Down . . .

When I was in my late teens, my family had moved there from Belfast. For some time before, my parents had felt that, as young Catholics living in a mainly Protestant area, my older brother and I were more vulnerable to attack by loyalists. My father had spent the previous ten years restoring an old, derelict, ancestral cottage that had been in the extended family since the nineteenth century. It had been a tumble-down ruin on the edge of a quiet village, but he had single-handedly transformed it from a pile of old stones into a modern home.

Two months before the IRA statement that brought about my reverie, as I sat in Belfast one evening watching the Republic of Ireland beat Italy in the World Cup finals in New York, that sleepy village became a place synonymous with political violence. At 10 p.m. on 18 June 1994, two UVF men entered The Heights bar in Loughinisland and indiscriminately sprayed the room with gunfire. Six men who were sitting quietly watching the match on television were killed instantly, including Barney Greene, at eighty-seven one of the oldest casualties of the conflict. The Loughinisland massacre became one of the many *causes célèbres* of the conflict, as no one was ever successfully prosecuted and allegations of police collusion have persisted. There have been a number of investigations over the years and several arrests, including that of a former police officer, who was questioned in 2010 about 'perverting the course of justice' and 'aiding and abetting' the killers' escape. But the lack of credible evidence has meant that nothing has ever stuck, and justice has evaded the victims' families.[23]

Now, as I drove back up North on 31 August 1994, I thought about Barney Greene and his wife (who were well known to my family) and about whether this was finally the point at which these random killings would stop. It was not the end, of course, but it did at least provide hope that it might be the beginning of the end.

***

Back in Belfast, Sinn Fein President Gerry Adams was smiling and waving and having his back slapped by those who could get near him. He accepted bouquets of flowers, and his confident speech was cheered by an expectant and jubilant crowd. However, it was largely a triumph of smoke and mirrors. Adams had little of substance to say about what the Provisional IRA had got out of the British in return for 'ceasing' its campaign, other than to praise the republican community for the sacrifices it had made in pursuit of Irish freedom and to reiterate the point that the IRA had not been defeated.

However, Prime Minister John Major was playing hard to get and wanted some guarantee from the IRA that its cessation was a permanent and complete one, rather than just another tactical manoeuvre that would create intense political problems for his government if the violence resumed. This guarded welcome was strikingly at odds with the reaction of the Irish government, which was happy to refer to it as an 'historic' day for Ireland. Within a week, a carefully stage-managed photograph was arranged in Dublin: a triple handshake involving Irish Prime Minister Albert Reynolds, SDLP leader John Hume and Sinn Fein President Gerry

Adams. This was an attempt to anoint the peace process and rebrand Adams as a legitimate political actor, rather than a paramilitary spokesman who was not allowed on the airwaves in Ireland, so dangerous were his views deemed to be. This was Ireland's version of the White House lawn moment in 1993, when a beaming President Clinton convened a 'historic' handshake between Israeli Prime Minister Yitzhak Rabin and PLO leader Yasser Arafat in front of a global audience.[24] One unionist politician described the Dublin handshake between the three leaders of Irish nationalism as 'nauseating', and many were unnerved by the speed with which Sinn Fein was being welcomed into the political process, despite the fact that the IRA had clearly not renounced violence.

Unionists' disdain was tinged with suspicion that the British may have done a deal with the IRA behind their backs, and they demanded assurances from the prime minister that this was not the case. The usually mild-mannered leader of the Ulster Unionist Party (UUP), James Molyneaux, reacted to news of the IRA ceasefire by saying that it had destabilized the whole population in Northern Ireland and 'was not an occasion for celebration, quite the opposite'.[25] Molyneaux was a modest, introverted individual and a rather dull public speaker who preferred to conduct politics in the committee rooms rather than on the streets. The adjective most frequently used to describe him was 'taciturn'. However, while he lost out to Paisley in terms of grabbing headlines or energizing the grass roots, he frequently out-manoeuvred his louder colleague by taking 'the long view'. He was certainly considered more reasonable by the British media and by John Major, who was aware that while it would be very nice to have Paisley on board for any British initiative in Northern Ireland, it was *essential* to have Molyneaux's private acquiescence, if not his public support. These were the halcyon days of the UUP, of course, when it was the largest party in Northern Ireland and a political force that had to be taken seriously by any British government.

Ian Paisley's reaction to the IRA ceasefire was typically more colourful and focused on the lack of remorse expressed by the IRA; he accused it of 'dancing on the graves of Ulster's dead'.[26] While Catholics on the Falls Road celebrated, this was not the mood in Protestant areas. The political logic was simple: if republicans were cheering and clapping in the streets, they must have secured major concessions from Britain to the detriment of the unionist community.

Prime Minister Major made concerted efforts to calm unionist fears, partly because he needed their support at Westminster to prop up his own flagging popularity. However, it was also clear that loyalist paramilitaries were unwilling to announce their own ceasefire until they were convinced that no under-the-table agreements had been reached between Britain and the IRA. This necessitated more talks between Major and the unionists' political leaders, which led at times to ill-tempered exchanges. On one occasion, a meeting between Major and Ian Paisley was 'terminated' by the prime minister after just ten minutes, when the DUP leader refused to accept Major's word that no deal had been done in secret with the IRA. This surprised everyone – including Paisley – because Major's public persona was of a buttoned-down, grey politician, not given to flamboyant or excitable gestures. Of course, this incident of 'the mouse that roared' made Paisley's ejection from Downing Street all the more newsworthy.

As ever, important dialogue was taking place behind the scenes at a more local level, to reassure loyalist paramilitaries that no promises had been made to the IRA. These took place in secret and were facilitated by respected Protestant clergymen – such as the Church of Ireland Archbishop of Armagh, Rev. Robin Eames, and the Presbyterian minister Rev. Roy Magee. Other informal third parties also played important roles, including Dublin trade unionist and peace activist Chris Hudson, who acted as an initial contact point between the UVF and the Irish government. Ironically, while the British refused to have any contact with loyalist paramilitaries in the absence of a ceasefire, the position of the Irish government proved more flexible, and both Magee and Eames acted as vital intermediaries between the UDA/UVF and politicians in Dublin.

The key to both the republican and the loyalist ceasefires was the care taken to bring along grass-roots activists and communities at the local level. The decisions were not dumped on people by the elite actors, but were explained and developed over time, to the point that paramilitary leaders on both sides, and their political representatives, felt confident that there was sufficient support to prevent splits or violent disintegration within their organizations. Gary McMichael, leader of the Ulster Democratic Party (which included people with links to the UDA), explained that getting loyalists to the point of declaring a ceasefire was a complex and fraught process that required prolonged and sensitive dialogue. By this stage, the two main paramilitary factions (the UDA and the UVF) had established a new umbrella grouping, the Combined Loyalist Military Command (CLMC), which presented a united front to the outside world and made sure that both organizations were able to share information and take co-ordinated decisions in relation to the ceasefire issue:

It was extremely difficult to bring the CLMC to a point where all the component parts agreed that they would end hostilities. By no means was it an easy ride and I understand that, even when the decision to announce a cessation was reached, there were elements within all of the groups which remained unconvinced that it was the right step.[27]

A key issue for Sinn Fein was to be able to demonstrate how the IRA cease-fire was having a direct impact on people's day-to-day lives. Those living in republican areas wanted to see signs of British demilitarization (such a reduction in army checkpoints and foot patrols). The Sinn Fein leadership understood that to sell the ceasefire within the republican heartland, it would have to be able to connect the decision of the IRA leadership to the lives of the people who supported and sustained it.

Precisely the same sort of calculations took place within the loyalist community, as both the UVF and UDA/UFF took soundings from their grass roots, explained their analysis of the political situation and tried to develop a response to the IRA cessation. As a result of such dialogue, the loyalists eventually announced a ceasefire under the umbrella of the CLMC on 13 October 1994.

Again this announcement was not cast in terms of a renunciation of violence and it contained two important caveats. First, the permanence of this ceasefire was entirely dependent on the permanence of the ceasefire by the IRA (and other republican groups that had not yet announced a suspension of hostilities). Second, it was declared on the proviso that the Union was secure and that no agreements had been made between the British government and republicans that would damage Northern Ireland's position within the United Kingdom.

To announce their decision, the CLMC held a press conference that was rich in symbolism. Gusty Spence, an iconic figure within loyalist circles who had reinvigorated the UVF in the 1960s, played a central role. Spence (full Christian name: Augustus) had moved with the times, from street-level gunman and leader of the UVF to a political strategist and active member of the Progressive Unionist Party (PUP). He had no time for those politicians who had incited others to commit acts of violence but who had not been ready to pay the price for this themselves. In 1966, he was sentenced to life for murder. Spence became a guru for other loyalist paramilitaries who arrived in jail during the 1970s, such as David Ervine, Billy Mitchell and Eddie Kinner. His enigmatic question to them on arrival – 'Why are you here?' – sought to get behind obvious operational answers, such as: 'Well, I shot someone dead and got caught.' Spence encouraged more fundamental soul-searching about the reasons why these people decided to engage in violence. Ervine, who later went on to become an influential member of the PUP and a key negotiator during the peace process of the 1990s, was fond of saying that 'the opportunities for reflection in prison are substantial'. He meant by this that the prison experience provided valuable space to sit back, analyse the situation and develop a more strategic political situation that understood violence as a methodology rather than an ideology.

In the 1960s, Spence (who had been a member of the British army until ill health forced him out) directed the UVF in the Shankill area of Belfast. He played a key role in its paramilitary activities, including shootings, bomb attacks and the fire-bombing of a house that resulted in the death of an old-age pensioner who was unable to get out of the burning building. His status as a loyalist folk hero was cemented when he escaped from prison during an authorized excursion to attend his daughter's wedding. His four months on the run were dotted with frequent appearances in Belfast and even an appearance on a television *World in Action* documentary, all of which earned him the sobriquet 'the Orange pimpernel'.

The Gusty Spence of the 1990s had become a reflective, grandfatherly figure, an enthusiastic pipe-smoker with the obligatory gravelly wheezing vocal delivery. Spence was the man chosen to deliver the CLMC ceasefire statement to the world, and it was a rather better stage-managed affair than its IRA equivalent had been two months earlier. On 13 October 1994, the expectant world media circus was invited up to Fernhill House, an imposing Victorian building that stood on a hill overlooking Belfast. This was no random location: the building was steeped in the history of the old UVF, its grounds having been used to train the local Protestant volunteers who had fought and died in the British army's Thirty-sixth (Ulster) Division at the Somme in the First World War. By 1994, it had become a local museum, charting the history of the Shankill area of Belfast.

Two things were interesting about the CLMC press conference, apart from the announcement itself. First (as was mentioned above), it was made clear that the decision to 'cease all military hostilities' was a conditional offer, made on the basis that republican violence had ended and no secret deals had been struck between the IRA and the British government. Second, and more surprisingly, there was a clear admission of responsibility – and even of contrition – for the violent acts of loyalist groups such as the UVF, the UFF and the RHC: 'In all sincerity, we offer the loved ones of all innocent victims over the past twenty five years, abject and true remorse. No words of ours will compensate for the intolerable suffering they have undergone during this conflict.'[28] Despite the caveat in the statement about 'innocent' victims and the slight ambivalence over such a category, this presented a rare occasion when loyalists had managed to beat republicans in matters of presentation. Both groups by this stage had one eye on their enemies and the other fixed firmly on their friends, as all sides held their collective breath to see if these ceasefires would hold, or if violent splinter groups would emerge to take to the field of battle once more.

## TOWARDS PUBLIC NEGOTIATIONS

With two sets of paramilitary ceasefires now in place, the ball was firmly in Britain's court. How would the government respond? Crucially, having conducted a clandestine whispering campaign with the IRA for several years, when would it engage in direct public talks with Sinn Fein and invite that organization into the full constitutional process? John Major's response to the tumultuous events that surrounded him in 1994 was rather less than the fanfare of trumpets some had hoped for, amounting to little more than a few muted notes of encouragement. In contrast to the reaction of the Irish and American governments, the British response was to give the ceasefires a cautious welcome. Major was nervous and his government was weak. He knew that if the IRA was not committed to non-violence and he opened public dialogue with Sinn Fein, his own political position would be fatally undermined. He was being savaged at Westminster by the 'Eurosceptic' wing of his own party, those he referred to as 'the bastards' in an off-the-cuff remark that he did not realize had been recorded. Even his attempts at swearing seemed polite, and as a journalist at the time remarked: 'He knows the words but he doesn't know the music.' This was part of Major's problem: while he was undoubtedly a charming and hard-working politician, he lacked charisma, colour and the ability to inspire others at moments of great emotional intensity. British satirists portrayed him as a grey man in a grey suit with a nasally speak-your-weight-machine voice and robotic personality. If people had only known that from 1984 to 1988 he had carried on an illicit affair with one of his Cabinet colleagues (Edwina Currie) he may have done something to counter his rather boring public persona (though people may have wondered where he found the time).[29]

Aside from the flushed imagination of Edwina Currie, Major lacked the ability to excite people, and patience and trust in him began to wane quite quickly after the IRA ceasefire, when he appeared to be placing obstacles in the way of talks with Sinn Fein. Major has subsequently admitted that his position was different from that of Clinton or Reynolds, and that he was subject to political realities that were not faced in Washington or Dublin:

> We needed to test its permanence for practical reasons – the unionists were unconvinced, the British House of Commons was unconvinced. We had in our mind a whole series of ways in which we could react but we needed some time to test that this wasn't a ploy before we began to move too far ahead.[30]

To say that Irish nationalists were underwhelmed by such caution would be to dramatically understate the mood. Many believed that there was more to Major's lukewarm response than statecraft alone, and that his agenda was dominated by more selfish considerations. Before he could invite Sinn Fein into talks, he needed time to win the support of the unionists, because they had the capacity to bring down his administration by voting against his government in the House of Commons. Major knew this, the unionists knew that he knew it, and (to use the Belfast vernacular) even the dogs in the street were aware of it.

It was now up to the British government to seize the initiative. How long would it take them to respond to the IRA ceasefire before announcing talks with Sinn Fein? In more melodramatic terms, would Major put lives in Northern Ireland ahead of the survival of his own government and his own political skin? Would he 'face down' the unionist veto and politicians such as the UUP's James Molyneaux, who called for a three-year 'decontamination' period for Sinn Fein before they could be invited into the democratic process?

It quickly became clear that the British government (and the unionists) wanted movement on IRA decommissioning before Sinn Fein was accepted into formal negotiations. For the British, this was a test of the IRA's commitment to non-violent methods and ultimately to the permanence of their cessation. After all, if you have given up the gun permanently, then what reason could there be to hang onto your military arsenal, and why would you be so determined to do so? This demand for prior decommissioning before negotiations could commence became known as

'Washington 3', following a speech in the US by Sir Patrick Mayhew, the Northern Ireland secretary of state, in March 1995, when he stated that 'actual decommissioning of some arms' was required to 'demonstrate good faith' and to indicate the beginning of a longer process.

For many republicans, however, this was a new precondition introduced by the British as a way of weaselling out of their previous commitments. Most republicans interpreted the demand for prior decommissioning as indicative of the untrustworthiness of British governments and as evidence that the unionist tail was wagging the British government dog: the first stalling tactic was to demand that the IRA must state that the ceasefire was permanent; when they failed to get such an assurance, they moved the political goalposts to demand up-front decommissioning before initiating inclusive negotiations. Major was never a hate figure within Irish nationalism in the way his predecessor Margaret Thatcher had been; but nor was he regarded with any affection. Perhaps this grey man was incapable of inspiring strong emotions either way, but his seemingly pedantic attitude towards the ceasefire exasperated many nationalists, who felt that a historic opportunity for peace was being squandered by an unimaginative and unambitious prime minister.

This was actually a misreading of Major, who had advanced the peace process significantly through his dealings with the Irish government. But public relations and good media coverage had never been his forte. In 1992, his government's economic policy had crash-landed and Britain fell out of the European Exchange Rate Mechanism (ERM) amidst rocketing interest rates. Billions of pounds were wiped off the value of the British economy. Major had attempted to salvage something from the wreckage by phoning the editor of Britain's largest tabloid newspaper, the *Sun* (a publication that had usually been sympathetic to his party), to see if he could smooth-talk its editor, Kelvin MacKenzie, into a more benign front page in the following day's edition. When Major asked him how the paper was going to cover the story, MacKenzie recalls telling the prime minister in his inimitably pugnacious manner: 'I said I've got a bucket of shit on my desk, prime minister, and I'm going to pour it all over you.'[31]

Republicans in Northern Ireland had access to much more potent substances, and their doubts about Major's ability to deliver serious political movement were clear from the outset, making concessions on decommissioning extremely unlikely. Sinn Fein's position was that weapons decommissioning was a matter for the Provisional IRA, not for it, and it should be given access to formal negotiations on the basis of its democratic political mandate. This was frequently followed up with suggestions that IRA decommissioning needed to be seen in the context of the overall demilitarization of the conflict (i.e. the removal of British army weapons and other military hardware).

Ultimately, underlying the whole debate on IRA decommissioning was a determination to ensure that internal splits were not caused by any suggestion that the IRA was 'surrendering' to the British. There was, of course, one other fundamental issue here, and there was no getting away from it: while the IRA held onto its weapons, it held onto its leverage; and while it was unclear precisely how much leverage the *threat* of renewed violence gave it, most people came to the reasonable conclusion that it was more than the organization would have if it had no weapons. To add to the uncertainty, no one was really sure exactly how many weapons the IRA had in the first place, which made assessments about decommissioning its arsenal rather difficult. Some informed sources claim that the IRA held around 3 tonnes of Semtex explosives, 600 AK-47 assault rifles, 60 Armalite rifles, 40 RPG-7 rocket launchers, 12 medium machine guns, 20 heavy machine guns, around 40 revolvers, 600 detonators and a few (two or three) SAM-7 anti-aircraft missiles.[32] Two important caveats need to be emphasized here. First, these are rough estimates rather than carefully audited inventories. Second, much of the worst IRA violence came from 'home-made' explosives, such as fertilizer and petrol-based fire bombs (e.g. the Bishopsgate bomb in 1993). This made it next to impossible to take away the capacity of the IRA (or anyone else) to gather materials for bomb-making purposes.

None of this prevented the issue of IRA weapons decommissioning being top of the political agenda and the basis of a power struggle between Sinn Fein/IRA on the one hand and unionists/British government on the other. Decommissioning was the ultimate bargaining chip and, as Major was to find out, would not be given away cheaply just to get into dialogue with an increasingly weak and beleaguered British prime minister.

While Major did not simply stall negotiations with Sinn Fein in order to preserve the life of his government, he did not take the initiative either, because he was always hamstrung by the need to maintain unionist support. What followed was an unhealthy stand-off for eighteen months, with Sinn Fein demanding immediate inclusive political negotiations and the British and unionists demanding urgent acts of IRA decommissioning in advance of formal talks. Both sides accused each other of bad faith, and mistrust spread like a cancer through the political classes and those who had elected them.

A route out of this impasse was urgently required if the peace process was to survive. If the British and unionists would not talk to Sinn Fein without prior IRA decommissioning, and if militant republicans would not give up their weapons in advance of inclusive political negotiations, then something would have to give. With the British government and Sinn Fein at loggerheads, outside help was desperately needed to prevent the peace process from total collapse.

# CHAPTER SIX

# BRINGING THE OUTSIDE IN: THE INTERNATIONAL DIMENSION, 1995–98

> Our day in Northern Ireland was indeed one of the most remarkable of our lives and a highlight of my Presidency. Today, almost two years later, I am still deeply moved by the warmth of the reception we were given and the palpable desire of the people we saw to come together in peace and reconciliation.
>
> President William Jefferson Clinton, Belfast, 1997[1]

THE LIST OF people who have turned up to switch on the Christmas-tree lights in Belfast is not an overly impressive one; the cartoon character Bob the Builder presided over affairs in 2009, while previous years had featured starlets from various reality television shows. However, 1995 was different: the forty-second president of the United States, William Jefferson Clinton, was making the first ever visit by a serving US president to Northern Ireland.

I was living in Belfast at the time and decided to attend the 'gig' at Belfast City Hall that evening. It was a curious and surprisingly uplifting experience, despite the depressing political stasis that existed at that time, in the period between the paramilitary ceasefires and the initiation of actual negotiations between the political parties. We were having 'talks about talks', tiresome but understandable clarifications about 'modalities', pettifogging and nit-picking over language, as all sides jostled for position and tried to buy time to ensure maximum advantage. This hiatus led to increased insecurity and frustration for both nationalists and unionists in Northern Ireland, and Clinton arrived in a tense and febrile political atmosphere. There was a sense that we were on the brink of momentous change, but few people were very clear about which direction this would go in. Others were worried that expectations would be raised beyond the political parties' capacity to deliver on them. It seemed like those in positions of political power were failing to get on with things and were getting bogged down in semantic argument. However, there were some forms of political power that went beyond the politicians – and beyond Northern Ireland for that matter. This power was less visible and less formal, but perhaps more dynamic and long-lasting. It was 'soft' rather than hard power. It was the ability to persuade rather than compel; to encourage and convince rather than demand or coerce; and to connect and build bonds of empathy, loyalty and mutual respect. President Clinton had this sort of power in spades and he deployed it to masterly effect in Northern Ireland.

The president's visit was scheduled for 30 November, and he would visit Belfast and Derry before going on to the Irish Republic, with First Lady Hillary Clinton also having a range of engagements with women's groups in the community development sector.

It was a surreal day, as the television news reported on the arrival of Air Force One at Aldergrove 'international' airport, amid scenes that we were used to witnessing in 'real' countries. As the enormous motorcade of bulletproof limos weaved its way slowly through Northern Ireland's blue-grey winter morning, its route was followed from the air by live TV with the usual 'breaking news' tagline. Local journalists in the studio speculated about what it all meant, in order to cover over the fact that nothing of any substance was actually happening. But of course, it was the imagery that counted, and it was clear that on 30 November 1995 Northern Ireland was *the* global media event – and for once it was a good-news story that even the most jaundiced local observers found it difficult to be negative about (though some managed nonetheless).

Clinton was visiting in an effort to bridge the divide that existed at the time: there were the British and the unionists (who were demanding weapons decommissioning prior to Sinn Fein being invited to the negotiations), while the republicans were pushing for immediate inclusive peace talks without extra preconditions. It was a sensitive and crucial visit that required a deft political touch, but it quickly became clear why Clinton had won the US presidential election three years earlier. He was as sure-footed as a mountain goat in the rocky terrain that confronted him and made the closely choreographed visit seem spontaneous, natural and effortless. He said the right things to the right people in the right places;

and, not content with herding the political cats in Northern Ireland, he managed to make most of them purr with satisfaction. His motorcade stopped on the Protestant Shankill Road for Bill and Hillary to get some provisions at Violet Clarke's fruit shop. They bought some oranges, among other things, and insisted on paying for them, which allowed the enterprising owner to subsequently put up a sign outside: 'President Clinton shops here.' They did not alight randomly, of course, but stopped close to the site of the 1993 Shankill bombing that had killed ten people (including the IRA bomber Thomas Begley). Again, it was a symbolic act of recognition that was understood as such by the Protestant community that lived there. The travelling road-show then moved on to the parallel Catholic Falls Road, only to grind to a halt once again for the Clintons to emerge and visit McErlains Bakery, where they happened to 'bump into' Sinn Fein President Gerry Adams. The two men shook hands, but they had worked out the camera angles to ensure that this would be done discreetly and would not become the main media story of the day, swamping the whole visit and annoying the unionists.

All of these set-piece events were worked out well in advance, with careful consideration given to ensuring that the president appeared even-handed to both nationalist and unionist communities. Every word he uttered had been carefully weighed to ensure that he did not cause offence to either side. The number of 'Derrys' and 'Londonderrys' were counted up, as were references to symbolic totems of British and Irish culture, so equal praise was heaped on the harp and fiddle of the Gael as it was on the Orange fife and Lambeg drum.[2] As a result of the 'site surveys' carried out by his pre-advance team, Clinton was to visit a non-sectarian manufacturing plant – Mackie's – and make a speech about the peace process, before going on to an economic rejuvenation meeting of local business leaders in East Belfast. In the afternoon, Clinton visited the mainly Catholic city of Derry and received a rapturous reception in the Guild Hall and in the streets of the city, where thousands of people had gathered to welcome him, waving the Stars and Stripes. He later returned to Belfast to do the honours at the switching-on ceremony at Belfast City Hall, standing in front of a giant Christmas tree imported from Nashville, Tennessee (which, rather bizarrely, is twinned with Belfast). The presidential party was billeted in the Europa Hotel in Belfast, which has the dubious honour of being the most-bombed hotel in Europe – an inconvenience that has since become a highly marketable piece of radical chic. It was a whirlwind schedule (even by Clinton's standards) and his attempt to visit his ancestral home in Co. Fermanagh had to be abandoned, as his team had decided that getting him and his travelling entourage there and back again would leave little time for his more important engagements.

One of my abiding memories of that evening in Belfast was of the security operation that had been put in place to protect the president, with impromptu iron turnstiles springing up along suddenly barricaded streets, and with individual body searches and metal detector scans of everyone who managed to squeeze into the centre of the city to swell the 80,000-strong crowd. The 'ring of steel' that was not capable of protecting the people who lived there through decades of political violence was certainly tightened by several notches that day, as the Secret Service and FBI took charge of the president's personal security. It took me over two hours to walk the fifteen-minute journey from my house in the Queen's University area into the city centre, as I queued, was intimately frisked by a man in a trench coat and dark sunglasses (despite the gunmetal grey sky overhead), got electronically scanned, was frisked again, queued up again, and was eventually vomited out through an iron turnstile in front of the City Hall, all of which added to the sense of occasion and expectation. In preparation for the president and first lady's appearance, local musicians Van Morrison and Brian Kennedy entertained us with songs such as 'Days Like This', a classic Van Morrison ballad that had already been taken up by the Northern Ireland Office in television advertisements promoting the ceasefires and the peace process. The two musicians, who had previously collaborated, were the perfect cross-community warm-up act in the sub-zero temperature: Morrison the Protestant from East Belfast and Kennedy the Catholic from West Belfast. Even the curmudgeonly 'Van the Man' seemed to be in a good mood, as his odd accent (Belfast with a hint of Los Angeles) warbled its rough semi-melodious way through the night air.

When he arrived, Clinton was greeted like a rock star by the waiting crowd and illustrated his political skills as he instantly connected with his audience, combining statesmanship and gravitas with optimism, humility and humour. The juxtaposition of the polished Clinton and Belfast's semi-articulate Lord Mayor Eric Smyth (who introduced him) was thankfully fleeting. When Smyth warned the restless crowd that his speech might 'go on forever', the chorus of 'We Want Bill' forced him to get on with it without any further delay.

It was clear that Clinton was a born communicator, able to give the person in front of him his total attention while looking out to his wider audience at the same time. At one point, he recalled that he had received a letter from a thirteen-year-old Belfast boy: 'Ryan, if you are out in the crowd tonight, here's the answer to your question. – No! As far as I know, an alien spacecraft did not crash in Rosswell, New Mexico in 1947.' He signed off by saying to his ostensibly Christian audience: 'When God was with us, he said no words more important than these: "Blessed are the peace makers, for they shall inherit the earth". Merry Christmas and God bless you all.'[3]

Clinton had a long-standing interest in Northern Ireland from his days as a Rhodes Scholar at Oxford in the late 1960s. He arrived in the United Kingdom at the very moment that the civil rights movement was disintegrating into violence, and he listened enraptured to the 'electrifying' maiden speech of Bernadette Devlin in the House of Commons. When he later recalled his interest in Northern Ireland, he agreed that the civil rights movement had grabbed his attention, as had one young woman at its forefront: 'Sure, I remember Bernadette. It was my second term at Oxford. I thought she was really something.'[4]

In April 1992, while still governor of Arkansas, Clinton was invited to speak at an Irish-American forum and was as surprised at the intensity of his audience as it was at his candour. Clinton remarked of this meeting: 'I was exhausted. It was late at night and it was almost like I was being put through an oral exam for a Ph.D. in Irish Politics.'[5] He was pressed on whether, if he was elected president, he would grant Sinn Fein President Gerry Adams a visa to enter the United States. Clinton's direct answer surprised many of the delegates, who were used to more banal and non-committal responses from their national politicians: 'I want to give you a precise answer to the question. I would support a visa for Gerry Adams. I think it would be totally harmless to our national security interests, and it might be enlightening to the political debate in this country.'[6] So even before becoming president, Clinton was well briefed on the history of the conflict.

The visit was a massive success on all fronts. Sinn Fein was delighted that Clinton had given his personal imprimatur to its right to be involved in the formal negotiations and had taken the trouble to stop and meet Gerry Adams. (He had already met and shaken hands with him in Washington earlier that year, but doing so in Belfast was of a different order entirely.) At a time when most other political leaders were crossing the road to avoid Adams, Clinton stopped his armour-plated cavalcade to greet him – and by extension, to shake hands with the rest of the republican and nationalist community in Ireland.

The British and moderate unionists were impressed by his dexterity and skill in managing not to offend the easily offended on either side, and took it as evidence of his potentially useful role as a third party in the wider peace process. The public reaction within and beyond Northern Ireland was overwhelmingly positive, and the whole event did him no harm at all in US domestic politics. With his re-election campaign already gearing up, the pictures of Clinton being lauded internationally as a peace maker, with crowds of people waving American flags, provided a positive backdrop for his bid to win another term in the White House (which he duly accomplished with relative ease in 1996). Clinton's slogan during his first election campaign – 'It's the economy, stupid' – was still accurate, but the pictures and headlines from Northern Ireland nevertheless put a useful gloss on his first term in office.

## AMERICA'S CHANGING POLITICAL RELATIONSHIP WITH NORTHERN IRELAND

The evolution of the United States (and to a lesser extent other international actors, such as the European Union) from passive observer of political violence in Northern Ireland to active participant in the efforts to end it was critical to the peace process. The United States provided the dynamic for change that altered the internal balance of power and the context within which the conflict took place, and was therefore a vital catalyst for change. While Clinton built on the work of others, he was committed to the efforts to secure an IRA ceasefire – and beyond that to the formal negotiations themselves from 1996 to 1998. The internationalization of the conflict altered the context and internal power structures in a way that facilitated political change. Equally importantly, the Clinton administration (and Irish-America more broadly) encouraged the unionist and loyalist community to engage with it and slowly won respect within that constituency for their efforts to make a positive contribution to peace.

This interventionist approach was a dramatic departure for US policy towards Northern Ireland, which had traditionally been careful to treat it within the context of its wider (and more important) relationship with the British government. Previous US governments, if they ever thought of Northern Ireland at all, tended to see it in security terms rather than as an issue that might be constructively moved forwards. During his period as US secretary of state in the 1970s, 'Henry Kissinger remarked that he spent no time at all on the Irish issue when he was in power because it was unsolvable.'[7] Due to a combination of pressure from Irish-American lobby groups and changes in the wider political context, such as the end of the Cold War, this attitude was to change dramatically between the 1970s and the 1990s.

The historical relationship between America and Ireland has been a close one for most of the last hundred years, even if the political relationship has been a little more distant and indirect. An organic link exists between the two countries as a result of generations of emigration from Ireland to the US, which has, in turn, provided layers of family links and the sinews of a shared identity between the two regions. In practical terms, of course, it is a relationship rooted in the reality that the US has a more important diplomatic and economic relationship with the government of the United Kingdom.

Formally, the US has treated Northern Ireland as a constituent part of the United Kingdom, and therefore as a purely internal matter for the UK government, rather than as an independent foreign policy issue. However, at the same time, successive US governments have attempted to maintain friendly diplomatic relations with their counterparts in Dublin and have sought to placate their own internal Irish-American constituency by demonstrating concern for the levels of political violence in Northern Ireland. Informally, US administrations have taken an unusual degree of interest in Northern Ireland at times, and have not always treated it as being purely a matter of UK domestic concern.

Today the United States accounts for over 35 million Irish-Americans, according to figures from the 2000 US census. The 1990 census showed that 43.7 million Americans (19 per cent of the total US population) defined themselves as being Irish-American.[8] The impact of Irish migration can be seen at the highest political level, with numerous US presidents claiming Irish descent. Incredibly, nearly half of all the presidents of the United States have been (or have claimed to be) of Irish or Scots-Irish extraction, including James Monroe, Andrew Jackson, James Buchanan, Ulysses S. Grant, William McKinley, John F. Kennedy, Ronald Reagan, Bill Clinton and – perhaps more surprisingly – Barack Obama: during his 2008 election campaign, Obama's ancestry was traced to Moneygall, a small town of around 350 people in Co. Offaly.

Despite the number of presidents who manage to find long-lost relatives in Ireland, the frequently quoted statistics about the number of Irish-Americans should be treated with scepticism. Such figures disguise a great shallowness of commitment for the vast majority, beyond the most disembodied of cultural celebrations on St Patrick's Day, and it has been demonstrated that 'there is no cohesive "Shamrock vote" in the US'.[9]

While this is undoubtedly true, the fact remains that, at particular pressure points in the conflict, Irish-America has played an important role and has had an impact on US government policy. British security policies during the 1970s – such as the response to the civil rights movement, Bloody Sunday, internment and allegations of police brutality – focused many Irish-American minds on what was happening in Northern Ireland. While the individuals concerned had no direct power to influence the political conflict, they were at times able to wield more subtle forms of power, especially in the context of how the conflict was understood beyond Northern Ireland. Such lobbying helped to shape international opinion and was critical to both the IRA's ability to pursue its 'armed struggle' and to Sinn Fein's subsequent attempts to replace it with dialogue and negotiation.

## LONG-DISTANCE NATIONALISM

One of the reasons why Irish-America reconnected with Irish politics when violence erupted in the late 1960s was that Irish-American civil society had evolved and developed over previous generations. Organizations such as the Ancient Order of Hibernians (AOH), together with a number of other cultural and sporting NGOs, had grown up around Irish neighbourhoods in the US. Equally importantly, this network was ideologically coherent in the early 1970s, and held the general view that Ireland had been a perpetual victim of malign British interference and exploitation. During the early years of the conflict in Northern Ireland, it was at this informal political level, as well as within the Washington elite, that Irish-American influence was felt.

The Irish Northern Aid Committee (known commonly as NORAID) was formed in 1970 and was openly supportive of the IRA's armed campaign. While NORAID was the most renowned Irish-American militant support group for the Provisional IRA, its influence was episodic and heavily dependent on events within Northern Ireland itself, with its major boost coming during the republican hunger strikes of 1981. It claimed to have over 80,000 members in 1972, though independent estimates put the figure much lower (in the region of 7,000–10,000 at its peak). According to informed estimates, 'between its founding [1970] and 1991 – when it ceased to report remittances – it officially remitted approximately $3.5 million to

Ireland to a Sinn Fein controlled charity that assisted the families of republican prisoners'.[10] While this was not a huge sum, it was supplemented by less official activities, not given to careful auditing, and by vital publicity and support for the Irish republican cause on the international stage. In a high-profile court case in 1982, NORAID's founder, Michael Flannery, admitted his role in a gun-running scheme to the IRA, but bizarrely managed to convince the jury to acquit him, on the grounds that he believed the shipment of arms to have been authorized by the CIA.[11]

Flannery was a flamboyant character, whose life story would make a rambunctious biopic set against the backdrop of twentieth-century Irish history. He was born in Ireland in 1902 and joined the IRA in 1916. He emigrated to the US in 1927 to help internationalize the fight for independence, eventually becoming the patriarch of militant republicanism. He founded NORAID in 1970 to provide financial and political support to the Provisional IRA. He remained opposed to the peace process till his death, falling out with previous allies such as Gerry Adams and opposing the IRA ceasefire in 1994. He is perhaps best known for being elected as grand marshal of the AOH St Patrick's Day Parade in New York in 1983. His installation was a propaganda coup for NORAID, but led to a boycott by other participants – including New York Governor Hugh Carey – who did not want to be seen endorsing his stewardship of the event. This controversy illustrates the point that NORAID's fortunes were episodic, as this came in the wake of the republican hunger strikes in Northern Ireland two years earlier, which had radicalized Irish-America for a short period. The previous year, Bobby Sands (who had died on hunger strike in the Maze prison in 1981) had been posthumously elected an honorary grand marshal of the parade. Flannery died aged ninety-two in September 1994, convinced to the end that armed struggle was the only way forward.

The Irish National Caucus (INC) was formed in 1974 as a lobby group. It was less militant than NORAID, though it was equally energetic in highlighting what it regarded as British government failures in Northern Ireland. Throughout the 1980s, the INC succeeded in generating support for the 'MacBride Principles'.[12]

## THE IRISH LOBBY

Influential Irish-American politicians such as Senator Edward Kennedy and Speaker 'Tip' O'Neill also adopted public positions critical of the British government, though these rarely impacted on US policy towards

Northern Ireland, due to the more important alliance with the UK. Typically, when a US president opened his mouth to speak about Northern Ireland, the State Department's words came out, and these were always carefully weighed to ensure that they would not cause any tension in the 'special relationship' with the British Cold War ally.

A group of Irish-American political heavyweights – Edward Kennedy, Tip O'Neill, Daniel Moynihan and Governor Hugh Carey, known collectively as 'The Four Horsemen' – issued statements and lobbied from the sidelines; but during the 1970s such pronouncements had more impact outside the White House than within it. These interventions were often striking in their simplicity, with Kennedy introducing a Senate Resolution in 1971 that called for a 'united Ireland' and the speedy withdrawal of British troops from Northern Ireland. While this played very nicely to his Irish-American constituency, it found little purchase within Washington policy circles.

Though they did not have a great deal of policy significance in the US, such interventions were extremely significant in Ireland and Britain, as they helped to expose the conflict in Northern Ireland to a global audience. Kennedy was a member of the most famous political dynasty in America, and what he had to say on most subjects was usually considered newsworthy by the media. His older brother's picture hung above the mantelpiece of many Irish living rooms and he had a profile that could shine a powerful light on alleged British misdemeanours in Northern Ireland. While these senior Irish-American politicians were careful to avoid making comments in support of IRA violence, their strident opposition to British policy was nevertheless used by militant republicans to justify and validate their campaign. This was an informal type of power that had no direct coercive impact, but it was no less significant for that.

This slightly one-dimensional approach to Northern Ireland within the Irish-American political elite only began to fracture in the mid-1970s, when SDLP leader John Hume and Sean Donlon, the Irish ambassador in Washington, began to convince Kennedy and others of the importance of separating out moderate Irish nationalism from the militant republicanism of Sinn Fein and the Provisional IRA. Hume and Donlon argued that, by doing this, they would have a better chance of impacting on British government policy through their own administration in Washington. If they could warm up the British, that would have a knock-on effect on the State Department, and in turn on the White House itself. The message was therefore to tone down the volume a little and to support achievable and low-risk policy objectives that could incrementally achieve change.

While the frequent interjections of these Irish-American elites had no sustained impact on US policy, there were still specific occasions when their moderate stance paid dividends. On Tip O'Neill's encouragement, President Carter made a statement on Northern Ireland in August 1977. While it contained little of any real substance, beyond a call for a form of government acceptable to both communities and other well-worn and non-controversial platitudes, its importance was that it was made at all. A direct line can be drawn between Carter's statement on Northern Ireland and the eventual hands-on involvement of Clinton in the peace process during the 1990s. For all its banality, this statement gave Northern Ireland a diplomatic identity that belied the region's status as an integral part of the United Kingdom and gave it a political presence that took it beyond being a matter of purely British domestic governance. It would have been unconscionable for the US to have said this about any other part of the UK (such as Scotland, London or Yorkshire) and it was a tacit signal that, while Northern Ireland might well be British, it was different from the rest of the United Kingdom.

Periodically within the Carter administration, the Four Horsemen played nice cop to NORAID and the INC's nasty cop. And to some extent, the former group benefited from the threat of the latter: the Four Horsemen were able to position themselves as representing a buffer between the White House and the radical NGOs with their demanding and potentially embarrassing policy agendas. The temperate and moderate stance of the Four Horsemen made them vital partners for London, Dublin and Washington in the management of the conflict; and if the words of the State Department came out of the mouths of US presidents, then the words of Dublin emanated equally strongly from the Four Horsemen:

> By the 1980s influential figures such as Ted Kennedy, Tip O'Neill, Hugh Carey and Patrick Moynihan were supporters of the Irish government's thinking on the north. Their joint 1977 St Patrick's Day statement . . . when they called on Irish-Americans to refuse to contribute to NORAID was a watershed in terms of mainstream Irish-American politics.[13]

As a consequence of their moderate objectives, the Irish-American political elites were able to prise policy decisions out of the US administration in return for controlling the more radical agendas of lobby groups such as the Irish National Caucus and other high-profile republican supporters. Carter risked embarrassing his close British ally by including the United Kingdom on an annual register of states 'deemed to have violated human rights standards' on account of Britain's treatment of prisoners in Northern Ireland. The State Department meanwhile suspended the sale of hand guns to the RUC in July 1979 in response to pressure from Irish-American elites. This was the price for Tip O'Neill squashing efforts by more radical activists to convene congressional hearings on Northern Ireland. These could have dragged the British government into a highly public defence against damaging reports from Amnesty International and the European Court of Human Rights over its mistreatment of prisoners in Northern Ireland. The activities of the Four Horsemen allowed the Carter adminis-tration to manage the expectations of Irish-America during the 1970s and helped both the British and Irish governments, which were concerned to reduce the political legitimacy of the IRA and the financial support it received. This, in turn, had an impact on militant republicanism's attitude to the sustainability of the 'long war' and to Sinn Fein's strategic pursuit of a political mandate and dialogue with the British.

While the activities of Irish-American elites *facilitated* rather than *caused* US policy change towards Northern Ireland, by the late 1970s a process had begun that led to major US involvement in the 1990s. It would have been difficult, if not impossible, for Clinton to have picked up the ball and run with it, if President Carter had not started it rolling in 1977.

## THE RISE OF CORPORATE IRISH-AMERICA

Time, money and social networks had transformed Irish-America from a beleaguered community at the start of the twentieth century into a powerful and wealthy group of political insiders by the end of it. Lawyers, business leaders, politicians, journalists and captains of industry moved forwards, intent on using their contacts and influence as a bridge between the US government and Northern Ireland. These individuals were more interested in quiet, unofficial fact-finding and facilitation than in public confrontation or mass campaigns. During Clinton's first presidential elec-tion campaign, some of these people surfaced in the guise of the organi-zation Irish-Americans for Clinton/Gore. This mutated after the election into a slightly more formalized grouping called Americans for a New Irish Agenda (ANIA), a broad coalition of influential Irish-Americans who epitomized the twentieth-century evolution of Irish-America from an immigrant community to an integrated, wealthy and highly networked sector of the indigenous population.[14] While they espoused an Irish nationalist outlook, they tried to shift Irish-American attitudes away from the assumption that the British were, by definition, the central cause of the political conflict in Northern Ireland. ANIA cleverly presented President Clinton with achievable policy options rather than an unattainable wish-list that would embarrass his administration or the UK government. Being asked to contribute to 'the process of peace-building' in Northern Ireland was a much easier nettle to grasp than telling the British to get out of Ireland.

Corporate Irish-America was keen to embrace Clinton within the Irish nationalist coalition rather than alienate him from it. As part of this effort, some unannounced and unofficial diplomacy took place in the full knowl-edge of the White House, but with enough distance to allow it to deny any involvement if the whole thing blew up in its face.

Niall O'Dowd, publisher of the *Irish Voice* newspaper in New York, led a delegation of influential figures within ANIA to Ireland in August 1993 to see if there was any potential for a ceasefire. It was a fact-finding mission which, they hoped, might be a means of opening some form of communi-cation between the White House and the IRA. In addition to O'Dowd, the group included a number of other heavy-hitters within the Irish-American community: Bill Flynn (a republican in both the Irish and the American sense of the word) was a former CEO of Mutual of America and chairman of the National Committee on American Foreign Policy; Bruce Morrison was an influential figure within the Clinton administration and a former classmate of the president's at Yale Law School; Chuck Feeney had become a billionaire businessman and was CEO of Atlantic Philanthropies; and Tom Moran was then serving CEO of Mutual of America. These were serious people with significant political and financial clout; they could open political doors quickly – and slam them closed even faster. They met Gerry Adams and listened to his analysis of the prospects for a peaceful resolution of the conflict; and, broadly speaking, they were convinced by what he had to say.

O'Dowd would later recall that the initial efforts to connect Sinn Fein to US policy makers were tentative: 'It was a strange world. You're groping around in the semi-darkness a lot of the time. You know the White House is out there, you know the IRA's out there and you are trying to make shapes out of shadows really.'[15] O'Dowd told his republican contacts that, while a formal IRA ceasefire might be difficult to arrange, it would be extremely helpful if there was a period of quiet while the American delegation was in Ireland. The IRA did nothing for ten days, until after O'Dowd and his colleagues had left. It was a smoke-signal to the high-level delegation (and indeed to the White House itself) that the IRA was both interested in exploring a route out of violence and had the capacity to deliver on it.

The activities of ANIA mirrored changes in the thinking of Sinn Fein. Though it had not publicly ditched its core objectives, by the early 1990s it was stressing the need for an inclusive engagement and negotiations leading to an agreed settlement.

To a degree, ANIA and the Clinton administration were reactive rather than proactive, taking advantage of the changes in republican thinking at the beginning of the 1990s, when Sinn Fein and the IRA were moving in a direction that made political engagement a possibility for Dublin and London, as well as Washington. The new phase in the politics of Sinn Fein had some interesting side-effects on their connection to radical Irish-American support groups. In particular, the relationship between NORAID and Sinn Fein became increasingly strained as the peace process developed through the 1990s. The erstwhile cheerleader for the IRA's armed struggle was effectively sidelined in 1995, with the formation of the Friends of Sinn Fein group, formed in the aftermath of Gerry Adams' first visit to the US the previous year. This was followed by Sinn Fein opening an office in Washington, headed up by Rita O'Hare, a republican from Northern Ireland and close ally of Adams.

This move was partly financed by corporate Irish-America, in the shape of Charles 'Chuck' Feeney, the Irish-American billionaire who was active within ANIA (see above). Feeney was an enigmatic, secretive character, who shunned the limelight but found that his philanthropic endeavours thrust him into it nonetheless. Originally from New Jersey, Feeney had become wealthy through his co-founding of 'duty-free' shops, and he went on to amass a fortune in his business life. Not that anyone would guess it from his behaviour or lifestyle: he lived modestly, frugally even, famously preferring to travel economy class, even on long-haul flights, and reportedly not even owning a house or a car. Unlike Bill and Melinda Gates, Feeney saw no need to personalize his philanthropic activities, quietly providing grants for academic research, to community groups and political parties for activities linked to education, development and reconciliation in Ireland. It emerged in 1996 that he had anonymously donated $600 million to the Atlantic Foundation, which for many years had funded community development initiatives in Ireland, and continues to do so. Through most of the 1980s, *Forbes* magazine listed him as the twenty-third richest living American (with an estimated fortune of $1.3 billion). But the magazine was wrong: he had signed most of his fortune over to his philanthropic company at a secret meeting in the Bahamas in 1984.[16] Chuck Feeney would probably detest it if a film of his life were to be made, but the screenplay would almost write itself and would have viewers feeling that truth was indeed stranger than fiction. Niall O'Dowd, one of the central 'fixers' between Sinn Fein and corporate Irish-America, has commented on the importance of Feeney's role in bringing republicans in from the cold:

> Feeney also took the considerable risk for a man of his stature of coming to the aid of Sinn Féin, shortly after the 1994 IRA ceasefire, when the party desperately needed funding to establish its political agenda. There was no other businessman on earth who would take the risk. Feeney [put] up more than a million dollars to ensure that the party was properly represented in America. His gesture was widely and deliberately misrepresented in much of the media as some sort of aid for the IRA. What he was doing was helping ensure that politics, not violence took precedence in the republican movement. He succeeded in helping Sinn Féin establish their American presence, to build on their links to successive White House administrations and to fully staff an office in Washington for a time.[17]

From this point onwards, Sinn Fein controlled publicity and fundraising in the US, made its activities more professional and sidelined those of NORAID. From the mid-1990s, Sinn Fein was at liberty to raise funds openly, at $500 a plate dinners in Manhattan and Washington, rather than covertly in back-street bars. It no longer needed such low-level fundraising, since it could now operate at the highest level. The move away from NORAID towards Friends of Sinn Fein in the mid-1990s epitomized this new era and is consistent with the strengthening links between the leadership of Sinn Fein and corporate Irish-America.

This was in turn networked into an emerging strategy in the White House, where key officials including Clinton, Commerce Secretary Ron Brown, National Security Advisor Anthony Lake and Nancy Soderberg, staff director at the National Security Council, looked at ways in which the US could underpin the developing peace process via an economic development package. Clinton and many of those around him believed that peace and prosperity were inextricably linked, and that improving the lives of people at the everyday level – through increased job opportunities and support for community-based amenities – would improve the prospects of those same people coming to realize the benefits offered by a non-violent future.

In an effort to co-ordinate this strategy, Clinton appointed Senator George Mitchell as his 'Special Advisor for Economic Initiatives in Ireland', a position that gradually evolved into Mitchell's more central role in the multi-party negotiations from 1996 to 1998 that led to the Good Friday Agreement itself.

The political context was now opening up, as key actors within both the Clinton White House and the Irish republican leadership in Northern Ireland realized that, while the door to progress might not be wide open, it was clearly not locked either. This triangle of relationships between Sinn Fein, corporate Irish-America and the Clinton White House developed into a virtuous circle of relationships, where a degree of mutual trust grew up between the main protagonists on the nationalist side. It was corporate Irish-America that was the facilitator of movement from the IRA, and it played a major part in the choreography of the peace process in the 1990s. It acted as matchmaker but did not *cause* the various actors to get together. This lobby linked up with the Irish-American political elite, and in particular Ted Kennedy and his sister, Jean Kennedy Smith, who had been appointed by Clinton as US ambassador to Ireland. Together with support from the Irish government, the Clinton presidency pushed the Northern Ireland peace process to the front of its foreign policy agenda. The days when the administration regarded the conflict as being purely a matter for UK domestic policy making were over.

## CLINTON'S CALCULATED RISK

There were clear signs from the beginning of his presidency that Clinton's administration was working independently of the British government and that it was not slavishly tied to an Anglocentric perspective on Northern Ireland. In personal terms, there was little love lost between Clinton and Prime Minister John Major, as the former suspected the latter of attempting to assist his opponent in the 1992 presidential election (the incumbent President George Bush Snr) by digging up dirt on Clinton's period as a student at Oxford. (In light of later revelations about Clinton's extracurricular appetites, it is perhaps a little surprising that the British found it so difficult to find anything incriminating.) Jonathan Powell (later to be Tony Blair's chief of staff) was a British diplomat in Washington at this time, and he set up the first phone call between Major and the newly elected President Clinton in December 1992. He later recalled listening in on their brief conversation: 'It was a very cold phone call, barely within the bounds of diplomatic courtesy. Clinton felt he owed Major little or nothing.'[18]

But Clinton soon settled into a cordial, if rather tepid, relationship with Major. The lowest point came in 1994, when Clinton clashed with the British government over his strategy towards Sinn Fein. The president wanted to co-opt that organization into the democratic process and test the mettle of the IRA ceasefire, while Major was still trying to keep it at arm's length and to control the pace of any official engagement. After a long diplomatic power struggle between the US and UK (and the White House and State Department), in January Clinton granted a visa for Gerry Adams to enter the US – before the IRA had called a ceasefire and in the teeth of fierce British opposition. Major was reportedly livid, as were members of Clinton's own administration, including senior officials in the State Department, the CIA and the Justice Department. The British were still trying to squeeze the pips out of the republicans and force them into a ceasefire; and they now felt their efforts were being undermined by Clinton's olive branch to Adams. Veteran Irish journalist Deaglan de Breadun later observed that 'the [British] Prime Minister's annoyance must have been all the greater when the Sinn Fein leader became the darling of the US media during his brief visit, but whether London liked it or not there had been a fundamental shift in US policy which would have huge effects further down the road'.[19]

It was not without political risk for Clinton, however: even if the IRA did not return to violence (which, of course, it did), his proximity to alleged 'terrorists' made him vulnerable to accusations from opponents in the US that his foreign policy activities were misjudged or irresponsible. During his presidential re-election campaign in 1996, his relationship with Sinn Fein was raised by supporters of his Republican opponent, Bob Dole. James Baker (a former secretary of state in George Bush Snr's administration during the 1980s) vilified Clinton during the Republican Party convention in San Diego: 'We have seen a representative of the IRA hosted in the White House just prior to its resumption of terrorist bombings in London. The result has been the worst relationship with our closest ally, Britain, since the Boston Tea Party in 1773.'[20]

Clinton later recalled that his visa decision was based as much on gut instinct as it was on consideration of actual evidence, but that he was prepared to take the risk of temporarily offending the British in the hope that it would produce a ceasefire announcement from the IRA: 'These kinds of things are always a judgement call. There's no rule book that tells you when this or that or the other thing happens. It was a judgement call. You asked me whether I think I did the right thing? I do.'[21] Casting a colder eye over events, Clinton's decision did him no harm at all in his relations with senior Irish-Americans at the helm of the Democratic Party, at a time when their support for his health and welfare reforms in Congress was desperately needed.

A few months later, in August 1994, Clinton again granted a visa – this time to allow veteran Belfast gunman Joe Cahill to go to the United States for meetings with Irish-American groups. Cahill was the 'Don Corleone' of the piece – one of the old guard, an IRA man since the 1940s who had devoted his entire adult life to the struggle. Cahill, then in his eighties, was not sent to rub shoulders with the Washington elite or to beguile the US media. His role, while less high profile than that of Adams back in January, was the equally vital one of reassuring nervous republicans in the US (many of whom had been slower to accept Sinn Fein's modernizing agenda) that the IRA had not gone soft. The thinking was that, if a republican with the 'street cred' of Joe Cahill could endorse a ceasefire, then even the hardest Irish-American nuts would crack. NORAID's Michael Flannery did not move from his position, but the vast majority were persuaded that the time was now ripe for republicans to engage in negotiations.

For Clinton, letting Adams into the US was one thing, but allowing in Cahill – a man who had been arrested for gun-running and who had been deported from the US on two occasions – was another matter entirely, and he was initially against the idea. On the eve of the ceasefire, Irish Prime Minister Reynolds tracked Clinton down during his holiday at Martha's Vineyard and a very frank phone call ensued. Clinton asked Reynolds if he had 'read Cahill's CV', to which the taoiseach replied that that was beside the point, since Cahill clearly had been a paramilitary. When Clinton said that he was unwilling to grant the visa unless he could be sure that this would be the final piece of the jigsaw that would immediately lead to an IRA ceasefire, the well-prepared Reynolds read out a section of a statement from the IRA army council, due to be released the following day, that announced a complete cessation of military operations. This convinced Clinton to take the final step and approve Cahill's visa, but he left Reynolds under no illusions that this was the end of the road unless the IRA delivered a ceasefire: 'Okay, we'll take another chance. But I never want to hear from you again if this one doesn't run. – Goodbye!'[22] The IRA duly announced its cessation of operations the following day and the vast bulk of Irish-American opinion came in behind it.

The importance of Clinton's decision to grant visas to Adams and Cahill was that it demonstrated to militant republicans that the US was a third-party presence that could (in American parlance) act as a 'game-changer', regardless of the wishes of the UK government or unionists. This helped Sinn Fein to argue that the US government could provide a catalyst for change, alter the structure of the conflict and act as a counter-balance to unionist efforts to veto political change.

## THE MITCHELL REPORT

Despite the trust that had been building between the Clinton administration, the Irish government and Sinn Fein between 1994 and 1996, the issue of weapons decommissioning had not gone away. It remained a roadblock to the peace process, and no amount of charming phone calls from President Clinton could remove it. Eventually, Senator George Mitchell, the US economic envoy and Clinton's 'special advisor' in Northern Ireland (along with a team of two others), was asked to square the circle, end the stalemate and provide a way forward for all concerned.[23]

Personally, Mitchell was a very measured individual – calm (and calming), with a considerable degree of gravitas and intelligence. Unusually for a politician, he was blessed with an ability to receive as well as to broadcast, and he was clearly someone with a hinterland beyond the political world. Mitchell was a political heavyweight, serving in the US Senate between 1980 and 1995, where he represented the state of Maine; he also held the prestigious position of majority leader in the Senate for six years during this period. He was close to Clinton, who trusted and respected his advice. One of Clinton's more unusual requests came in September 1996, when he was preparing for the forthcoming presidential candidates' debate: he asked the former senator to impersonate Bob Dole, Clinton's

Republican opponent. Folders containing all of Dole's speeches and public statements for the previous two years were shipped to Mitchell in Northern Ireland:

> It was heavy going, but I read it all. I laughed at my plight. All day long I listened to Northern Irish politicians giving essentially the same speeches over and over again. Then, late into each night, I read the words of an American politician giving essentially the same speeches over and over again. And I wasn't being paid for either.[24]

Mitchell was a man used to finding pragmatic solutions to political problems, doing deals and squaring circles between implacable adversaries. He also had an astonishing personal commitment to the people and the place, both of which grew on him over time: 'I am not objective. I am deeply biased in favour of the people of Northern Ireland. Having spent three and a half years among them, I've come to like and admire them, to enjoy being with them.'[25] Mitchell's professional commitment and his personal qualities were all put to the test during his sabbatical in Northern Ireland in 1995–98.

Mitchell's trouble-shooting team met and took soundings over several weeks, speaking to all the main players (apart from Paisley, who refused to participate). Largely as a result of talking to the RUC and the Irish police, the team concluded that Sinn Fein was not capable of getting the IRA to decommission in advance of negotiations. Mitchell records that when he asked the chief constable of the RUC, Sir Hugh Annesley, whether Adams could persuade the IRA on this, his answer was unequivocal: 'No, he couldn't do it even if he wanted to. He doesn't have that much control over them.'[26] This realization convinced Mitchell that prior decommissioning – the crux of the British position – was a non-starter. However, before he published his report, his team was summoned to London to meet Major and his officials for a 'progress' report. When asked how they were getting on, Mitchell emphasized the assessment of the RUC chief constable that Sinn Fein could not deliver on prior decommissioning. The British then produced a rabbit from the hat, in the shape of a letter from Annesley, clarifying and modifying his remarks – but, as Mitchell reflected, not substantively revising his conclusions: 'I felt sorry for Annesley, he had been truthful with us, and now, because his opinion didn't fit with the government's policy, it became obvious that his honesty with us had gotten him in trouble with his superiors.'[27]

It was crystal clear that the appointment of Mitchell was another attempt to stall for time and to use the independent grouping as a shield to hide behind, in the hope that it would simply ratify the British position. When it became clear to Major that this was unlikely and that the report was liable to recommend 'parallel decommissioning' (i.e. where decommissioning happened at the same time as formal talks began), he used a more direct approach: 'His words had a steely candour. If we recommended parallel decommissioning he would have to reject the report. He didn't want to, but he would have to.'[28] While this was all done perfectly politely, everyone in the room knew the game that was being played: Major was trying to lean on Mitchell and threaten him with the prospect of complete failure before the report was even written; Mitchell and his colleagues were indicating that they were not going to be pushed around by the prime minister or act as puppets of the government.

Convinced that prior IRA decommissioning was impossible, but wanting to provide some mechanism to re-frame the whole issue and allow all sides to move forwards, Mitchell's team developed a set of principles of non-violence, with the recommendation that all those seeking involvement in negotiations should commit to them. These Mitchell Principles would eventually underpin the subsequent negotiations in 1996–98 and were an attempt to move the debate from the *physical act* of decommissioning to the *intellectual case* for non-violence. If everyone committed themselves to 'exclusively peaceful methods' and could be held to that promise by their opponents and independent third parties, then the actual weapons themselves became less important. This was a creative and ingenious attempt to resolve the impasse, and was based on the adage that it is not the guns themselves that cause harm, but the people who use them.

On their own, this series of pledges to non-violent principles may have done enough to bridge the gap, but by this point another problem had loomed onto the horizon. The UUP, now led by the legal academic and enthusiastic Orangeman David Trimble, had requested that elections should be held in Northern Ireland prior to any formal negotiations. This was largely an attempt by Trimble to get a mandate for any dialogue, in order to protect himself from accusations by Paisley that he was 'selling out' the unionist community and to ensure that he did not move too far ahead of his support base.

Trimble had become leader of the UUP in 1995, shortly after playing a high-profile role over a contested Orange parade in Drumcree, where he had walked hand in hand with Ian Paisley in celebration, after a stand-off over the route of the parade had finally been resolved in favour of the Orange Order. At the time, Trimble was considered to be a 'hardliner', elected by a frightened and insecure group of unionists who were anxious for someone who could stand up for them amidst the tumultuous events that surrounded them. Personally, Trimble came across to those beyond his immediate circle as an irascible and tense individual, a jumpy man with a short fuse, who frequently appeared red-faced with anger as he jabbed his debating points across the media. To some, he was a hard man with brains; to others, he was a 'head-banger'. This was, of course, a simplistic reading of a complex individual; but it would be fair to say that he was often ill at ease in social situations, lacking the easy-going charm of some of his more urbane colleagues.

The election issue (like everything else) quickly became politicized: Trimble demanded it, while the SDLP and Sinn Fein rejected the idea as just another delaying tactic that was likely to polarize an already nervous electorate. Unsurprisingly, the British government supported the idea of an election and even privately lobbied the Mitchell team to put something in its report to the effect that an election would be helpful. The final report did not 'recommend' an election, but it did comment – in a brief paragraph towards the end – that if it reflected the popular will (which it did not), an elective process might help to build confidence in the negotiations.

John Major responded officially to the Mitchell Report in the House of Commons on 24 January 1996. Given the positive reaction it had received from other parties and media commentators, he had to praise it (albeit faintly). But of the document's sixty-two paragraphs, the only one that the British took up in policy terms was the one relating to the holding of elections prior to negotiations. This was Major's way of sidestepping his demand for prior decommissioning: aligning the British government with another unionist policy and pushing talks with Sinn Fein farther into the distance.

## THE END OF THE BEGINNING

Gerry Adams and John Hume both raged at Major for pandering to the unionist position and, as they saw it, for undermining the peace process. The IRA delivered its verdict sixteen days later, communicating its opinion the way it knew best.

On 9 February 1996, Jamie Thompson had just returned home to his apartment in the Docklands area of London. He was a computer consultant living in the Canary Wharf area of the city and was unwittingly about to find himself at the centre of an international news story. While he was busy trying to locate an episode of the Simpsons on his video recorder, he heard a strange rumbling sound outside his building. The IRA had detonated a half-tonne bomb from a lorry parked in an underground car park near the Docklands Light Railway:

> The apartment block was shaking and I remember thinking stupidly enough that it was an earthquake. I was focussed on my briefcase, because it was just swaying from side to side as the rumbling noise got louder. The windows on my balcony started to flex inwards and just at the point I thought they were coming in, the briefcase fell over and there was this almighty boom. I'd never heard anything like it before. I went to my balcony, looked out the window and saw a huge pall of smoke rising from the direction of South Quay.[29]

Thompson found himself in the middle of an IRA bomb attack that killed two people, injured dozens more and caused an estimated £85 million worth of damage to commercial premises in the Docklands area of London. The IRA ceasefire was over. The blast wave could be felt a quarter of a mile away, but the physical impact was nothing to the political shock wave that went around the world, as it looked to most people that the peace process in Northern Ireland was over.

The IRA had finally run out of patience with the British government and had concluded that Major was incapable of moving forwards or delivering on what it thought had been promised. This was no knee-jerk reaction, of course, and it later emerged that the IRA had been planning the attack since the previous September.[30] From Major's point of view, he had perhaps finally clarified that the IRA's ceasefire was indeed not permanent; but this was cold comfort, as it looked as though the peace process was in tatters amid the glass and debris that littered London's Docklands area. Gerry Adams was 'saddened', but he blamed John Major. The prime minister blamed the IRA and spoke of 'dark shadows' hanging over the peace process, while the Irish government attempted to calm things down and counselled people to avoid hasty or emotional reactions that might have negative long-term consequences.

After the usual hand-wringing, the British and Irish governments announced that multi-party talks would commence on 10 June, following elections to a Forum, and that these negotiations would exclude Sinn Fein on account of the breakdown of the IRA ceasefire. It was difficult to avoid the conclusion that the bomb had acted as a catalyst, galvanizing the British government into action. The intention was to entice the IRA to renew its ceasefire, in order to allow Sinn Fein to participate in the talks. This got nowhere, of course, as it was a tease that had been tried before. The IRA had decided to await the inevitable arrival of Tony Blair as prime minister before proceeding any further.

When John Major was jolted into announcing the creation of an elected Forum and the commencement of multi-party talks in June, there was an obvious answer to the thorny question of who should chair the process.[31] The choice of George Mitchell was not, however, altogether uncontroversial: the unionists were worried about the senator's role and about the fact that he was 'imposed' on them by the British and Irish governments through a set of 'ground rules' issued in April 1996. The DUP was the most vocal in this respect, but there were also senior people within the UUP who questioned Mitchell's personal independence and integrity. UUP deputy leader John Taylor suggested that his appointment as chairman 'was the equivalent of appointing an American Serb to preside over talks on the future of Croatia . . . It's a non-runner.'[32] The UUP, while not officially opposed to Mitchell and his two colleagues, was uneasy about the ground rules for the all-party negotiations, which conferred discretionary powers on the chairman.

All of this resulted in one of the most bizarre beginnings to a process of political negotiation ever recorded, unusual (even by Northern Ireland standards) for its level of excruciating pedantry. While Mitchell and his team were appointed to chair the negotiations, they all had to wait in an ante-chamber adjacent to the multi-party discussions, while the politicians discussed the procedural rules of engagement. While seven of the ten parties involved accepted the team, the other three unionist parties wanted further reassurances about its role. Robert McCartney of the UK Unionist Party (UKUP) complained that the undemocratic process by which Mitchell was appointed had undermined the ethos of the negotiations and was designed to achieve a predetermined outcome. DUP leader Ian Paisley accused Mitchell of being 'a crony of Gerry Adams', and alleged that he would be presiding over the negotiations like a 'sort of pope'.[33] The results of this dispute were unedifying, as Mitchell and his two colleagues sat around for two days listening in to the parties discussing whether or not they were appropriate third-party mediators in the process.

After the many months of preparation for the start of the multi-party talks, it seemed at the last minute that the starter's pistol had jammed.

Mitchell accepted his humiliating treatment with typical good grace, but was incredulous at the circumstances of his formal acceptance. Shortly after midnight, Mitchell and his colleagues were asked to enter the room, only to find a British government representative sitting in the seat that had been assigned to him as chairman. The man sprang up at the last minute, when Mitchell was within a few feet: 'Evidently, the governments feared that the DUP and UKUP would occupy my seat and refuse to leave, requiring their expulsion by force. That would further delay the proceedings and cause a public furore. So a British official was assigned to my seat until I got there. As I sat down and listened to that story, my unease grew.'[34]

Formal multi-party talks duly began on 10 June 1996, though Sinn Fein was predictably excluded on account of the IRA's ongoing sporadic violence. Ever media aware, the Sinn Fein delegation turned up at Stormont anyway, and was photographed standing solemnly against the iron gates peering in, just in case anyone had forgotten that they had been excluded from the democratic process. These talks went on for a year without Sinn Fein, but it became increasingly clear that Major's government was fatally undermined and that it would not survive the May 1997 British general election. The talks were going nowhere without Sinn Fein, and everyone knew it. The pithiest exhibition of public attitudes to the political soap opera going on around was displayed on a billboard outside St Anne's Cathedral in Belfast: 'You can play a part in the political talks. Come in and say a prayer!'[35] Everyone was gearing up for the new regime in London; it seemed clear that a new dynamism and political pragmatism would be brought to the process.

## INCLUSION AND NEGOTIATION

George Mitchell's task as a mediator became much more dynamic when Tony Blair replaced John Major as the British prime minister after a landslide Labour victory in May 1997. Blair arrived in Downing Street to a fanfare of hope and optimism. 'Things can only get better' was his election campaign song, and it seemed to many that his victory had delivered them from the Narnia of Conservative rule – where it was forever winter . . . but never Christmas. Blair wanted to talk to all shades of opinion in Northern Ireland. Blair was good at talking, especially in 1997, when his popularity was high and he had not yet been responsible for starting any wars himself. He was convinced that if he smiled his smile and talked to a political opponent for long enough, that person would eventually see the logic of his argument.

Back in 1997, Blair's toothy grin reached across the Irish Sea, and his election was quickly followed by a resumption of the IRA ceasefire. He was not going to make the same mistake that Major had, and his huge majority in parliament meant that he had much more room for manoeuvre than his predecessor.

For Tony Blair and the British government to meet Gerry Adams and Sinn Fein was a huge and necessary step, signalling that they were an important and legitimate political constituency. It would be the first meeting between a British prime minister and the Sinn Fein leadership for over seventy-five years (since Lloyd George in 1921), and regardless of the substance of the discussions it was another crucial starting point in the peace process. Because of the symbolic and sensitive nature of the meeting, it was convened in Belfast rather than London and was downplayed as much as possible by Downing Street. So Blair combined it with other, seemingly more important engagements, going first to Derry to open a new factory and meet SDLP leader John Hume. As though trying to put off the inevitable, he then went to Portadown, where he visited an army barracks and met representatives of the RUC. Finally, he visited UUP leader David Trimble in his constituency, before travelling back to Stormont to meet the parties engaged in the talks – including a delegation from Sinn Fein.

The meeting took place on 13 October, when Sinn Fein President Gerry Adams gave the prime minister a present of an Irish harp made from ancient bog oak, commenting (rather churlishly) that he hoped it was the only part of Ireland that Blair would keep.[36] Despite the tense atmosphere and lack of any real movement on either side, this was the first direct meeting between the British government and Sinn Fein for over two generations. As usual, symbolism rather than substance was the key, and both sides were keenly aware of the sensitivities of their various constituencies. The fact that Blair shook hands with Adams incensed some unionists, who waved surgical rubber gloves at the prime minister in a subsequent walkabout in Belfast. Even the supposedly 'liberal' unionist stalwart Ken Maginnis was unimpressed by Adams' demonstration of social courtesy, with a riposte that was as blunt as it was ignorant: Adams, he claimed, collected handshakes 'like a Comanche collects scalps'.[37]

Blair spent much of his time performing a political balancing act, as he tried to stop the edgy UUP leader, David Trimble, from leading his party out of the process, while at the same time allowing Sinn Fein to enter it. Paisley's DUP was, from the British perspective, an unfortunate (if predictable) casualty, withdrawing from the process when Sinn Fein was admitted; but the UUP was essential if the talks were to progress. Blair also understood the importance of presentation and political symbolism. His first speech outside London was given in Northern Ireland and was specifically designed to reassure nervous unionists that the new Labour government did not favour a united Ireland (though that had been party policy when Labour was in opposition during the 1980s).

Blair picked the Royal Ulster Agricultural Show to sound some melodic notes for unionist ears. In a passionate speech, he declared that unionists had nothing to fear, as any agreement would have to come from within Northern Ireland rather than being imposed from the outside. Furthermore, any such deal would have to be ratified in a referendum of the people within Northern Ireland and by a vote in the House of Commons. He even went out of his way to say that Northern Ireland was a key component of the United Kingdom, which he 'believed in' and 'valued'. Unionist blood pressure duly lowered, he swiftly turned around and started talking direct to Sinn Fein, to reassure it that the government was committed to an inclusive talks process that would deliver political change. Blair built the 1997–98 negotiations on the basis of working out how to keep everyone inside the lifeboat and what needed to be said to those who looked as though they were about to jump out of it. He later reflected that this was an entirely pragmatic strategy, which at times strained the limits of truth and accuracy: 'Politicians are obliged from time to time to conceal the full truth, to bend it and even distort it, where the interests of the bigger strategic goal demand it be done. Without operating with some subtlety at this level, the job would be well-nigh impossible.'[38] Put another way, Blair was claiming that it was fine to conceal the full truth from people – and even to mislead them – if that served a greater purpose in the longer term.

The arrival of the Blair government brought renewed energy to the peace process and to the negotiations, which had been flagging since well before the IRA had blown Sinn Fein out of the negotiations by ending its ceasefire in February 1996. Blair brought with him a sense of direction and dynamism that had been lacking before. He wanted to get a deal done, to cut through to the key divisions between the parties, and he believed that he had the political skills to bring unionists and nationalists together.

At one level, the multi-party talks chaired by George Mitchell represented a new departure in the political process. For most of the period up to the mid-1990s, the general approach taken by the British government was to find political consensus between the constitutional parties, as a way of marginalizing the radical extremes of militant republicanism and loyalism. This was also intended to starve them of international sympathy and support from Irish-America and elsewhere.

Up to this point, the formal political process had been a rather elite pursuit, remote from the everyday lives of grass-roots communities, especially in urban interface areas where sectarian friction was often at its sharpest. However, the multi-party talks of 1996–98 took a different approach. As talks among the constitutional parties were frequently undermined by continuing violence, and as it was clear that those parties had little control over such violence, the militants were given a seat at the table. Their participation in the negotiations was based on agreed principles of non-violence and was accepted by the British and Irish governments, assisted by the international mediation of George Mitchell and, less directly, President Clinton.

From this perspective, the negotiations that were chaired so ably by Mitchell broke through the normal elitist channels of the established party system in Northern Ireland. Republicans and loyalists were represented at the talks by Sinn Fein and by the Ulster Democratic Party (UDP) and the Progressive Unionist Party (PUP), which 'provided analysis' to the UDA and UVF, respectively. At the denouement of the talks in April 1998, members of the Provisional IRA and the UDA/UVF were in direct contact with their political colleagues over the terms and wording of the agreement, especially in relation to the sections on weapons decommissioning and prisoner release schemes. Mo Mowlam, the Northern Ireland secretary of state at the time, admitted that, at the eleventh hour, the British government sat down face to face with leaders of the Provisional IRA to ensure that they were on board: 'We sat down with Sinn Fein. We sat at one end and they brought in some people who were obviously members of the [IRA] Army Council. You don't ask names – you just say hello and get on with it.'[39]

In addition to the paramilitary factions, there was a broader range of voices at the table, including those of women and a much stronger component from the community development sector. Due to the dearth of female political representation, a party had formed called the Northern Ireland Women's Coalition, many of whose members were drawn from the trade union movement and community-based NGOs. The Women's Coalition played an active and influential role in the negotiations, though subsequently it faded away as the main parties 'shot their fox' and appointed more women to senior positions.

The inclusion of Sinn Fein along with the UDP/PUP and Women's Coalition gave the impression that these negotiations were different from those that had gone before and were more connected at the community level. It would also be fair to say that they helped to introduce more flexible and creative terminology and human relationships into the process.

One example of the way in which the traditional political elites were 'grounded' within the negotiations was provided when Secretary of State Mo Mowlam decided to visit loyalist prisoners in the Maze prison, in January 1998, to persuade their organizations to maintain their ceasefires and their support for the talks process. This was a significant political risk for Mowlam, but she took it because she was convinced that loyalist opinion within the jail was critical to the wider peace process. Blair's chief of staff, Jonathan Powell, later recalled that Mowlam did not consult the prime minister before taking the decision, but that ultimately her judgement was right:

> She didn't think of consulting us and went straight ahead and announced she was going to the Maze to meet the UDA prisoners. We didn't approve and if she had asked us we would certainly have said no. But in the event she was right and we were wrong. Her visit had the effect of reassuring the loyalists that she took them seriously . . . Her instinctive reaction turned out to be the right one.[40]

Mowlam epitomized the fresh new approach to dialogue in Northern Ireland from 1997 onwards, and she proved a foil to George Mitchell's more straight-laced chairing of the process. While it was an incongruous and unnerving sight to see a British secretary of state seeking the tacit approval of paramilitaries in prison, it would have been inconceivable that her predecessor, the rather blimpish and stuffy Sir Patrick Mayhew, would have done so. Again, like the meeting between Blair and Sinn Fein, the point here was a symbolic one: to indicate that the view of these people was important and that the political elite understood the necessity of engaging with those at the sharp end of the conflict.

Mowlam was a former university academic and had a direct and informal manner that went down well with the Northern Ireland public, though not always with some unionist politicians. David Trimble was not the only unionist who felt that Mowlam had a nationalist bias, and he called for her resignation several times from 1997 onwards. Eventually he insisted on dealing directly with Tony Blair, which kept Trimble on board but undermined Mowlam's position. Aside from the political differences, many unionists were unnerved by her informal (and at times crude) style and by her capacity for swearing 'eyeballs out' at both colleagues and opponents when she felt the need to do so. She was a bit too 'touchy-feely' for some tastes, though she was seen as a breath of fresh air by others. As one observer put it at the time: 'Mo has the disarming air of a kindly school-mistress charged with the task of keeping some unruly but basically loveable gangs from killing each other.'[41]

In 1997, it came to light that Mowlam was undergoing treatment for what turned out to be a malignant brain tumour. Her illness did nothing to diminish her commitment to the peace process, but public awareness of it contributed significantly to the warmth extended to her by people of all political persuasions in Northern Ireland.[42] The treatment caused her hair to fall out and she sported a blonde wig in public, though frequently ripped it off when it got too itchy. This caused some initial consternation during private meetings with nationalist and unionist politicians. George Mitchell later commented that this flourish 'was one of many ways she had of breaking the tension'.[43] In 1997, having promised her consultant that she would tell Blair the truth about her illness, she told him that the tumour was benign, so that he would not take the Northern Ireland portfolio away from her. She lied to both her physician and Blair: the tumour killed her in August 2005.

Mowlam was unusually popular for a politician, both in Northern Ireland and in Britain. She seemed to represent an integrity that her other colleagues lacked, not least her leader. Her common touch and direct nature connected the formal political process with grass-roots communities in a way that made people feel that they could talk to her – and that she would listen to them. This ability to close the gap between the policy process and people at the community level who were on the receiving end of such policies was crucial to the success of the talks process during 1997–98.

Perhaps only Northern Ireland could construct a human drama of this nature: a politician so committed to the place and its people that she drew positive energy from trying to resolve its political problems. This role quite possibly kept her going, as she had initially been given only three years to live when told about the disease in 1996. But as well as killing her, that brain tumour had certain potential side-effects, including disinhibition, anger, intellectual decay and impaired judgement, and those could have jeopardized the very political process that she was dedicated to helping.

Her decision to visit loyalist paramilitary prisoners was widely regarded as an act that shored up the peace process and maintained the ceasefires. But it was also seen as an audacious political risk – even a reckless act – by some of her critics at the time. Could the tumour have produced this behaviour? If so, then Mowlam's cancer could be said to have made a positive contribution to the peace process before killing the woman at the centre of it. Mowlam's deputy minister, Adam Ingram, believes that her illness was a factor in her behaviour and in her drive to secure an agreement in the time she had left:

> My objective assessment is that Mo was a major catalyst in the change in Northern Ireland. A lot of people know she injected momentum into the process, and when you step back from it and realise that she knew she had a terminal illness – she was in a rush to get things done and that was put to the advantage of the peace process. It kept the momentum going.[44]

## THE CONSTRUCTIVE AMBIGUITY OF THE PEACE PROCESS

When the negotiations formally began between the political parties in Northern Ireland, international mediation played a crucial role in bringing people together at the right time, as well as in keeping them apart when necessary. Talks chairman George Mitchell had absorbed some initial hostility over his appointment and gradually began to wade his way through the treacle of the negotiations themselves. Patience was a key skill in this regard, as it took months to establish a set of 'ground rules' before the participants even got onto procedural issues (never mind talking about the actual areas that divided them). It was progress of a sort, but tortuous and tedious nonetheless. It took from September 1996 until October 1997 for the parties to negotiate a set of procedures and a vague agenda for the discussion of the substantive issues. Then for another five months – October 1997 to March 1998 – the general issues were outlined and discussed. The political adversaries circled one another in the ring, cautiously waiting for the other to lead with a jab so they could land an effective counter-punch. The result was a lot of shadow-boxing, but there was no evidence of any real progress for most of this time.

The actual detailed bargaining and hard arguing took a little over two weeks at the end of March and beginning of April 1998. Mitchell's approach to mediation was akin to Muhammad Ali's 'rope-a-dope' style of fighting, where he would let opponents pummel him furiously and tire themselves out, while he defended himself on the ropes and conserved his energy. Once they were exhausted, he would open up on them and win the fight. In the end, Mitchell got the punch-drunk parties together and announced a deadline of a week, during which they would 'eat, sleep and negotiate'. This was not imposed on them, but was done with the agreement of all the parties, since they themselves had realized by this stage that the open-ended timeframe was actually preventing progress rather than enabling it.

The deadline was a calculated risk, as Mitchell had made a judgement that the main parties had been brought to the point where they wanted to sign up to an agreement, though he was also conscious that forcing the pace might precipitate a collapse of the process if the fine detail was unacceptable to them. As he later recalled: 'I was convinced that the absence of such a deadline guaranteed failure. The existence of a deadline couldn't guarantee success – but did make it possible.'[45]

By this stage the media was permanently camped outside Castle Buildings at Stormont, where the talks were taking place. It was a disorienting maze of a building, which did little to help the stress levels of those inside it. At this point the process lurched from breakthrough to breakdown, with hopes being raised and dashed daily. Politicians would emerge blinking into the lights of the broadcast media to make generalized statements about how the talks were progressing, and these were then analysed by pundits and by other parties in the talks. Even the body language of the participants was studied for signs of change; and if Martin McGuinness laughed, or if David Trimble walked even faster than usual, there would always be someone on hand to explain what this meant for the fate of the talks process.

Sinn Fein had by this stage brought its own film camera into Castle Buildings, aware (as always) of the importance of controlling the narrative of events without the unreliable intermediation of the professional media. There were some surreal moments when politicians giving live interviews on the steps of Castle Buildings were applauded by their colleagues watching them either from the windows of the building or on TV. Sinn Fein's chief negotiator, Martin McGuinness, commented on how the momentum built up in the negotiations as they entered their final days: 'There were people passing one another in corridors. It was just like people rushing out of the Stock Exchange in New York trying to get to a telephone or pass on information before some other buyer; it was a frenetic negotiation.'[46]

1 Sir Edward Carson, flanked by his unionist lieutenants, signs the Solemn League and Covenant on 'Ulster Day', at Belfast's City Hall on 28 September 1912.

2 This mural on Beechmount Avenue, off the Falls Road, commemorates the 1916 Easter Rising.

3 Members of the Provisional Irish Republican Army (PIRA) check vehicles and passengers at a 'checkpoint' on the Lecky Road in the Bogside area of Derry in 1971.

4 A member of the public is stopped and searched by a British army patrol on Westland Street in the Bogside in August 1972. Questions are also likely to have been asked about his identity, home address and where he was going.

5 A mural by the Bogside Artists' collective, painted in 1997 to commemorate the 25th anniversary of Bloody Sunday and depicting a group of men carrying the body of Jackie Duddy, accompanied by Fr. Edward Daly. In front of it stand Martin McGuinness and Duddy's sister Kay.

6 Rev. Ian Paisley outside Canterbury Cathedral in protest against the concelebrated Pontifical High Mass in commemoration of the 800th anniversary of the martyrdom of St Thomas à Becket, July 1970.

7 A group of rioters attack the RUC in Belfast, a scene so commonplace in the 1970s that the photograph is undated.

8 Six people died in this no-warning bomb attack by the Provisional IRA in Donegall Street, Belfast on 20 March 1972. This picture captures the immediate aftermath as emergency services, soldiers and passers-by attempt to help victims of the explosion.

9 Peace People founders Betty Williams (left) and Mairead Corrigan (right) show off telegrams of support at the 'Women for Peace' Rally held in Belfast in August 1976.

10 Sinn Fein President Gerry Adams waves to the media after talks with the Prime Minister Tony Blair on 11 December 1997. Pictured (left to right) are Michelle Gildernew, Martin McGuinness, Gerry Adams, Lucilita Bhreatnach, Martin Ferris and Siobhán O'Hanlon.

11  Tony Blair (centre), David Trimble (left) and John Hume (right) pictured on the last day of campaigning for a Yes vote in the referendum on the Good Friday Agreement on 21 May 1998.

12  Historic handshake between Queen Elizabeth II and Martin McGuinness at the Lyric Theatre, Belfast on 27 June 2012, while First Minister Peter Robinson looks on.

13 This mural on the Falls Road makes a connection between the Falls Curfew in 1970 with imprisonment of dissident republican Marian Price in 2013.

14 This loyalist mural on Dee Street, off the Newtownards Road, depicts the UFF with typical imagery of the Crown, the Red Hand of Ulster and the political boundary of Northern Ireland.

Delegations from the main parties (who were still not talking directly to one another) weaved through the media bottleneck at the front of Castle Buildings like prize fighters with their entourages. Journalists shouted questions at them in the hope of a quote; cameramen tripped over their equipment and fell on their backsides in the general melee. At times it was reminiscent of preparations before a fight in the school playground, with the nervous would-be pugilists shouting 'hold me back' to anyone who would listen, and dearly hoping that someone would!

George Mitchell used the credibility and influence he had built up with the parties over several years very skilfully at the critical denouement of the negotiations. By this stage he was doing much more than simply relaying messages from one party to another, and was providing political judgements and assessments across all sides in the process. He was firm, fair and used the power of his influence deftly to push the process slowly forwards to the point where an agreement could be secured. One of his assistants, Martha Pope, who was heavily involved in the negotiations herself, has commented on Mitchell's importance to the overall success of the process:

> Well, I guess if I had to sum it up I would say that he played a very, very important role, and . . . that his judgment and his gravitas and his intelligence enabled him to keep talks going for two years, in the face of violence and discouragement, and I think he gained the respect of every single person in that room, and without his engagement it probably would not have occurred, ultimately.[47]

Mitchell was, of course, fully supported by Clinton, who gave the leaders of Northern Ireland's political parties unparalleled access to a US president, to the point of personally phoning both Gerry Adams and David Trimble at the eleventh hour to reassure them and try to convince them to accept the deal.

In the final stages, the Good Friday Agreement was produced through hard bargaining, intense pressure and best guesses on all sides about what the various constituencies would accept. From this perspective it was a 'lowest common denominator' form of political agreement, which presented people with a set of 'least-worst' options, rather than the fulfilment of their dreams and aspirations. This is, admittedly, a rather downbeat assessment of the Good Friday Agreement, but it is nonetheless a realistic one. It was a significant political compromise that seemed to square the circle of incompatible national identity claims, while sharing power between them.

In broad terms, the contents of the negotiations were well known. The whole process was based on two fundamental principles. First, any future political structures would be based on 'parity of esteem' between the unionist and nationalist communities, which would require a system of power-sharing between them. Second, the negotiations had to manage the rival British and Irish identities of those who lived in Northern Ireland. The negotiations themselves were sensitive to this, in that they were held in three locations (Belfast, London and Dublin) to reflect the three different nationality claims involved. There were three strands of negotiations: Strand 1 was concerned with relations within Northern Ireland; Strand 2 focused on cross-border relations between Northern Ireland and the Irish Republic; Strand 3 centred on relations between Ireland and Britain.

Unsurprisingly, perhaps, unionists were keen to make progress on Strand 1 issues and were least interested in reaching agreement on Strand 2 (cross-border institutions between Northern Ireland and the Irish Republic). It was the reverse with Sinn Fein, which focused most of its attention on how the negotiations would go beyond internal political institutions and build in an all-Ireland dimension.

In the broadest of terms, the UUP and the minor loyalist parties really wanted to secure a system of political devolution in Northern Ireland, based on recognition that Northern Ireland was part of the UK and on the consent of the majority of the people who lived there. Sinn Fein (and the SDLP) wanted an agreement that reached out beyond Northern Ireland and that provided sufficient checks and balances within the system to protect the nationalist minority from domination by the unionist majority. While Sinn Fein worried about getting corralled within an agreement that produced an 'internal' solution in Northern Ireland, unionists worried about the power and remit of the cross-border bodies, in case these undermined their support. Both Sinn Fein and the loyalist parties also focused on specific issues, such as the terms of prisoner release and the proposed reform of the RUC, while the UUP obsessed about the sequencing of IRA weapons decommissioning and Sinn Fein's entry into government.

As Sinn Fein and the UUP (the main unionist party participating) wanted to go at different speeds over the various strands, the negotiations settled on a formula that interlinked them all. The 'riddle of the strands' moved forwards on the basis that 'nothing was agreed until everything was agreed', to prevent one side gaining concessions on its agenda and then obstructing progress on other items in the negotiations.

As the talks reached their conclusion, the main sticking point remaining was whether the central political structure should be a power-sharing executive (which the SDLP and Sinn Fein wanted) or a committee-based system (favoured by the UUP). The extent of cross-border bodies was also of major concern to the unionists and loyalists. David Trimble was well aware that this had played a part in destabilizing the power-sharing executive in 1974, destroying the political career of his predecessor, Brian Faulkner. The timing of weapons decommissioning and the release of paramilitary prisoners were likewise massive stumbling blocks in the negotiating process as the clock ticked down to the 9 April deadline set by George Mitchell for an agreement to be reached. Unionists were also very concerned that the Irish Republic should reform Articles 2 and 3 of its constitution, which in their eyes laid political claim to Northern Ireland. However, while this was an important element, it was not a critical sticking point in the negotiations, as transforming them into aspirational form simply involved recognition of the political reality that had existed for at least a generation.

Of course, attitudes to the negotiations varied widely, and while some preferred to see their glass as half full, others saw it as half empty. Paisley's DUP had walked out of the multi-party talks when Sinn Fein was re-admitted in 1997, following the resumption of the IRA's 'ceasefire'. Since then it had acted as a 'spoiler' in the political process, accusing Trimble of 'selling out' the unionist community and generally taking every available opportunity to claim that the British government was doing a grubby deal to placate the IRA, and that this would prove disastrous for the people of Northern Ireland.

As the negotiations approached the deadline of 9 April, Paisley led a late-night protest rally up to Castle Buildings, where the negotiations were taking place. This temporarily grabbed the media spotlight from those inside and led to a rowdy press conference, at which the DUP leader was finally outflanked by the loyalist delegation, including former paramilitary prisoners from the UVF and UDA. They gate-crashed Paisley's impromptu gathering, shouting 'Where are you taking us, Ian?' and 'Show us your number, Ian!' Such heckling was a pointed reference to the fact that, despite Paisley's bombastic rhetoric, he had never spent a significant amount of time in jail for his beliefs, or been issued with a prison number like many of those who were now supporting the PUP and UDP within the negotiations. The emperor was exposed as having no clothes, and for once the 'Big Man' looked vulnerable and humiliated. Paisley's evening was not improved when he was assailed by Dr Joe Hendron, former SDLP MP for West Belfast, who shouted out during the press scrum: 'You say you're a man of God – well tonight's the night to prove it.'[48] It was a PR disaster for Paisley and the DUP, and for a fleeting moment it looked like they were yesterday's men, soon to be swept aside by the forces of moderation.

While the opposition of the DUP was transparent, it was unclear at this stage which way the UUP was going to jump. While Trimble had one eye on the DUP, his other was firmly fixed on his own party, many of whom were growing uneasy as the deadline approached. On the evening of 9 April, he convened a meeting of his senior party executive in Belfast, where he was heckled by a small group of angry and discontented unionists: 'The talks are a disaster for unionists. Trimble is selling us out like De Klerk sold out the white South Africans.'[49] Paisley's constant criticism had worried some people that Trimble may have 'gone soft', and his support within the party began to melt away like snow off a ditch on a sunny spring morning.

The issue of Sinn Fein's participation in government *before* IRA decommissioning had commenced was a difficult one for Trimble and the rest of the Ulster Unionist Party to accept. This was a matter that Sinn Fein had refused to compromise on, and it had said repeatedly to Tony Blair and others that it would not accept the principle of tying IRA decommissioning to Sinn Fein participation in government. It was a 'walking' issue for them, a deal-breaker.

As 9 April approached, the mood of expectation was palpable. Tony Blair and Irish Taoiseach Bertie Ahern had both arrived earlier in the week to take direct control of the negotiations, in an effort to get the parties across the finishing line. Immediately after his arrival, Blair provided some unconscious humour, when he commented that: 'A day like today is not a day for soundbites, really. But I feel the hand of history upon our shoulders with respect to this, I really do.' With their jackets off and sleeves rolled up, both prime ministers got stuck into the detail of the remaining issues. Key concerns on the unionist side were the precise terms of IRA weapons decommissioning and the relationship between this and Sinn Fein's participation in government, together with the scale and remit of the North–South bodies to be established between Northern Ireland and the Irish Republic.

The discussions between Blair, Ahern, Mitchell and the Northern Ireland parties were finally distilled into a draft agreement, commonly

referred to as the 'Mitchell Document', which was distributed to the negotiating parties on the evening of 6 April. The title was a misnomer, however,
as the section on Strand 2 (North–South bodies that would connect
Northern Ireland and the Irish Republic on issues of common interest)
had actually been written by the two governments, but was presented by
Mitchell as his own work. This diplomatic sleight of hand was seen as a
reasonable piece of subterfuge, on the grounds that either the unionists or
the nationalists (but probably both) would have rejected it if they believed
it to have been written by the two governments, but would be more likely
to accept its terms if it came from an independent third party.

The draft was roundly condemned by the UUP, which was incensed at
the scale of the proposed North–South bodies and sceptical about the
guarantees relating to IRA weapons decommissioning. Trimble shook
with rage in George Mitchell's office, making it clear that this was totally
unacceptable to him and his party and was not the basis for a deal. The
UUP negotiating position had originally been 'guns *before* government'.
This was subsequently watered down to 'guns *and* government', and many
of his party were concerned that they had now ended up with 'guns *after*
government'. While some had been prepared to hold their noses and
swallow hard in accepting the second of these positions, the third triggered their collective gagging reflex. Trimble's deputy leader, John Taylor,
delivered a very public rebuke to the Mitchell document on the very day it
was distributed, reacting in particular to the scale of North–South bodies
initially envisaged: 'Clearly this paper is unacceptable to unionists . . . I
wouldn't touch it with a 40 foot pole.'[50]

Eventually the text was reworded in a way that reassured unionists and
also linked the idea of paramilitary decommissioning and the holding of
office; but crucially for both Sinn Fein and many unionist sceptics, such as
Jeffrey Donaldson, it decoupled the two issues. The wording that was
finally agreed upon and included in the Good Friday Agreement was
turgid and ambiguous. While it stated that the achievement of decommissioning was central to the overall process, it required nothing 'up front'
and was not a prerequisite for Sinn Fein's participation:

> All participants accordingly reaffirm their commitment to the total
> disarmament of all paramilitary organisations. They also confirm
> their intention to continue to work constructively and in good faith
> with the Independent Commission, and to use any influence they may
> have, to achieve the decommissioning of all paramilitary arms within

two years following endorsement in referendums North and South of the agreement and in the context of the implementation of the overall settlement.[51]

This convoluted paragraph could be read in a number of ways, and working 'constructively and in good faith' while 'using any influence' were matters of degree rather than transparent benchmarks. Proving that people were *not* acting in good faith or using any influence they *may* have would be next to impossible. This was part of the 'constructive ambiguity' of the whole peace process in Northern Ireland. In other words, unless the language was sufficiently elastic to allow it to be read differently by the opposing sides, neither faction would sign up to it. In such circumstances, the only way of moving forwards was to build multiple meanings and layered opaqueness into the language.

While it was hoped that a commonly accepted view would eventually emerge once suspicion and mistrust had subsided, the initial 'agreement' had to be couched in terms that allowed the parties to 'agree to disagree' over the details. This allowed the process to move forwards and eventually to conclude successfully, but it stored up problems for the future when rival interpretations of what was meant by it, came to the surface. At an earlier point in the process, this had led one local humorist to ask the following rhetorical question: 'What do you get if you cross the peace process with the mafia? Answer: An offer that you can't refuse, but can't understand.'

David Trimble was well known for having a short fuse, and the machinations within the UUP on 9–10 April left him understandably tense and nervous about whether he could bring his party and the wider unionist constituency with him. The deadline of 9 April came and went, due largely to difficulties within the UUP over the terms of the deal. Trimble had left the negotiations late on 9 April, thinking an agreement was in place, only to return early the next morning to hear of serious discontent within his party. This was principally over the lack of linkage between decommissioning and Sinn Fein's participation in government. A meeting was hastily arranged between Trimble's team and Tony Blair. The prime minister listened to their worries but refused to reopen negotiations. The deadline of midnight on 9 April had already been missed by several hours, and it was time to finally decide one way or the other.

By this point inside Castle Buildings even the food had run out and the coffee machines had run dry: it was time to starve the groups out of the negotiating chamber, like troublesome house guests who had overstayed their welcome and kept drinking the whiskey. SDLP chief negotiator Seamus Mallon recalls the scene: 'I went down to get my breakfast – nothing left, couldn't get anything. Coffee machines were turned off, everything was cleared out of the canteen. I said at least I'll have a smoke: I went to the cigarette machine, empty! That was it.'[52]

In the end, Trimble was convinced to accept the deal through diplomatic sleight of hand by Tony Blair. The UUP wanted some form of written guarantee that connected decommissioning and the holding of political office. While Blair could not change the agreement, he wrote a letter to David Trimble which tried to give him the type of undertaking he needed. In late afternoon, the following text was hand-delivered to the unionist room in Castle Buildings by Blair's chief of staff, Jonathan Powell:

> This letter is to let you know that if, during the course of the first six months of the shadow Assembly or the Assembly itself, these provisions have been shown to be ineffective, we will support changes to these provisions to enable them to be made properly effective in preventing such people from holding office.
>
> Furthermore, I confirm that in our view the effect of the decommissioning section of the agreement, with decommissioning schemes coming into effect in June, is that the process of decommissioning should begin straight away.[53]

It was rather fitting, given the halting nature of the negotiations, that even at the point of agreement it looked like the whole process was on the brink of collapse. Trimble and a few of his key lieutenants, including John Taylor, read the letter that had been hastily written by Blair and felt that it was strong enough for them to proceed. It was only a fig leaf to hide their embarrassment over Sinn Fein entering government without prior IRA weapons decommissioning, but it was a necessary one. However, it was not a large enough fig leaf to prevent some of Trimble's senior colleagues from jumping overboard at the last minute and denouncing the deal.

## STRIKING A DEAL

It was already 4.30 p.m. on 10 April. The other participants in the negotiations, not to mention everyone else in Northern Ireland and the global media camped outside, were sitting by their televisions or radios, waiting and wondering what on earth was going on. First it was all off, then it was all back on again. The broadcast media – always anxious to be first with the news – were desperate to announce the result, whether positive or negative. But the problem was that they had to rely on guesswork, on snatched conversations with one of the participants, or on deliberately slanted briefings by the parties themselves or by Blair's chief of staff.

The result was that people had turned on the television on the morning of 10 April to be told that the deal was done, only to find out at lunchtime that it might be undone. The local newspapers were no clearer, the early edition of the *Belfast Telegraph* announcing that agreement had been reached on 9 April, while the later edition toned this down considerably by reporting that the deal had hit a 'snag'.[54]

It was now Good Friday, of course, and if nothing else the religious calendar demanded an outcome, one way or the other. Could a crucifixion be followed by a resurrection in Northern Ireland? The world was watching. Tony Blair was waiting. And so was President Clinton. More importantly, everyone in Northern Ireland had their fingers crossed and was desperate to know whether their politicians had finally managed to reach an agreement.

Local musicians, led by folk-singer turned peace activist Tommy Sands, had been mounting a vigil outside Castle Buildings, singing ballads in support of the talks. They wanted to demonstrate that there was popular 'non-political' support for the efforts of the politicians to reach a settlement, and it added a surreal (if more harmonious) note to the final days of the negotiations.

And the weather was behaving even more perversely than is usual for springtime in Northern Ireland: bright sunshine one minute, followed by dark clouds and slanting rain the next. We had all the seasons and all the emotions on display in one chaotic and confusing afternoon – fear, anxiety, hope, respect, joy, anger . . .

By late afternoon, word finally came through that a deal had been reached between all of the parties in the talks. The Good Friday Agreement (also called the Belfast Agreement) set out the terms of a new multi-party accommodation in Northern Ireland. Its fundamental principles were based on non-violence and power-sharing between the nationalist and unionist political parties. A new 108-seat Assembly was to be established, along with an Executive drawn from party strength in the Assembly (subject to cross-community representation). A committee system would hold ministers in the Executive to account. And the whole structure was to be headed by a 'first minister' and a 'deputy first minister', one of whom had to come from the nationalist and the other from the unionist community. In other words, the system was based on a mandatory coalition, with unionists and nationalists having a mutual veto written in to the new structures.

On top of this, there was to be a new set of cross-border bodies established to reflect relations between Northern Ireland and the Irish Republic, while a British-Irish Council was to be established to consider relations between Ireland and Britain. At a more direct level, paramilitary prisoners were to be released 'on licence' within two years, and a new commission would examine possible ways of reforming the RUC to make it more representative of, and accountable to, the community.

It was a densely worded and, at times, convoluted document. But it held out the prospect that, at last, a realistic agreement had been reached between unionism and nationalism that dealt with the underlying grievances of the two communities. Unionists had a devolved assembly based on the consent principle, with Sinn Fein signed up to the democratic process (even if IRA decommissioning had yet to commence), while the hated Articles 2 and 3 of the Irish constitution were also being transformed to their satisfaction.

For its part, Sinn Fein had a way forward that it could present as being an equitable political system, with check and balances that would prevent unionist domination, as well as embryonic cross-border bodies that it could 'sell' as staging posts to eventual Irish reunification. In addition, republican (and loyalist) prisoners were to be released early, and the future of the RUC was to be reviewed by an independent commission.

There were also significant sections in the Good Friday Agreement that focused on rights and safeguards and on equality of opportunity, including the establishment of a new Human Rights Commission. Finally, it recognized that it was the 'birthright of all of the people of Northern Ireland to identify themselves and be identified as Irish, or British, or both, as they may so choose, and accordingly confirm that their right to hold both British and Irish citizenship is accepted by both governments'.[55] This allowed nationalists and unionists to 'agree to disagree' about their contested nationality claims and to opt into one, or other (or both) as they chose.

A talks process that had begun on 10 June 1996 had finally concluded on 10 April 1998. Given the length of time the negotiations had taken, the final acts seemed a little hurried as the various parties delivered short statements to the assembled media in very blustery weather outside Castle Buildings. Both the British and the Irish prime ministers were understandably upbeat, as they had wrestled victory from the jaws of defeat at the eleventh hour. It even seemed as if Tony Blair could control the weather: his joint press conference with Bertie Ahern was conducted in reasonable conditions, with a moderate breeze and a hint of watery sunshine. But when UUP leader David Trimble had his turn to speak to the media, it began to snow heavily, making him look even more forlorn. It was a portent of the winter winds that would subsequently engulf both him and his party in the months and years to come.

Despite the collateral damage on the unionist side, talks Chairman George Mitchell hastily convened the closing plenary session. The speeches and hugs commenced and the process was concluded. Mitchell closed proceedings with the same understated panache he had demonstrated throughout the preceding two years. His tone was reassuring, like an experienced airline pilot who had just made a perfect landing despite having a hole in the fuselage that had resulted in some of the more demanding passengers being sucked out at high altitude: 'I have that bitter sweet feeling that comes in life, I'm *dying* to leave, but I *hate* to go.' Mitchell had certainly earned the praise that was heaped on him at the conclusion of the negotiations. At an earlier point, when the process was at a critical stage, he had to choose between remaining in Belfast to hold things together and returning to America to visit his brother Robbie, who was on his death bed with bone marrow cancer. To his credit, he stayed to herd the political cats in Northern Ireland, but knew that 'I would never see Robbie alive again'.[56] Unfortunately he was to be proved correct, as his brother died a few days later.

Now his job was done, and it was up to the politicians in Northern Ireland and their supporters to implement what had been negotiated.

# CHAPTER SEVEN

# THE INCOMPLETE AGREEMENT, 1998–2002

This is a phase in our struggle. That struggle must continue until it reaches its final goal.

Gerry Adams, Sinn Fein, 10 April 1998

THE PROBLEM WITH massive highs is the deep lows that often follow soon afterwards. In Northern Ireland, the euphoria that surrounded the Good Friday Agreement (GFA) did not last for long. The very next day, the *News Letter* front-page headline read: 'Trimble Facing Revolt', which indicated the level of concern about the Agreement within the unionist community.

The problem lay not just in what it contained, but also in what was missing from its carefully worded text. While those who had negotiated it had pored over every word and punctuation mark, ambiguity persisted over what it really meant. This was indicated by the remarks of Gerry Adams and David Trimble: even before copies of the Agreement had been printed, the two leaders were saying dramatically different things about what it signified for the political identity of Northern Ireland. The reason for this divergence was that they were more concerned about calming their nervous supporters and preventing splits in their parties than they were about demonstrating that they had reached a historic compromise with their former enemies. In truth, the word 'compromise' was on few people's lips, and certainly not those of the politicians, who sought sanctuary by posturing to their core constituencies.

This highlights a fundamental problem that lies at the heart of the Northern Ireland peace process. In effect, the Agreement was not an agreement at all: it was an 'agreement to disagree' over readings of the likely political future of Northern Ireland. So Trimble could accept the GFA on the basis that it strengthened the Union, while Adams did so on the grounds that it represented a stepping-stone to Irish unity. But both readings could not be right – could they? This apparent paradox was not lost on the electorate, many of whom wondered who was correct. As often happens at times of heightened tension, the more politically insecure tended to believe the worst-case scenarios. A clearly exhausted and relieved Tony Blair claimed that the Good Friday Agreement represented an 'either/or' choice for the people of Northern Ireland – violent mayhem or peaceful co-existence: 'The essence of what we have agreed is a choice. We are all winners, or we are all losers. It is mutually assured benefit, or mutually assured destruction.'[1] His assumption was that people would plump for the former rather than the latter, but this was far from clear-cut, and one thing that united unionists and nationalists was the irritation they felt towards outsiders telling them what they should or should not do.

## LET THE PEOPLE DECIDE

It was critical that the GFA should gain popular support from across the community in Northern Ireland – not just to help the political elites implement it, but because there was to be a referendum in Northern Ireland to decide whether it should be accepted or rejected. One of the big selling points of the initiative was that the 'consent' of the people would be sought before it was introduced. It was hoped that this would give the electorate a sense of 'ownership' of the peace process and prevent the agreement falling apart, in the manner of the 1974 power-sharing executive. Ian Paisley had helped to destroy that initiative, and he was still saying 'no' in 1998. He was, of course, a past-master at scaring the unionist electorate into the polling booths to vote for his populist and moralizing messages. By having a referendum in Northern Ireland, it was hoped that the community would feel it was being given a say in its own political future. Given the litany of previous failures, it was vital to reassure the general public that the political system was being designed by them, rather than imposed in the manner of the 1985 Anglo-Irish Agreement, the 1974 power-sharing executive, or even partition itself in 1921.

As part of this charm offensive, the British government arranged for a printed copy of the GFA to be delivered to every home in Northern

Ireland. Its front cover showed a young family on a beach at sunrise (or possibly sunset), with the words *'It's Your Decision'* emblazoned across it. As a way of demonstrating how this new era reflected the 'parity of esteem' between British and Irish identities, the agreement was also available in the Irish language.

There were two referendums on 22 May 1998, and both were of critical symbolic importance. The 'consent' principle was at the core of the GFA, to reassure unionists that the constitutional future of Northern Ireland was a matter for the people to determine and would not change without the consent of the majority of those who lived there (or more precisely, a majority of those who were on the electoral register). This also allowed David Trimble to argue that ultimately the electorate was sovereign, and that while he may have negotiated the GFA and be 'recommending' unionists to support it, they would have the final decision to accept or reject it. He hoped that this would provide him with a mandate from his party and from the wider unionist community to implement the Agreement, and in the process consign his political tormentors (such as Paisley) to the sidelines.

Sinn Fein was also keen on the idea of a referendum, though for different reasons. In formal ideological terms the party did not actually recognize Northern Ireland. For them it was the bastard child of Irish partition in 1921. So why would they care about the consent of those who merely lived in one part of the island of Ireland? The answer, of course, was that there was also a referendum on the GFA in the Irish Republic at the same time. Sinn Fein's immediate response to the Agreement had been positive but wary. This was typical of its leaders' generally non-committal negotiating style, where they nearly always left themselves enough wiggle-room to make sure that they had sufficient space to manoeuvre if they could not sell their position to the republican grass roots:

> While the document produced this morning contains elements which are positive, there are others yet to be resolved. So much more has to be done. I have always made it clear that our negotiating team will go back to the Ard Chomhairle (National Executive) of Sinn Fein. We will assess the document in the context of our peace strategy: Does it remove the causes of conflict? Can it be developed and is it transitional? As in the past we will approach this development in a positive manner . . . Sinn Fein will ask all those questions also. When we have democratically come to a conclusion we will let you know.[2]

In many ways the GFA was a 'hard sell' for Sinn Fein. It did not have Irish unity. It did not even have a promise of Irish unity (even a vague one). It merely had a *right to aspire* to Irish unity, while recognizing the legitimacy of Northern Ireland and operating a set of political structures under the sovereign control of the British parliament. This was hardly what Bobby Sands or his nine comrades died for on hunger strike – or, for that matter, what any of the others on the pantheon of martyred republican heroes had given their lives for. Those republicans whose glasses were half full chose to see it as a staging post to Irish unity; as a transitional moment on that journey – one that would hasten their ultimate goal. For those who saw their glasses as half empty, however, this was little more than a soft-landing for the admission of republican defeat.

While Sinn Fein went off to consult (and convince) grass-roots republican communities to look at the GFA through green-tinted spectacles, it could at least point to the two referendums in Ireland as evidence that, regardless of the here and now, in wider terms politics was developing on an all-Ireland basis. So it could sell the consent principle in a more holistic manner than the unionists, since the consent of *the whole island of Ireland* was being sought for this political change. For the first time since the last election before partition in 1919, Irish national self-determination was being enacted. This idea of the Irish people acting as one political unit had been a republican mantra ever since Northern Ireland came into existence, and the dual referendums were vital elements of political symbolism for the republican constituency.

They were two processes rather than one, however, as there was a bit more to the Southern plebiscite than to its Northern counterpart. The reason that the Republic of Ireland was having a referendum was not primarily the symbolic act of national self-determination, nor the useful demonstration of popular support for the Agreement. Part of the negotiations concerned the relationship between the two parts of Ireland and, in particular, the Republic's historic constitutional claim on Northern Ireland contained in Articles 2 and 3 of its constitution.[3] Unionists had felt threatened by these for some time, and the reform of those articles had become an act of faith for the Irish government in its effort to convince unionists that it was a non-threatening neighbour. As the Republic of Ireland has a written constitution, this change had to be ratified by the electorate in a referendum, as well as through parliamentary legislation. So the referendum in the Republic had this added dimension, which was not part of the Northern vote.

## SELLING THE AGREEMENT

While the negotiations were tough, convincing the wider community that the GFA was acceptable (or even desirable) was never going to be an easy task. Although there was a general sense of relief for many that a route out of violence may finally have been found, there was little euphoria about its detailed contents. For one thing, it was a densely worded document, and while it was delivered to every home in Northern Ireland, the vast majority of people read the media reportage of its contents rather than the Agreement itself and formed their views from their existing party allegiance.

As the initial comments of Adams and Trimble indicated, the process of selling the GFA was not helped by the fact that the political elites were sending out contradictory messages about its contents and significance. While many people would happily sign up to the sentiments behind the grandiloquent language of the 'declaration of support', the devil was very much in the detail:

> We acknowledge the substantial differences between our continuing, and equally legitimate, political aspirations. However, we will endeavour to strive in every practical way towards reconciliation and rapprochement within the framework of democratic and agreed arrangements. We pledge that we will, in good faith, work to ensure the success of each and every one of the arrangements to be established under this agreement.[4]

Few would disagree with such laudable goals, but many people (especially on the unionist side) remained unconvinced about the terms and conditions of the GFA and about whether the promises made by their opponents would be honoured. While Trimble could point to his personal letter from Tony Blair, Sinn Fein was quick to remind him that this lay outside the terms of the GFA: it was the private view of the prime minister, was not formally connected to the terms and conditions of the Agreement itself and was therefore not binding on Sinn Fein or anyone else.

For two years, the people had sat and watched the political elites negotiate the GFA. Now the baton was passed to the wider community in Northern Ireland, which was invited to vote on the Agreement in a referendum on 22 May. There was more heat than light during this period, and no shortage of motivated and opinionated commentary on what should happen next. The 'No' campaign was quickly into its stride because it had been preparing itself since the DUP walked out of the negotiations in 1997. Its slogan was 'It's Right to Say No' and the pitch was very much at an emotional and moralistic level. The campaign was led, of course, by the DUP, but it drew in other dissenting voices, such as Robert McCartney's tiny but vociferous United Kingdom Unionist Party and senior 'dissident figures from the UUP'.[5] Westminster MPs from the UUP such as Willie Thompson, Willie Ross and Roy Beggs joined Paisley and Peter Robinson (the DUP Deputy Leader) at a rally in the Ulster Hall on 23 April, demonstrating that the 'No' campaign was a cross-party one and that mainstream UUP voters could vote against the Agreement without feeling that they were joining the Paisleyites or switching their political allegiance to the DUP. Willie Thompson was a blunt and irascible unionist farmer from Co. Tyrone who prided himself on telling it as he saw it – a character to some, to others a curmudgeon. He had a high profile within the UUP, having been elected MP for West Tyrone at the 1997 general election. The media loved his 'shoot from the hip' attitude, which frequently gave them colourful copy. The sprightly fifty-eight-year-old came out of the blocks like an Olympic sprinter at the beginning of the referendum campaign, making it clear that he did not support either the GFA or the policy of his party: 'It's a complete disaster. Trimble has conceded on almost every point he said he would stand on. It has weakened the Union and is completely unacceptable and I will be voting no in a referendum.'[6]

The most interesting aspect of what was quite a co-ordinated and slick campaign was that virtually none of it focused on the central political architecture of the GFA. Little was said against power-sharing, or even against the North–South bodies that were to be established. There was a claim that the GFA would 'destroy' the Union and Northern Ireland's place within it, but the main focus was on the prospect of Sinn Fein being in government without decommissioning, prisoners being released from jail within two years and the planned commission on the future of policing in Northern Ireland. The message was a clear and simple one: the GFA was immoral and was rewarding murderers at the expense of the innocent victims of violence. The DUP's anti-Agreement campaign leaflet tried to mobilize support through unionists' antipathy towards Sinn Fein, as well as through the suggestion that the GFA was an interim step on the way to Irish unity, rather than a final settlement. This allowed Paisley to connect the GFA with the heritage of the past, as well as with fears for the future of the Union:

The Agreement is a staging post to a united Ireland and has come about by abject surrender to IRA/Sinn Fein. A 'Yes' vote is a vote which the enemies of our Province and those who have surrendered to them are calling for. You have the opportunity to save Ulster for the Union and for your offspring by voting 'No' . . . Stand up for Ulster! Stand up for your children and your heritage! Stand up for your children and your children's children! Let the world know that the Ulster people will not be bullied, bribed or butchered into accepting fascist rule. It is suicidal to do otherwise.[7]

By contrast, the 'Yes' campaign was initially leaderless and incoherent. For one thing, the parties campaigned separately rather than together, giving out different messages to the electorate. The PUP understandably tried to counter DUP claims by campaigning on the basis that the GFA strengthened rather than weakened the British character of Northern Ireland. Its referendum literature led with the slogan 'Progress, Union, Peace' (which conveniently coincided with the party's acronym – PUP).[8] The SDLP message was strikingly different, in that it focused much more on the future being a matter for the people of Northern Ireland to determine for themselves. Its election leaflet for the referendum, subtitled 'Our Shared Future – A Key Decision', claimed that 'people could feel that history was in the making. Now it is up to the people to make history, make it the **People's Agreement** by voting **Yes** in the referendum on May 22nd.'[9]

The UUP was hopelessly split by this point, with six of its ten Westminster MPs in the 'No' camp. Trimble seemed as irascible as ever, repeating (like a broken record) that the GFA represented a victory for unionism. His efforts at rational debate in the media scored some hits against his unionist opponents, but he was on the back foot for much of the campaign and at times appeared impatient and petulant during media appearances. In one highly charged appearance on BBC Northern Ireland's *Hearts and Minds* programme, he screamed at his inquisitor, Noel Thompson, that he was 'distorting the facts'. Afterwards he reportedly told the programme's producer that 'it was the nearest he'd ever come to punching someone'.[10]

In the end, due to the inertia of the political elites, an independent, non-party 'Yes' campaign set itself up. It was formed by civil society activists who felt that a more urgent and co-ordinated campaign in support of the GFA was needed, in order to prevent its critics from strangling it at birth. Like a pop-up shop, a company was quickly formed, funding was applied for (and generously provided by the Joseph Rowntree Reform Trust (JRRT) among others) and the organization hastily tried to engage with the political parties that were supporting the Agreement.

There was suspicion from many within the political elite at this sudden eruption of civil society activism. Were they trying to steal the glory? Were they going to muddy the ideological waters or the identity of the party? On a more practical level, were they going to stand as candidates in the planned election to a new Assembly if there was a positive outcome to the referendum? The UUP was initially disparaging towards this effort to supplement the elite actors from outside the formal party system. One senior figure within the party leadership was reported to have said that 'when this Campaign is over, these people should be cleaning the streets, where they belong'.[11]

The GFA had shaken up the political universe in Northern Ireland to a point where it had disoriented many. David Trimble's UUP was suffering from the greatest schizophrenia, as half of the party supported the GFA, and thus the same policy as the SDLP and Sinn Fein. Meanwhile, the other half of the party was attacking its own leadership in the media and at public rallies with Ian Paisley. This partly explains why the political parties were such uneasy bedfellows. Reaching a negotiated settlement with one another when formal distances were maintained was one thing; but emerging from their sectarian trenches and arguing the same case together was something else entirely. Even the lure of financial support was not enough to convince them to unite in a joint campaign. Quintin Oliver, the former director of the Yes Campaign, recalled that, during the initial meeting, the representative from the JRRT tried to appeal to the parties in material terms, in the hope that this would get them on board an integrated effort to support the Agreement:

> 'These people have pledges of £50,000,' he explained. 'I have promised to match that by giving them another £50,000. If you agree here to form a joint strategy committee, I will give you another £100,000. That will give you £200,000 in total, which may be enough to run a decent campaign. Will you take it?' 'No,' they said. 'We need time to consult and to think.'[12]

They were perhaps still a little punch-drunk from the negotiations and concerned that the pace of change was too fast. The UUP negotiators managed to get through the whole process by barely speaking to the Sinn

Fein delegation, even to the extent of refraining from exchanging basic social pleasantries. One of Gerry Adams' favourite ploys was to say hello to unionists when they were least expecting it. These greetings at times met with understandable consternation. Former UUP negotiator Dermot Nesbitt recalls one particularly close encounter with the Sinn Fein President: 'I was standing in the toilet relieving myself when suddenly I felt a hand on my shoulder, and realised it was Gerry Adams who was inquiring about my well-being. Lost for words and for want of anything better to say I said "I didn't realise you were so big." '[13]

Given how new the idea of 'agreement' was to many of the politicians in Northern Ireland, their suspicion about getting too close to one another is understandable. There was also an election to a new Assembly scheduled for June (assuming the GFA was supported in the referendum) and this was also in the minds of the main party strategists.

In the end, the independent Yes campaign settled for a looser form of co-operation with the UUP, SDLP, Sinn Fein and the smaller parties, but it played a significant role in communicating public support for the GFA through an active publicity campaign. This involved regular media 'stunts' and endorsement from well-known public figures, such as boxer Barry McGuigan and actor Kenneth Branagh. This ensured a high media presence and great street visibility. One of the most iconic moments of the period came at a concert held in support of the GFA, when Bono (the lead singer of U2) held the arms of David Trimble and John Hume aloft in triumph on stage. It was the enduring media image of the period and signalled a unity of sorts between the main parties on the eve of the poll. The two political leaders looked excited, if a little dazed by the sudden adulation – even if their formal shirt-and-tie look was a little out of line with the young audience and the *über*-cool image of their aging rocker turned potential matchmaker.

Relations between the independent Yes campaign and the political elites developed from their initial frosty suspicion into more cordial co-operation, though it was always an uneasy alliance. These tensions were illustrated when the civil society activists attempted to get an endorsement from Nelson Mandela for the Yes campaign. Mandela was a global icon who could bring gravitas, prestige and media interest, and his endorsement in Belfast would provide the perfect climax to the campaign. Eventually a message was got to him via intermediaries in London, Geneva, New York and Cape Town, and amazingly he said 'Yes' to 'Yes'. He was to be in Geneva the day before the vote and could come over to Belfast to put his seal of approval on the peace process. The Yes Campaign team was elated, as this would be a major coup, and it approached the two main political parties to get their agreement. However, the SDLP's response was luke-warm, as it had already made its own plans for the eve of the referendum. The reaction of David Trimble's UUP was more interesting and illustrated once again how politics in Northern Ireland was viewed through a particu-larly narrow prism:

> Yes, he is an international moral icon, but he is also the world's best example of a former paramilitary turned political and national leader – and all without decommissioning . . . It will be used by our opponents against us to hammer away at the key issues of prisoner release, paramilitaries in government and decommissioning.[14]

After a heated and emotional campaign, the referendums eventually produced an overwhelming mandate for the Good Friday Agreement across the island of Ireland. In the North, 71 per cent of the electorate voted 'Yes' to the question 'Do you support the Agreement reached in the Multi-Party Talks', while only 29 per cent voted 'No'. The turnout was 81 per cent, the highest ever in the history of the 'state'. The numbers in the Irish Republic were even more impressive, with an overwhelming 95 per cent of people voting in favour of the Agreement and reform of Articles 2 and 3 of the constitution, though the turnout was much lower, at 55 per cent. The raw numbers were equally impressive: 2,119,549 voters across the island of Ireland voted 'Yes', and only 360,627 'No'.[15] Interpreting the numbers on an all-island basis is, of course, a bit of 'creative accounting', as it was the consent of people within Northern Ireland that really mattered in terms of its future survival.

Whichever way the figures were tallied up, it was (initially at least) a triumph for the pro-Agreement supporters and a defeat for the No campaign. The turnout was massive and the overall majority in support of the GFA was healthy and robust. The episode illustrated once again, however, the inability of the political elites to win the trust of the elec-torate without the assistance of more informal, community-based initia-tives. The independent Yes Campaign played a significant part in securing the positive result. It was much more media savvy than the political parties and it used networks from across civil society to create the sense of a shared agenda in support of a peaceful future – networks that were not available to those within the formal political process. Proving cause and effect is extremely difficult, of course, but it is reasonable to conclude that, had the informal political activism of the Yes Campaign not supplemented the efforts of the political parties, rather less than 71 per cent would have voted in favour of the GFA.

I voted 'yes' in the referendum. While I was aware of all the imperfections of the GFA, I felt that this was a crucial moment in Northern Ireland's political history and a crucial moment for the island of Ireland itself – perhaps the most crucial there would be in my lifetime: electoral participation by the wider community would have a direct material effect. Normal elections come and go, but this was different; and for me, a 'yes' vote meant a future for my family and friends, while a 'no' vote signalled a return to the past.

I was aware by this point that I would soon be leaving Northern Ireland for an academic job in Britain, which made the experience all the more poignant. At a conference in Belfast around the same time, a colleague chided me for leaving when the peace process was just about to take on institutional form. 'Northern Ireland needs people like you now', he proclaimed rather melodramatically. I laughed at the conceit of the idea and at the irony of my situation. Like a reworking of Beckett, having spent many years like Estragon waiting for the Godot of the peace process to arrive, it had persistently failed to show up and now I had to leave.

I remember being at the King's Hall in Belfast, where the referendum vote was being counted and where the candidates and academic commentators were giving interviews to the assembled media. It was an intense and emotional atmosphere inside and outside the building, and we were all strung out amid rumour and counter-rumour about the likely outcome. Party leaders came and went, followed by their loyal entourages and – in the case of the larger parties – by clusters of journalists looking for quotes. Early exit polls suggested a majority of people had voted 'yes', but the scale of the majority was critical. The Agreement needed a strong endorsement, as a narrow majority would have left it extremely vulnerable to attack from its opponents.

Eventually the result came in around mid-afternoon. There were scenes of jubilation among the Agreement's supporters. I remember Ian Paisley and some of his deflated colleagues being heckled as they left the building, like a defeated boxer with his entourage, to the chant of 'Easy, Easy, Easy'. Less charitable souls were heard to remark on his exit: 'F*** off home, Paisley, you're finished!'[16] It was a humiliating exit for this colossus of political figures. Had the stakes not been so high, I would have felt sorry for him; but as they were, I didn't.

While Paisley was bloodied by the referendum, he remained unbowed and pointed out to some incredulous journalists that while, yes, he still supported the democratic process, and yes, a large majority of the people of Northern Ireland had voted in support of the GFA, only a very small majority of the *unionist* community had come out in favour of it. He was right, and this was an important caveat to all the talk about the brave new peaceful world that Northern Ireland was about to enter. Local newspaper coverage was unreserved in suggesting that the outcome was 'resound-ingly' in support of the GFA. The *Belfast Telegraph* editorial was gushing: 'Historic Yes. The Verdict: A Bright New Dawn for Northern Ireland'.[17] The reality was that Northern Ireland's morning skyline was a little more grey than forecast, and scattered heavy showers of opposition to the Agreement were imminent.

The simple fact was that unionists found the GFA much more difficult to stomach than nationalists, partly because of what was in it over the pace of prisoner releases, but also because of what had been left out of it. The future of the RUC was uncertain and was to be determined by an independent commission, while there were no explicit guarantees on the decommis-sioning of paramilitary weapons. The following postings on a BBC News interactive discussion website at the time provide a flavour of unionist displeasure at what had been agreed by the community's politicians:

> Despite international pressure and massive bribes only slightly more than half the Unionists voted for the Stormont Sellout. Many of them voted because of the assurances Tony Blair gave on the campaign trail, promises that weren't in the agreement because the IRA/SDLP coalition wouldn't agree to them.[18]

> To some the cheers and celebrations that have accompanied the Good Friday referendum may be a cause for celebration – but for the keener observers some will remember Neville Chamberlain bran-dishing a piece of paper crying 'Peace in our time!' How wrong he was. It is truly ironic that Gerry Adams and co are giving lectures to bona fide democrats on observing the wishes of the people when Mr. Adam's [*sic*] pals have been doing their level best to reduce the electorate through the bomb, the bullet and punishment beating. Nobody minds giving peace a chance, but at what price?[19]

Media coverage of the referendum disguised a significant gap between unionist and nationalist attitudes to the GFA. An independent election survey found that in the referendum 57 per cent of Protestants had voted for the Agreement, compared with 99 per cent of Catholics. By 1999, support for the Agreement within the Protestant community had fallen to 53 per cent, and by 2000 only a minority supported it – 47 per cent.[20] 'Since then, less than half of the Protestants interviewed in the surveys have said that they would vote yes if the referendum was repeated. In 2003, for example, 96% of Catholics and 46% of Protestants said they would vote yes again.'[21]

So, while the GFA seemed on the surface to unite opinion in Northern Ireland, it has always divided it, and unionist support has never been more than lukewarm. When Peter Weir (who defected from the UUP to the DUP in the wake of the GFA) was later asked by a journalist if there was anything in the Good Friday Agreement that he liked, his response captured the mood of many of its critics: 'It was very nicely typed.'

In part, the attitudes of unionists and nationalists towards the GFA were reflective of wider default settings within the two communities. In broad terms, nationalists took the view that political reforms over recent years (while imperfect) were going in the right general direction. Time and history were on their side, and they could afford to wait a little longer for their aspirations to become realities. As the general picture looked acceptable, they did not need to spend too long examining the detailed brushstrokes.

Many unionists felt precisely the opposite: namely that their British identity and Northern Ireland's position within the United Kingdom had been steadily eroded over the previous thirty years. Like limestone cliffs battered by generations of relentless ocean waves, chunks of their sea defences had been washed away over time, while the unionist house inched closer and closer to the cliff edge. Many felt that time and history were not on their side and that the GFA represented the distillation of the forces that had been ranged against them since the 'Troubles' began in 1969: a duplicitous British government; an avaricious Irish state; a violent Irish republicanism within Ireland; and a hostile and meddling international community beyond it. It is difficult for people who are insecure about the future to embrace the very change that they fear could destroy them, especially if it is couched in such pathological ambiguity. This partly explains why so many unionists voted 'no' in the referendum.

The positive result in the referendum opened the way for elections in June to a new Assembly, from which the governing cabinet-style Executive would be drawn. I was at the election count in Belfast City Hall, and I watched the adrenalin-pumped candidates as the votes came in. I was reminded of one Northern Ireland politician at a previous election who, on being defeated, uttered the immortal line: 'The people have spoken – the bastards!' Sinn Fein politicians moved around in clusters, the cut of their suits giving a clue as to their role within the organization. The loyalists were also there in strength, though they seemed less confident, their suits sometimes fittingly awkwardly around limbs that had been toned by long sessions in the prison gym. This lack of confidence about their electoral prospects was entirely appropriate, as they found it much more difficult to get people to vote for them than did their republican counterparts.

## BEYOND THE GOOD FRIDAY AGREEMENT

Convincing reluctant unionists to see their political glass as being half full rather than half empty was a perennial problem in the peace process and had been a key aspect of John Major's and Tony Blair's management of the negotiations. While nationalists and republicans did not like it, the unionists were the crucial constituency in the referendum and in the June Assembly election. Could enough unionists be kept on board, despite their obvious discomfort, for long enough to see the fruits of political stability start to come through? Even among the unionists who voted *for* the GFA in the referendum, fewer than 50 per cent supported the establishment of a commission on the future of policing.

Reform of the RUC was an elephant in the room of the peace process, and it was left out of the terms of the GFA. It was pushed down the pipe (like the precise terms of weapons decommissioning) because it was thought impossible to get agreement on it. This was one of the central fault-lines that ran through the whole peace process. On the one hand, constructive ambiguity allowed the separate factions to move forwards and bought some time for structures to become established and relationships to be built. On the other hand, if there was no convergence in the narrative of what had been agreed to, that risked making the fundamental disagreements more difficult to resolve. This is exactly what happened, as both sides accused the other of breaking their promises and failing to live up to their commitments on the Agreement.

For republicans, the RUC was a political and oppressive force, a belligerent in the conflict rather than an objective protector of the rule of law. The 'securocrats' within Special Branch had a self-interest in the status quo and were a symbol of the British Crown that was at odds with Irish nationalist rights to 'parity of esteem'. For many unionists, the RUC was part of their identity and family history, their buffer and protector from IRA violence, and a source of continuity with the past. It was impossible to reach an agreement on policing within the GFA, and so the issue was fudged and left for a later date. An independent commission was to be established to look into the issue of policing, consult the communities and provide a report with recommendations that could be acted upon.

Unsurprisingly, the campaign for the June Assembly elections was dominated by anti-Agreement unionists' claims that the RUC would subsequently be destroyed by the GFA, and that members of the Provisional IRA who had killed many RUC officers would be released without having surrendered a bullet. Their colleagues in Sinn Fein, meanwhile, would be allowed to enter government and help shape the destruction of a police force that had been the first line of defence for the people of Northern Ireland for over thirty years.

These unionists did not much like the actual political structures of the GFA either, but tugging at the emotional heart-strings of unionists who were already worried about whether they were 'doing the right thing' was much more effective than debating the finer points of consociational democracy or complaining about the remit of the institutions.

In the end, this internal battle for the heart of unionism during the Assembly elections produced a near dead heat between the two sides: thirty pro-Agreement unionists were elected to the Assembly and twenty-eight unionists from anti-Agreement parties. This was vitally important, as the institutions required 'parallel consent' between unionists and nationalists in order to function. It was already teetering on the brink of collapse, as defections from the 'yes' camp to the 'no' camp were much more likely to occur than the other way around, especially as IRA decommissioning failed to take place, as prisoners were released and as the RUC was downsized to bring it into line with its new civilian role.

While many people became consumed with the outcome of the first Assembly election and the continuing arguments surrounding who promised what to whom in the GFA, a shocking reminder of the past arrived just after 3 p.m. on Saturday, 15 August 1998. The place was Omagh town centre. That day, with the ink on the GFA barely dry, Northern Ireland suffered the largest single act of paramilitary violence in the history of the conflict. A car bomb exploded in the town centre, killing twenty-one people instantly; a further eight died either on their way to hospital or shortly afterwards, and 200 were left injured.

The roll call of the dead was horrific. Avril Monaghan was seven months pregnant with twins and had four children aged under seven. She was in town with her eighteen-month-old daughter Maura and her mother, Mary Grimes, who had recently celebrated her birthday. All three of them, together with the two unborn children, were killed in the blast. Breda Devine was only twenty months old and had been taken into Omagh by her mother in search of a wedding present. Breda was killed instantly and her mother received 60 per cent burns to her body. Oran Doherty (aged eight), James Barker (aged twelve) and Sean McLoughlin (also twelve years old) were from Buncrana, Donegal, in the Irish Republic, and were all killed in the explosion. Two Spanish students from Madrid, Fernando Baselga and Rocio Ramos, who were on a student exchange programme, were also killed in the blast.

The scene was one of utter devastation. People scrabbled through the collapsed buildings to pull victims out from amidst scattered limbs and charred body parts. Buses and cars were used to ferry the dead and injured to hospital or to the impromptu morgue that was set up nearby.

Though a warning had been telephoned to a Belfast news agency forty minutes before the bomb detonated, the police claimed that it was confusing and did not provide accurate enough information to clear the area. The town was packed with Saturday shoppers and the bomb ripped through the main street. Soon afterwards, a newly formed republican splinter group, the 'Real IRA', admitted responsibility for the attack but blamed the RUC for the deaths, as it had not acted on the warnings provided. Its statement that 'we offer apologies to the civilians' was of little value to those whose loved ones lay scattered beneath the rubble or who had themselves been disfigured by burns and flying debris from the blast.

The primary motive of the Real IRA in this attack was to derail the peace process and damage implementation of the GFA. These republicans saw the Agreement as woefully inadequate in terms of its ability to deliver political change and, more specifically, Irish reunification. It was not a case of 'agreeing to disagree', as there was a visceral bitterness within this small but significant grouping that they had been duped by the Sinn Fein and Provisional IRA leadership, which had sold off its republican heritage for the trappings of office, amid vague hopes of political change. The Real IRA was a tiny radical fringe within the republican community, but an important one nonetheless. The bombing ironically united nationalists, unionists and the vast majority of republicans against them, but the Real IRA knew that the attack would remind everyone that the tradition of militant republicanism had not gone away.

Eventually the inevitable question was asked: what sort of peace process is it that blows innocent men, women and children into oblivion while they are doing their Saturday afternoon shopping? All the political parties (including Sinn Fein) issued unequivocal condemnations of the bombing. Tony Blair visited some of the victims and issued a statement shortly afterwards calling on the parties to unite to defeat the bombers' attempt to undermine the peace process: 'What happened on Saturday is in the past. If we give up and return to it, then they do win. Evil will have secured its objective. We can defeat it, if we refuse to be deflected.'[22] President Clinton issued a similar entreaty to the politicians to pull together to overcome their differences and visited the scene of the bombing shortly afterwards on his second visit to Northern Ireland.

In the past, a bombing of this magnitude might have blown any political initiative off course; but the Omagh bombing brought unionists and nationalists together in grief and emboldened the politicians to search harder for a way forward. By September, Trimble had held his first face-to-face meeting with Gerry Adams – a meeting that both men described as 'cordial and businesslike', even if no actual progress was made on the decommissioning issue. Given that Trimble and the rest of his party had refused even to speak directly to Adams during the multi-party negotiations from 1997 to 1998, this was a positive step forward. The police investigation into the bombing was more problematic. Initially, numerous suspects were arrested and questioned about their responsibility for the attack, but all were released without charge. In 2002, Colm Murphy was convicted of conspiracy to commit the bombing, but his conviction was quashed in 2005 on account of irregularities in police evidence. The RUC was publicly rebuked for its handling of the bombing investigation by Police Ombudsman Nuala O'Loan in 2001, and specifically for its poor leadership, bad judgement and lack of urgency in its enquiries. In March 2001, a £2 million civil action was launched by the victims' families against Murphy and several others suspected of involvement in the bombing, including Michael McKevitt. The case dragged through the courts for eight years, but eventually concluded in June 2009. It found that the defendants were responsible for the bombing and were jointly liable for damages of £1.6 million to the victims' families.

Back in 1998, a 'Day of Reflection' was held in Omagh a week after the bombing, and over 40,000 people attended a cross-community service. Prayers were said and hymns were sung, and all the main politicians were in attendance, apart from Tony Blair, who was on holiday in France. Despite all of formalities, it was an informal moment that had the most powerful impact. Local singer Juliet Turner sang 'Broken Things', a haunting and beautifully simple song about the slow and difficult process of mending broken hearts. It was a spell-binding, spine-tingling moment of hope amidst the pain – a signal that all was not lost – and it was greeted by spontaneous and prolonged applause from the audience.[23] It was the image that went around the world from the aftermath of the Omagh bombing and it carried more meaning and more power than the words of any politician.

## DYSFUNCTIONAL DEVOLUTION, 1999–2002

While the Omagh bombing made it very clear to the advocates of the GFA that they needed to make progress towards implementing it in full, they were no closer to working out how to do that. David Trimble and the dwindling number of his colleagues within the UUP who supported the GFA made a massive strategic error in tying their policy to a decision that was entirely beyond their control: by adopting the position that the UUP would withdraw from the institutions of the GFA if IRA decommissioning was delayed, he placed himself and his party in the hands of republican strategists. So in this game of 'political chicken', Sinn Fein and the IRA set the agenda, while the UUP could only threaten to crash the institutions it had agreed to establish, to the delight of its opponents in the DUP, which had been unable to destroy the agreement itself through the democratic process.

The IRA was reluctant to decommission for a number of interconnected reasons. First, it was intent on managing tensions within the republican movement and preventing any splits from emerging. Any hint that it was 'surrendering' weapons to the British government would have incensed many of those within its core constituency and raised the likelihood of a major fracture within both the IRA and Sinn Fein. Republicans tried to push the idea that the best way of ensuring that decommissioning took place was not to ask too many questions about it and to recognize 'the silence of the guns' rather than demand that they should be handed in. As one senior Belfast republican put it at the time: 'If you want the IRA to go away . . . let them – you don't kick a dog to see if it's still asleep.'[24] This missed the point, of course, that unionists wanted the IRA to be 'put to sleep', rather than wait in trepidation for it to awaken from its slumber. Second, the position of Sinn Fein was that decommissioning was not a prerequisite for its participation in government and was actually linked to the full demilitarization of the conflict and the complete implementation of the GFA, neither of which had been fully achieved. Third, the IRA realized that decommissioning was a major card – one that it was not going to play until it could be sure that it would have the maximum impact. It provided political leverage, which would significantly reduce once the IRA had decommissioned; consequently there were benefits to be had from taking this slowly.

The decommissioning of paramilitary weapons applied, of course, to loyalist organizations, as well as to republican ones, but the former received much less attention than the latter. There were two broad reasons for this. First, unionists had made it 'their' issue, in an attempt to slow the pace of change and postpone the inevitable day when they would have to recognize the democratic mandate of Sinn Fein and enter government with it. In part this goes back to the point that nationalists were more confident about the general picture than unionists and looked to the future with less trepidation. Thus, the fact that loyalist paramilitary groups had not decommissioned their weapons was seen by nationalists as a price that had to be paid for wider gains within the political process. Unionists, however, worried about each of the individual brushstrokes of the peace process like a neurotic and highly strung artist, and were not at all sure that they would like the portrait when it was finished. More ignobly, unionists seemed much more concerned about the guns of republicans than about those of loyalists. When pressed by the media on this, the politicians would often add that of course loyalists were under contract to decommission as well; but they never threatened to pull out of the GFA's institutions if the loyalists failed to do so. The grubby, if pragmatic, reality was that loyalist guns were unlikely to be used against unionist politicians or those who voted for them, whereas republican ones might be.

The second broad reason why decommissioning became an issue for republicans rather than loyalists was connected to the political success of the former and the relative electoral failure of the latter. Sinn Fein had developed a powerful democratic mandate that gave it a right to a place in the Executive and to a significant bloc of representatives in the Assembly. Loyalist political parties – the Progressive Unionist Party and the Ulster Democratic Party (connected to the UVF and UDA/UFF, respectively) – remained extremely small, and although they had a presence within the negotiations and made a vital contribution to the GFA in 1998, they failed to build on this public profile in subsequent years. The fact that Sinn Fein was going to hold ministerial office in the Executive, while the loyalist parties were not, made the decommissioning issue more relevant for republicans than for their loyalist counterparts.

The lack of agreement over the issue of decommissioning caused a number of delays in setting up the Executive following the June Assembly election. It was clear at this point that unionist support was wavering, and so the UUP responded by refusing to set up the Executive until there was some movement on decommissioning. A whole year passed as each side argued with the other about what the GFA did or did not say about the requirements concerning weapons decommissioning. Final deadlines were set and missed and set again. The 'final' deadline for the formation of the Executive was set for 30 June 1999. When this was missed, it was revised to 15 July.

The slippage in the timetable of setting up the institutions, combined with the bad blood between the political elites over allegations of broken promises on the GFA, weakened public confidence in the process. The public bickering encouraged the doom-merchants, who claimed that the main political actors either did not want to, or were not able to, co-operate with one another. At times, this stand-off descended into an embarrassing farce as the UUP and Sinn Fein tried to make the other 'blink first'.

On 15 July 1999, when the parties were finally required to nominate ministers to the new Executive, the UUP refused to participate, in protest at the lack of IRA decommissioning. As the DUP and Alliance Party refused to nominate their ministers as well, the ludicrous process continued with the SDLP and Sinn Fein taking up *all* the ministerial positions and holding office for ten minutes! The GFA's requirement for cross-community selection in the Executive was then ruled to have been contravened and the process was suspended, pending a review by the long-suffering former talks chairman, Senator George Mitchell.

This fiasco marked an inauspicious start to the new era that the local media had foretold a year before, and it was not until 29 November 1999 that the Executive was finally formed, with UUP leader David Trimble becoming 'first minister' and the SDLP's Seamus Mallon, the nominee of the largest nationalist party, 'deputy first minister'. The trigger for this was a dramatic three-hour meeting of the UUP's ruling Ulster Unionist Council (UUC), at which David Trimble secured a narrow majority of 58 per cent in a vote authorizing him to take the UUP into government in the absence of IRA decommissioning. There was, however, the significant proviso that the UUP would withdraw from government in February if the IRA failed to disarm by that date. Trimble had managed to seize the initiative and put the ball firmly back in the republican court: 'We've done our bit. Mr Adams, it's over to you. We've jumped; you follow.'[25] While this vote triggered the end of direct rule and the implementation of the structures of the GFA, it also started a time bomb ticking – one that would detonate in February if the IRA had not delivered on the decommissioning issue.

Power was finally devolved back to Northern Ireland from Westminster at midnight on 1 December 1999, with the simultaneous amendment to Articles 2 and 3 of the Irish constitution. The following day, the power-sharing executive and other institutions were set up to govern Northern Ireland – a full 601 days after the GFA had been reached.

Unfortunately, this apparent new dawn in Northern Ireland proved to be another false one. First Minister David Trimble was trying to lead the UUP at a time when it was virtually unleadable: it was split down the middle over the GFA and was at war with itself over whether the Agreement should be supported or opposed. While the UUP waged internal war, the DUP ramped up its rhetoric against the UUP, and its leader in particular, for taking the decision to enter government with Sinn Fein. At his party's annual conference, Ian Paisley launched an attack on David Trimble that was vitriolic even by his standards, calling him a 'salesman prepared to besmirch his heritage, split his party and destroy his country. Every vote cast today [for Trimble] is a vote of shame, a vote for darkness, a vote that tramples on the graves of innocent victims and a vote that not only tramples on them, but dances upon their graves.'[26]

Trimble limped along from one crisis meeting to the next, but by this stage he was following as much as he was leading. He was in an unenviable position, as his dwindling authority within the UUP made it harder and harder to convince sceptical unionists to participate constructively in the institutions of government. The numbers were against him, too, as an equally split unionist community had elected supporters and opponents of the GFA to the Assembly in an almost equal proportion. As unionists watched power being shared out, Sinn Fein taking its seats in the Executive,

North–South bodies being developed, prisoners preparing for early release and the RUC being prepared for a radical overhaul, many became more and more disillusioned. On the other side of the equation, there was minimal movement from the IRA over weapons decommissioning, and while it claimed to be 'constructively engaging' with the Independent International Commission on Decommissioning, few unionists believed it. By early 2000, the prevailing mood within the UUP and the wider unionist community was that in this new era of give and take, they had done all the giving and republicans had done all the taking.

It was clear by February 2000 that while the UUP may have jumped, the IRA had not followed. A second meeting of the UUC was looming, at which it looked certain that the UUP would withdraw from the Executive and cause its inevitable collapse. Even by the standards of Northern Ireland's faltering peace process, the situation now looked desperate. There was no chance of the IRA decommissioning, and, given the narrow margin of the previous meeting in November, there was equally no conceivable chance that Trimble could get past the UUC again (even had he wanted to). The peace process now looked doomed to hit the rocks, and both unionists and nationalists braced themselves for the impact.

To prevent a crash-landing of the institutions, British Secretary of State Peter Mandelson suspended the Executive on 11 February 2000, the day before the UUC meeting was due to take place. This came as no great surprise to anyone, but it incensed both the SDLP and Sinn Fein, which claimed that Mandelson had acted with undue haste. He had caved in to unionist demands, despite being in possession of what Gerry Adams referred to as 'a new and significant proposition' from the IRA that was of 'enormous significance' in terms of breaking the deadlock over the decommissioning issue. But for both the UUP and the British government, this eleventh-hour initiative lacked the clarity they were looking for and so Mandelson pulled the plug on devolution before Trimble could collapse it by walking out.[27] After a mere seventy-two days, direct rule returned to Northern Ireland amidst recriminations, which predictably flew between the unionist and nationalist political parties, and resigned cynicism across the wider community. It was both a tragedy and an embarrassment for the peace process, as the chronic lack of trust between the political elites and concern about disenchantment within their grass-roots support created the impression that Northern Ireland was simply incapable of governing itself.

The DUP accused the UUP of serious political misjudgement for taking the promises of the IRA at face value and wagged an 'I told you so' finger at its main unionist political rival. While the DUP was implacably opposed to the GFA, it nonetheless took part in the structures of government that were formed. In public, it defined this as a type of critical engagement and a way of holding others to account, and so it took up the posts it was entitled to, but did not participate in meetings of the Executive. It decided to 'rotate' its two ministerial positions (i.e. changing its ministers periodically), in an effort to disrupt the new institutions. This was a difficult balancing act for the DUP: on the one hand, it wanted to destroy the new political system; on the other hand, it was participating in it and claiming that those in ministerial positions would do a good job and fulfil their responsibilities effectively. The more practical reason for this awkward stance was that if the DUP did not take up its two ministerial posts, they would have been reallocated to pro-Agreement parties (the UUP and the Alliance Party), thereby significantly strengthening the system. Peter Robinson, the DUP deputy leader, conceded this point shortly after the restoration of devolution in May 2000: 'We do not intend to play into Trimble's hands by allowing our ministers to be replaced by compliant agreement supporters . . . We shall not hesitate to be the whistle-blowers – exposing each of Trimble's further concessions to Sinn Fein/IRA.'[28] Robinson was later to look back on this period and suggest that necessity had been the mother of invention in terms of the DUP's role: 'In the end we opted to rewrite the rules of government and create a new category of Minister. We became Ministers in Opposition.'[29]

The lack of IRA decommissioning led to a reduction in unionist support for the GFA, fatally constrained Trimble's room for manoeuvre and damaged his leadership of the UUP. While he managed to limp along for several years and to drag his party into the devolved structures of government, he was unable to build them effectively. His authority within his own party ebbed away as the UUP vote slid inexorably downwards at subsequent elections. His relations with both the SDLP and Sinn Fein also worsened, as nationalists felt he was reluctant to get on with implementing the GFA. His tendency to lapse into sectarian language when under pressure did little to build bridges with nationalists either. Following a particularly tense meeting of his party's Ulster Unionist Council in May 2000, at which he squeezed out just enough support to go back into the devolved structures (suspended since February), Trimble lashed out at Sinn Fein. In response to a question from a journalist, he responded that republicans needed to be 'house-trained in democracy and brought to heel'.[30] This did little to placate his unionist opponents, but incensed both Sinn Fein and the wider nationalist community, many of whom interpreted it as evidence of the unreconstructed bigotry that remained within the unionist psyche. Sinn Fein's Bairbre de Brún commented: 'It's the kind of sectarianism which led to the second-class citizenship that Catholics and nationalists have known throughout the history of the state. It led to much of the conflict and it needs to be left behind.'[31]

While Trimble succeeded in getting just enough support from the UUC in repeated crisis meetings during this period, his leadership of the UUP and the embryonic political institutions suffered a death by a thousand cuts. His opponents within the party grew steadily in strength and confidence and shackled him increasingly tightly to the delivery of IRA decommissioning. When Trimble first called on the UUC to support him in joining the Executive, a very healthy 72 per cent of its 860 delegates did so. As we saw above, by November 1999 this had dropped to a narrow 58 per cent, which gave him just enough support to trigger devolution on 1 December. By May 2000 his support had dwindled to 53 per cent. And so it continued. Every attempt to shore up support for his policy dented his political leadership further. Trimble hung on for as long as he could, but in the years that followed, his grip loosened steadily and his authority slowly drained away both within his party and beyond it.[32]

## SECTARIAN REALITIES AFTER DEVOLUTION

We have a problem in this society with sectarianism at all levels. It permeates right through all sections of our society. It determines where people live. It determines where people shop. It determines where people socialize. It determines how people engage with each other. All of that is inherent within our society and needs to be dealt with in a root and branch manner if we are to ever move into a society fit for purpose . . . Because if we don't, it has the capacity to come back and haunt us in many different ways.[33]

Outside, in the real world, the GFA meant little, especially to those living in urban interface areas. The uncomfortable truth was that, beyond the level of general rhetoric, the GFA did not connect adequately with communities in a way that would help to encourage integration or reconciliation. Regardless of whether power was or was not devolved to Northern Ireland, the sectarian dynamics of society were as visceral and virulent as ever. Here was the rub: the internal machinations within the UUP and the IRA made very little difference to the day-to-day lives of the wider community. More worryingly, perhaps, the periodic stop-start-stop-again nature of devolution between 1999 and 2002 seemed incapable of dealing with the experience of sectarian tension at the ground level. This led many people to regard the sometimes-functioning Assembly and Executive (and by extension the GFA itself) as an expensive political decoration, rather than as a set of institutions that could provide political stability and augment the quality of their lives. Looked at from this perspective, the GFA had not stopped paramilitary violence; it had not significantly improved community relations; it seemed incapable of mediating the summer 'marching season' or the more controversial Orange parades; and finally, it could not arrest communal segregation, as Catholics and Protestants seemed just as anxious to live separately from one another as they did before 1998. In short, when the ambitious language of the GFA was set against the sectarian reality of what was happening in Northern Ireland, it was found sadly wanting.

One of the defining characteristics of the conflict in Northern Ireland has been the apartheid-style separation of the Catholic and Protestant communities. People have lived apart, worshipped apart, been educated apart, played apart and have even been buried in separate graveyards: 'Within the Belfast City Cemetery there is an underground wall. The reason why such a wall exists is to separate the Catholic dead from their Protestant counterparts.'[34] This pattern of separation was primarily a result of structural factors, such as the segregated educational system and the development of Protestant and Catholic employment patterns over generations; but it was also a result of people's behaviour during the conflict. Marrying into your own community and living within it was often a much easier and safer option than going beyond it; in fact, an NGO – the Northern Ireland Mixed Marriages Association – was formed during the conflict to provide information and assistance to those who did marry outside their community. The figures from the 2001 census on residential segregation are stark and suggest that a majority of the population live in areas that are either 90 per cent Catholic or 90 per cent Protestant: '67.3 per cent of Catholics and 73 per cent of Protestants live in such places. A mere 10.7 per cent of Catholics and 7.0 per cent of Protestants live in places that are between 41–60 per cent Catholic or Protestant or places that could be described as "mixed".'[35] The political conflict and the physical dislocation that resulted from it led many people to seek sanctuary within their own communities. The irony of this herd mentality, however, was that such physical separation provided a much easier and more visible target for the violence and made those who lived in segregated areas much more likely to be killed or injured than those who were dispersed more widely. Once again the figures are quite striking:

> One-third of the politically motivated attacks resulting in fatalities between 1966 and 2001 took place within 250 metres of an interface; over two-thirds of deaths (but representing only 53 per cent of Belfast's population) occurred within 500 metres. More than three-quarters of deaths occurred in areas which were over 90 per cent Catholic or 90 per cent Protestant. In overall terms death was closely tied to places that were highly segregated, militarised, close to interfaces and socially deprived.[36]

To put it more starkly, while sectarian attitudes permeated the whole of Northern Ireland society, those most likely to be caught up in the violence – as both perpetrators and victims – were young men living in working-class urban interface areas. While people understandably felt safer when corralled within their own communities, this residential separation also made it much easier to target people for attack.

The sectarian separation is often visible, the most obvious example being the so-called 'peace line' in North Belfast and the other fences or security barriers that blot the urban landscape. However, there are many other less-visible demarcations of division, such as bridges, bus signs or other road markings which denote the religious and political boundaries of the area. This is so ingrained that people become self-regulating, for fear of veering into potentially threatening or unwelcoming territory.

The peace process and the arrival of inclusive power-sharing held out the prospect of a post-conflict environment where these divisions would become more fluid and malleable. The GFA included an ambitious section on 'reconciliation and victims of violence', which made clear that the vision was to bring the unionist and nationalist communities closer together, while acknowledging the rich historical, political and cultural diversity that existed: 'An essential aspect of the reconciliation process is the promotion of a culture of tolerance at every level of society, including initiatives to facilitate and encourage integrated education and mixed housing.'[37] This is a laudable objective and something we would expect from a reconciliation process; but the GFA was less clear on the means by which this goal might be achieved. In fairness, it should be remembered that the Agreement was a broad framework, which set out the basic political geometry of the region rather than worked through all the specific calculations about how it was to be implemented. However, the lack of delivery mechanisms or connections between the political elite who negotiated it and the wider community who would experience it reduced the practical relevance of the GFA for many people at the grass-roots level. For some of those living in urban interface areas, it was the worst of both worlds, as they lived in an atmosphere of heightened political tension and sporadic violence, while the paramilitary groups who could have been relied on in the past to provide a degree of order were observing ceasefires (to a greater or lesser extent).

Disagreements over political strategy and manoeuvring over the spoils of war led some loyalists to turn on one another. A vicious feud emerged in 2000–02 between the UVF (which was broadly in support of the GFA) and the UFF (which was largely against it). Tensions also arose between the UVF and a splinter group, the Loyalist Volunteer Force (LVF), previously led by Billy Wright (aka 'King Rat'), before his assassination in 1997 by the Irish National Liberation Army. Loyalist shootings increased from 33 in 1997/98 to 124 in 2001/02 as these paramilitary factions fought it out.[38]

This phase of internal feuding was partly political, but it was also a turf war between organizations and personalities for control of the 'war economy'. The conflict had created personal fiefdoms for a number of people at the top of loyalist paramilitary organizations, several of whom had lined their pockets through extortion rackets and drug dealing in working-class areas. The British government had informally turned a blind eye to this low-level criminality for three reasons. First, it was more concerned with the bigger picture, namely the level of sectarian violence and the possibility of getting loyalist support for the peace process. Second, there tended to be a bigger security focus on republican violence and on the threat posed by the Provisional IRA. Third, the security services such as MI5 and the police Special Branch put up with (and at times encouraged) drug dealing and other forms of criminal activity in exchange for intelligence from informers.

A number of colourful personalities fought one another for control of their paramilitary groups – and, by extension, for control of criminal activity within their areas. Perhaps the most notable within this rogues' gallery was Johnny 'Mad Dog' Adair, who controlled 'C Company' of the UFF in the Lower Shankill area of Belfast. To continue the metaphor, Adair wanted to be 'top dog' within loyalist paramilitarism, and he relished his reputation as a 'hard man' within his community. Before the loyalist ceasefires of 1994, Adair, a rather squat, bald-headed and unusually muscular figure, was interviewed by a locally born journalist, Maggie O'Kane, for the *Guardian* newspaper. In response to the ice-breaker about whether he had ever given a Catholic a lift in his car, he reportedly replied 'only a dead one'.[39] Adair's attempt to take control of loyalist paramilitary activity eventually failed and resulted in his imprisonment and the exile of his supporters to various locations in Scotland and the North West of England in 2001.

The early years of the twenty-first century saw a rise in republican para-military violence, even though the Provisional IRA (like the UVF and UFF) was supposed to be observing a ceasefire. Figures from the Police Service of Northern Ireland indicate that there were 323 victims of 'paramilitary-style attacks' in 2000/01; the following year, this figure only dipped marginally – to 302.

The development of unionist and loyalist politics from 1998 onwards has not mirrored events within the republican community, and there has been no upsurge in 'dissident loyalist' violence. There are a number of reasons for this, the most important being that, when the Provisional IRA left the stage, loyalist paramilitaries found it difficult to identify a target. As a result, their violence turned inwards rather than being directed outwards at the republican community. Second, many loyalists felt that the agreement reached in April 1998 had significant benefits for them (such as prisoner release), and in political terms it did not signify a threat to Northern Ireland's constitutional position within the United Kingdom.

Loyalist paramilitary violence against the nationalist community has not re-emerged because the majority of those involved in it do not feel that Northern Ireland's position within the UK is in danger and because (aside from the low level of dissident republican violence) they lack a visible enemy with which to engage. Nevertheless, sectarian attitudes within loyalist communities have remained stubbornly intact, and while the GFA did not make the paramilitaries worried about Northern Ireland's consti-tutional position within the UK, friction has frequently surfaced at the local level.

## THE HOLY CROSS DISPUTE

Well do we have a real peace? We definitely have a peace of sorts. [Northern Ireland] is unrecognizable from what it was in the early nineties and going back even further than that. Nothing's perfect, nothing ever is. But it is still pretty clear that there are some deeply negative elements out there and some strange attitudes as well.[40]

An emblem of the times was provided between September and November 2001, when sectarian tensions boiled over near the Holy Cross girls' primary school in North Belfast. To the outside world, this fitted neatly into the narrative of Protestant bigotry, as an angry mob of loyalists repeatedly heckled a group of Catholic schoolgirls walking to the Holy Cross school in the (Protestant) Glenbryn district of the (mainly Catholic) Ardoyne. The images of the dispute captured global media attention, not only because it looked like an attack by snarling adults on a group of defenceless children, but also because the last time people looked, Northern Ireland was supposed to be basking in the glow of a peace process:

The protests became very vociferous and violent and pictures travelled the world of hectoring Protestant mothers spitting hate at cowering, frightened Catholic schoolchildren. Bottles of urine were thrown at the children and the Ulster Defence Association (UDA) even lobbed a pipe bomb into the middle of a group of schoolchildren which exploded, but luckily injured no one.[41]

The dispute dominated the local media for months, and in his memoir of the incident a local Catholic priest, Fr Aidan Troy, chairman of the school's board of governors, recalled just how extensive the coverage was:

Between June 2001 and February 2003, The *Irish News* and *Belfast News Letter* published a total of 279 articles on the protests, together with 150 photographs and 3 cartoons ... The *Belfast Telegraph* gave extensive coverage on an almost daily basis. Papers in the Republic of Ireland covered the events on a daily basis ... BBC News 24 carried regular accounts that were broadcast around the world and seen by airline passengers ... Some American TV companies also had journalists covering the events ... It was clear that the media interest was enormous.[42]

Predictably, the issue escalated from latent tension into a small skirmish, and then into a much wider and more serious incident involving two nights of rioting. Each morning, the police ended up having to form a human corridor, through which the children were escorted into the school, to the accompaniment of a spitting and jeering loyalist mob shouting 'Fenian whores' at eight-year-old children. Fr Troy describes the scene on the morning of 5 September 2001 quite vividly:

> As we made our way to school – children, parents and priests – a bomb was thrown towards us. It exploded before it reached us, injuring police officers and a police dog . . . Parents scooped children up in their arms and ran in every direction . . . At this stage it was not clear if there were other bombs . . . It is amazing how quickly we all react under threat of death or serious injury. When eventually the road was clear and everyone had reached the safety of the school grounds, shock hit me such as I had never experienced before. I began to tremble with fear of what might have happened.[43]

This stand-off continued for over five months, both sides becoming entrenched and engaged in a power struggle over the demonstration of their 'rights'.

The reality was a little more complicated than the media pictures suggested, as the loyalists saw the building of this school as evidence of Catholic encroachment into *their* territory and of the further marginalization of the Protestant community in the area. This fed into their sense of being physically, politically and culturally squeezed out by the peace process. So to that extent, the Holy Cross incident was the backlash that followed this loss of community confidence. This in no way excuses the actions of those involved, but it is an important contextual detail in helping to understand the rationality of their actions.

What did the spirit of the Good Friday Agreement or its institutions contribute to the resolution of the Holy Cross problem? Apart from the rhetoric of individual and group rights, the answer was 'very little indeed'. In fact, it was community-based mediation from the local clergy and the leadership of clerics such as Fr Aidan Troy and his Presbyterian colleague Rev. Norman Hamilton that helped to calm the situation, rather than any actions or statements on the part of the political elites or the terms of the GFA, most of which focused on the wider political framework. This local-level co-operation had a longer-lasting impact, and a relationship was built from the ground level upwards that arguably was much more valuable than the rhetoric contained in the GFA about 'safeguards' and 'rights'. The mediation over the Holy Cross dispute evolved into the creation of the North and West Belfast Parades Forum, which included church leaders, political representatives, community workers and even paramilitaries themselves.[44] These people, in their different ways, had credibility within the community and a close understanding of its political dynamics. They had no executive power to pass or enforce legislation, but they did have 'soft power', which was arguably more useful and durable. They enjoyed influence, loyalty and standing in the communities they lived and worked within. Over time they built relationships that were directly relevant to the concerns and needs of those communities. Norman Hamilton recalls that this gradually allowed him to make a contribution on contentious community issues in co-operation with loyalist paramilitary actors, as they were all – in their different ways – informal leaders and opinion formers within society:

> You sometimes have some very uneasy discussions, so you talk politics and you talk parading and you talk community stuff, but at the same time you are building real relationships with the paramilitary guys there ... For me, the [principle of] building relationships has ... come out of saying, these folks, like the churches, are part of the fabric of this society, for good or ill, and in the normal course of what you might call social dialogue and social intercourse, we will be engaging with each other.[45]

While the GFA was a very inclusive type of negotiation, it was constructed in the main by the political elites. As a result, it was a very top-down agreement, which focused primarily on constitutional structures within Northern Ireland and on arrangements for North–South bodies. Beyond that, it defined political and cultural rights and safeguards at a relatively abstract level, without specifying how those rights might be applied in practice to the policing of contentious parades or to disputes such as that at Holy Cross school. There is quite a long section in the GFA on 'human rights', which, on the face of it, would seem to lend itself very easily to the management of such community tension. There is a series of laudable principles, including 'the right of free political thought; the right to freedom and expression of religion; ... the right to freely choose one's place of residence; ... the right to freedom from sectarian harassment'.[46]

Everyone found such rights unproblematic in theory; but in practice people tended to interpret them in zero-sum terms, so that the granting of such rights to one community meant their elimination for the other.

What was missing here, of course, was any semblance of a joint understanding by unionists and nationalists of how these rights might be applied equally to *everyone* in Northern Ireland, rather than be used in a sectarian tug of war between the two sides. This has been an enduring problem for the GFA. It lacks mechanisms for interpreting its agreed values and principles in ways that connect and integrate the nationalist and unionist communities into interdependent relationships, rather than separating and dividing them:

> All of us like to invoke human rights standards to back up our stance on something, but not all of us are good at seeing the other side of the argument and at weighing up objectively whether the points on the other side more than counterbalance those on our own side. In short, making human rights assessments is a tricky business and anyone who asserts categorically that he or she knows the 'correct' human rights answer to a problem is very often over-simplifying the problem or refusing to recognise some of its more intricate aspects.[47]

The GFA made a genuine attempt at outlining a series of general principles that might govern new institutions and social relationships; but it was less able to mediate conflicting interpretations of these principles in situations such as the Holy Cross dispute. This goes back, of course, to the constructive ambiguity that underlies the whole peace process and to the fact that the political elites themselves have taken different meanings from the GFA ever since George Mitchell adjourned proceedings on 10 April 1998.

## 'STORMONTGATE' AND THE DONALDSON AFFAIR

Truth can sometimes be stranger than fiction. The final chapter in this first phase of devolution came in autumn 2002, when David Trimble finally ran out of room to manoeuvre. Following yet another fractious meeting of the UUC in Belfast, he announced in September that his party would withdraw from the Executive on 18 January 2003 (precipitating its collapse), if republicans had not demonstrated by then that they had left violence behind for good, through *actual acts* of decommissioning.

On 4 October 2002, events took a more dramatic turn, when the Sinn Fein offices at Stormont were raided by the police as part of an investigation into an alleged IRA 'spy-ring' at Stormont. Two days later, Sinn Fein's head of administration at Stormont, Denis Donaldson, was arrested and charged with 'possessing documents likely to be of use to terrorists'. The following day, the DUP tabled a motion in the Assembly calling on Sinn Fein to be excluded from government. Martin McGuinness responded by suggesting that if the institutions were again collapsed by the British government at the behest of unionists, then the Good Friday Agreement itself might be 'dead in the water'.[48]

Trimble issued what was to be his final ultimatum, to the effect that he would withdraw UUP ministers from the Executive in seven days' time, if the British government had not by then expelled Sinn Fein from office. To save the political system from a potentially more damaging crash-landing, the British once again pre-empted a UUP walk-out by suspending devolution at midnight on 14 October 2002. Direct rule returned and was to remain in place for the next five years, the institutions mothballed. The GFA was now in suspended animation, the payment of the politicians' salaries being one of the few points of continuity during this period.

By this stage it was clear that the relationship between the UUP and Sinn Fein had broken down irretrievably and that Trimble's leadership of his party was in terminal decline. Denis Donaldson's arrest was simply the *coup de grâce* for this phase of devolution. It triggered (rather than caused) the suspension of the institutions of government, but it was a fascinating and tragic episode nonetheless – for Donaldson personally and for the peace process generally.

In many ways, Donaldson was emblematic of the whole story of Northern Ireland and its journey through violent political conflict into the more complex uncertainties associated with the peace process. Denis Donaldson was a physically inconspicuous man: short, weedy with a nasal Belfast accent – generally unremarkable. He was also evidently charming, sociable and (as it turned out) extremely devious. He came from a well-known republican family and had an impeccable 'war record', being active in defending Catholics from loyalist attack in the Short Strand area of Belfast in 1970. This was an iconic moment in the development of the Provisional IRA and in its split from the Southern Marxist faction. The defence of the Short Strand was the antidote to the cutting graffiti 'IRA = I Ran Away' and marked a new and more direct phase of militant republicanism in the North. Donaldson had also associated with republican icons such as Bobby

Sands during his time in the Maze prison, though he was not as close to the leadership or to Sands himself as he often liked to suggest. He became an important figure in Sinn Fein from the mid-1980s (not a general, but certainly more than a foot soldier), playing a vital role in liaising with Irish-American groups during the 1990s. While he was well known within republican circles as an inveterate womanizer, few thought him anything other than 'dependable' and 'sound' during his time in the IRA and as a Sinn Fein administrator.

While Donaldson did not keep his womanizing much of a secret, he was more adept at hiding the fact that he had been a British informer – an agent, a 'tout' – for over twenty years. Like a scene from a le Carré novel, the British security forces (in the shape of police Special Branch) staged a raid on Stormont buildings, publicly arrested their own agent, and accused him of leading an IRA spy-ring at Stormont. Local journalist David McKittrick has pointed out that – even by Northern Ireland's murky standards – this was an unusually convoluted episode:

> One of the ironies in this saga is that the IRA instructed him, a police informer, to start spying at Stormont, co-ordinating the collection and photocopying of confidential documents. That is presumably exactly what he had been doing for British intelligence: collating documents and information on the activities of Sinn Fein and the IRA, and passing them to police. The IRA, in other words, ordered the British spy to start spying on the British – a tribute to his skill in avoiding suspicion.[49]

Donaldson's double life was eventually laid bare at an excruciating press conference in 2005, when the now disgraced republican expressed contrition for his past deeds. He commented (rather enigmatically) that he had become a British informer in the 1980s 'after compromising myself during a vulnerable time in my life'. Precisely what he meant by this was left unexplained, though he did admit to taking money from Special Branch in return for information and apologized to anyone who had suffered as a result of his activities. He went into 'hiding' in Co. Donegal, but was murdered in April 2006 – though not, it would seem, by the Provisional IRA. In the past, anyone exposed as being a 'tout' would inevitably have received a swift visit from the IRA's 'Nutting Squad';[50] but the Provos were trying to convince everyone at this point that they had left violence behind, so killing Donaldson would have given ready ammunition to unionists and would have damaged

Sinn Fein. Though at the time of writing no one has yet been charged with his murder, in 2009 the Real IRA claimed responsibility and suggested that Martin McGuinness might be next on its list of targets.

One enduring and unanswered question remains from this bizarre episode: why did the British security services arrest and expose their own agent, and in the process precipitate the collapse of the devolved structures of government for what turned out to be a five-year period? A number of theories have been advanced, including one that by the time of his arrest Donaldson had ceased to provide valuable information. He may have been their agent, but he clearly did not tell them everything, especially if that information was likely to implicate him as the source.

The cold reality was that he was an expendable asset. Some believe that he was deliberately exposed because the security services had other agents higher up the Sinn Fein chain of command who could be pressured more effectively by making an example of Donaldson. As ever within the world of covert intelligence, secrets and shadows are the stock in trade, and fact and fiction can be difficult to unravel.

Another theory suggested that the 'securocrats' attempted to deliberately sabotage the peace process, in order to protect their positions of power. RUC Special Branch and other intelligence services had lost their dominant role and faced being downsized. The RUC Special Branch was also threatened with being radically restructured to take account of its new civilian role. The logic goes that the security agencies therefore had a more obvious motive for disrupting devolved government than did David Trimble, Tony Blair or Gerry Adams. If true, this would indicate the greatest constitutional crisis within British politics in recent history, amounting to the subversion of the democratic process and of the wishes and interests of the government itself.

In addition, 'Stormontgate' (as it became known) facilitated a narrative that placed the blame for the collapse of devolution on the IRA, rather than on David Trimble and the UUP's imminent and inevitable departure from government. The alleged IRA spy-ring was denied by republicans as fiction, dreamt up by British intelligence to wreck the peace process and then place the blame on Sinn Fein and the IRA. At his 2005 press conference, Donaldson himself said that the so-called spy-ring was a total fabrication, though – given his long record of lying and double-dealing – he was not perhaps the most credible of witnesses.

Before he became aware of Donaldson's role as a British agent, Martin McGuinness had alleged that police 'dirty tricks' lay at the heart of the issue, and that Stormontgate was 'a carefully constructed lie created by the Special Branch in order to cause maximum political impact . . . Its effect politically has been to collapse the institutions and personally it has damaged the lives of the four people originally charged and their families . . . This operation is as blatant an example of political policing as you are likely to find.'[51]

While Adams publicly attempted to downplay the whole thing and to distance Donaldson from Sinn Fein, the affair sent a shock wave through republican circles. If he was a 'tout' and had been for over two decades, and if the rumours were true that he had been hung out to dry by the British to pressurize more high-profile informers within Sinn Fein, then who could be trusted? An article in the local *Down Democrat* newspaper about republican discontent in the South Down area of Northern Ireland was typical of the mood among republicans at the time: 'We cannot trust anybody anymore. It's as simple as that. When you have a major player like Donaldson turned over as a British spy it could be your brother or sister who is also on the paid informer list.'[52]

Regardless of who was ultimately responsible for Donaldson's arrest, its political impact was clear, in that it forced the British to suspend the structures of devolved government. It also dealt another blow to Trimble's leadership and led to further gains for the DUP at the expense of its UUP rivals. Direct rule was returned and would last for five long years, while the political blocs within both unionism and nationalism radicalized and realigned.

With no functioning institutions, with a politically crippled David Trimble leading a hopelessly divided Ulster Unionist Party, and with both unionists and nationalists throwing around buckets of bad blood about whose fault it all was, the forecast for the peace process in Northern Ireland looked increasingly gloomy.

# CHAPTER EIGHT

# DELIVERY, DELIVERY, DELIVERY, 1999–2010

[The structures of government] have been good for the peace process. Let's underline that, they are good and strong [structures] for the peace process. We don't kill 110 people a year anymore; we only kill two or three. So it has been remarkably good for the peace process, but pretty poor on governance, because we have 104 out of 108 [Members of the Legislative Assembly] in government . . . we've only got four independents and a rag-bag of opposition.[1]

THE OLD SAYING 'be careful what you wish for – you might get it' could be applied to the arrival of devolved government in Northern Ireland after 1999. The peace process had struggled for years to find a way of devising a form of regional government that the majority of unionists and nationalists could buy into. The key question now was whether the institutions and the politicians could actually deliver for the people who lived there.

Devolution did not grant Northern Ireland any tax-raising powers, but it did transfer legislative and administrative responsibility in key areas such as health, education, the environment, culture and the arts to locally elected politicians. A cabinet-style 'Executive' was formed, based on party strength within the elected 108-seat Assembly and led by the 'first minister' and the 'deputy first minister'. A series of ten departments and other parliamentary structures were established around the areas of responsibility that had been devolved from the Westminster parliament.

This was, in other words, a whole new political infrastructure, a visible edifice of government that those who lived in Northern Ireland could engage with. There were now departments with budgets to spend, policies to deliver, responsible ministers and an Assembly and committee structure to perform oversight functions and debate the issues. This may all sound quite normal– even mundane – within a modern, liberal-democratic region. However, for Northern Ireland it was quite a new experience, both for the politicians and for those who elected them.

In the old days of direct rule, before the structures of the GFA were implemented, Northern Ireland had been treated like a political infant and most of the important decisions were taken for it by people who, for the most part, did not live there. Because of the polarization of the political parties and of the wider community, the people of Northern Ireland were considered incapable of running their own services in health and education or of passing legislation on the environment or tourism. This was often referred to as the 'democratic deficit', because decisions were taken 'on behalf of' people by political parties who did not even stand for election in Northern Ireland.

Beyond the new political institutions that were established, the criminal justice system also experienced significant change in Northern Ireland during the move to devolution. Following the report of the Independent Commission on Policing Reform, chaired by Conservative Party grandee Lord Patten, the Royal Ulster Constabulary was reconstituted as the Police Service of Northern Ireland (PSNI) in November 2001. This was both a symbolic and a practical step to distance the police force from its over-riding security function and convert it into a body that was capable of exercising civil functions and that was acceptable to both the unionist and the nationalist community in Northern Ireland. These changes went beyond removal of the word 'Royal' from the title, as the governance structures of the PSNI made it more transparent and accountable to the wider community. A new policing board was established, with greater cross-community participation and oversight powers, while a new office of 'policing ombudsman' was established to investigate complaints made against the PSNI by anyone within the community who felt they had been mistreated. In an effort to fast-track the religious imbalance in the policing service, 50–50 (Protestant–Catholic) recruitment was adopted by the PSNI from 2001, in order to send a signal to the nationalist community that this was its police force, too.[2]

Once the knots in the GFA were untangled sufficiently for the new structures of government to be established in 1999, the nature of politics changed quickly. The political elites had to shift gear dramatically. For over a generation they had been powerless critics of the political process, watching helplessly and shouting from the sidelines as decisions that would affect their constituents were taken by others. Suddenly, from 1999 onwards, politicians who could justifiably claim 'good verbal communication skills' found they had to expand those skills sets to become managers, budget holders and bureaucrats. Those who were voting for them, meanwhile, suddenly had choices to make that had not previously been available. The social and economic agendas of the political parties now mattered; they could not simply pad out their manifestos by focusing on the 'constitutional question', security policy and issues of cultural identity. Once 'power' and resources had been devolved from London to Belfast, people had to start making choices and taking responsibility for the outcome of their policies. Given the financial constraints that were imposed by Westminster, politics began to centre on a series of very practical questions. Which hospitals should remain open? Why did fuel and energy cost more in Northern Ireland than in the rest of the UK, and what was the new regime at Stormont doing about it? What was happening to the future of education and the threatened reform of the grammar-school system? Finally, how was the devolved government in Northern Ireland going to juggle the identity-based issues that had not been resolved by the GFA, such as the future of policing or securing agreement over flags, emblems and contentious parades?

The centre of political gravity had now shifted from Westminster to Belfast. Previously, career politicians (aside from those within Sinn Fein) used to prize a seat in the Westminster parliament as the most prestigious position on offer. It brought stature, profile, salary and media attention. Why? Because that was the centre of power.

More substantially, perhaps, it gave Northern Ireland MPs the chance to 'chip in' to debates that affected Northern Ireland and to lobby those in power direct. However, this changed quite quickly after devolution and all its associated political apparatus arrived in Belfast. Westminster became more remote from the day-to-day issues in Northern Ireland, as suddenly there were ministers issuing press releases, developing policies and spending public money. While ultimate sovereign power remained with Westminster, everyday authority over people's lives and livelihoods was now firmly located at Stormont.

## EDUCATION, EDUCATION, EDUCATION

Some people were initially shocked at the new realities which devolved government had presented. Perhaps the most vivid for many unionists was the fact that in 1999 Martin McGuinness became the minister in charge of the education of their children (and those of nationalists, of course) in Northern Ireland's 1,400 schools. Under the rules established for the formation of the Executive, each qualifying party got to nominate a minister for a department of its choice, with the largest parties going first and having more ministers than the smaller ones. When it came to Sinn Fein's turn, McGuinness was proposed for the education ministry, which resulted in some gasps in the chamber and hissing from the public gallery.

The unionist and nationalist middle class was especially concerned that Sinn Fein's stated policy was to bring an end to the eleven-plus exam. This system of academic selection of children at eleven years of age (ten in some cases) was regarded by Sinn Fein (and many others) as especially damaging to those children in urban working-class communities, and as perpetuating middle-class privilege.

Ending the eleven-plus 'transfer test' became identified as a 'Sinn Fein issue' from 1999 onwards, with the result that other parties opposed it – even those whose own constituents were being disadvantaged. Speaking in his capacity as president of the National Union of Students–Union of Students in Ireland (NUS–USI) in 2011, Ciarnan Helferty commented: 'if parties were honest in terms of who they actually represented and who would benefit from some of the changes, the positions would almost be reversed. You would have unionists supporting the abolition of the 11+ and nationalists doing the opposite.'[3]

Like many subsequent high achievers, McGuinness had failed his eleven-plus, and his pledge to end this selection test would (ironically for an Irish republican) have brought Northern Ireland into line with the rest of the United Kingdom. McGuinness's arrival as education minister in 1999 quickly led people to become much more interested in what he was going to do to schools, and how this would affect their children, than in what he did or did not do while he was a leading member of the Provisional IRA. This is not to underplay the fact that people's attitudes did not change much, certainly initially, but their priorities certainly did.

They need not have worried too much about McGuinness's commitment to the issue of education or academic standards. Many years previously, before the peace process had gathered momentum, his daughter told her secondary school in the Bogside area of Derry that she wanted to leave school early to pursue a career as a model. When the school agreed that this was in her best interests and gave her its blessing, the former member of the IRA army council went to see the headmistress to stress that his daughter was not leaving school until she had the chance to take exams that might lead on to higher education. As the story goes, she defied her father and left school anyway.[4]

The management of education policy goes to the heart of the challenge for devolution. For over a decade, it has been at the centre of disagreement between the political parties and has resulted in deadlock, gridlock and confusion. None of this has augmented the educational experience of children in Northern Ireland (or their parents), who often seemed to be the last priority rather than the first.

Sinn Fein held the education portfolio from 1999 to 2002 and has done so again since 2007, once devolution was restored from suspension. Through the tenures of its three Sinn Fein ministers – Martin McGuinness, Caitriona Ruane and John O'Dowd – the flagship policy of ending academic selection at eleven years of age has been pursued. However, fourteen years after devolved government first arrived and Sinn Fein took over the education portfolio, the eleven-plus transfer test has proliferated rather than been abolished. Thus, while the last 'official' test was held in November 2008, many grammar schools in Northern Ireland have simply privatized the selection process and set their own entrance exams, which are largely based on the eleven-plus model. So instead of having the exam removed, many children now face separate exams for each of the different schools they apply to. From the perspective of many parents and their children, therefore, the impact of devolved government has been, first, to create instability (despite the passage of legislation abolishing the transfer test in 2001, it remained until 2008) and, second, to then make the trauma of selection more painful for children rather than less.

Similar frustrations emerged over further and higher education, with long delays in decision-making over the new level of university top-up fees resulting from a lack of coherent direction from within the Executive. Speaking on behalf of the NUS–USI, Ciarnan Helferty made the point that, while organizations such as his had greater access to the policy process as a result of devolution, this had not translated into any significant impact on the decision-making process: 'For far too many of the issues that we care about and that students care about . . . we've seen paralysis and indecision . . . Whatever big-picture issue you have in education, we seem to either have paralysis or failure.'[5] Education policy, in other words, is being made within the confines of existing sectarian divisions, rather than helping to re-shape or transcend old ways of thinking.

## DEVOLUTION AND THE MEDIA

Another sign that the political centre had shifted after the arrival of devolution was provided by the fact that the local broadcast and print media shifted their emphasis from London to Belfast. Significantly, the secretary of state, who from Willie Whitelaw in 1972 onwards had been one of the most important political voices in the region, became a much less significant actor. The post was still there, but the person occupying it acted more often in the role of referee rather than player, and gradually, as the institutions have become more stable, the role has diminished accordingly.

More fundamentally, the media's previous focus on security issues and on coverage of the machinations surrounding the peace process was supplemented and eventually overtaken by reporting on specific issues. The media did initially concentrate on areas of political division, particularly the pace of IRA weapons decommissioning, Trimble's leadership of the UUP and the likelihood of the whole system collapsing. However, this concern was gradually replaced by a focus on issues such as the state of the health service, the future of post-primary education, employment and overall economic management. It is difficult to be definite about the extent to which the media was leading or following the interests of the wider community, but it certainly altered the day-to-day agenda within which politics in Northern Ireland took place.

Thanks to fair employment legislation brought in by the British government in the early 1990s to deal with discrimination (and to placate external criticism from the US), all government jobs had to be advertised in the three main newspapers. The *Irish News* was traditionally read by Catholics; the *Ulster News Letter* was read by Protestants; and the *Belfast Telegraph* traditionally had a softer 'unionist lite' flavour, with a more mixed readership.[6] Because of their divided readerships, it had become a legal requirement for the same government jobs to be advertised in all three newspapers, a cost which used to be shouldered by the British Treasury. With devolution and then the economic downturn, this is now coming straight out of Northern Ireland's block grant at a time when there are many other competing priorities.

The editor of the *Irish News* commented that the arrival of devolved government had forced the newspaper to adjust to the new environment and rethink its role:

> We've had to change the content of the *Irish News* and the approach of the *Irish News* and the structures of the *Irish News* beyond all recognition . . . The readership of the paper was at its highest in the 1970s when there was mayhem on the streets, but in those days broadcasting was at a relatively early stage and to find out what was going on you had to read the papers. We were selling 60–70,000, the *News Letter* was selling 100,000 and the *[Belfast] Telegraph* was selling over 200,000. It was just incredible. But there was no commercial radio, there was no satellite broadcasting, UTV [formerly Ulster Television] was very limited and the BBC was very low key as well. Now it's just so different, you can get your news from almost anywhere.[7]

A memo from the Office of the First Minister and Deputy First Minister[8] in December 2011 suggested that job advertising in the media needed to be streamlined, given the economic difficulties facing the region: 'Media organisations have to recognise that in this new era of intense pressure on public finances, government advertising budgets will decline. The purpose of advertising is to deliver effective communication and not to act as a subsidy.'[9] Then in April 2012 it emerged that the Executive was indeed seeking to streamline the way in which it advertised government jobs, with some estimates suggesting that this could result in the closure of 20 per cent of the local newspapers in Northern Ireland, with substantial job losses.

The print media in Northern Ireland (as elsewhere around the world) has struggled to cope with its changing environment, especially in the wake of the economic downturn, which has affected readership and advertising revenues. Reporting on momentous political events such as the Good Friday Agreement or the human tragedies produced by violent conflict was always going to be easier than covering the boring minutiae of 'normal' politics. However, the decline in sales of Northern Ireland's local papers has been dramatic and has mirrored the drop in the level of political violence since the early 1990s. According to the Audit Bureau of Circulations, readership of the liberal unionist *Belfast Telegraph* dropped from 132,617 in 1990 to 53,771 at the end of December 2011. The *Irish News* has also seen its circulation decline from 43,353 to 41,932 in the same period. The *News Letter*'s readership likewise fell – from 34,338 to

22,548.[10] In April 2012, the *Tele* (as it is affectionately known) took the decision to stop printing a second evening edition on account of the drop in its sales figures and the general malaise within the newspaper industry. This contraction in Northern Ireland media coverage has been mirrored outside the region, as *The Times* closed down its Northern Ireland correspondent's post in 2011, following the example already set by the *Daily Telegraph*, the *Economist* and Reuters.

Economic recession, combined with the arrival of social media and the mundane reality of devolved government, has forced broadcast and print journalism to rethink what is 'newsworthy' in Northern Ireland. For better or worse, in the twenty-first century the world no longer watches as keenly as it did in the twentieth: in June 2012, the Irish Open Golf tournament at Royal Portrush received much wider media coverage than some of the ongoing issues surrounding economic redevelopment and community reconciliation.

Devolution has clearly had an impact on the media in Northern Ireland. However, the extent to which it has brought with it a new form of politics that engages effectively with people's needs and concerns is more hotly contested.

## TO STABILITY AND BEYOND?

> I don't know too many people outside of this region who consider the way that we design our social housing, or run our education system, or provide public services, to be normal. I don't know too many people from divided societies who agree that it should be the height of your ambition to continue with a separate and a separated society. If government isn't about being able to lead the conversation about how we change this, without undermining who we are, without in any way threatening or diluting identities or the right of people to enjoy their identities, then I think government has failed.[11]

In the run-up to Christmas 2007, two men sat down together on a big, red, leather sofa in Northern Ireland and engaged in cordial and at times jovial conversation.[12] Out of context, this type of banter would be unremarkable; but in Northern Ireland, of course, context is all. The two men were Ian Paisley and Martin McGuinness attending the opening of the new IKEA superstore near Belfast on their first official engagement as the new first and deputy first ministers of Northern Ireland. There have not been many more unlikely turnarounds in the entire political history of Northern Ireland than the relationship between these two former arch enemies. Paisley, vilified as 'the demon doctor' by former unionist leader Brian Faulkner in the 1970s, and McGuinness, dubbed 'the Godfather of terrorism' by his enemies, were the most unlikely of double-acts. The event generated one of the worst puns in recent memory from the *Belfast Telegraph* – 'Sofa, so good for new IKEA' – in its commentary on the progress of this new phase of devolved government.[13]

The imagery was somehow fitting, as the diagrams produced by the Swedish giant for erecting its self-assembly furniture are no less complicated or frustrating than the plans designed by the DUP, Sinn Fein and the other political parties to restore devolved government to Northern Ireland. While the sofa was undoubtedly built to IKEA's usual high standards, it was too early to determine in 2007 if all the requisite nuts and bolts had been supplied for this latest attempt to revive devolved government.

How did Northern Ireland's political universe flip so dramatically between 2002, when the system seemed to have collapsed in upon itself, and 2007, when Paisley and McGuinness could sit comfortably together on a sofa? The answer is that the whole structure of politics in Northern Ireland changed between 2002 and 2007, as did the personalities at the top.

By 2003, the DUP had become the largest unionist party, as it fed off the disintegration of its UUP rivals like a parasite devouring an unfortunate host. The parallel with the natural world is a good (if grisly) one, as the relationship between the two parties was reminiscent of the *Glyptapanteles* wasp from Central America, which lays its eggs inside young caterpillars. The eggs hatch and the larvae feed on the caterpillar's body fluids. When they are fully developed, they eat their way out through the caterpillar's skin, attach themselves to a nearby branch or leaf and wrap themselves up in a cocoon until they have time to pupate. To add insult to injury, the larvae paralyse the caterpillars and prevent them from pupating themselves, thus keeping them in the condition of a perpetually weakened larder for the wasp grubs. In the context of Northern Ireland politics between 2003 and 2007, the DUP was the wasp, the UUP was the caterpillar and the cocoon was Stormont, where the DUP eventually transformed itself into the largest unionist party prepared to enter government with Sinn Fein, having devoured and digested its unionist rival.[14]

It is a well-known (if unwritten) rule that divided parties do not win elections, and by 2003 the UUP had been ravaged by internal division. Under the circumstances, it did extremely well in the 2003 Assembly election to have a net loss of only one seat. However, the trend in UUP support by 2003 was unmistakably downwards. The party was divided by its 'support' for the GFA, by personal animosities and by the continuing experience of electoral decline. The 2003 Assembly election witnessed its relegation to third place, behind the DUP and Sinn Fein, in terms of its overall percentage of the vote, though this was masked somewhat by the fact that it won more seats than Sinn Fein.

The 2003 election was the second to the Northern Ireland Assembly since the GFA of 1998. It was unusual, in that the structures of government had been suspended for a year by this stage, and so candidates were standing for election to a political system that was not actually functioning. The devolved powers of the Assembly and the work of the Executive had all been transferred back to the secretary of state for Northern Ireland in 2002, which left it unclear what the politicians would be doing once they got elected. Within unionism, the old debates were rehearsed. However, although the DUP attacked the UUP for weakening Northern Ireland's constitutional position within the United Kingdom through its operation of the GFA, there was also a much more pragmatic message for its supporters. It was now claiming in its election literature that it would renegotiate the GFA rather than destroy it, and the tagline on the front page of the DUP's manifesto was 'Protecting the Taxpayer. Controlling the Cost of Government'.[15] Another sign of the times was provided by the simple title of Sinn Fein's manifesto for the election: 'Agenda for Government'.[16] While there were the traditional nods here towards the goal of Irish reunification, the main focus was on the importance of restoring the structures of the GFA as the means of promoting equality and political change.

The big winners at the 2003 Assembly election were the DUP and Sinn Fein, but the fact that voters did not know when (or indeed if ever) the people they were electing would have anything to do made the atmosphere a little surreal. The system had been mothballed for a year and the prospect of Sinn Fein and the DUP reversing this seemed unlikely to many observers. In 2003 the DUP won only three seats more than its UUP rival (thirty to twenty-seven), but it quickly widened this gap after the election by appealing to high-profile but disaffected members of the UUP. Senior figures such as Jeffrey Donaldson and Arlene Foster defected to the DUP in 2004, which also served to weaken the UUP. When Peter Robinson later reflected on the reasons why the DUP had advanced into its leadership position, he pointed to this as one of the foundational moments:

> This event, in my view, created a new dynamic in Ulster politics. The DUP had instantly broadened its appeal and reached meaningfully into middle Ulster. The momentum was with the DUP and the UUP was on the back foot. Though we did not know it at the time David Trimble still held out hope of an early comeback for the UUP. His theory was that the DUP would prove intransigent in talks and the electorate would then reject an unreasonable approach. This was an error we were never likely to make. We had learned enough from the history of the process, had waited long enough to find ourselves in this position and knew enough about politics, to ensure that this was not going to happen.[17]

For its part, by 2003 Sinn Fein had eclipsed the SDLP as the largest nationalist party. This was partly due to the fact that senior leadership figures such as John Hume and Seamus Mallon were reaching the end of their careers. The big personalities were going and the SDLP did not have people of equivalent stature to replace them. Mark Durkan became the new leader of the SDLP and, although highly capable, he did not have the profile or 'record' of his counterparts in Sinn Fein. Gerry Adams and Martin McGuinness were seen by nationalists in Northern Ireland as being 'authors' of the peace process, in a way that the new wave of SDLP leaders were not. In organizational terms, Sinn Fein was much more effective at election times than its SDLP rival. It understood the single-transferable vote system as well as any political scientist and it ran its election campaigns with military precision, to ensure that as many of its candidates as possible were elected with the smallest majorities and thus the fewest 'wasted' votes.

Of course, the reasons go beyond the personalities and relate to the wider political context. In the 1970s, 1980s and perhaps for a good part of the 1990s, Sinn Fein supported the 'armed struggle' of the Provisional IRA. This made it difficult for a lot of Catholics to vote for it and imposed a 'ceiling' on the Sinn Fein vote that the party found hard to break through. This was hardly surprising, given that the Catholic Church regularly condemned the actions of the Provisional IRA and called on people not to support the continuation of violence. Many found it difficult to balance support for the shooting and bombing of the IRA while at the same time signing up to their Catholic faith and the Ten Commandments (though some, of course, did succeed in squaring this apparent circle). The peace process, the IRA ceasefires and the Good Friday Agreement changed all of that, and as the Sinn Fein discourse moved from a defence of ideological war to advocacy of peaceful democratic change, the votes followed in their thousands.

These trends initially looked disastrous for the peace process and for the future of devolved government. The increased support for Sinn Fein and the DUP in the 2003 Northern Ireland Assembly election suggested a radicalization within the electorate, a narrowing of the centre ground of politics and a widening sectarian gulf between the unionist and nationalist communities. If it had proved so difficult for the UUP and SDLP to establish the devolved institutions, then the chances of their more radical counterparts doing so appeared negligible, not least because one of them (the DUP) had set its face so firmly against the whole system of government to begin with. This was certainly how Tony Blair's chief of staff, Jonathan Powell, read the situation in the immediate aftermath of the elections: 'All our hopes about building agreement out from the centre in Northern Ireland were dashed by the election of 26 November 2003. The DUP and Sinn Fein came out of it as decisively the largest parties on either side and we now had to make peace between the two extremes.'[18]

But looks can be deceptive, and Powell was wrong. While it did take some time for the DUP and Sinn Fein to agree a way forward, once they had done so it was clear that they were committed to the arrangement and that they could deliver on the promises they had made. To view this as a radicalization is to look at Northern Ireland through the wrong end of the political telescope: it was not so much the electorate that was moving as the parties themselves. Both were shifting onto the centre ground because that was where the votes could be found. The DUP had moved from fierce opposition to the devolved structures, through a period of critical engagement, and finally to an enthusiastic defence of the political system. If anything, Sinn Fein had moved further, from an initial position of abstentionism to a *de facto* recognition of Northern Ireland and the legitimacy of its political structures within the United Kingdom. As Noel Doran, editor of the *Irish News* put it: 'In some ways, the DUP have become the Ulster Unionists and Sinn Fein have become the SDLP and that's not necessarily a bad thing.'[19]

Critics of the Good Friday Agreement (and the peace process more generally) had often maintained that it was built on foundations of sand. Its structures enshrined and actually rewarded sectarian divisions, and would make political moderation unlikely, if not impossible. The sort of devolved government created by the GFA could not function, because those involved in it would always be pulling in different directions. Its structures would therefore lack coherence and be doomed to collapse, due to the inherent contradictions within the system. This rather pessimistic perspective seemed like good judgement from 2002 to 2007, as the devolved structure hung in suspended animation and as the political elites seemed once again to dance on the head of an ideological pin over the conditions needed to restore it.

However, while the public mood music that sounded in pronouncements from the DUP and Sinn Fein was shrill and minor-key for much of this time, the melody was by this point well known to those involved. Both parties adopted antagonistic public positions, while they inched towards formulating a basis on which co-operation would be possible. This was accelerated by the fact that when they became the largest parties within their respective communities, the political ball lay at their feet, and responsibility for whether or not devolution was restored now rested with them.

The British government set about trying to find out whether there was any scope for co-operation between the DUP and Sinn Fein, and by 2004 the two parties were setting out their stalls. In December 2004, Paisley sought to reassure his supporters that the DUP had not gone soft by suggesting that the IRA should 'wear sackcloth and ashes', but his party was committing itself to going into government with Sinn Fein if IRA weapons decommissioning was completed and independently verified. Sinn Fein had a shopping list of its own, including an amnesty for republicans 'on the run' and full implementation of the GFA, but by this stage it was desperate to get back into government.

## THE RESTORATION OF DEVOLUTION

The final pressure that pushed the IRA into decommissioning its arsenal of weapons came ironically not from its enemies, but from its friends; and not through the formal political system, but via informal networks and 'soft power' relationships.

The post-9/11 mood in the United States of zero tolerance towards 'terrorism' had led to a chill in relations with Irish republicanism. This was not helped by the arrest of three members of Sinn Fein in Colombia in August 2001 on a charge of training Revolutionary Armed Forces of Colombia (FARC) guerrillas in bomb-making techniques or by the 'pilgrimage' of Gerry Adams to Cuba in December 2001. The Sinn Fein president's condemnation of the war in Iraq in 2003 rubbed salt into open wounds and irritated many Americans, even those who did not support President Bush's 'war on terror'. During this period, Sinn Fein's stock was plummeting, both with the Bush administration and across sections of Irish-America, many of whose members were having intellectual difficulty in supporting the 'good terrorism' of the IRA, yet condemning the 'bad terrorism' of Al Qaeda.

Relations deteriorated further in December 2004, following a £26 million robbery of the Northern Bank in Belfast. At the time, this was the largest bank robbery in UK history, and blame for it was laid squarely at the door of the IRA by the police and by both the British and the Irish government. The final straw for many was the murder of Robert McCartney[20] in a Belfast bar in January 2005 amid widespread allegations that the IRA had attempted to block investigations and had intimidated witnesses to prevent them from giving evidence to the police about who was responsible. All of these incidents suggested to sceptics that the IRA had clearly not decommissioned its weapons and was not about to wind up the organization. It was also, of course, supposed to be observing a cease-fire, and an IRA statement offering to 'shoot' those responsible for the murder did little to reassure anyone.

The cumulative effect of all this was disastrous public relations for Sinn Fein, which saw doors that were once open to it being slammed closed in the US. Ted Kennedy refused to meet Gerry Adams on St Patrick's Day in 2005, choosing instead to meet Robert McCartney's sisters, who were at the forefront of a public campaign to find those responsible for their brother's murder. It was all the more galling for Sinn Fein that the McCartneys were a republican family and that they publicly castigated the IRA for its descent from freedom fighters into gangsterism.

The rumbling discontent over the failure of the IRA to decommission its weapons reached a crescendo in 2005, as friends of Sinn Fein within America finally lost patience. Even Peter King, an ally of NORAID who had compared Gerry Adams to George Washington and who had supported the 'armed struggle' in the past before there was any sign of a peace process, called on the IRA to disband and said that if it did not, then he would publicly condemn it. None of this pressure caused the IRA to do something that it did not want to do, but it did trigger what it now realized it had to do. Finally, on 28 July 2005, the following statement was released by the Provisional IRA:

> The leadership of Oglaigh na hEireann has formally ordered an end to the armed campaign. All IRA units have been ordered to dump arms. All volunteers have been instructed to assist the development of purely political and democratic programmes through exclusively peaceful means. Volunteers must not engage in any other activities whatsoever.[21]

That was it. The war was over and the roadblock of IRA decommissioning had been removed, opening the way for a deal to be done between Sinn Fein and the DUP over the restoration of devolution. By September, the Independent International Commission on Decommissioning had verified that the IRA had 'put all its arms beyond use', though some unionists still worried that it had squirreled some away just in case.

After that, it took just over a year before the parties, meeting in the Scottish golf resort of St Andrews, hammered out an agreement on the restoration of devolution. This refined the terms of the GFA and set a timetable for the devolution of policing and justice powers, which Sinn Fein had wanted. In typical fashion, even this was a messy and paradoxical affair, as the DUP and Sinn Fein (the critical partners) did not negotiate directly with each other, and nor did they immediately even admit that they had reached an agreement! As usual, both were concerned about splits within their respective parties and gave tacit rather than active support to the St Andrews deal. While the DUP had complained bitterly in the past about the 'constructive ambiguity' of the GFA and the lack of straight-dealing with the Ulster people, it found itself involved in much the same thing in 2006. So while it refused to endorse the St Andrews agreement, it allowed its mechanisms to proceed nonetheless.

This set the clock ticking for the restoration of devolution, which would follow new Assembly elections on 7 March 2007. It was promised that devolved government would be restored to Northern Ireland on 26 March. Both the DUP and Sinn Fein emerged from the subsequent election with increased mandates, while the SDLP and UUP continued their decline. The proposed date for the return of devolution predictably slipped, when the DUP leadership expressed fears that it needed more time to ensure that it could carry the majority of the party and its supporters with it. 'Devolution Day' was eventually agreed on for 8 May 2007.

Not for the first time, right up to the eleventh hour both Sinn Fein and the DUP were sending out conflicting signals to their supporters about what they had agreed to. Martin McGuinness told a group of republican supporters in April that the St Andrews agreement represented the next stage in the journey towards Irish reunification: 'I truly believe that we are on a countdown to a united Ireland. [Republicans] must try to understand the anxieties of unionists for whom such change was a terrifying prospect.'[22]

Paisley, like Trimble before him in 1998, argued that the resolute nego-tiating of the DUP had forced Sinn Fein into surrendering its war machine, at the same time as recognizing the legitimacy of the police and the authority of British political institutions.

Given the discordant lead-up, Devolution Day on 8 May was a surreal moment, when even the most cynical of observers was surprised and taken aback by the gusto with which both Sinn Fein and the DUP embraced their new partnership. It did feel like the Rubicon had been crossed. For once, rather than declaring victory for their own 'tribe', the two sides suggested that they were embarking on a *joint* enterprise for the benefit of all the people in Northern Ireland. Paisley went first: the man who had said 'no' for a generation was now saying 'yes', without caveats or qualifi-cations, without side-swipes at his political opponents, and even with a hint of humility:

> From the depths of my heart I can say to you today that I believe Northern Ireland has come to a time of peace, a time when hate will no longer rule. How good it will be to be part of a wonderful healing in this province. Today we have begun the work of plenty and we will all look for the great and blessed harvest.[23]

McGuinness followed this up with less dramatic but equally enthusiastic language and addressed remarks directly to his now DUP 'partner' in government:

> I want to wish you all the best as we step forward towards the greatest yet most exciting challenge of our lives. Ireland's greatest living poet, a fellow Derry man, Seamus Heaney, once told a gathering that I attended at Magee University that for too long and too often we

speak of the others or the other side and that what we need to do is to get to a place of through otherness. The Office of the First and Deputy First Ministers is a good place to start. This will only work if we collectively accept the wisdom and importance of Seamus Heaney's words.[24]

I happened to be in Belfast on 8 May – and I was glad to be there. While academics are expected to be dispassionate observers, I had a lump in my throat: I knew that I was witnessing the end of a political conflict that had shaped my own life. It did not mean, of course, that sectarian conflict had been eradicated; but it presented the best chance of reducing the animosity to a minimum. To achieve these lofty ideals, devolved government would have to make a difference to people's everyday lives and relationships. Saying it was one thing, but delivering on the grand rhetoric would prove to be much more difficult.

## THE CHALLENGES OF DEVOLUTION: THE RECORD OF DELIVERY

Issues do have to be addressed about how we create a more func-tioning system – because we do have a rag bag of weasels in a sack around that Executive table.[25]

Back in the 1970s or 1980s, the idea that cross-community power-sharing would be running at Stormont in the context of relative peace and stability would have seemed like a distant dream to many. The suggestion that it would be operating through a coalition between Sinn Fein and the DUP, together with three other smaller parties, all sitting around the same table, would have sounded like the wild ravings of someone under the influence of drugs or alcohol, or both. But the vision is no longer so dismal, and we all now hope and expect the political system to actually do some-thing to improve the health and well-being of the people who live in Northern Ireland. There is now a justifiable and healthy demand for ministers to manage their budgets efficiently, to deliver devolved services effectively, and to provide a responsive local tier of government that can tailor legislation to specific needs and challenges facing the young, the elderly, the unemployed, the disabled and those suffering from social exclusion – in other words, to offer Northern Ireland-focused solutions to Northern Ireland-based problems.

The question that now arises is: has devolution delivered on the challenges it has faced? The short answer (to quote in full a former Lancaster University student's UK Politics exam answer) is: 'To some extent – but not entirely.'[26] It would be fair to conclude that devolved government succeeded in its first full term (2007–11) in delivering *stability* to Northern Ireland. Given the challenges facing the Executive and the wider society, this was no small achievement, and the 2007–11 administration was the first in forty years to run for a full parliamentary term. This represents a large tick in the positive column. However, it failed in large part to get beyond that and to deliver effective governance that made a positive difference to people's lives. A Programme for Government was eventually agreed in 2008, but it was not delivered effectively. Stephen Farry, a leading figure in the centre-ground Alliance Party of Northern Ireland and minister for higher education and learning, has suggested that we are at a transitional point in the history of devolved government, somewhere between negotiation and implementation:

> There is probably a shift in what you are seeing from the politics of the peace process ... to the politics of governance ... Part of the difficulty, of course, is that while we may move in the direction of the narrative of politics changing in terms of what would be viewed as routine issues in other societies, the nature of our party system is unlikely to change for the foreseeable future, where you have essentially a form of identity politics.[27]

This gap between traditional political attitudes and the practical challenges of governance gave rise to criticism from various quarters, including from the smaller political parties (notably the SDLP and UUP) and from across a range of civil society groupings. The main accusation was that the structures of devolved government had been hijacked by the two most powerful blocs within it, namely the DUP and Sinn Fein. Instead of a multi-party coalition within the Executive, which shared out responsibility between all its different groupings, the reality (according to such critics) was that government had become a cynical carve-up by the DUP and Sinn Fein, while smaller voices were drowned out. SDLP Member of the Legislative Assembly (MLA) Conall McDevitt commented that devolved government was failing to achieve its potential because the political culture of the two larger parties remained within a sectarian mindset:

It strikes me that it is not maybe sectarianism that is the elephant in the room but partisan politics. Because as well as having a problem with sectarianism as a society, we have deeply partisan politics in this place and certainly with the big two. Sinn Fein and the DUP are deeply partisan parties, in that they will not countenance anything that is not *from* their party, *of* their party, *for* their party. Now that is bad politics in a consociational system. Partisan politics will never work, or will never be able to work here. What you need is more consensual, bi-partisan politics in order for the consociationalist model to work well.[28]

Peter Weir of the DUP responded to such criticisms by suggesting that the SDLP, as part of the devolved government, wanted to take credit for positive issues but to avoid responsibility for the more difficult policy areas:

I think there is a slight element of cop-out by the likes of the SDLP . . . If there is something good that the Executive does they will claim as much credit for it as anybody else. If there is something that they think will create difficulties then they will simply distance themselves from it and try to pass this off as the big parties pushing against the weak. To some extent, some of the parties try to have their cake and eat it.[29]

What is clear from the record of devolved government in 2007–11 is that its structures were dysfunctional: the DUP and Sinn Fein dominated the system, while the SDLP and UUP maintained a form of critical engagement with the Executive. They held ministerial office and sat in meetings of the Executive, but at the same time acted as oppositional voices within it. This lack of collective responsibility within the Executive damaged its ability to deliver over key policy goals such as health, education and economic development. Towards the end of its term, the Executive lost any semblance of internal coherence, with the UUP and SDLP refusing to support the budget. Other flagship policies, such as the Programme for Government, either faltered or stalled altogether.

While the DUP and Sinn Fein had now become the dominant parties within the political system and the two of them held a monopoly over the offices of first minister and deputy first minister, neither was free from criticism or crisis. Sinn Fein continued to be vilified by radical militant factions for 'selling out' on its republican heritage and for bending the knee to British rule in Ireland. Violence remained a background threat during the period and kept Sinn Fein pinned down between condemning the violence of splinter republican groups, yet constantly reiterating its steadfast commitment to the same objective of Irish reunification.

The popularity of unionist political leaders also experienced some ebb and flow during the 2007–11 period of devolution. The UUP had already seen its support base disintegrate, with several leading figures defecting to the DUP. After David Trimble resigned in 2005, his replacement, Sir Reg Empey, also failed to reinvigorate the party, and he too resigned following a humiliating result in the British general election of May 2010, when the UUP failed to return a single MP to Westminster. He was, in turn, succeeded in September 2010 by Tom Elliott, who pledged to return the UUP to the top spot in unionist politics in the years ahead. He failed in this quest and, after another poor electoral performance in 2011, was replaced as leader by former local television journalist Mike Nesbitt. Like a football team that goes through too many managers in a short space of time, the UUP lacked continuity, coherence and cohesion. Good players left to join other teams, while relegation to the lower leagues beckoned.

The DUP had profited, of course, from the decline of the UUP; but it faced its own challenges after 2007, when it moved from its well-honed position as a party of opposition to become a party of government. It no longer had the luxury of booing from the sidelines; it now had to engage in the sort of pragmatic compromises that it used to condemn others for taking. As sure as night follows day, when the DUP decided in 2007 that the time was right to go into government with Sinn Fein and to revive the devolved institutions that had been in limbo since their suspension in 2002, other factions emerged to claim that it was misguided in doing so. Traditional Unionist Voice (TUV) was formed in 2007 by Jim Allister, a former member of the DUP and long-standing critic of the peace process. In an episode of rich poetic irony, the TUV has tried to do to the DUP what the DUP had done to so many others in the past, by accusing it of betraying the unionist community. The TUV's website indicates its opposition to the GFA and to the idea of sharing power with Sinn Fein, and condemns the DUP for perpetuating what it sees as an unacceptable political system:

> TUV was formed in December 2007 to give voice to Traditional Unionists throughout Northern Ireland who reject unrepentant

terrorists at the heart of government and who feel betrayed by those who ushered them into government. In essence we occupy the ground forsaken by those who for the sake of office sacrificed their principles ... The very least we have achieved is to keep the brakes on DUP concessions. But our ambition is much greater. We want an end to the obscenity of unreconstructed terrorists in government and an end to the system which ever let them in.[30]

The good news for supporters of the peace process is that the TUV seems to be a taste that many unionist voters have yet to acquire. Despite Allister's high public profile in Northern Ireland, the TUV has failed to break through politically and the DUP remains by far the largest unionist political party, and looks set to remain so for the foreseeable future. While Jim Allister won a seat at the 2011 Assembly election, he is effectively an independent within Stormont – a maverick who is capable of making headlines, but not able to impact at the policy level.

Peter Robinson succeeded Ian Paisley as DUP leader and first minister in 2008. Although he lost his East Belfast seat in the 2010 British general election, this owed more to the personal sleaze that surrounded him and his wife Iris than to unionist opposition to structures of government in Northern Ireland. In the run-up to the 2010 Westminster general election, Iris Robinson (who had also been an elected MP at Westminster, as well as a member of the Northern Ireland Assembly) was in 'rehab' following tawdry stories about a sexual affair she had been conducting with a nineteen-year-old man and associated allegations of financial misconduct linked to her affair: the fifty-nine-year-old MP, MLA and local councillor had failed to declare an interest when her lover's application for a grant for his business came before the local council, of which she was a member. Her husband gave an excruciating television interview, in which the apparently crushed and humiliated first minister reported that his wife had tried to commit suicide at the family home the previous March, when he found out about her affair, and was now receiving treatment for mental illness.

The story led to a feeding frenzy among the tabloid newspapers in Ireland and Britain. It contained the perfect mixture of titillating ingredients: power, sex, money, alleged corruption and religious bigotry, sprinkled with the fairy dust of personal hypocrisy. Iris Robinson was depicted as being an unhinged and besotted lover, and there were further lurid allegations in the *Daily Mail* newspaper that she had also had an affair with the nineteen-year-old's father, but he had died of cancer.[31]

While this led to a degree of juvenile sniggering in Northern Ireland and to a surge of requests on local radio for Simon and Garfunkel's classic theme tune to *The Graduate* – 'Mrs Robinson' – many people felt that she had been impaled on a stake of her own whittling. Iris Robinson had previously made much of her religious faith, and had publicly invoked the Bible in 2008 to defend her view that gay and lesbian people were 'sick' and needed to be cured. She went a step further in a statement to the Northern Ireland Grand Committee on 17 June 2008, during a session on risk assessment and management of sex offenders, when she said that homosexuality was actually worse than child abuse: 'There can be no viler act, apart from homosexuality and sodomy, than sexually abusing innocent children.'[32]

DUP leader and First Minister Peter Robinson just about managed to survive his wife's anti-gay remarks and her extramarital affair, but there then followed allegations about his own business dealings with a number of property developers – allegations that did little to improve his political reputation. While an inquiry subsequently cleared Peter Robinson of any impropriety, these 'special circumstances' (rather than any sudden meltdown in DUP support for devolved government in Northern Ireland) may help explain why he lost his East Belfast seat in the 2010 general election.

These machinations and disturbances at the top of government fed into frustrations at the wider community level over the apparent inability of the devolved structures to respond effectively to people's concerns. David Ford, minister for justice and leader of the Alliance Party, commented that: 'There is too little incentive for ministers to co-operate and almost every incentive to dig your heels in.'[33] This political paralysis was also partly due to the fact that the system itself was designed to give both the unionist and the nationalist community a veto and to provide protections and safeguards to both sides. As Peter Weir of the DUP pointed out, devolution was established on this basis, rather than with the explicit purpose of delivering on a series of coherent and unified policy goals:

> As a system [of government] it is quite well equipped to stop particular things and block particular things. Therefore from a unionist or a nationalist perspective you can stop something which you think could be fairly unpalatable for your community from happening. Forcing a minister to do a particular thing, it's very difficult in that regard and I think that is an inevitable weakness of the system.[34]

This slightly negative perspective on how the dynamics of the political system have affected the record of government was emphasized rather directly by Justice Minister David Ford. This was an extra ministerial position, created as a result of agreement over the devolution of policing and justice responsibilities to Northern Ireland in February 2010. It was an extremely sensitive area, and deciding who could be accepted as the minister was driven more by negative than by positive factors:

> The reason why I am justice minister is not because they all love me, it's because they all hate other people more! I mean, let's be completely blunt about it. The DUP would not have a nationalist minister, nor would they have an Ulster Unionist minister. Sinn Fein would not have a unionist minister nor would they have an SDLP minister . . . So there wasn't much choice [other than to appoint a member of the Alliance Party].[35]

The evolution of a political system based on what people would not accept, rather than on what they could unite around, partly explains why it has struggled to deliver on its policy agenda. The Alliance Party's Stephen Farry suggested that the political system was capable of functioning reasonably well in areas where the parties could agree over general policy, but would grind to a halt once more divisive issues came onto the agenda:

> Where the parties agree on things, progress happens. Where they don't, it gets parked. If something doesn't really touch a raw nerve across the unionist/nationalist divide then the parties can find a way to resolve it. Anything that remotely creates a difficulty in that sense gets vetoed by one or other side and then it actually gets parked.[36]

Criticism of the record of government was also heard across civil society, with trade unions, community development organizations and the business sector voicing concerns over either the pace or the direction of policy. Nigel Smyth, Director-General of the CBI in Northern Ireland, suggested that devolved government had brought stability, but was less impressive in terms of its record of delivery:

> I don't think we should underestimate the progress that has been made. I think we've gone from the 'war' to the 'peace' and I would be

positive on that. Have we gone to good government? The answer is that we have not. [The system] is not designed to deliver good, efficient government [that is] agile and responsive. So that is where you would see the frustration of business coming in.[37]

A new NGO emerged in 2010 with the title Platform for Change. It launched a petition calling for a 'step-change' in the nature of politics in Northern Ireland, where political power was 'genuinely shared, not shared out'.[38] This was a reference to the common allegation that devolution amounted to a sectarian carve-up by Sinn Fein and the DUP, rather than a properly functioning democratic system:

> While the Good Friday Agreement raised deeply felt hopes that a new future lay ahead, disillusionment has grown in subsequent years, with the post-agreement institutions as often in abeyance as in operation. Commitment to the common good has repeatedly been trumped by a partisan political agenda, frustrating widely shared aspirations for the focus to shift to day-to-day economic and social concerns. Most pressing among these, the political impasse over academic selection has displayed a cavalier attitude to the concerns of parents, teachers and children.[39]

While this represents a small faction within the liberal intelligentsia, it nonetheless captures the essential criticism of the experience of devolution for many people. The system was stable but dysfunctional and mired in sectarian gridlock and paralysis.

The 2008 Programme for Government (PfG) declared that devolved government aimed 'to build a peaceful, fair and prosperous society in Northern Ireland, with respect for the rule of law and where everyone can enjoy a better quality of life now and in years to come'.[40] However, prosperity was torpedoed by the global economic crisis that hit the UK and Ireland from 2008 onwards, while the PfG's other objectives met with varying degrees of success.

The commitment of the 2010 British coalition government to reduce the budget deficit had obvious knock-on effects in Northern Ireland. The devolved government had its budget cut by £128 million in 2011, which left it in the unfortunate position of looking like an enforcer of austerity rather than a creator of prosperity. The more fundamental problem was that the 'mandatory coalition' of parties, with their separate agendas and priorities, could not agree on a coherent set of policies and 'was unable to overcome entrenched sectarian attitudes and behaviours'.[41]

For long periods of time in its first full term, the devolved government seemed gridlocked. There were lots of arguments between the political parties, but very little action to deal with the practical issues that people were worried about, linked to ongoing community sectarianism, the future of the education system or the funding of the health service. May Blood, a community leader who had lived and worked in the Shankill area of Belfast for the previous thirty years, encapsulated the sense of disappointment that many ordinary people felt about the inability of the formal political process to deliver on the ground:

> Politics on the Shankill I would say has taken a big dip. From 1998, when the Good Friday Agreement was signed, there were enormous promises made around that, [but] they were never fulfilled ... The Agreement at this time means nothing to them, and if you speak to people on the [Shankill] Road, they will tell you they are fed up listening to the politicians and they are sick of politics. My big fight now is to get people to vote ... If you look at health, all we hear about is cuts in the health programme, and yet health on the Shankill is a big, big issue. If you look at education, it's in a mess. If you look at planning, who knows where that's going, and people have just said to themselves 'it's not working'.[42]

This sense of disappointment, disillusionment and cynicism about the inability of the formal political system to deliver at the ground level or to address the practical, economic and social problems that people were facing in Northern Ireland was a frequent motif of the 2007–11 period. The leading voluntary and community sector group – Northern Ireland Council for Voluntary Action (NICVA) – summed up the general mood in its 2011 policy manifesto:

> No one can be in any doubt that, in many ways, Northern Ireland is a very different place now than it was 10 years ago. However, for many people and communities, life hasn't changed much and statistics on poverty, inequality and inclusion show that in some cases problems are getting worse.[43]

Northern Ireland is not the only place where people are bored and frustrated by their political systems; but for many other societies this is partly a result of a blasé attitude towards ageing institutions that are worn with the comfort of old carpet slippers. Northern Ireland's formal political system was still in its infancy in 2007–11 and should still have been able to generate some lustre, vibrancy and even excitement among those expected to participate in it. The fact that it could not, and that people felt disconnected from it in terms of 'bread and butter' issues, was a problem for the wider peace process. If the devolved institutions could not deal with sectarianism, unemployment and the litany of other problems that people faced on a daily basis, then what was the point of the GFA or the peace process more generally? The heady days of 1998 were long gone. If they bothered to participate in the democratic process at all, those who made their way to the polling stations walked with more of a trudge than a skip.

## A LACK OF COHESION

Despite all the press conferences and political gravitas of Stormont between 2007 and 2011, there was a clear gap between the rhetoric of policy statements such as the 2008 PfG and the practical effect these had on people's everyday lives. It proved relatively easy for the multi-party coalition to agree on a series of vaguely progressive principles, but it seemed much more difficult to crystallize these into coherent policies that mattered to people. Once again, one of the underlying reasons for this was that disagreement over fundamental direction lay at the heart of government. One of the more prominent illustrations of this was provided by the Cohesion, Sharing and Integration (CSI) consultation document in 2010,[44] which became a centrepiece of the devolved administration's efforts to connect into wider community relations issues.

CSI was actually a significant revision of the 2005 flagship policy on community relations *A Shared Future*.[45] It was not lost on people that the *Shared Future* document had been written by the Northern Ireland Office while the devolved government was suspended and that its reworking by the local parties in 2010 represented a fundamental change of direction.

Critics were quick to point out that CSI had very little to say about sharing or integration by the communities and was actually based on celebrating and perpetuating the diversity and separation of unionist and nationalist traditions.[46] SDLP MLA Conall McDevitt argued that the

CSI strategy was incapable of dealing with sectarianism because it totally failed to promote community integration and shared values in Northern Ireland:

> Envisaging the future of this community needs to go way beyond the bi-communal, bi-polar separate but equal future for Northern Ireland. It needs to actually understand that integration will be the order of the day in the decades ahead and that there is a duty on government to promote that, be it integration in housing and public services, be it integration in education. If government can't step up to that mark and if government can't set the standard for society to follow, well then, what right does anyone in political authority have to ask more of any section of society? So CSI doesn't just fail to deliver, it fails even to envisage what it is we should be working towards.[47]

A wide array of different civil society organizations also criticized CSI as either too vague and unspecific to be implementable or actually flawed at the philosophical level. The following response to CSI from the Chartered Institute of Housing makes the point several times that it is unclear either what CSI aims to achieve in terms of cohesion, integration and sharing, or what mechanisms it will put in place to achieve it: 'We would suggest that CSI defines what is meant by the terms cohesion, sharing and integration and also by shared future, shared neighbourhoods and shared housing. Clarity on what is actually intended by these terms would be helpful in taking the programme forward.'[48] The Rural Community Network (RCN) also welcomed the fact that a strategy had at least been agreed between the DUP and Sinn Fein; but, like other observers, it expressed disappointment over the ambiguity at the heart of the policy:

> Whilst RCN would endorse many of the sentiments included within the document we would be concerned that the programme does not clearly define cohesion, integration, community relations, sectarianism or segregation. The failure to set out clear definitions means that the programme is more ambiguous than it should be and many of the key terms are open to interpretation. This lack of clarity fundamentally weakens the programme. We would also be concerned that the Programme does not clearly set out an action plan for implementation with clear timescales, resource allocations and hoped for outcomes.[49]

From the perspective of community development initiatives such as the Belfast Interface Project, CSI was a relatively useless policy, which failed to provide either the intellectual framework or the financial means to implement the values that it espoused:

> We need to tackle the sectarianism that is inherent right across the society here . . . [CSI] was generally lambasted, not for the fact that the document didn't say all of the right things; it just didn't give any substance or any detail to it, or any way of implementing it. If you were kind, you would say that it was deliberate because they were letting the people decide. If you were being unkind you would say that it was an absolute mess and it needed to be rewritten again.[50]

The CSI strategy was clearly an area of policy failure for the outgoing devolved government in 2011, but there was at least a recognition that delivery of a more coherent set of goals around issues of community sectarianism would become a critical benchmark for the 2011–15 administration. The problem here is that there remains both a psychological and a physical gap between the political rhetoric and the sectarian reality in Northern Ireland. While politicians and many of those who vote for them talk of the need for sharing and integration by unionist and nationalist communities, they actually do very little in practice to achieve it. While people are quick to speak of their support for integrated education, the vast majority of parents still educate their children separately, live in religiously and politically segregated communities, socialize apart and bury their loved ones in different graveyards.

There are dozens of examples of how the real-world experience of division in Northern Ireland continues to evade the aspirational goals of the peace process. One of the more ironic was provided by the decision to erect a barrier in the grounds of a religiously integrated school as part of a wider effort to manage violence between Catholic and Protestant residents in this part of North Belfast:

> In May 2007 the [Northern Ireland Office] announced that an eight metre high fence was to be built in the playground of Hazelwood Integrated Primary School on Whitewell Road in north Belfast to protect the houses and residents of Old Throne Park from attack . . . while the barrier might well provide some sense of security and safety to the residents of Old Throne Park it also served to reinforce in a

very visible way the ongoing divisions and territoriality that persists in parts of Belfast.[51]

Justice Minister David Ford has indicated his intention of mediating community tensions so that mechanisms other than erecting physical barriers between the two communities are found:

> It is very easy to put up a wall as a way of dealing with a short-term issue, [but] it is quite hard to take them down. I'm quite proud of the fact that one of the things I did last summer [2010] was to refuse to extend a so-called 'peace wall', and said that instead we needed to put more money into the community safety unit and into direct engagement on the ground with young people . . . I took action last summer not to extend the peace wall but instead to put the resources into dealing with the community relations issues.[52]

However, the reality is that since 1998 this mechanism has increased rather than decreased in frequency of use, and the number of barriers and peace walls in the Greater Belfast area has risen significantly, because communities feel under threat of sectarian attack from their neighbours. The task of taking them down will only be accomplished if the unionists and nationalists who live in their shadow believe that doing so will make them no more vulnerable to attack. At present they do not believe that, and it will require a step-change in the political culture of Northern Ireland before they do.

As the editor of the *Irish News* points out, despite the agreements made between the party elites, and despite the new political structures that have resulted from them, the basic sectarian fault-lines that run through Northern Ireland remain largely in place:

> This is a divided society. You can't revel in that [and] you can't retreat into the trenches. But you still have to recognize that there are basic differences out there and that they are always likely to endure in some shape or form. But they have evolved, they are different and if [sectarianism] is largely below the surface then that has to be a good thing.[53]

The sad reality is that the conflict mindsets that built up over several generations are alive and well in Northern Ireland and will take more than a set of policy documents to change. A culture of sectarianism does lie beneath the surface of society and remains the bedrock on which Northern

Ireland is built. While much of this is latent and understated, it continues to threaten the peace process, as some people are still prepared to kill those they regard as posing a threat to their political and cultural identity.

The perhaps frightening truth is that nineteen years after the initial ceasefires, fifteen years after the Good Friday Agreement and six years after the full implementation of devolved government, sectarian attitudes seem stubbornly undiminished in Northern Ireland. While devolution has delivered stability, it has so far failed to develop policies capable of promoting reconciliation within the wider community. Unless this is addressed and remedied in a way that changes the mindsets of unionists and nationalists, a dark shadow will remain over the future of Northern Ireland and over the long-term viability of the peace process.

# CHAPTER NINE

# DISSENTING VOICES, 2010–12

AT AROUND 10 P.M. on 26 April 2012, a mother from Derry brought her eighteen-year-old son to an alleyway in the city to be shot. This was done 'by appointment', on the orders of the republican vigilante group Republican Action Against Drugs (RAAD). He was 'kneecapped' shortly afterwards for alleged drug dealing and other anti-social activities in the Creggan area of the city. The brutal choice he faced was either to turn up to face the summary justice of his self-appointed accusers or have them attack his home, which would have put the rest of his family in danger. The grisly 'code of conduct' that is often followed in these cases is that those who turn up for their 'punishment' get shot through soft-tissue areas or through the front of their legs, while those who do not get shot through major bone-mass areas or through the back of the kneecaps or ankle joints. As the exit wounds are larger than the entry point of the bullets, being shot in the back of the knee can cause much more lasting damage to the victims, including permanent disability. This comparatively 'lucky' individual was shot once in either leg and still has a bullet lodged behind his right kneecap, as surgeons feared that removing it might cause further damage. When his mother was asked why she did not contact the police to tell them her son had been threatened, she said: 'We hold staunch republican views . . . I also believe that it was better he is shot in the legs now, than shot in the head further down the line.'[1]

It is hard to imagine a more dismal vision of 'post-conflict' Northern Ireland than this form of 'Hobson's choice'. It could have been an exchange straight out of the 1980s, but it reflects the everyday reality for some people living in Northern Ireland today. In the 1980s, these punishment beatings led to the formation of a community-based NGO called FAIT (Families Against Intimidation and Terror – see chapter 4). It was initiated by families scarred by the trauma and brutality of these mutilating attacks, some of which led to the death of those involved. While FAIT eventually disintegrated amid embarrassing allegations of corruption and financial mismanagement, it was quite successful in terms of getting the media to focus on punishment attacks and on those who could be held responsible for them.

Fast-forward to 2012, and we have a similar chain of events unfolding with the creation of MOVE ON (Mothers Opposed to Violence Everywhere in Our Neighbourhoods). The emergence of this grouping mirrors that of its predecessor over twenty years ago, though there is no connection between the two. Karen Mullen, one of MOVE ON's founding members, suggested that it was driven by a group of mothers who felt they had to do something to try to protect their children in the face of such intimidation and the inability of more formal policing and justice structures to come to their aid:

> It became apparent, through the reliable community grapevine, that a number of parents were expected to present their sons at a specific location to be shot by RAAD, and if they refused their children would be blasted with shotguns. So the message was really simple – bring your wains to be brutalised or we will brutalise them even worse . . . Faced with the decision to allow their children to be brutalised with shotguns or present them to be shot, in the interest of their children's safety, and their own, [parents] decided on the lesser of two evils . . . After these events we decided that it was not enough to react in anger after such incidents, but we needed to organise as mothers to do what we could at grassroots level to prevent such actions and offer support to other isolated mothers who have lived this nightmare. MOVE ON was created.[2]

We were, of course, meant to be past all this, and the time when NGOs emerged to deal with the traumas associated with paramilitary violence was supposed to be a distant footnote to the 'Troubles'. In the vernacular of the twenty-first century, such activity was clearly 'trending' in Derry and elsewhere across Northern Ireland during 2012.

On 3 April, at 10.30 p.m., a gang burst into a house in Strabane, intent on dealing with a twenty-six-year-old man who had missed his 'appointment' with RAAD. The man was beaten with an iron bar and shot in one knee in front of his partner and her eight-year-old daughter. An attempt to shoot him in his other knee only failed because the gun jammed.

On another occasion, a father from Derry explained the brutal reality of life for some people living in Northern Ireland today. He was forced to accompany his son – who had been accused of involvement in a bar-room brawl – to 'an appointment' with RAAD: 'I could have went to the police. But we're not living in a normal society . . . That was probably my easiest option – to do that and it was the second-hardest thing I [have] done in my life. The first was burying my daughter.'³

These violent incidents demonstrate two wider themes. First, while a lot has changed in Northern Ireland since the height of the conflict, there are also some points of continuity. The persistence of vigilante groups exercising social control in urban working-class areas is one such instance. Second, the existence of devolved government and a reformed policing and justice system acceptable to both unionist and nationalist communities has made little difference to the immediate sense of security of people such as Karen Mullen or those her new organization is trying to help.

Despite the fact that Northern Ireland's devolved government employs over 160 journalists, there were few press releases from the Office of the First Minister and Deputy First Minister (OFMDFM) following these events: such bad-news stories do not fit the narrative of how Northern Ireland is moving forward to a more hopeful and prosperous future. The list of press releases from OFMDFM in April and May 2012 focused on congratulating Ulster for reaching Rugby Union's Heineken Cup Final and a blizzard of announcements about new training initiatives and investment decisions. There was little comment on the fact that at the end of April at least five men had been ordered by RAAD to leave Derry or face being shot. Nor was there a press release from OFMDFM supporting the 200 people who turned up to a rally in Derry's Guildhall Square at the end of April to protest about RAAD's activities. Such a reminder of the dark days of the past was out of kilter with the new image of Northern Ireland as a place that was slowly coming to terms with and getting beyond its violent past. It would also highlight an uncomfortable truth in Northern Ireland: namely, that in 2012 the formal political system, with its institutions, public statements and photo-opportunities, mattered much less to some of the people who lived there than the whispered orders of RAAD, the Real IRA, the UFF or the UVF, which still controlled what happened at street level in certain areas of Belfast and Derry. Even the Department of Justice, which focuses on issues of sectarianism, policing and hate crime, was strangely silent on these horrific attacks: no statements were released from its well-equipped media centre.

Statistics released by the Police Service of Northern Ireland for the period 1 April 2011 to 29 February 2012 paint a gloomy picture. They report twenty-seven 'punishment beatings' in this period and forty-four casualties as a result of paramilitary-style assault. Perhaps more worryingly, they record sixty shooting incidents (though their methodology includes shots fired by the police!), fifty-one bombing incidents and 166 firearms recovered over the same period.[4]

In terms of the police response, the prosecution rate for these 'punishment attacks' stood at a derisory 4 per cent in June 2012. This illustrates once again the lack of connection for some groups within society between the political structures of devolved government in Northern Ireland and the experience of living there. The police were vocal in condemning such attacks, but they appeared powerless to stop them. In April 2012, PSNI Chief Constable Matt Baggott announced a new telephone 'hotline' to encourage people to come forward with information on such attacks. This is unlikely to help much, given that the contact numbers for the police are already well known to most people; the point is that they either do not want or are too afraid to contact the police about criminal activity taking place in their areas.

The inability of the police to prosecute the leaders of RAAD and prevent these punishment attacks from taking place demonstrates the gap between the formal political system and life as it is lived at the community level in Northern Ireland. Despite all the public condemnations, and regardless of how often the PSNI chief constable (or even Sinn Fein) tells people to provide information on those who are responsible for the attacks, they are likely to endure for some time. In simple terms, despite the radical reform of the Royal Ulster Constabulary and its transformation into the PSNI over a decade ago, many republicans still do not trust or accept the police. They also do not believe that the police can protect them from paramilitary factions such as RAAD, whose members live in their midst. There is a Catch-22 problem here, of course: without the co-operation of the communities, the police are unlikely to be able to prosecute those responsible for the attacks; but until they can demonstrate such a capacity, those same communities are unlikely to co-operate with them.

At a more general level, this demonstrates how the formal political system can be subverted at the ground level by the informal political culture: for the mothers and fathers who felt obliged to deliver their children up to be brutalized, the police had failed them, the politicians had failed them and the peace process had failed them. The condemnation from the police amounted to little more than a cacophony of empty rhetoric: these parents had to watch their children hobbling around on crutches as they convalesced from their wounds.

Punishment shootings have been predominantly (but not exclusively) a problem in republican rather than loyalist areas. Nevertheless, in 2002, the infamous Belfast loyalist Johnny 'Mad Dog' Adair was reported to have sanctioned a 'punishment attack' on his eighteen-year-old son, Jonathan 'Mad Pup' Adair, by his own UFF battalion in the Lower Shankill area of Belfast, on account of his alleged 'anti-social' behaviour. It was no coincidence that Adair junior was shot though soft tissue rather than through bone, a 'courtesy' that was not always extended to victims of such attacks. A UDA source from the Shankill area explained the brutal logic of the attack, pointing out that even 'Mad Dog' Adair was not above the 'kangaroo courts' of paramilitary 'justice':

> Johnny Adair is a man of principle and integrity, and that integrity would have been in question if his family had been treated any differently from anyone else's, and he wouldn't have wanted to be treated differently ... The young buck would be told to turn up at an appointed time or they would call at his house for him. You obey. The only alternative is to leave the country. Jonathan was shot in the balls of the legs. The intention was to hurt and scare, but not to cripple, otherwise he would have been blasted behind the kneecaps. Now he's back home, licking his wounds. There's no question of him being thrown out but I'm sure Johnny and Gina will reprimand him for the shame he has brought on the Adair family.[5]

Attacks such as these encapsulate the conundrum presented by Northern Ireland today. It was *supposed* to have had a peace process during the 1990s that brought an end to a generation of politically motivated violence that had killed around 4,000 people since 1969 and had maimed thousands more. This process was *supposed* to have delivered a political alternative to violence, with the Good Friday Agreement of 1998. Finally, following all the wrangling between the politicians in the decade that followed, this was *supposed* to have resulted in the paramilitary factions on both sides renouncing their campaigns and joining the democratic process. Job done, then, as far as relatively detached observers and the international media were concerned.

Of course, *real* peace in Northern Ireland has been elusive, and a nagging question remains to be answered: why, despite all the new political engineering put in place during the peace process, does politically motivated violence and vicious sectarianism still exist? More generally, what more needs to be done to transform the seemingly reluctant peace in Northern Ireland into something rather more enthusiastic?

## LOSING CONTROL

On 7 August 2010, Karen Cole strapped her young daughter into the child seat in her car, turned on the engine and drove off from her home to go shopping. This is an unremarkable, everyday event for millions of people in the UK, Ireland and around the world. But this was Kilkeel in Northern Ireland, the woman was a Catholic police officer and a bomb had been attached to the underside of her car. Luckily for both mother and daughter, the device fell off when the car started moving and failed to explode.

Part of the reason why the attempted bombing of Karen Cole gained such notoriety was that the woman's uncle, Martin Connolly, a local councillor, consistently refused to condemn the attack on his own niece, despite repeated requests to do so from the media, other politicians and even members of his own family. Connolly had left Sinn Fein in 2007 when the party finally agreed to give its full support to the police in the context of the devolution of new policing and justice structures for Northern Ireland. Connolly had rebranded himself as an independent republican and had become critical of Sinn Fein's role in the government of Northern Ireland. Up until this point, Sinn Fein and the wider republican community had regarded the police as part of an oppressive British security presence and as a political force dedicated to upholding what republicans regarded as the illegitimate status quo in Northern Ireland. While the implementation of the GFA was slow and tortuous, the second phase of devolved government, from 2007 to 2011, did eventually bridge the gap between Sinn Fein and the police. After a series of reforms to make the structure and practice of policing more acceptable to the nationalist community, Sinn Fein decided to formally endorse the reconstituted Police Service of Northern Ireland and accept its legitimacy. This led to disagreements within the republican community, and some, like Martin Connolly, felt that they could no longer remain within Sinn Fein. Such people were either cast out (or cast themselves out) and would have either to take an independent stance or align themselves with other republican groups critical of Sinn Fein's position.

The story of Karen Cole encapsulates the working logic of militant republican groups who want to maintain armed resistance against what they see as the British military and political presence in Ireland. The device planted under her car had been put there by the dissident republican group Óglaigh na hÉireann (Volunteers of Ireland). It saw this woman as a 'legitimate target', since she was a representative of 'Crown Forces' and therefore guilty of helping to perpetuate British rule in Ireland. Rather than seeing the participation of people like Karen Cole in the reformed policing system as a new beginning for accountable and representative government, these dissident republicans regard such 'collaboration' as part of a larger political lie: namely that British rule in Ireland can be ended by democratic methods and that there is a viable alternative to the use of violence for the achievement of their political objectives.

From one perspective, it looks both absurd and callous that anyone would refuse to condemn an attempt on the life of a family member, and Connolly was himself condemned by, among others, Gerry Adams for being 'an eejit'.[6] From another angle, however, Connolly was being more consistent than some of his erstwhile colleagues in Sinn Fein when he refused to engage in 'the politics of condemnation'. The president of Sinn Fein himself, Gerry Adams, had refused to condemn countless acts of violence during the 'armed struggle', including the actions of Thomas Begley, who blew himself and nine other people up in the Shankill Road bombing of October 1993 (see chapter 5).

There are important aspects of political context here that help to explain Adams' public position – not least the fact that he was trying to manoeuvre his own movement (and those who supported it) into dialogue with the 'enemy'. In addition, violence in Northern Ireland in the early 1990s was far from being a one-way affair, and there were few voices to be heard from within British government circles condemning acts of violence carried out by the police and the army in the same period. Whatever one's view of his personal or political ethics, Connolly can at least claim some consistency.

Orange parades are an annual feature of Northern Ireland and they have frequently witnessed sectarian rivalry since the peace process began in the 1990s. The month before the attack on Karen Cole, Sinn Fein politicians and former Provisional IRA stalwarts had struggled to control the rioting in Belfast that accompanied an Orange parade held in Ardoyne during the

July 'Marching Season'. The disdain with which former militants are sometimes treated nowadays by younger elements within the republican community illustrates two wider themes. First, senior figures within the old guard of the Provisional IRA are no longer feared the way they once were. Back in 1995, a Belfast rally heard a call from the crowd to 'bring back the IRA'; Gerry Adams' unscripted response was 'they haven't gone away, you know'. During the peace process in the 1990s, this off-the-cuff riposte was regularly held up by unionists as an indication that the Provisional IRA was waiting in the wings with its weapons and ideology intact. However, a decade and a half after the remark was made, it is clear that they *have* gone away. The people on the ground know it, and as a consequence their coercive control and ability to maintain discipline at the local level has largely evaporated.

This has touched a nerve with republicans of a certain vintage, as in the late 1960s the largely dormant IRA had been accused by some of inaction in the face of sectarian attacks on Catholics. Partly as a result of this, internal factionalism over the strategic direction of the IRA – and, explicitly, whether to go down a political or a military route – led to a split in the republican movement and to the birth of the Provisional IRA in 1969. Senior republicans are all too aware of their own past and have been anxious to avoid history repeating itself in the context of 'dissident' violence.

## THE REPUBLICAN 'DISSIDENTS'

The 'punishment' attacks meted out by RAAD are a mild irritation in comparison to the actions of more politically motivated groups that are frequently grouped under the canopy of 'dissident' republicans.[7]

The choice of targets of these dissident groups (such as Catholic police officer Karen Cole) is primarily directed at destabilizing the peace process, whereas RAAD tends to be more focused on narrower objectives aligned with social control. While there is some overlap of personnel, RAAD is restricted to Derry and has a large element of former members of the Provisional IRA, who are more interested in flexing their muscles as community policemen than they are in destabilizing the peace process. Some of them are not even opposed to the Good Friday Agreement and are not as politically motivated as those within the hard core of the dissident camp. The moderately good news here is that RAAD is not against the peace process in principle, but emerged because a small number of former members of the Provisional IRA who initially supported the GFA and its institutions became increasingly disillusioned with the course of events. The breaking point came when Sinn Fein started to support the police and, with the DUP, signed up to the devolution of policing and justice in 2007.

The leaders of RAAD want to retain control of 'anti-social behaviour' in parts of Derry, and they focus on drug dealing in particular. They believe that their brand of summary justice will do this more effectively than the efforts of the PSNI. From this perspective, therefore, the activities of RAAD are (at the moment) pragmatic rather than ideological. Their violence is linked to 'internal housekeeping' within relatively small areas of Derry (mainly the Creggan estate) rather than to the wider political objectives of those 'dissident' republicans who are committed to the militant pursuit of Irish reunification. In this sense, they are not sectarian and at the moment they restrict their violence to 'their own' republican areas of Derry, rather than targeting those within the unionist/loyalist community.

At the end of July 2012, it was reported that a number of republican splinter groups had decided to merge under a unified leadership. The new group called itself simply the 'Irish Republican Army' and claimed that its new united structure would enhance its organizational coherence and increase its capacity to wage an armed struggle against the continued British presence in Ireland. This rebranding connected RAAD with the 'real' dissidents of the Real IRA, though the Continuity IRA continued its discontinuity with these other organizations.

Up until this point, the conventional wisdom was that the more long-standing 'dissident' groups, such as the Real IRA, posed more of a threat, in part because they had indicated a wish to extend their violent activities to mainland Britain. The Real IRA, the Continuity IRA, Óglaigh na hÉireann and other micro-groups (e.g. Saoirse na hÉireann – Freedom of Ireland) all vilify Sinn Fein for moving into the democratic process, just as the Provisional IRA before them used to vilify the Workers' Party[8] and Official IRA. While Gerry Adams and Martin McGuinness are still revered by the majority of republicans in the North (if not the South) of Ireland, they are seen as traitors to the cause of Irish republicanism by these radical groupings that have emerged since the 1990s.

In an attempt to open a political space to oppose Sinn Fein, the 32 County Sovereignty Committee was established in 1997, with close links to the Real IRA. This had a degree of traditional republican credibility, as it was initially fronted by Bernadette Sands-McKevitt, the sister of 1981 Irish hunger-strike leader Bobby Sands and partner of Michael McKevitt, the former quartermaster general of the Provisional IRA.[9]

These various republican groups reject the peace process and the GFA, reject Sinn Fein, reject the new policing structures and continue to believe in the capacity of 'armed struggle' to bring about the political reunification of Ireland. They have also demonstrated – through deeds as well as words – that they have the ability and desire to kill and injure those they regard as responsible for the continuation of the British presence in Ireland.

While the Good Friday Agreement of 1998 triggered a new phase in the activities of these militant republican splinter groups, it was not the cause of their emergence. This had more to do with the wider history of republicanism in Ireland, where 'splitting' is part of the organizational DNA. The Provisional IRA was itself a splinter group in 1969, and Sinn Fein's slow acceptance of the electoral route saw splits over its decision to end its abstention policy in parliamentary bodies in the North and South of Ireland. This strategic shift led to the formation of the Continuity IRA in 1986, though it remained relatively dormant until the Provisional IRA provided space for it to operate, first when it announced its 1994 ceasefire and then when it put its weapons 'beyond use' and made clear that it had ceased all military operations. There is an old joke that whenever republicans form up into a new grouping, the first item on the agenda is organizing the split!

Although they are frequently referred to collectively as the 'dissidents', it would clearly be a mistake to see them as a cohesive group with coherent tactics. They would be united in feeling that the Provisional IRA ended its armed struggle prematurely and that physical force is the only route to Irish political reunification; but beyond that they are highly factionalized. Sometimes it all borders on the farcical: the Continuity IRA, for instance, has itself split into three groups, each of which claims the name as its own. One is based in Limerick, and the other two are in Belfast, under the control of rival individuals. All three claim to represent the 'Continuity IRA' and all have separate 'army councils',[10] though given the tiny numbers involved, there must be a significant amount of 'double-jobbing' going on. The Real IRA can be traced back to 1997, though it has also split into at least two factions, one of which operates as Óglaigh na hÉireann (though this is not the same organization as the Strabane-based Óglaigh na hÉireann, which emerged in 2006 but has since 'ceased trading').[11]

Clearly, the membership and critical mass of these various splinter groups have varied over time. Also given their activities, their precise profiles are a matter of some conjecture and confusion. While this perhaps limits their ability to unleash a co-ordinated and sustained campaign of violence, it also makes it more difficult to control and disrupt them. It has even been suggested that the organizational labels are so transient and unreliable that the police focus on the particular individuals involved, rather than waste time mapping the groups they adhere to: 'What's important is who did it, rather than what group did it.'[12]

To add an extra layer of ambiguity, not all of those who take shelter under the umbrella of 'dissident republicanism' actually participate in or advocate 'armed struggle'. Some are merely former republicans who are disenchanted with the strategy of Sinn Fein, but who stop short of recommending a return to violence in response.

Despite their organizational chaos, the militant republican factions that persist have demonstrated their ability to inflict significant damage to life and property in Northern Ireland. The Real IRA was responsible for the Omagh bombing in August 1998 that killed twenty-nine people. While none of these groups has managed to carry out such a 'spectacular' since 1998, they have maintained a sporadic level of bomb attacks and shootings, targeting Catholic members of the police in particular.

Evidence also emerged in 2009 that dissident republican groups were using new technologies to attract younger recruits and to tap into a constituency that felt socially excluded, disadvantaged and disconnected from Sinn Fein and the new structures of government that it represented. 'Social media' has also been used by militant republicans to help them identify possible targets for attack. In January 2012, for instance, members of Óglaigh na hÉireann planted a bomb under a woman's car on a Belfast housing estate when they learned that her British soldier boyfriend was staying in the area. They used his Facebook page to identify him – not difficult, given that he had posted a picture of himself in uniform sitting on a tank: 'His comments revealed who he was, what he did and where he was staying. After the attack it is understood the young woman who is dating the soldier was ordered from her home by dissident republicans.'[13] A community worker in Craigavon, who wanted his identity protected for fear of reprisal from the dissident groups involved, said that local sectarian skirmishes in the area were often recorded by those involved and uploaded onto social media sites, which then fuelled further disturbances: 'You can see all the recordings when there is rioting. And they're taping them on their mobile phones, put it on the sites and the kids see it so they can recruit and keep control.'[14] The argument of some academic commentators is that social media help to sustain (rather than to create) sympathy and energy for dissident republican groups:

> It has an important support function in terms of providing an 'always-on' space for discussion, consumption, and production of Irish Republicanism and thus a potentially educative role in terms of introducing 'newbies' to VDR [violent dissident republican] ideology and potentially interesting them in 'real world' activity while also acting as a 'maintenance' space for the already committed.[15]

Social networking sites such as Facebook and Bebo had a number of 'Real IRA' support groups, which were investigated by the police in April 2009 following an upsurge in violence by dissident republicans the previous month. There are numerous online militant support networks and websites, the most popular being the Irish Republican Forum, which is reported to have over 15,000 registered members.[16] One online group on Bebo, called Support the Dissidents, had a membership of 117 people in April 2009. A posting from this website indicates the extent to which some were prepared to voice their antipathy towards the peace process and the leadership of Sinn Fein:

> The Republican cause has been betrayed by traitors such as Gerry Adams and Martin McGuinness. [They] are enemies of Irish republicanism. Traitors, and sell outs ... These men represent a British party. The Provisional IRA has disgraced themselves on a national and local level. The signing of the Good Friday Agreement is surrender to the British forces and a surrender of the beliefs the men of 1916 died for. Is this what our martyrs fought for?[17]

Interviewed by the republican newspaper *An Phoblacht* shortly before rioting took place in the Ardoyne area of Belfast in July 2010, former Provisional IRA commander Bobby Storey criticized the dissident activists and their supporters for having no backing and no strategic alternative to Sinn Fein's policies:

> These groups openly admit that they have no chance of achieving an end to partition by their armed actions. Their stated goal is to 'prevent normalisation' in the Six Counties ... This is no justification for any loss of life, and for the destruction of other lives through

imprisonment. It is a huge price to be paid for such a narrow, dead-end goal ... The approach of these groups is anti-democratic. They fail to engage with the broader community in any positive way and treat the opinions and will of their neighbours with disdain and hostility.[18]

This article makes for fascinating reading, given the traditional attitude of militant republicanism towards the need for popular support and its antipathy towards the capacity of the democratic process to deliver political change in Ireland. In an interesting throwback to the traditional republican mindset, militant groups such as Óglaigh na hÉireann and the Real IRA treat the Sinn Fein electoral mandate with the sort of contempt that the Provisional IRA used to display towards the Irish Dail Eireann, and the partitionist structures that followed the emergence of the Free State in 1921. The fact that Sinn Fein has a mandate from the people and that it is organized on an all-Ireland basis does not dissuade the dissidents, because they, like the Provisionals before the peace process, believe in physical force rather than in democratic politics.

The economic downturn has aided the dissident critique, and while poverty and unemployment are not a causal factor in the rise of dissident republican violence, the recession experienced since 2009 has made it easier for such groups to argue that the peace process has brought little to the lives of urban working-class Catholics in Northern Ireland. Some of the statistics indicate the scale of youth unemployment and explain young people's disaffection with the political status quo: the youth unemployment rate in Northern Ireland stands at 16 per cent, and nearly 43 per cent of those unemployed have been without a job for more than a year. The Conservative government's plans to reduce the UK budget deficit also look set to have a disproportionate impact on Northern Ireland: the public sector employs 31 per cent of the workforce in Northern Ireland, compared with a UK average of 19 per cent, and so cuts in this sector are likely to hit the region particularly hard and further increase disaffection among disadvantaged groups, which can be exploited by dissident republican factions.

It is also important to recognize that there is a constituency within Irish republicanism that agrees with much of the 'dissident' critique, but is unwilling to support a return to violence.[19] The Republican Network for Unity (RNU) is an example of a small group that rejects the current strategy of Sinn Fein, but stops short of condoning (or condemning) militant groups such as Óglaigh na hÉireann. The fact that the RNU sent 'comradely greetings' from its *Ard Fheis* in 2011 to Óglaigh na hÉireann suggests that it views the latter's activities as legitimate at some level. The RNU has clearly embraced the new media and is reported to be 'active on both Twitter and Flickr; @RepublicanUnity had 152 Tweets and 217 Twitter followers in August 2011, while RNU's Flickr account had over 200 photos posted'.[20] In August 2012, the RNU was listed on Twitter as having 479 Tweets and 499 followers.

Anthony McIntyre has been among the most prominent of the 'non-violent dissidents' over the last several years, and his book *Good Friday: The death of Irish republicanism* presents a relentless attack on current Sinn Fein policy and the manner in which the leadership of that organization betrayed the republican memory: 'The republican struggle is over ... Republicans without republicanism are little different than constitutional nationalists. The blood spilt was a costly fuel with which to power the ambitions of self-proclaimed establishment politicians. The ends corrupted the means.'[21]

The sustained intellectual critique of republicans like McIntyre, together with evidence of bolder operations by militant dissidents and the lower-level skirmishing of young nationalists within urban interface areas, indicates that the political credibility and authority of the Sinn Fein leadership, which has so far prevented a split in the movement, is increasingly under strain.

## THE POLITICAL LOGIC OF REPUBLICAN VIOLENCE

Why do incidents such as the Karen Cole attack matter? They are important because they demonstrate the gap between the formal political process and life as it is lived in Northern Ireland today. Moreover, they signal that this gap is widening and that the political system (and the peace process more generally) is becoming increasingly fragile. While it is easy to dismiss instances of street unrest as low-level sectarianism or the type of thuggish behaviour by angry young men that can be witnessed across countless cities in Britain and Ireland today, that would be too sanguine.

While much of it may be 'recreational violence', carried out by bored and frustrated teenagers with street-corner bravado, it is nonetheless carefully orchestrated, directed and strategic. In large part its purpose is to embarrass Sinn Fein politically, draw the police onto the streets in their public-order capacity and force a British military response; that would require Sinn Fein to choose between supporting the police or supporting the nationalist community in Ardoyne and elsewhere.

This would put Sinn Fein in an extremely difficult position, as it would risk either offending its core political constituency within key republican and nationalist areas or alienating its partners in government within the unionist community, many of whom are still getting used to the idea that the IRA and Sinn Fein actually support the police and the rule of law. Peter Robinson, the DUP leader and first minister in Northern Ireland, has been weakened by recent personal and political scandals and, if Sinn Fein did not support a security response to serious dissident violence, he would find it extremely difficult to resist unionist allegations that he was in government with 'terrorist sympathizers'.

So while the media response to dissident violence such as that aimed at Karen Cole has featured adjectives such as 'cowardly', 'sickening' and 'murderous', in fact the words that should have been used were 'rational' and 'strategic'. The dissidents know that, by raising the security threat in Northern Ireland, they will squeeze the political space available to Sinn Fein and limit its room to manoeuvre, eventually forcing it closer to the unionists and the DUP. Sinn Fein's narrative that it is pursuing republican goals through the democratic system will then look increasingly at odds with reality, and the dissident argument that Sinn Fein has been co-opted into oppressive British rule in Ireland will appear more coherent. Sinn Fein, the police and unionist political leaders know that this is the logic behind dissident violence and they are trying to make sure that they do not inflame it further by over-reacting at the local level.

At a broader level, the dissident factions are saying that the conflict is not over and that, despite the arrival of Sinn Fein in the new devolved institutions, Northern Ireland is not normalizing or moving into a new era of peace and stability. This had done precious little to boost Northern Ireland's tourist image as a post-conflict area: on 27 August 2010, as a result of the rising levels of sectarian violence in the region, the Australian government issued a travel advisory warning to its citizens about the dangers of visiting Northern Ireland.

Events at the beginning of October 2010 provided another illustration of the way in which dissident republican violence is intertwined with the surrounding political environment. On 4 October, the Real IRA detonated a 200-pound bomb in Derry, causing substantial damage to surrounding properties. A warning had been given to the police, who evacuated people from the area, so no one was killed or injured. The bomb was carefully timed to coincide with the appearance of Deputy First Minister Martin McGuinness at the Conservative Party Conference in Birmingham. While

McGuinness was forced to condemn the Real IRA as 'conflict junkies', it highlighted the group's argument that Sinn Fein had been co-opted into the British political establishment. More broadly, for many former members of the Provisional IRA it provided an unwanted political symmetry: some of them had helped plan the attack on Margaret Thatcher at the Conservative Party Conference in 1984, which nearly killed the prime minister and several members of her government.

While there has been an attempt not to over-react to such attacks, it is clear that the attention of the police and other elements of the British security apparatus is being inexorably drawn back to Northern Ireland by the low-level, but sustained paramilitary activity of dissident groups. In the first half of 2010, there were over forty attacks or attempts to bomb a range of targets in Northern Ireland, compared to twenty attacks in the whole of 2009. While many of these were quite amateurish in comparison to the sophisticated operations of the Provisionals, the capacity of the dissident attacks to kill and injure has grown in recent years. In September 2010, the head of the British security service MI5 took the unusual step of speaking out publicly about the threat posed by dissident republican violence. Jonathan Evans commented that when his organization assumed lead responsibility for intelligence gathering in Northern Ireland in 2007, the working assumption within MI5 had been that the security risk posed by dissident violence was low and would fade away as devolution bedded down and the democratic structures gained momentum and credibility:

> Sadly that has not proved to be the case. On the contrary we have seen a persistent rise in terrorist activity and ambition in Northern Ireland over the last three years. Perhaps we were giving insufficient weight to the pattern of history over the last hundred years which shows that whenever the main body of Irish republicanism has reached a political accommodation and rejoined constitutional politics, a hardliner rejectionist group would fragment off and continue with the so-called 'armed struggle' . . . Therefore, while we do not face the scale of problems caused by the Provisional IRA at the height of the Troubles, there is a real and increasing security challenge in Northern Ireland.[22]

While the record of MI5 in the history of political violence in Northern Ireland is far from blameless, his comments represent a marker being put down for the future by those whom Sinn Fein used to refer to as the 'Securocrats'. The clear signal in this speech was that dissident violence was getting worse and that a significant security response may be necessary in the future to protect the civilian population in Northern Ireland and across Great Britain.

On 2 April 2011, Catholic police officer Ronan Kerr was killed in Omagh by a car bomb, responsibility for which was later claimed by a group believed to be composed of experienced members of the Provisional IRA, rather than the new wave of 'dissident' republicans active since 1998. On 20 June 2011, several nights of rioting took place at the interface between the predominantly Protestant Newtownards Road area of East Belfast and the mainly Catholic Short Strand district. This was orchestrated by the Ulster Volunteer Force and was met with retaliation by republican dissidents, who shot two people, including a press cameraman. In scenes reminiscent of the 1980s, around 400 people engaged in pitched street battles with each other and with the police, amid flurries of petrol bombs and plastic bullets.

Research conducted in October 2010 indicated some level of empathy within the nationalist community for the dissidents' argument. The survey suggested that one person in seven in the nationalist community (14 per cent) had 'some sympathy for the reasons' why dissidents wanted to maintain their violent campaign. While this is not the same as saying that this number actually *supported* the use of violence, it nonetheless illustrates that some potential exists for the dissident critique of the political status quo. The other striking aspect of this highly respected study is that this sympathy came overwhelmingly from young males under the age of thirty-five. This suggests that the most militant elements within the republican community are people with little or no knowledge of the phase of conflict that took place from 1968 to 1998.[23]

## THE POLITICAL LOGIC OF LOYALIST VIOLENCE

> Our war of thirty years isn't going to be like the Vietnam War. It's not going to be people trying to sweep it under the carpet and say it never happened or it shouldn't have happened. Now, the war in this country happened and the people that fought it didn't fly in from another country. They were born and bred here. They fought and defended what they thought was their cause, whether it be republican or loyalist and it's not something that is going to be swept under the carpet.[24]

While republican paramilitary groups such as the Provisional IRA have tended to dominate international media coverage, violent factions have also been active within loyalist communities of Northern Ireland, though the fact has frequently been ignored by outside observers. The primary reason for this is that, while loyalist paramilitary factions have also splintered since the peace process began, their continuing violence has been directed inwards at themselves, rather than outwards as part of an attempt to destabilize the political process. The violence is thus internalized within the loyalist community rather than directed at external targets such as republicans or Catholics more broadly. Their violence has revolved around personal and organizational feuds over territory and post-conflict turf wars for control of racketeering in 'their own' areas, rather than bomb attacks on people or property. To that extent, loyalist groups are no longer politically motivated, and nor are they particularly interested in engaging in sectarian murder. Unlike their republican counterparts, there is no likelihood of loyalist paramilitaries exporting a bombing campaign to mainland Britain, with all the security worries that would entail. So, in blunt terms, they are less of a threat to the wider community than are dissident republicans – or at least less of a threat to those who live beyond their immediate control. They are seen as being a criminal problem rather than a political one.[25]

A secondary reason why there has been less focus on loyalist than on republican violence is that the connection between the paramilitaries and the political process itself has diminished. While loyalist groups such as the UVF, RHC, UDA, UFF and LVF have fed off one another since 1998, their political representatives – the Progressive Unionist Party and the Ulster Democratic Party – have spiralled into oblivion. There is little connection left, therefore, between formal political representation and the continuing activities of the remnants of loyalist paramilitary organizations.

The less positive news is that, while loyalist violence is perhaps less destabilizing to the wider political process, it is proving persistent and difficult to eradicate. This has been compounded by a lack of central leadership and strategic political direction, as identified by the final report of the Independent Monitoring Commission (IMC) in 2011:

> In contrast to PIRA, loyalist groups are finding it very difficult to contemplate going out of business. Indeed, one striking feature of the changes we have described has been how PIRA, however slowly, transformed itself under firm leadership and has gone out of business

as a paramilitary group while loyalist groups, lacking comparable direction, have struggled to adapt.[26]

Loyalist paramilitary groups have decommissioned most of their weapons, but they have not fully disintegrated and could potentially re-emerge if dissident republican violence grows in scale or is targeted more directly at the unionist community. However, they have lost their political *raison d'être* and much of their support within urban working-class areas. Added to this, the police now have time to turn their attention more directly to loyalist criminal networks and have less reason to put up with the racketeering and extortion of the past. Finally, there are a number of loyalist ex-paramilitaries working at the grass-roots level to support the peace process and to convince those who are wavering to do likewise. One commentator explains the importance of this role to the wider process of conflict transformation in Northern Ireland:

> Former combatants play a vitally important role mediating with active paramilitaries and mediating with the most vulnerable parts of their communities. If they did not do this job, no statutory body – by their own account – could replace them. This would leave a volatile loyalist constituency without progressive leadership – a factor that would inevitably damage the peace process in Northern Ireland, particularly given the current slide into criminality.[27]

This presents a potentially unpalatable but realistic scenario – one that is not confined to loyalist paramilitary violence. On the one hand, those involved were (and some still are) perpetrators of violent crime and key actors in non-political criminal activities, such as drug-trafficking and racketeering. Viewed through this lens, they continue to have a damaging effect on the communities they live in and they should be pursued and removed through the criminal justice system. On the other hand, however, within their communities these people and the remnants of their paramilitary organizations have credibility, respect and the leverage to promote acceptance of post-conflict policies, such as restorative justice schemes. The brutal truth is that some of them are much more powerful gatekeepers than are the politicians sitting in government up at Stormont; and whether we like it or not, their opinion matters. Many of them (particularly former members of the UVF) are engaged in conflict transformation initiatives, active citizenship schemes and youth development programmes, in an attempt to build the non-violent capacity within working-class loyalist communities.

To ignore such people, sneer at their efforts to build a sustainable and peaceful future, or attempt to remove them from society because of their past criminality may be counter-productive. It would risk taking away what little glue exists in some urban working-class loyalist areas and making anti-social behaviour and violent sectarianism more likely. It has been argued by some commentators that such people can operate beyond the formal political sphere, in a way that would be impossible for elected politicians or the police.

There is also a suggestion that the experience of political conflict has given both loyalist and republican paramilitaries a shared experience that provides a common ground for dialogue in the post-conflict environment: they are all ex-combatants and share similar problems as they attempt to reintegrate into civilian life. As the central political division has been removed/suspended, it is easier for these people to see their mirror image on the other side of the sectarian fence. Leaving aside the issue of Ireland, many loyalist and republican ex-combatants hold strikingly similar views, such as on the exploitation of working-class communities within the capitalist system in terms of employment levels, on educational attainment and on wider health and welfare issues:

> One former combatant commented on the irony of former paramilitaries engaging in reconciliation while politicians have made slower progress. Many loyalist former combatants agreed that they have found it easier to talk to their former republican enemies than to transcend class divisions within unionism itself. Indeed, co-operation and dialogue between republican and loyalist former combatants' groups is one of the most important contributions to the post-conflict transition.[28]

Like all such processes, of course, some former combatants are much more useful than others in the context of post-conflict peace-building, and there remains a belief and an intent in some quarters that those found guilty of criminal activities should be 'brought to justice' for what they have done in the past, regardless of what they are contributing to society today.[29]

These internal tensions have led to incoherence across loyalist paramilitary activity, with some former militants happy to move into democratic, community-based activism, but others determined to use the remaining paramilitary infrastructure to criminal ends: 'The loose brigade structure ... means that different parts of the organisation have moved in different directions, and while ex-prisoner organisations have provided a role and a purpose for some, others have continued with criminal activity.'[30]

The question as to why loyalists have been reluctant to wind down their paramilitary activities has no simple answer. While it is easy to stereotype them and obsess endlessly about their potential to destabilize the peace process and go back to violence, the more critical issue is: what are they doing today and what do they want to do tomorrow?

The picture is varied, of course: at one extreme there are some loyalist paramilitaries who seek to continue an ideological rear-guard action against what they regard as a creeping process of Irish reunification through the devolved institutions in Northern Ireland. At the other extreme are those paramilitary leaders who have profited from the war economy and seek to capitalize on the infrastructure of their organizations to capture resources from illegal racketeering. In between these rather one-dimensional positions are those who see their paramilitary organizational shell retaining some value, even as it enters a non-sectarian, non-violent phase. It may connect such individuals to others within their community and so have value as a provider of social capital and personal prestige.

On another level, there are certainly some ex-combatants who see the continuation of the loyalist paramilitary infrastructure as an important transitional phase for their community – keeping the old roof trusses and rafters in place until the refurbished house of loyalism can be built up around the old shell, rather than having it all suddenly collapse in a heap, endangering the loyalist residents and their nationalist neighbours. Unsurprisingly, loyalist paramilitary activities are complex, multifaceted and evolving; but it seems clear that there is an equilibrium of sorts between, on the one hand, the profiteering and gangsterism and, on the other, the positive efforts to manage peaceful change through proactive civilianization and restorative justice programmes.[31] It should also be remembered that even those who continue to engage in paramilitary violence today rarely do so for ideological reasons. The profit motive has now replaced the sectarian motive, and violent attacks are much more likely to be motivated by personal animosities or squabbles over resources than they are by political or religious differences.

The murder of Bobby Moffett by the UVF in May 2010 demonstrated that the transition within loyalist paramilitarism remains a fragile one.

This killing on Belfast's Shankill Road shocked the local community, but it was the result of a personal feud between Moffett and the UVF commander in the area, rather than any political disagreement linked to the peace process. Moffett was a well-known loyalist himself, with connections to the Red Hand Commandos, and though his murder was carried out in broad daylight on one of Belfast's busiest roads, no eyewitnesses came forward to the police with information.[32] The silence was deafening. Like the parents of the young men who are summoned for punishment shootings by RAAD, many people still regard these paramilitary factions as powerful forces within their community and remain afraid of them. A special report from the Independent Monitoring Commission claimed that the murder had been 'officially sanctioned' by the leadership of the UVF, despite the organization's claims in 2009 that it had totally decommissioned its arsenal of weapons.

The Moffett case demonstrated that the UVF is still capable of exercising discipline; but it also indicated that the organization is no longer as iron-clad as it once was. Moffett was a popular local figure, and opposition to his murder meant that the UVF had to resort to threatening text messages (which were largely ignored), warning people that if they attended his funeral they would be shot, too. The result was a massive turnout from the community to demonstrate its opposition to the murder and its defiance of the UVF itself. As a direct consequence of Moffett's murder, Dawn Purvis resigned as leader of the Progressive Unionist Party, citing her disillusionment with the fact that the UVF was not committed to a conflict transformation agenda.

## TALKING TO THE DISSIDENTS

The broad picture across both loyalist and republican paramilitarism is that the ideological energy has gone out of most of the organizations, while those that remain have divided and sub-divided on a number of occasions, which has reduced their coherence and strategic capacity. While the dissident threat (and the reaction to it from security agencies such as MI5) has tended to grab media attention, it should not be exaggerated. There is clearly an intention on the part of some militant republicans to destabilize the political process through violence, but there is less evidence that they can sustain their activities either in terms of military capacity or in terms of political support within republican communities. It is, of course, very possible that one of these groups will manage to pull off a 'spectacular' and kill a large number of people in the next few years; but the political impact of this would be likely to damage rather than increase support within the nationalist community in Northern Ireland.

At the end of April 2012, the army defused bombs in Belfast and Newry, either of which could have killed dozens of people and maimed many more. According to the local police commander, the Newry bomb was a 600-pound device – larger than the 1998 Omagh bomb – that would have killed anyone standing within fifty metres and seriously injured anyone within a hundred metres of the blast.[33] The Belfast bomb was mistakenly planted under a car that used to be owned by a police officer but that had since been sold on to someone with no security connections at all. These militant factions clearly can and intend to kill people on a large scale, but suggestions by some academic commentators and by the media that this violence is an increasing military or political threat are alarmist and perhaps even self-fulfilling. These groups want to create the impression that the war is continuing, that they have a legitimate level of support to continue with their campaign, and that this is capable of disrupting the current phase of devolved government in Northern Ireland.

Obsessing about the 'dissident' threat is precisely what such groups and individuals want, as that allows them to set the security agenda and forces Sinn Fein, the DUP and the British government to take them seriously. This is clear from the fact that both Sinn Fein and the British government have already tried to establish links with some of these militant factions, in order to determine whether they could be encouraged to declare a cease-fire. In August 2010, Sinn Fein President Gerry Adams invited representatives of the dissidents to talks with Sinn Fein, though the offer was rejected as a 'stunt' by the 32 County Sovereignty Committee. Adams' argument sounded remarkably similar to the one that former SDLP leader John Hume had put to him over twenty years earlier, though the irony was ignored by Adams himself:

> These groups have the absolute right to disagree with the Sinn Féin strategy. They have every right to oppose us politically and in elections. Indeed they have done in the past and the republican community has delivered their verdict. There is a peaceful and democratic path available to a united Ireland – the vast majority of republicans are on it. As the party elected by republican communities to lead, we have a responsibility to provide political leadership. This is what we are doing.[34]

While Sinn Fein found it difficult to engage in talks with the dissident groups, it was convinced in 2010 that the British and Irish governments were doing so, despite their public denials. In August 2010, Deputy First Minister Martin McGuinness told the local media he was convinced that contacts were ongoing between the British and Irish governments and representatives from the dissident groups, despite point-blank denials from the British secretary of state, Owen Paterson. McGuinness himself had been down that road before, of course, so could be forgiven for thinking that the private and public processes might not be in total alignment. The militant groups for the most part felt that talking to the British government was pointless, unless the main issue on the agenda was the British presence in Ireland. As this was not on the table for discussion, dialogue would be unproductive and would merely lead to the sort of mistakes they felt Sinn Fein had made before them.

While there is clearly a potential for violence among groups such as the Real IRA and for re-engagement among former members of the Provisional IRA who are disenchanted with the modest progress towards Irish political unity, this has so far failed to gain political traction. At times, such violence has actually achieved the opposite objective, bringing the DUP and Sinn Fein closer together, rather than exploiting the divisions between them. This was seen most vividly in the reaction to the murder of PSNI Constable Ronan Kerr in 2011.

In terms of the overall level of violent crime, Northern Ireland today is one of the safest regions of either the UK or Ireland. Ronan Kerr was the only sectarian fatality of 2011, and while there was plenty of sectarian skirmishing, no Catholics were killed by Protestants, no Protestants were killed by Catholics, no members of the security forces were killed by paramilitaries (aside from Kerr), and no paramilitaries were killed by the security forces:

> The security figures for the year show a decline in all forms of paramilitary activity. There was an overall drop of a quarter (27%) in bombings and shootings compared with the previous year, and a sharp decline also in the number of casualties from paramilitary attacks: down from 94 to 73, a drop of 22%. Taking all these statistics together the year 2011 emerges as the least violent since the police first began compiling statistics in 1969.[35]

The average tourist is statistically less likely to be the victim of a violent assault in Belfast than in many other major cities. That did not stop a senior manager at Lancaster University asking me to complete a 'risk assessment form' for a student trip I was organizing to Northern Ireland a few years ago. This again demonstrates the lag between the perception and the reality of Northern Ireland, as he would not have dreamed of asking me to do the same if I was taking my students to London, Manchester or Dublin.

## CONCLUSION

> Paramilitary violence is still a real issue. Dissident republicans are an active and serious threat, especially at the moment against members of the PSNI. They apparently seek to undermine community policing. Loyalists, though they have decommissioned and with varying degrees of success have led members away from crime, have yet to inspire confidence that they are capable of finally going away as paramilitary organisations, as PIRA has. Some members and former members of all groups remain heavily involved in a wide range of serious crime, exploiting the contacts and expertise they acquired during the Troubles and thereby presenting a challenge to law enforcement which is significantly more serious than it would otherwise have been.[36]

While violence and sectarian hatred persists in Northern Ireland, those engaged in it are numbered in the hundreds rather than the thousands. Perhaps more importantly, the political grievances and ideological drivers that underpin this activity are much less cohesive today than they were during the 1970s and 1980s. While young rioters can still be heard shouting 'SS-RUC' at the police, they have to ask their elders what the RUC was. While the PSNI is disliked by some, it is not reviled by a cohesive section of the community in the way the RUC was, and its popularity index (if such a benchmark existed) would compare favourably with those of other police forces across the UK, such as the London Met.

In June 2012, Judith Gillespie, deputy chief constable of the PSNI, was awarded a silver *fáinne*[37] for passing her Irish-language exams and was reportedly one of 200 PSNI officers who had expressed an interest in learning Irish. She received her award personally from Sinn Fein's culture, arts and sports minister, Carál Ní Chuilín, who described the moment as being 'very, very significant' in relations between the police and the nationalist community. Ní Chuilín herself was a former member of the Provisional

IRA and served four years in jail on explosives charges, so it is clearly not just the PSNI that is undergoing a process of change.

The point here is that while sectarianism is finding new forms and causes, these are not as structurally embedded as those that led to the outbreak of violent conflict in 1969. Put simply, it is more difficult to claim today that there is no democratic alternative to 'armed struggle' or that unionists have a permanent veto on change underwritten by a belligerent and hostile British presence in Ireland. This is still claimed by some, of course, but the steam has largely gone out of the argument, not least because the republican community is at the centre of government and the democratic process, while both the British and the Irish states have long argued that the sovereignty of Northern Ireland is a matter for the people who live there.

Without underestimating the violent potential of dissident republicans, all they have managed so far is to provide cohesion to the security situation and to the relationships between Sinn Fein, the DUP and the PSNI. Justice Minister David Ford points out that the devolution of policing and justice powers to Northern Ireland, and Sinn Fein's acceptance of the new policing structures, is having an impact in terms of its day-to-day relationships with the PSNI: 'If you know your local area commander, and you call him John – or even call her Emma – rather than calling them 'chief inspector' or some of the other things they used to get called in days gone by, it does make life slightly different.'[38] Ford believes that these closer relationships have provided the climate needed for community-based policing to effectively tackle the threat posed by the remnants of violent paramilitary activity in Northern Ireland.

While republican militant factions have demonstrated their capacity to survive and to carry out bombings and shootings on a sporadic basis, it is highly unlikely that their activities will reinvigorate the 'armed struggle' in Ireland. Violence may very well increase, and the capacity to use it remains and may accelerate over the medium term, but the key to the future of Northern Ireland lies in the extent to which the majority of both communities in the region feel that the political system and the structures created in the aftermath of the Good Friday Agreement of 1998 are capable of making a positive impact on their lives. For this to happen, the political system needs to be capable of demonstrating that it can deal with dissident violence in a manner that does not divide nationalist and unionist opinion, but instead serves to unite nationalist and unionist political parties, together with their respective electorates, in a joint political and security response. This will be a difficult but not impossible balancing act, and it will be helped greatly if the formal political process can demonstrate a positive relevance to the lives of the people who live in Northern Ireland.

Reluctant though peace might be in Northern Ireland, it is likely to take some time before conflict relationships change to the point where people can embrace their less violent society more enthusiastically. In order for this to happen at all, the political structures in Northern Ireland have to survive and will have to provide real meaning and relevance to those who live there in the years ahead.

# CHAPTER TEN

# LOOKING TO THE FUTURE, 2012–13

Our peace process has demonstrated that with imagination and dialogue and a commitment to achieve peace it is possible to rewrite the script. A remarkable shift that has taken place. We can never forget our past and our history but I am interested in writing a new history for future generations, one that is inclusive and prosperous for all our people.

Martin McGuinness, speaking at the Political Studies Association dinner, Belfast City Hall, 4 April 2012

THE WHOLE PREMISE of devolved government and of the wider peace process in Northern Ireland is that the people who live there are primarily defined as being equal citizens, rather than as unionists or nationalists. The 'new history' referred to by McGuinness was based on the idea that a post-conflict society was being built that would break through the patterns of sectarianism that had so scarred relationships in the past. However, reminders of this sectarian past are never too far from the surface, suggesting that it would be unwise to exaggerate the progress that has been made in recent years.

One of the sparks that lit the bonfire of the post-civil-rights phase of violence in Northern Ireland related to the fact that the political system discriminated against sections of the population in the allocation of jobs and housing. A central driving force of the civil rights movement and of general nationalist disillusionment with the political process was that there was no transparent 'points system' in Northern Ireland for the allocation of public housing, which instead was controlled for narrow political advantage by unionist-run councils. In the 1960s, housing was connected to voting and local political control, which made the allocation of houses vitally important for the maintenance of sectarian political geography.

Many people had assumed that a generation of direct rule and the subsequent peace process would have consigned such glaring anomalies to the history books. But in Ireland history has a knack of repeating itself (or at least stuttering), and in May 2012 the announcement of plans for the redevelopment of the old Girdwood army barracks in North Belfast looked worryingly familiar. The former Girdwood site was a twenty-seven acre parcel of land right in the heart of the sectarian fault line in North Belfast. It was supposed to be an emblem of the new, peaceful era: the Ministry of Defence handed over the site in 2006 as part of the British military demobilization, so that it could be used to provide houses and amenities for an area that had suffered more than most during the conflict and that desperately needed regeneration. Unfortunately, the provision of new houses raised the old spectre of sectarian geography, with fears that providing houses for Catholics (who most needed them) would push the beleaguered Protestant community farther out and give Sinn Fein more votes in the area, at the expense of the DUP. The Girdwood redevelopment exposed the fact that while the 2011–15 Programme for Government contains the rhetoric of inclusiveness, sharing and progress, sectarian realities remain and continue to drive political behaviour in Northern Ireland.

For a start, it took five years for the devolved government finally to agree on a way forward for Girdwood, which goes to illustrate once again the tendency of the system to promote inertia, due to the difficulty of securing cross-party agreement between unionists and nationalists. The impasse was only broken because the time limit on a possible £10 million redevelopment grant from the European Union was about to expire and Sinn Fein and the DUP wanted to divvy the money out to 'their' areas rather than see it wasted.

Second, the Girdwood plan broke a golden rule that had been observed ever since the reforms that were introduced in the wake of the civil rights sit-in protests of the mid-1960s (chapter 2), which did so much to expose the partiality and favouritism within the old Stormont system – that public housing should be allocated on the basis of objective need, rather than on the basis of religious denomination or unaccountable political manoeuvring. The Girdwood plan appeared to be a sectarian 'carve-up' between the main parties (and particularly between Sinn Fein and the DUP), as a certain number of houses would be built for nationalists and a certain number for unionists – despite the fact that the overwhelming pressure for housing in the area came from the nationalist rather than the unionist community.

The Northern Ireland Housing Executive (set up during direct rule in the early 1970s) was now coming into conflict with the political imperatives of housing policy under the direction of the Department for Social Development (DSD) and the DUP minister concerned, Nelson McCausland. Using public money, the Housing Executive prepared a glossy leaflet entitled 'Modern Homes in Lower Oldpark' to market the plan to build new social housing, but allegedly only sent it to those deemed to be living in Protestant areas.[1] So while there was an 'urgent need' to provide homes for Catholic families in the area and little demand from the declining Protestant population, the Housing Executive and the DSD were leafleting other areas of Belfast in an effort to create need and shore up the Protestant population in the area. This would have the knock-on effect of keeping the DUP vote stable against Sinn Fein in the context of a young, rising Catholic population and an older, declining Protestant community.

Finally, while the announcement of the Girdwood plan was couched in terms of cross-community regeneration, with the building of a multi-use sports field that could accommodate games from both traditions and a 'community hub' at its centre, it was clear that *integrated housing* was not on the agenda. Instead, Catholics were to be housed at one end of the site and Protestants at the other, the two communities separated by a quarter-mile chasm of cross-community infrastructure.

It was marketed by both the DUP and Sinn Fein as an example of a 'shared space', but it is more likely to be a contested space, divided by the very facilities that are supposed to bring the communities together. The move away from the allocation of social housing based on individual need to one based on ethnic group membership and a political turf war between unionists and nationalists was more reminiscent of the pre-civil-rights period than of the ideals expressed in the peace process or documents such as the PfG.

If this is indeed the 'future', then it looks more like sectarian apartheid than any form of cohesion, sharing or integration that could break down barriers between unionists and nationalists. Former civil rights activist Eamonn McCann warned of the dangers inherent in allowing housing to be allocated on the basis of sectarian politics:

The resonance of this question with Derry is very clear. I mean what is obviously happening in Girdwood is that houses are going to be built, but the houses are not going to be allocated on the basis of need . . . It is very significant indeed and anyone who understands the role of housing shortage, of housing provision, of housing allocation forty years ago . . . the way in which that played out to detonate the Troubles, which rumbled on for decades – anyone who looks back on that experience now and considers what's happening in North Belfast on the Girdwood site must really tremble for the future . . . I think what we are seeing is the sectarian manipulation of the allocation of public resources.[2]

The 'master plan' for the redevelopment of Girdwood was initially agreed by all the main parties – with the exception of the Alliance Party, which criticized the plan on the grounds that it would entrench rather than transform segregation in the area. This also precipitated Alliance's decision to withdraw from a cross-party working group at Stormont that was exploring ways of improving community relations and developing the 'shared future' vision for Northern Ireland. Party leader David Ford commented in May 2012 that his party had 'lost . . . faith in the integrity and value of this process. From now on, we believe that the debate about how we achieve a genuinely shared future should take place in public, not behind closed doors.'[3] Suspicious that the Girdwood decision was linked to a wider set of agreements between the DUP and Sinn Fein (linked to the redevelopment of the Maze prison), the SDLP withdrew its support for the plan, having initially supported it.

One way of interpreting this whole incident is positive. The DUP and Sinn Fein were getting over inertia within the political system by horse-trading over difficult issues and packaging hard policy choices so that there was give and take on both sides. Thus, Sinn Fein compromised on the principle of housing allocation being based on objective need, in return for the DUP lifting its veto over the regeneration of the Maze. Sinn Fein had gained movement on converting the H-Blocks into a commemorative conflict-resolution centre, while the DUP had got agreement on the building of around thirty houses that would protect its precarious vote in North Belfast at the next election. Both parties had conceded ground in one area, but gained it in another, allowing both policy areas to advance. Is this sort of pragmatic bargaining not what politics is supposed to be about in 'normal' societies?

The more negative way of looking at it is that it was a private deal that subverted and hijacked the five-party coalition in the Executive – a behind-the-scenes carve-up for narrow political self-interest, which excluded smaller parties from access to the decision-making process.[4] The North Belfast branch of the Irish Republican Socialist Party was quick to seize on the 'old history' parallel, with a pamphlet headlined 'Caledon 1968 – Girdwood 2012':

> As we approach the 50th anniversary of the Civil Rights Association, after 40 years of conflict and associated conflict management, over 2500 deaths the northern Ireland state has arrived back were [sic] it started, a state founded on intolerance, bigotry and discrimination. In a shady sectarian carve up by the DUP/SF in relation to the former Girdwood Barracks site has left local working class communities and those requiring social housing reeling as once again equality measures have been ignored in favour of sectarian division.[5]

The longer-term implications for public policy being made on the basis of sectarian carve-ups of this nature are worrying and leave a question mark over the capacity of devolved government to break down the suspicion and antipathy between the unionist and nationalist communities.

## PUBLIC ATTITUDES

The people of Northern Ireland are the happiest in the United Kingdom. This unexpected finding comes from statistics released in February 2012 by the Office for National Statistics. Admittedly, the methodology of this survey was relatively blunt, with one of the questions asking people: 'How happy did you feel yesterday?' Even so, the fact that more people in Northern Ireland than elsewhere in the UK felt able to provide a positive response demonstrates how much the region has moved on in recent years.

Northern Ireland is in a slow – at times stumbling – transition from war to peace. Despite the persistence of community sectarianism and the fragility of the peace process, Northern Ireland is gradually changing from a society ravaged by the reality of violent conflict to a place that is merely traumatized by its memory. For some who complain about the slow pace of change, the persistence of sectarian division or the inadequacies of policy delivery, this is not enough. For others, the mere fact that Northern Ireland has reached a point of relative stability is a cause for cautious celebration.

There is an old Irish anecdote, whose punch line concludes: 'If you want to get to there, then you shouldn't start from here.' A more helpful piece of guidance is that building peaceful relationships after generations of violence is a painful process and takes time to achieve. We should approach the next phase of Northern Ireland's political development with this in mind. Things are evolving imperfectly and at times imperceptibly, but few modern political systems are without their flaws, even those that have had centuries to polish off the rough edges of their revolutionary or colonial pasts.

Two key questions will need to be answered if Northern Ireland is to move from its current uneasy stability and reluctant peace to a new phase of development, characterized by increased cohesion and mutual respect between the unionist and nationalist communities. First, can Northern Ireland deal effectively with the enduring sectarianism that still plagues its society? This is the bedrock for continuing community division, where sporadic violence can easily be triggered either by occasional sectarian tensions or by the gravitation of people towards the activities of those paramilitary groups that remain. However, sectarianism is not an urban working-class phenomenon, and while it may manifest itself more obviously in interface areas, it percolates through all aspects of a society that remains chronically divided. This point was rather clumsily made by a DUP junior minister, Jonathan Bell, at a community relations conference in May 2012: 'Many communities may not paint their kerb stones or put out flags, but scratch the surface and you find the prejudice and the hate whispered behind closed doors or joked about in golf clubs or over dinner parties.' While Bell later apologized for these remarks, after being criticized by Northern Ireland golfing associations, the general point is that sectarianism cuts across all classes, religions and age groups and across both genders. It is also clear that combating sectarian attitudes lies at the heart of devolution's task of fully implementing the peace process and connecting government with the well-being of local communities. If sectarian attitudes can be reduced, that will also make the formal political structures more relevant to the wider communities. Closing this gap between the political system and the everyday lives of the people will offer the best chance for Northern Ireland to convert its current reluctant peace into a much more enthusiastic one.

The second question that presents itself relates to the comment by Martin McGuinness at the start of this chapter. Can Northern Ireland manage to 'write a new history for future generations' that is not infected by its violent past? Maya Angelou, one of the great voices of post-war

American literature, once said that 'History, despite its wrenching pain, cannot be unlived, but if faced with courage, need not be lived again.'[6] If Northern Ireland is to achieve this, then it has to be able to deal with its past in a manner that defuses the incendiary history of conflict. This involves being able to agree on the shared legacy of political violence and to commemorate the past in a way that decouples it from the present. There are some recent examples of this being done in artistic and imaginative ways, though remembering remains a fraught and difficult issue. In April 2012, the 'Everyday Objects Transformed by the Conflict' art exhibition included pieces such as a CS gas canister used by the police during the Battle of the Bogside in 1969, which had been converted into a table lamp, and a bin-lid that had been used in nationalist areas as a means of communication and dissent.[7]

## POPULISM AND POPULARITY IN NORTHERN IRELAND

People in Northern Ireland undoubtedly want to move on from the dark days of the past, and they like the fact that devolution provides a tier of government that can be responsive to local issues. The danger is that the political parties court popularity among their constituencies by 'playing to the sectarian gallery' or taking short-term decisions that they cannot afford. The outlook for the political development of Northern Ireland seems likely to be dominated by stability on the one hand and political populism on the other.

In the past one of the main difficulties was that political structures in Northern Ireland were either inherently fragile or simply absent, as the local parties and those who voted for them could not agree on how to govern themselves. We have moved on significantly today, to a point where the political system is defined by the stability of relations between Sinn Fein and the DUP and where only a tiny minority seek to overturn the institutions and precipitate further political crisis. The main arguments now revolve around the inability of the political structures to function effectively and democratically, rather than around the legitimacy of their existence. In basic terms, none of the main parties wants to be held responsible for taking decisions about the economy or the provision of local services that will be unpopular with the people who have voted for them. In the old days of direct rule, responsibility for this could be placed on unelected ministers and civil servants; but devolved government introduced a new dynamic. The financial crisis and recession have left Northern Ireland's political parties struggling to match their shrinking block grant to the rising public expenditure priorities that face them. At times there has been a tendency to avoid taking the decisions altogether, or to push them further down the political agenda in order to avoid conflict and unpopularity. Like a bad doctor, several of the main parties have told their supporters what they want to hear, rather than confront them with the seriousness of their condition. This populist approach has protected the parties during election campaigns, but is storing up problems for the future, especially given the relatively large size of the public sector in Northern Ireland in comparison to the rest of the UK. Unlike England, Northern Ireland has free NHS prescriptions and it has consistently resisted the introduction of water charges, even as its utility infrastructure declines. It has followed the devolved administrations in Scotland and Wales by deciding not to impose university fees of £9,000 in 2012/13 as the majority of universities in England have done. This was a popular decision in Northern Ireland, but it will cost around £40 million a year; and that will have to come from elsewhere in the fixed block grant provided by the UK Treasury. Nigel Smyth, director-general of the Confederation of British Industry (CBI) in Northern Ireland, suggested that, although Northern Ireland has achieved a level of political stability, questions remain about its long-term economic management:

> We've got the cheapest housing rents in the UK with the best housing quality . . . our domestic rates are the lowest in the UK . . . you don't pay your water charges, disposable incomes are very high, it's a nice place to be from that perspective. We've got free prescriptions and you've got all those sort of things. From a business perspective, these are nice populist [policies]. Of course people like them – of course we'd like to pay no tax, but are we actually building a 'sustainable economy'? And [the CBI] would be a bit more challenging on those sorts of things.[8]

Given the existing economic climate, it seems inevitable that in the years ahead the devolved government will have to confront some of these issues more directly and will have to take decisions that are based on longer-term sustainability, rather than on short-term populism.

Whatever the future holds in store, for the moment people have come to like having devolved government in Northern Ireland. While there is frustration and disappointment over some of the decisions that are taken (or not taken), people seem to like the idea that Northern Ireland has some level of control over its affairs. While few people have 'traded in' their core identity as unionists and nationalists for access to local government, there is evidence that interest in issues relating to health, education and the local economy has been sustained over time and is connected to public support for devolution. When the 2007 Northern Ireland Life and Times (NILT) survey asked whether the Assembly should focus on 'constitutional' or 'policy' issues, only 12 per cent opted for the former, while 65 per cent of people said that the latter should have priority.[9] The implication of this response was strengthened further by two other questions in the survey. First, when the 'constitutional' issue was broken down further and people were asked about the most significant priority that the Assembly needed to address here, a majority (53 per cent) opted for 'the devolution of policing and justice', and only 9 per cent said that a 'United Ireland' was the most significant priority. While 26 per cent said that 'securing Northern Ireland's position in the United Kingdom' was the most significant issue, this was still well below the figure for policing and justice (a goal that has now, of course, been achieved).

A broader identity-based question asked by the 2007 NILT survey under-lines this general picture. When people were asked whether they regarded themselves as 'unionist', 'nationalist' or 'neither', the responses were 36 per cent, 24 per cent and 40 per cent, respectively, with the 'neither' option being chosen by nearly half of those under the age of forty-five.[10]

While overall approval ratings for the structures of government are a little volatile, there is plenty of evidence to suggest that voters in Northern Ireland accept that the political system is worth having and is an improve-ment on the direct rule that preceded it. The NILT survey of 2010 found that 65 per cent of people felt that the Assembly had achieved either 'a lot' or 'a little', while only 32 per cent said it had achieved 'nothing at all' or it was 'too early to tell'. More tellingly, when the survey asked what the government of Northern Ireland should be getting on with at the moment, the responses demonstrated the way public attitudes have become focused on pragmatic policy issues rather than on the identity politics that domi-nated debate during the conflict. Only 9 per cent said that the government should focus on 'strengthening the union with Great Britain' and only 4 per cent suggested that it should be 'working for a united Ireland'. Some 31 per cent said that the government should be getting on with 'improving cross-community relations in Northern Ireland', and 26 per cent suggested that 'tackling the level of unemployment' should be the government's top priority.[11]

These figures illustrate that now that Northern Ireland has established its own set of political institutions, people's focus revolves around how these structures are going to affect their lives in terms of the provision of local amenities, the education of their children and the sorts of issues that dominate politics within 'normal' societies.

When people were asked if their politicians should be working with others in different communities to pursue compromise and reconciliation, an overwhelming 83 per cent either agreed or strongly agreed, while only 2 per cent disagreed and 0 per cent strongly disagreed.[12] When the 2010 NILT survey asked whether they felt that relations between Protestants and Catholics were better than five years ago, 62 per cent said they were better and only 3 per cent said they were worse (though 33 per cent felt they were the same).[13] Asked if it was a good thing that the Northern Ireland Executive existed, 82 per cent of respondents agreed and only 6 per cent disagreed – this was similar across nationalist and unionist communities (89 per cent and 83 per cent, respectively). Asked whether it was a good thing that Peter Robinson and Martin McGuinness had to work together for the benefit of everyone in Northern Ireland, an over-whelming 90 per cent agreed and only 4 per cent disagreed. When asked whether the Executive was helping to bring peace and stability to Northern Ireland, 75 per cent agreed and 10 per cent disagreed.

Of course, these types of surveys can produce overly positive results, as people are frequently keen to appear more moderate in public or when they are phoned up by market research companies, than they are in private. However, even with this caveat, the figures are quite encouraging and are indicative of a general trend towards political pragmatism in Northern Ireland since the arrival of devolution. That can only provide hope for the future. Noel Doran, editor of the *Irish News*, points out that, from a nation-alist perspective, political progress is palpable in terms of everyday life, even if more long-term aspirations for Irish reunification have not been fully met:

> What people do tend to look at are the simple things, like the roads. The roads have improved so dramatically. In terms of the self-esteem of nationalists, to be able to drive to Dublin in an hour and a half, it may not be a major political breakthrough – but it's brilliant! ... Things like that make a big, big difference [for nationalists]. I mean, you could commute quite easily from Belfast to Dublin now. People do much larger distances in London and it means you are closer, the

island is smaller and everybody's closer together. All those things have an impact. It's not the be all and end all, but it definitely helps.[14]

## COMMEMORATION AND DEALING WITH THE PAST

Billy Giles was a killer. He joined the UVF in 1975 and murdered a Catholic workmate in 1982. He served fourteen years in jail. Shortly after taking part in a BBC television documentary, he hanged himself in his living room. He left a suicide note that indicated both personal remorse and an inability to cope with what he had done:

> I was a victim too . . . please let our next generation live normal lives. Tell them of our mistakes and admit to them our regrets. I've decided to bring this to an end now, I'm tired.[15]

Was Billy Giles a victim? If so, was he the same sort of victim as those who burned to death in the La Mon fire bomb in 1978 or the children blown to pieces in the Omagh bombing in 1998? Should we grieve for him as someone caught up in difficult political circumstances, or condemn him as a murderer who deserves no more sympathy than he extended to the person he killed?

These questions go back to a wider and more fundamental issue that faces many societies emerging from political violence. How should we celebrate or remember the victims at the end of a violent conflict? Whatever we do will be politically charged and risks damaging the fragile peace that has been established. To forget the victims or to engage in a collective amnesia about the past is one option, though this will frustrate and anger those who have suffered as a consequence of the conflict. To remember the victims is equally contentious, as this will inevitably be selective and may focus minds on the divisions of the past, at the very time they should be turned to the present or the future.

'Forgive and forget' is a rather trite phrase, but it does hint at important choices that have to be made. Those who say that they will forgive but will never forget are likely to do neither. Can Northern Ireland really move forward as a non-sectarian society if people are not prepared to forgive one another for the past? Most psychologists (if not political scientists) would agree that repressing or denying grief or trauma has a corrosive effect on the individual and that the feelings are likely to explode to the surface at a later date. Should we collectively forget our violent past (or even reinvent it) as a means of self-medicating ourselves into a more peaceful future? One of the reasons why peace is so challenging is that it forces us to make difficult choices over how to remember the past – or more precisely, over *which parts* of the past deserve to be remembered. A fine line must be trodden, allowing the conflict and its victims to be defined and commemorated in ways that will not dredge up unresolved issues about whose fault it was and wider issues of cultural legitimacy. The fact that this has to be managed by political elites that still disagree fundamentally on the causes of the conflict and on how the narrative of remembrance should be written only adds to the difficulty. At this level, things were easier during the conflict, as none of these matters were on the table: the focus was on short-term survival, getting to work the next day and hoping that the streets would be quiet at night.

In an effort to map out some feasible options in terms of how to deal with the past, the British government established a working group, which reported its conclusions in 2009.[16] This was officially known as the *Report of the Consultative Group on the Past*, but everybody referred to it as the Eames–Bradley Report, after its two lead authors. This demonstrated the sensitivities involved in commemorating victims, where issues of victory, defeat and legitimacy remain contested. To take the most basic of points: *who* should be remembered? Who should be offered support in terms of trauma counselling, education and retraining, financial help and so on? The *innocent* victims of violence? And who are they, exactly? A bystander caught in an explosion? A policeman killed outside his house? An ex-combatant like Billy Giles who commits suicide due to depression? A member of the IRA killed by his own bomb? A hunger striker? The answers to these questions remain highly political and emotive, and while relatives of the security forces find it easier to see a divide between the legitimate defenders of the rule of law and the paramilitaries, the ex-combatants[17] on both sides prefer a more holistic and inclusive attitude towards the notion of victimhood.

Avoiding hierarchies of victimhood, yet at the same time preventing a dilution of the term to the point where it includes everyone and satisfies no one, was a problem that the Eames–Bradley Report failed to resolve. Its headline conclusion in 2009 was that the relatives of all those killed during the conflict should receive a one-off payment of £12,000. This was a well-intentioned attempt to avoid differentiating between victims, but it was politically naive and demonstrated the difficulty in dealing with the past, when the conflict is 'suspended' rather than 'ended'. This 'recognition payment' was regarded as a derisory sum of money, a crass attempt to buy off private grief and an egregious failure to value *innocent* victims over the guilty *perpetrators* of violence.

Victims surely have a right to be remembered, but at the time of writing (December 2012) disagreement remains over the definition of the term itself. In the formal legal sense, it was defined by the Victims and Survivors (Northern Ireland) Order 2006, which classified a 'victim' as a person who has been physically or psychologically injured as a result of a 'conflict-related incident'. Use of this phrase creates scope for both state and non-state actors to be regarded as victims (i.e. both a soldier and a paramilitary). A narrower definition was provided in a draft directive debated at the European Parliament in May 2012, which sought to establish minimum standards for the rights and protection of victims of crime. By this defini-tion, a victim is a person 'who has suffered harm, including physical or mental injury, emotional suffering or economic loss, directly caused by a *criminal* offence' (my italics). This is a much narrower definition of a victim and would have important implications for post-conflict commemoration projects. It was developed within the EU to address 'crime' rather than 'violent conflict', a distinction that renders its application to Northern Ireland politically significant. This more restrictive EU definition was taken up by the new leader of the Ulster Unionist Party, Mike Nesbitt, in a debate in the Northern Ireland Assembly on 8 May 2012. Nesbitt was himself a former member of the Victims Commission, and he emphasized the importance of distinguishing between those responsible for the conflict and those who suffered as a consequence of it.[18] Sinn Fein's Francie Molloy responded that this effort to create 'second-class victims' would lead to conflict, just as the creation of second-class citizens had in the past.[19]

These definitions matter – that is why they lead to such emotional exchanges. They also indicate how the issue of commemorating the victims of violence is another front for community disagreement – the memory of the dead being used to retrospectively define legitimacy in the conflict. For some, restorative justice schemes involving ex-combatants are the way forward – such people were brutalized by political circumstances and would not otherwise have acted as they did: as Billy Giles said, they were victims, too. For others, this fosters a no-blame history, which absolves those who killed and maimed of guilt – the emphasis on the historical and political context is merely a sleight of hand to distract us from the hard reality that some people pulled the triggers, lit the fuses and detonated the bombs, while others did not.

The inauguration of the Victims and Survivors Service in May 2012, after ten years of delay and argument over its remit, suggests that progress in this area has been slow. There is, of course, no final answer to the question of how to deal with and commemorate the past, because there is no consensus or agreed narrative on what caused it in the first place.

## THE REGENERATION MAZE

One of the most emblematic examples of the challenges facing the devolved government (and the rest of society) in commemorating the conflict was provided by the decision in 2012 to develop the Maze prison into an 'international peace centre'. It took over a decade for the Northern Ireland government to reach agreement on this, as it connected into issues of wider legitimacy within the conflict. Would such a centre glorify the violence of the past and be a 'shrine' to terrorism, as some unionists feared?[20] Others of the population believe that a peace centre of this kind could provide a public space, where people can reflect on the past and learn lessons from it – lessons that even could be applied in societies beyond Northern Ireland. After twelve years of wrangling between unionists and nationalists over the future of the Maze/Long Kesh[21] (MLK), in March 2012 the Office of the First Minister and Deputy First Minister published an information pack as part of the move to recruit a chair and board members of the Maze/Long Kesh Development Corporation (MLK DC). While the pack cast the project as primarily a 'regeneration' project of a 347-acre site, the scheme is much more than that. MLK is a political site, first and last, though talking about its economic potential made it less difficult for some to come to terms with its obvious commemorative role.[22]

By contrast, the Titanic Quarter development in Belfast, with its new Titanic Belfast visitor centre, is a regeneration project designed to bring tourist revenue into Northern Ireland by focusing on a theme that bypasses sectarian tensions. *Titanic* is the new 'brand' and can be seen on everything from wall murals to a swathe of tourist merchandise (of varying quality). Who could not be proud that Belfast wants to be known for having built the most famous ship to have sunk in modern history?

April 2012 marked the centenary of the sinking of the *Titanic*, an event that was commemorated very actively in Northern Ireland and beyond. This was a non-controversial issue and did not particularly offend either the unionist or the nationalist community (though *sotto voce* reference was made on more than one occasion to the fact that the workforce that built the ship was overwhelmingly Protestant, as Catholics found it difficult to get employment in the shipyard). The next ten years will see centenary commemorations that may prove much more divisive, including the Easter Rising and the Battle of the Somme (2016) and the formation of Northern Ireland itself (2021). How the devolved government and the wider community mark these anniversaries will tell us much about the capacity of the region to deal with its divided history, and about its ability to move forward beyond it.

There is plenty of evidence to suggest that Northern Ireland is moving forward as a society to a point where the history of political violence becomes decoupled from contemporary political debate. It is likely to take several more generations for the pain and bitterness of the conflict to fade, but in time such commemorations will lose their political significance. In May 2012, the Northern Ireland Assembly Commission announced that an approach had been agreed between the main parties, and the hundredth anniversary of both the Easter Rising and the Battle of the Somme would be marked at Stormont in a 'fitting and respectful' manner. If these two events are commemorated in 2016 in a way that connects unionists and nationalists rather than divides them, then it will be clear that Northern Ireland has begun to cast off the shackles of identity politics.

There are already signs that this process is under way, as efforts are being made to confront the past and prevent the dead hand of history from affecting future relationships. One example of this was provided by the conclusions of the Saville Inquiry into Bloody Sunday, which finally upheld the innocence of the fourteen people killed by the Parachute Regiment on 30 January 1972. The previous Widgery Report into Bloody Sunday had been a whitewash, exonerating the actions of the British army and implying that the deaths were almost self-inflicted. This had been a running sore in the conflict, an open wound that made it impossible for those concerned (and many within the wider nationalist population) to patch up their relationship with the British state. Saville took twelve years to release his 5,000-page report on 15 June 2010. Some felt that the cost (£191 million) was too much to pay – the price of political guilt that ignored all the other bloody days of the week caused by republican and loyalist paramilitaries. Some unionists asked why this event was singled out for attention, while countless IRA massacres – such as Bloody Friday in 1972 – were ignored.

But Saville allowed the vast majority of nationalists in Ireland to move on from Bloody Sunday, not just because he laid responsibility for it squarely at the door of the British army, but also because of the immediate response from British Prime Minister David Cameron. British politicians have rarely admitted responsibility for misdeeds so categorically or convincingly as Cameron did on this occasion. His words were unambiguous, fulsome and accepted by the vast majority of nationalists who heard them:

> There is no doubt. There is nothing equivocal. There are no ambiguities. What happened on Bloody Sunday was both unjustified and unjustifiable. It was wrong . . . what happened should never, ever have happened . . . and for that, on behalf of the government – and indeed our country – I am deeply sorry.[23]

This is only one example, of course, and it represents a partial dealing with the past driven by pragmatic political imperatives. However, it does demonstrate that Britain and Ireland are capable of mending and moving on from their violent past.

## THE ROYAL PROGRESS

While Saville was explicitly concerned with the events of Bloody Sunday, his report should be seen as an important building block for the future development of wider relationships between Ireland and Britain in the years ahead. These relations are slowly normalizing and adjusting as the memory of political violence in Northern Ireland recedes into the past. A clear signal of this new 'post-conflict' phase was sent out in spring 2011 with the state visit of Queen Elizabeth II to the Republic of Ireland. This four-day event (17–20 May) was hugely symbolic for both countries. It was the first time that a British monarch had visited independent Ireland (i.e. the Republic of Ireland/Free State). The last time royal feet trod on Irish soil (beyond the border with Northern Ireland) was when King George V visited in 1911 – when there was no border, and when there was no Northern Ireland or Republic of Ireland. The Queen's 2011 visit would never have taken place without the Good Friday Agreement and the subsequent arrival of devolved government and political stability in Northern Ireland. It probably would not have happened without the Saville Report either, given the Queen's titular role as commander-in-chief of the British armed forces and her son Prince Charles' role as colonel-in-chief of the Parachute Regiment. The security implications and political sensitivities of a visit before this new era of détente would have made it impossible, which partly (but *only* partly) explains why an invitation had never been issued in the past.

While the visit was governed by the formal protocol of such occasions, there were nonetheless poignant and important moments. The Queen laid a wreath and bowed her head at the Garden of Remembrance in Dublin, at the graves of the old IRA men and women who had fought against Britain for Irish independence in the early twentieth century. This had royal watchers and correspondents muttering about what a big deal it was, as the Queen rarely bowed her head (apart from on Remembrance Sunday) – and normally never to those who had killed members of the British army. She also visited the Gaelic football stadium Croke Park, where British soldiers had shot and killed fourteen people in 1920, during the Irish War of Independence, in reprisal for an earlier IRA attack.

During her visit, the Queen gave a keynote speech to an invited audience, which included the first minister of Northern Ireland, Peter Robinson.[24] This again attempted to draw a line under the past and to mark out a new beginning for the two countries. While references to the British role in conflict in Ireland were oblique, they were there nonetheless and were easily picked up by the ultra-sensitive hearing of everyone in the audience: 'It is a sad and regrettable reality that through history our islands have experienced more than their fair share of heartache, turbulence and loss . . . with the benefit of historical hindsight we can all see things which we wish had been done differently, or not at all.'[25] The Queen opened her speech in the Irish language, to audible gasps from the assembled guests: 'A Úachtaráin agus a chairde' (President and friends) was a deliberate mark of respect for the cultural and political independence of Ireland and was warmly received by those in the audience who could understand it. Irish President Mary McAleese (a native of Ardoyne in Belfast) mouthed 'wow' under her breath and went on to remark that Ireland and Britain were forging a 'new future, a future very, very different from the past, on very different terms from the past – and I think the visit will send the message that we are, both jurisdictions, determined to make the future a much, much better place'.[26]

This closer Anglo-Irish relationship is providing a new context within which Northern Ireland can develop, and there is already evidence that some movement is taking place. While Sinn Fein complained that the visit was premature and that relations between the two countries would never be normalized until the partition of Ireland was ended, it did not actively oppose the visit. Though they did not attend any of the official functions connected with the Queen's visit, the party leaders in fact had asked not to be invited, as they wanted to avoid being accused of deliberately snubbing the Queen or of damaging relations with the DUP or unionists in Northern Ireland more generally. Following the expression of regret from the Queen for the past history between the two countries, even Gerry Adams managed to find something positive to say about the British monarch: 'I believe that her expression of sincere sympathy for those who have suffered as a consequence of our troubled past is genuine.'[27] While his judgement on the royal visit was not without substantial caveats, the fact that he had anything to say (beyond denunciations of the British presence in Ireland) was significant enough in itself.

It was left to 'dissident' republican groups to lead the protests and throw the brickbats, which they did – to huge levels of disinterest from everyone except those in charge of security for the visit. A few hundred members of the 32 County Sovereignty Committee and Republican Sinn Fein protested as loudly as their limited numbers would allow, while an improvised bomb was defused by the Irish army on the eve of the Queen's visit. But such opposition was drowned out by the enthusiastic applause of many more who felt that the Queen's visit had closed a chapter on Ireland's violent past and opened a new one – one based on mutual respect and friendship between the peoples of Ireland and Britain.

## NO MORE 'THEM AND US'? THE FUTURE OF SECTARIANISM

> The fact that the causes of sectarianism, the costs of sectarianism, the manifestations of sectarianism are not top of this Executive's agenda is an indication of how unable the big two [parties] currently are to tackle the elephant in the room. And without a shadow of a doubt, future Executives . . . if they do not put sectarianism and tackling its causes, its cost and its manifestations at the heart of everything they do, and if they do not lead from the top down declaring war on bigotry, then this system, and the politics within it, will absolutely fail its people.[28]

A key question for Northern Ireland is whether the stability of the new political system can facilitate a set of policies capable of removing the ingrained sectarian attitudes that persist. That would obviously take time anyway, but it remains to be seen whether the limitations of the political system will even *allow* it. To put it in the bluntest possible terms, if a culture of sectarianism is woven into the very fabric of the political institutions themselves, how can devolved government possibly deliver policies that tackle this culture effectively or get beyond it?

Since 2003, the Community Relations Council (CRC) has held a 'community relations week' in an effort to raise awareness of the issues surrounding sectarianism and as a means of highlighting the positive work taking place in cross-community initiatives run by Catholics and Protestants in Northern Ireland. One of the centrepieces of the week of events in 2012 was a conference held in Belfast's new Titanic Centre entitled 'No More Them and Us'. This brought community relations practitioners together with Minister for Justice David Ford and other senior figures across the main political parties in Northern Ireland. Tony McCusker, chairman of the CRC, pointed out that, despite all the good community relations work that has been done, sectarianism and division remain an endemic problem in Northern Ireland society:

> The number of interfaces in Northern Ireland was twenty-two when the Belfast Agreement was signed; today the number is as high as eighty-eight by some estimates. We still see flags and emblems as prominently displayed during the marching season as before the Agreement. Deep divisions in housing and education also remain. To add to this, racism in our society is now apparent.[29]

When Justice Minister David Ford is asked about the rise in the number of 'peace walls' that divide people in Northern Ireland, he makes a point of saying that they have not increased since he has been in office and that he is working with communities to have them taken down. Ford gave a keynote address at the 2012 community relations conference, where he pointed out that the devolved government needed to come up with a clear strategy that can provide local communities with a coherent message and a means of tackling sectarian division:

> History will not forgive us if we squander the opportunity presented by an end to violence to tackle the underlying divisions of this society ... Above all, we must move past preening ourselves for moving on from the disaster of the 1970s and face the challenge to act to make change.[30]

This was an implicit criticism of the failure of Sinn Fein and the DUP to come up with an agreed (and coherent) cohesion, sharing and integration (CSI) strategy that can be implemented effectively (see chapter 8).

Both main parties have been slow to bring forward 'CSI II' because neither party actually wants to promote integration between the nationalist and unionist cultures in Northern Ireland. Instead, they want a community relations approach that values and provides resources for both identities separately, rather than integrates unionists and nationalists under a common identity. Ford bemoaned the fact that Sinn Fein and the DUP were likely to asset-strip the vitality of such a strategy by developing an anodyne policy that would achieve 'maximum acceptability' across both communities, rather than an ambitious policy that would challenge people to confront division and separation: 'But we won't bring about "an end to them and us" by settling for the lowest common denominator – we'll only achieve it by setting the bar high, and working in every department to reach it.'[31]

The current Programme for Government highlights the achievement of CSI as one of its thematic goals between now and 2015: 'We will work towards our goal of a shared and better future for all; all of our policies and programmes across Government will be built upon the values of equality and fairness and the ethics of inclusion and good relations.'[32] The title page of the PfG has the strap-line 'Building a Better Future', and it has positive images on its cover, including the Titanic Belfast Centre and the new £14 million 'Peace Bridge' in Derry, which was opened in June 2011.

However, there remains a paradox at the core of the PfG and within the Executive itself: how can it deliver a policy that seeks to build a shared future for all, if it does not possess any overarching strategy for reconciliation itself? It remains to be seen whether the 'mutual accommodation' model advocated in the current draft of the CSI strategy can deliver the PfG's ostensible goals between now and 2015 (and beyond). It is more likely that the focus will remain on shoring up the economy with a variety of tokenistic gestures towards mutual respect between the two *separate* traditions of unionism and nationalism. This contains hints of Terence O'Neill's strategy in the 1960s, as he hoped that the rising tide of economic rejuvenation would 'lift all boats' (though his confusion of behavioural symptoms with the structural causes of conflict was to prove disastrous for Northern Ireland within a few years).

An acceptable balance has yet to be found between respecting the diversity of the two traditions – unionist and nationalist – and encouraging sharing and integration between them. However, unless sectarianism is tackled at a structural level by the devolved government in Northern Ireland, through the implementation of an agreed cohesion, sharing and integration strategy, then division is likely to remain, and attitudes and behaviour are unlikely to change. In this event, the gap between the rhetoric of formal politics and the sectarian reality for the wider community will continue to undermine the political structures that exist and the notion of the 'peace process' more generally.

Clearly, Northern Ireland's journey out of political violence has been anything but smooth. It has been characterized by as many setbacks as breakthroughs. But the people who live there are gradually emerging into a new set of political, social and cultural relationships. While these are still bedding down, the political vacuum that had sucked the air out of public debates on social and economic policy since the 1970s has been replaced by a new set of political institutions. Imperfect as these are, there is now no shortage of political representation in the region – from the complex system of power-sharing in the Northern Ireland Executive to a new Human Rights Commission and oversight bodies on policing and across other public services.

Many of these structures may not be functioning as efficiently as one would hope, and some may be highly flawed, misconceived or even unnecessary. However, they are not doomed to inevitable failure, as some have suggested, and they will sink or swim on the basis of their record and their ability to demonstrate a relevance to the people who live in Northern Ireland. While some commentators think the structures of the Good Friday Agreement unhelpfully cast sectarian divisions in 'marble' rather than transforming them,[33] others believe that this form of power-sharing across a mandatory coalition of unionist and nationalist blocs has the potential to work as a political settlement.[34] The political system does appear to have the capacity to lumber forwards, whatever its imperfections. It might be ungainly, but it could become more sprightly and graceful if the structures and institutions were to evolve in ways that make them relevant and acceptable to the people who live in Northern Ireland.

## DISMANTLING THE UGLY SCAFFOLDING

Northern Ireland's current political situation is clearly an outcome of its divided past. It has resulted in a form of consociational democracy that builds a complex array of safeguards into its structures, in order to prevent one community from being dominated by another. It tries to encourage a spirit of interdependence and co-operation across unionist and nationalist representatives, without which political gridlock would ensue. This has led to a unique and unwieldy set of political structures, with a governing Executive that is composed of all the main parties and no formal opposition to hold it to account. The question for the future is whether this 'mandatory coalition' will remain, forcing everyone into their traditional sectarian pigeon-holes, or whether it will evolve and loosen up once the fears and insecurities subside. When the then leader of the SDLP, Mark Durkan, took part in an event in 2008 to mark the tenth anniversary of the Good Friday Agreement, he pointed out that the need to define political representatives in sectarian terms as 'unionists', 'nationalists' and 'others' was a condition of the past rather than a prospectus for the future:

> I remember, at the time, saying that the system of designation was necessary because of what we were coming from but should not be necessary where we were going. I argued that such measures with their arguably sectarian or sectional undertones should be bio-degradable, dissolving in the future as the environment changed. Most, if not all of us, had such future adjustments in mind when we wrote the review mechanisms into the Agreement. As we move towards a fully sealed and settled process we should be preparing to think about how and when to remove some of the ugly scaffolding needed during the construction of the new edifice.[35]

The fact that the SDLP was thinking about a future beyond the existing sectarian arithmetic of a mandatory coalition between unionism and nationalism might suggest that tomorrow's political structures will be less rigid than they are today. A review of the mandatory coalition arrangements is due at the end of the Executive's current term in office in 2015, and the DUP is keen to move to a system of voluntary coalition (as is Alliance). It would certainly suit the smaller parties (UUP, Alliance and the SDLP) to investigate some form of voluntary coalition (though they would have to reassure nationalists that there would be no reversion to unionist majority rule). Sinn Fein is firmly set against any such thing (as are most nationalist voters), as it fears that this would allow Sinn Fein's electoral mandate to be bypassed and would enable unionists to move back to a majority-rule form of 'democracy', as practised between 1921 and 1972. Sinn Fein effectively has a veto over any change of this nature, and it is difficult to see the party accepting it. However, as Northern Ireland's recent history demonstrates, nothing is impossible, and it is more likely than not that the political system will evolve further over the next ten or twenty years in a manner that increases its flexibility and dexterity. The DUP's Peter Weir suggested that, despite the current difficulty in selling the idea to nationalists, his party saw it as a feasible long-term aspiration:

> The interpretation that's been put on voluntary coalition [by Sinn Fein and the SDLP] is pure majority rule, and that is not what anybody is particularly envisaging. I think, given the level of attach-ment the nationalists have to more or less the current structures, it is going to be difficult to wean them away from that and I think that at best it may be something that can only be done over a long period of time . . . The safeguards would be that you would be shifting towards a situation of weighted votes rather than run on a cross-community basis, but that would inevitably mean that you would have a cross-community element to any side of it.[36]

The scar tissue of the conflict makes it unlikely that nationalists would find an end to mandatory coalition palatable in the short (or even the medium) term. As the Alliance Party's leader, David Ford, points out, there is still insufficient trust between unionist and nationalist communities for such policies to be reformed:

> We think that [political] evolution would be seen to be happening and would then have the opportunity to develop, if we could move to our preferred model, which would be something like weighted majorities and voluntary coalition. But the blunt reality is, I know that if I talk about that, three-quarters of Sinn Fein MLAs will think I mean to exclude them and when any unionist talks about it, 100 per cent of them know it means to exclude them.[37]

Such a voluntary coalition would open up the possibility for the smaller parties to hold the balance of power and enter a coalition, which could potentially exclude one of the larger parties. This is one of the reasons, of course, why Sinn Fein is fundamentally opposed to it. While this type of reform seems unlikely at the moment, significant changes are already taking place in how the political system operates, and in the years ahead these are more likely to accelerate than to go into reverse. There is certainly plenty of evidence that the future will be defined not by a 'grand coalition' (as originally envisaged by the GFA in 1998), where all the main parties are in government together, but by a 'duopoly' of the DUP and Sinn Fein. The 'junior' partners (represented by the UUP and SDLP) are likely to become further marginalized, to the point that they may leave the Executive and either form two separate opposition parties or else join in a new type of merged opposition group that transcends their traditional nationalist and unionist labels.

Early signs of the potential change to come were evident in 2011, when the UUP looked seriously at leaving government altogether and forming an opposition. In 2012, John McCallister contested the UUP leadership election with an explicit commitment to take the party into opposition if he won. He lost.[38] The SDLP has taken a more cautious approach, denying that it was going to become an opposition party, yet casting the devolved government as a DUP/Sinn Fein coalition (despite the fact that the SDLP is also a member of it). Former SDLP leader Margaret Ritchie epitomized this attitude at the SDLP annual conference in November 2010, when she appealed for co-operation across traditional ethno-national lines with centrist unionists:

> I say there is scope for the centre ground to regain the centre of government, and I want to say to the Unionist Parties that we are ready to work with them to move on to the next horizon . . . I honestly believe that the SDLP and fair-minded unionists could resolve the many issues that were too much for the DUP and Sinn Fein.[39]

Most of this speech was a critique of the performance of the devolved government rather than a defence of its record, and it provides evidence that the traditional nationalist/unionist waters are beginning to muddy a little as the political system evolves. While Ritchie's resignation as SDLP leader in 2011 will slow down the party's movement towards a more centrist political position, it is unlikely to reverse it over the longer term, as it will be in the party's interests to move out of the long shadow being cast by Sinn Fein.

Peter Robinson, leader of the DUP and first minister of Northern Ireland, delivered a major speech in March 2012, illustrating the type of evolutionary change that is taking place. Neither the venue (Dublin) nor the occasion (the Edward Carson Lecture) was chosen at random. It was a statement by Robinson to the effect that unionists were confident enough, in the capital of Irish nationalism, to define their political allegiance as one that is open to all and threatening to none:

> I have said on many occasions that from a party point of view I want to see more Catholics supporting the DUP. I have no doubt that there are many Catholics in Northern Ireland who have much more in common with the social and economic policies of the DUP than they do with either Sinn Fein or the SDLP and I welcome some early signs of modest progress . . . For unionism to prosper in the decades to come it must be inclusive and not exclusive. I want to see a broad and inclusive unionism that can embrace all shades of those who support Northern Ireland's present constitutional position. Unionism must reach far beyond its traditional base if it is to maximise its potential. That means forming a pro-Union consensus with people from different religious and community backgrounds.[40]

## TROUBLED TOURS

We even have a tourist industry now. Visitors are eager to take black-taxi tours on which they can see the murals they used to watch as the backdrop to television news reports of rioting and visit the other 'greatest hits' of the conflict from a safe distance, facilitated by a range of colourful and enterprising local entrepreneurs.

Derry, meanwhile, has been selected to be the 'UK City of Culture' in 2013, which will bring a much-needed financial boost to the North West, lots of activities celebrating the cultural richness of the area and just as many positive headlines for the city and for Northern Ireland more generally. Of course, this is not without its overtones of the past. The bid was from 'Derry/Londonderry'. This was emblematic of the fact that rival identity claims persist and need to be accommodated alongside each other. Some republicans also noted with dismay that it was going to be the *UK* City of Culture and suggested that this was a further attempt at British political co-option under the guise of culture and entertainment. Such 'British-branding' was seen as linked to the 400th anniversary of the creation of 'Londonderry' during the plantation and an attempt to connect *legitimate* aspects of Irish culture with *illegitimate* British celebrations of the past. Dissident republican groups have backed up their words with deeds, and in October 2011 bombed the City of Culture offices in Derry. In October 2012, Lonely Planet's 'Best in Travel 2013' awards named the city the fourth-best city to visit in 2013 – behind San Francisco, Amsterdam and (perhaps less obviously) Hyderabad.[41]

Belfast has also received its share of tourist accolades in recent years. Lonely Planet's 2007 *Bluelist* named it one of the top cities in the world to visit. The tourists who come can sample a rich cultural array of events, including the Belfast Festival and the more recently established Belsonic Festival, which in summer 2010 hosted audiences of over 5,000 people on each of its eight consecutive nights. Even Lady Gaga came to town when Belfast hosted the MTV Europe Music Awards in October 2011. This was a global media event that generated around £22 million in revenue for Northern Ireland (though this figure is admittedly rather speculative).[42]

The new Titanic Belfast Centre and the Maze/Long Kesh 'international peace centre' also look set to make a substantial contribution to the tourist economy over the next ten or fifteen years. At the end of 2011, National Geographic's *Traveler* magazine named Belfast 'one of the world's top destinations' for 2012, with the editor-in-chief, Keith Bellows, suggesting that: 'It was great, the food, the incredible atmosphere and don't take this wrong, in many ways it reminded me of Cuba, what it was like there seven or eight years ago.'[43] This positive publicity has already been seized upon by organizations that are trying to attract people to Northern Ireland, such as Queen's University (though the reference to Cuba is not always included). As a prelude to the opening of the new Titanic Belfast exhibition centre, over 140 tour operators visited Northern Ireland on in April 2012. One of them commented that the region was now being marketed alongside more established locations: 'We used to include Northern Ireland as part of our UK or Ireland tours, but now we are marketing the province as a short break destination alongside the likes of Paris or Prague.'[44]

The conflict itself has been turned to profit by private entrepreneurs, with numerous guided tours on offer which combine the region's grisly past with its stunning scenery. Paddywagon Tours, for example, seeks to enable (exploit) the tourist fascination with Belfast, now that people feel safe enough to actually visit the place:[45]

> The North is quickly becoming a must-see for any traveller arriving in Ireland. This tour enables you to focus on Belfast, in the little corner of our Motherland so ever present in world headlines since 1969 but now experiencing a new dawn. We introduce you to local guides and characters and customs of both the Ulster Irish and Ulster British communities while you travel in the black Cab tour of Belfast.[46]

Paddywagon Tours is based in Dublin and was presented with a Tourism Ireland award by the Irish government for its 'outstanding contribution to Irish Tourism' in 2004.

Allen's Tours in Belfast runs a series of hop-on-hop-off, open-top double-decker bus tours that combine popular representations of Northern Ireland's history, politics and geography. The company's website demonstrates the dexterity with which the conflict has been repackaged into heritage and our violent history airbrushed into edgy charm:

> Belfast is an enchanting and welcoming city with something to offer even the most diverse and demanding of visitors. Recently voted 'Europe's Friendliest Regional Capital' it is a compact and charming city of contrasts, in addition to being an epicentre for political, cultural and historical intrigue. Our exciting tour takes in all that the city has to offer from the bustling University Quarter where architecture, academia and a vibrant social scene are all spectacularly combined, to the notorious political murals of East & West Belfast which depict in their own unique way the turbulent events of the so called 'Troubles'. We also visit amongst other places the infamous Titanic Quarter, home to colossal cranes of Harland & Wolff and the final location of the recently returned SS Nomadic, tender to the ill fated Titanic and only surviving vessel from the White Star Line. Our tour aims to capture the unique charm and distinctive ambience of Belfast as well as provide a definitive sense of history, heritage and culture for this fiercely proud and extremely hospitable city.[47]

These tourist buses zigzag across Belfast and Derry on a daily basis and can regularly be seen hauling up the big hill to Parliament Buildings at Stormont and stopping by the few sectarian murals that remain dotted around the city. To this extent, the conflict has become a commodity to be consumed by the growing tourist economy; but of course Northern Ireland is not alone in that regard. I was reminded of this when Martin Bell, former BBC foreign affairs correspondent, showed me a pen he had bought in Sarajevo many years after the war there, made by local entrepreneurs from a spent high-velocity bullet cartridge.

Not all of Northern Ireland's new wave of tourists are quite as gullible as the visiting academic from Britain, who believed a black-taxi driver's quip that he would have to get permission from the local IRA commander before he could take any photographs on the Falls Road. He returned to the safety of his hotel, wide-eyed from his 'walk on the wild side' and slightly flushed by his apparent brush with local paramilitary chic – an incident which illustrates merely that the external perception of Northern Ireland has been slow to catch up with its more mundane reality.

## CONCLUSION

> One thing that we can be sure of is that nothing stays the same. In my forty years in politics it is clear that only those who can adapt to changing circumstances remain standing.[48]
>
> First Minister Peter Robinson, MLA

The political history of Northern Ireland has been dogged by sectarian division, structural inequality and violent conflict between nationalist and unionist communities. Indeed these dynamics pre-date the existence of Northern Ireland and were a causal factor in its birth in the first place. Everybody's shoddy compromise in 1921 was ripped apart by political violence in the second half of the twentieth century, before Northern Ireland tried to reinvent itself as a 'post-conflict' society at the beginning of the twenty-first. Most of the lines dividing the map of the world into countries have been forged out of violence, of course, and so Northern Ireland is not unique in that respect.

As a youngster in Belfast, I remember a common piece of graffiti on the walls in 1976: '7 years is too long. Don't make it 8.' This plea turned out to be a hopelessly optimistic one, as eight years became eighteen and then twenty-five. A whole generation of people lived through a vicious era of sectarian violence, while the British and Irish governments vacillated between wilful ignorance and destructive engagement. It was a brutalizing experience for all involved, as violence always is. Negative stereotypes were built up and nourished by all sides, as humanizing your enemy makes it devilishly difficult to kill him – or to accept murder being committed in your name. Sectarian murders were always justified as 'regrettable' and 'defensive' violence, a consequence of wider political structures and dynamics. Even those who did not directly engage in such violence frequently 'understood' it. Violence was a product of structural conflict, not an activity of choice to be enjoyed by those engaged in it – though many of those involved did enjoy the power they held, and a smaller number took a sadistic pleasure in killing their victims. The British government spent thirty years defending its security policies, even when these

were causing violence to escalate rather than decline. Even worse, it sometimes claimed that the conflict was unsolvable, primordial and inevitable.
Arrogant disdain was passed off as statecraft, as though allowing the two
sides to slug it out would yield catharsis and result in more robust and
sustainable policies.

Politics meanwhile became debased, as it was clear that violence
'worked', while local politicians were unable to establish institutions to fill
the vacuum. The years 1968–2004 were a time of vicious circles, with tit-
for-tat murders and industrial-scale lying on all sides. A propaganda war
shadowed the actual 'undeclared war', as all sides attempted to gain legitimacy and support within Northern Ireland and beyond.

During these years, unionist and nationalist communities became inured
and resigned to the everyday diet of murder, mayhem and political failure.
The society became structured around its sectarian divisions, with separate
housing provision, separate educational facilities and even segregated
graveyards. Public policy took these divisions for granted and even planned
services around them, rather than attempting to disrupt or transform
them. While community activism emerged from time to time, in sporadic
attempts to deal with the symptoms of violence and in the absence of
progressive political leadership, it mostly revolved around disconnected,
single-issue campaigns which were, at times, stunning in their simplicity
and naivety. Their inability to get beyond the immediate symptoms to the
underlying structural causes of the conflict was an enduring problem for
civil society engagement and left the majority of initiatives unable to do
more than provide palliative care to those affected by the violence.

This is the context within which we should look at Northern Ireland
today and think about its future development. Where once, in the 1970s
and 1980s, there was unremitting gloom and despondency, now the mood
is much more positive. Today, the vast majority of people in Northern
Ireland are content to park their ultimate political aspirations and get on
with the more immediate issues that affect their lives. Unionists still want
to be British and nationalists still want to be Irish, of course: little has
changed at that fundamental level. However, the new political dispensa-
tion allows everyone in Northern Ireland to choose between these two
alternative forms of citizenship, to opt in to the one of their choosing,
rather than have an identity foisted upon them.

Sectarian hatred and the threat of violence remain as a spectral presence
over Northern Ireland's future; but this built up over several generations,
and it is unrealistic to expect anything else. The violent conflict raged for

at least thirty years, and it is going to take that long (as a minimum) for a post-conflict society to emerge. This longer-term perspective is also important because the violent behaviour of the past (and present) has been rooted in the dysfunctional political, economic and cultural structures of society. This has layered sectarian attitudes across all aspects of society, making them robust, ingrained and slow to change. Reform of these structures is ongoing, but it will take time for people to gain confidence that these do not pose a threat to their identity or their interests, or to those of the community they feel part of.

The political system is evolving in new and interesting ways, some of which were not envisaged at the outset. There are problems, and there is as much incompetence and corruption in Northern Ireland as there is in any other political bureaucracy. However, for the most part people are no longer interested in killing each other over rival nationality claims or religious labels.

The 'war' is over, but the 'peace' is only just beginning. It remains to be seen how effectively the political process deals with community sectarianism and other issues of policy delivery. What is certain, though, is that a general absence of political violence (notwithstanding the activities of 'dissident' republicans) and a functioning political process provide the best chance for the region to overcome its violent past. When Queen Elizabeth II visited the Irish Republic in June 2011, she spoke about the importance of 'being able to bow to the past, but not to be bound by it'. This sits neatly with the aspiration set out at the beginning of this chapter by Martin McGuinness – to write 'a new history for future generations'. That seems a fitting note on which to conclude and a reasonable basis upon which to believe that Northern Ireland can move forward into the next phase of its political development.

# POSTSCRIPT

*SLÁN AGUS BEANNACHT.* Loosely translated as 'Goodbye and God bless', that is what Martin McGuinness said to Queen Elizabeth II when he shook her delicate, white-gloved hand in Belfast on 27 June 2012 during her diamond jubilee tour of Northern Ireland. When she visited in 1977 to celebrate her silver jubilee, the graffiti scrawled on the Falls Road in Belfast conveyed a rather more brusque message: 'Victory to the IRA. Stuff the Jubilee.'[1] What a difference twenty-five years can make.

While the Queen's official visit to the Irish Republic in 2011 was more important, it would be difficult to imagine a moment that encapsulated the peace process more neatly than this brief encounter in Belfast's Lyric Theatre. The former IRA commander was making peace with the titular head of the British army, the defender of the Protestant faith and the head of state of the UK, despite the record of violence and antipathy between the two sides. The Provisional IRA murdered the Queen's cousin, Lord Mountbatten, in 1979, when (it is widely believed) McGuinness was playing a senior role in the organization and would have been involved in planning the operation.

While the British media focused on the Queen's magnanimity in meeting McGuinness, it was the deputy first minister who was taking the greater political risk. The event was carefully stage-managed, with McGuinness sucking through his teeth like a rogue builder pricing up a kitchen extension in the weeks beforehand, claiming it was 'a huge ask' for his party. The final decision was announced only days before the visit and was sold as a 'concession' by Sinn Fein and as a grand gesture in support of the peace process. Typically, Sinn Fein managed to sell something it *had* to do as something it *chose* to do, and thereby to occupy the moral high ground.

The chosen venue of the Lyric Theatre was a relatively neutral space (in comparison to Stormont), and it was made clear on a number of occasions that the event was a stand-alone celebration of the contribution of the arts to reconciliation in Northern Ireland and was *definitely not* connected to the Queen's jubilee celebrations. There was a cross-border dimension, too, and the president of Ireland, Michael D. Higgins, was also in attendance. Despite all the attempts to choreograph the event, right-wing British politicians and left-wing Irish republicans both interpreted this as Sinn Fein's final act of supplication to the British Crown. Former Conservative Home Secretary Norman Tebbit (whose wife Margaret was crippled by the IRA in the Brighton bombing of 1984) commented that it signified nothing less than that both McGuinness and Sinn Fein 'now accepted the sovereignty of Her Majesty over Northern Ireland'. Anthony McIntyre, a long-standing critic of Sinn Fein strategy during the peace process and a former member of the Provisional IRA, claimed that the handshake had 'been made possible by the earlier negotiated surrender of the IRA'.[2] It was noted by McIntyre and many other observers that Sinn Fein's longer-term strategy was concerned with expanding its support base in the Irish Republic, and that McGuinness's act of conciliation would assist that development in the years ahead.[3]

The imagery surrounding the handshake between McGuinness and the Queen was beamed around the world, and this in itself is emblematic of the wider peace process in Northern Ireland: it was a photo-opportunity that dominated the debate between the political elites. The meeting made little practical difference to the lives of the people on the ground or to the problems they faced, the grievances they nurtured and the hopes they cherished. The future of the peace process in Northern Ireland will be determined by the extent to which the formal political system connects with the lives of the people who live there and proves itself capable of delivering policies that improve the circumstances of both unionist and nationalist communities.

At the time of writing, the disconnection between what is happening at the top of the political system and the attitudes of people within the broader community is widening rather than narrowing. Politicians and the institutions they operate are failing to mediate continuing sectarian tensions at the local level, presenting a real and present danger for the peace process in Northern Ireland.

All of these issues came to a head in late 2012 following the decision of Belfast City Council on 3 December to fly the Union flag only on a small number of designated days, rather than, as before, continuously. Sinn Fein had wanted the flag removed altogether on the basis that the Irish Tricolour was not flown and that one political identity should not be given preferential treatment over the other. However, they eventually supported the Alliance Party's compromise proposal to fly the Union flag on eighteen specific occasions during the year.

This decision was widely regarded by unionists and loyalists as another attack on their British identity and protests broke out across East Belfast within minutes of the decision. These demonstrations continued throughout most of the Christmas period in 2012 and resumed at the beginning of January 2013. While nationalists might not appreciate the analogy, they grew in significance in a manner not dissimilar to the civil rights marches during the late 1960s. Peaceful demonstrations were accompanied by sporadic violence and public order policing, which included the use of water cannon and plastic bullets. The protesters claimed they had a right to freedom of speech and peaceful demonstration, while the politicians and the police warned increasingly about the threat to public order.

As tensions increased so did the power of the protests, the collective fear of the wider community and the interest of the local and global media. By the end of the first week of January 2013, over 100 people had been arrested for public order offences while more than 60 members of the PSNI had been injured as a result of nightly rioting in East Belfast and across other towns such as Ballymena and Carrickfergus. Christmas trading in Belfast was badly affected as shops either closed early or saw potential customers evaporate, scared away from the commercial centre of Belfast by the prospect of being caught up in the violent disruption. While the City Hall sported a banner saying 'Happy Christmas Belfast' and the streets were festooned with luminous decorations such as 'B Festive', there was precious little peace and goodwill on offer over the holiday period. The public image of Northern Ireland as being a stable place for external investment, painstakingly built up over several years by the main political parties, lay in tatters at the beginning of 2013 as loyalist protesters and police exchanged volleys of petrol bombs and plastic bullets on a nightly basis. By the middle of January the PSNI estimated that the cost of policing these protests had reached over £7 million.

The explanation for these protests is complex. Many unionists have been alienated by the peace process and the removal of the Union flag was a tipping point for those who saw it as emblematic of a long-term attack on their British identity. While nationalists might well point out the poetic irony of the fact that loyalists could not accept the result of a majority vote by Belfast City Council, they would be unwise to dismiss the reality of these grievances. Unionist alienation is their problem too as the peace process requires two willing partners rather than one. While the flag was the trigger point the problems run much deeper, with a large number of unionists believing that their British identity is being steadily whittled away and that the democratic process is not working for them.

While the majority of loyalists protested peacefully during this period against what they regarded as an attack on their political and cultural identity, a minority gratefully accepted the chance to encourage, plan and participate in acts of violence, intimidation and destruction. At a more mundane level, teenagers, and even children as young as ten and eleven, took part in 'recreational' violence in their local areas as a form of entertainment.

Initially, unionist politicians within both the DUP and UUP raised the collective temperature by distributing leaflets blaming the Alliance Party for the decision, and suggesting that the removal of the flag cast into doubt Alliance's commitment to a 'shared future'. The DUP denied allegations that this was an attempt to oust the Alliance Party's Naomi Long as MP for East Belfast, though this did not prevent Long and several of her colleagues from being attacked and sent death threats. As violent disorder spread across Northern Ireland, the DUP and UUP tried to distance their respective parties from it and condemned the violence that resulted. It soon became clear that few people were listening and that the politicians were powerless to stop either the ongoing protests or the violence that accompanied them. This situation was not helped by the fact that unionist politicians were sending out mixed messages, participating in many of these demonstrations while at the same time calling for them to be brought to an end. A sinister presence lay behind the flags protest in the form of the East Belfast UVF, which was widely believed to be orchestrating the violence.

In an effort to regain the initiative, the leaders of both main unionist parties came up with the idea of a unionist flags forum that they hoped would channel energies through the political process rather than through continued street disturbance. However, in the short term at least, this failed to capture the public imagination, as violent disorder disrupted normal life and reminded everyone old enough to remember of the dark days of the 'Troubles'.

This upsurge of street violence and wider community dislocation at the beginning of 2013 laid bare the brittle condition of the peace process in Northern Ireland. It also provided a salutary lesson about the necessity to connect the formal political process (and its institutions) with the perceptions and grievances across the wider community. Unless this is done, and done quickly, then not only symbolic advances such as the meeting between Martin McGuinness and the Queen, but the peace process itself will be engulfed by the forces of community sectarianism.

For lasting peace to be achieved, the formal political system has to deliver on its symbolic rhetoric in a way that makes people feel it is relevant to their grievances and their aspirations. Not all of the responsibility should be left at the doors of Stormont, of course, as the unionist and nationalist communities will have to grasp the opportunities that are offered to them and that they themselves create. Northern Ireland has come a long way since 1969, but it has a long way still to go.

# NOTES

CHAPTER 1: THE COLLISION OF RELIGION AND POLITICS, 1690–1920

1. The year 1690 is an iconic date in Irish political history – the year of the Battle of the Boyne. The date functions as both a statement and a slogan in the context of political divisions in Northern Ireland.
2. This was the date under the old-style Julian calendar; under the Gregorian calendar the battle is commemorated on 12 July.
3. The Irish thesaurus is a political battleground, with numerous phrases loaded in a way that provides a useful code for locals and a potential minefield for unwary outsiders. During the 1980s, local radio personality Gerry Anderson coined the term 'Stroke City' for the region (Derry/Londonderry) as a humorous, but nonetheless pragmatic, alternative for those who would rather not play the sectarian name-game.
4. R.F. Foster, *Modern Ireland 1600–1972*, Penguin, London, 1989, p. 155.
5. Quoted in Jonathan Bardon, *A History of Ulster*, Blackstaff Press, Belfast, 1992, p. 224.
6. R. Crawford, *Loyal to King Billy: A portrait of the Ulster Protestants*, Gill & Macmillan, Dublin, 1987, pp. 2–3.
7. 'Gay activist's "King Billy was a homosexual" claim sparks furore', *Belfast Telegraph*, 28 July 2008, available at: www.belfasttelegraph.co.uk/news/local-national/gay-activistrsquos-lsquoking-billy-was-a-homosexualrsquo-claim-sparks-furore-13922468. html
8. Paul Arthur, *The Government and Politics of Northern Ireland*, Longman, Harlow, 1984, p. 3.
9. Daniel Defoe, *The Parallel; or Persecution of Protestants the shortest way to prevent the growth of Popery in Ireland*, London, 1704.
10. 'Ulster-Scots and the birth of America', Ulster-Scots Society of America website, available at: http://www.ulsterscotssociety.com/about_ulster-scots.html
11. From the United Irish Catechism, 1797. Reference to the 'four quarters' relates to the four provinces of Ireland – Ulster, Munster, Leinster and Connacht – uniting as one.
12. Trevelyan was advising the Chairman of the Famine Relief Commission, Sir Randolph Routh, that it was unnecessary to grind hard Indian corn more than once to make it suitable for human consumption.
13. Christine Kinealy, *This Great Calamity: The Irish famine 1845–52*, Dublin, Gill & Macmillan, 2006, p. 297.
14. 'The Stricken Land' was written by Jane Francesca Elgee, a young Protestant who became a member of the radical nationalist Young Irelander movement. She published

this poem under the pen name of 'Speranza' in *The Nation* magazine in 1847. Elgee was to become the mother of Oscar Wilde.

15. There had been a disastrous potato famine in 1740 and more than a dozen partial or total crop failures between 1816 and 1842.
16. St John Ervine, *Craigavon*, Ulsterman, London, 1949, p. 183.
17. 'The Ulster Covenant', History Journal website, available at: http://www.history-journal.ie/archives/war-in-ulster/142-the-ulster-covenant.html
18. P. Buckland, *James Craig*, Gill & Macmillan, Dublin, 1980, p. 89.
19. Quoted in A.T.Q. Stewart, *The Ulster Crisis*, Faber, London, 1969, pp. 55–6.

## CHAPTER 2: WHY POLITICS FAILED AND VIOLENCE BEGAN, 1921–72

1. J. Brewer and G. Higgins, *Anti-Catholicism in Northern Ireland 1600–1998*, Macmillan, Basingstoke, 1998, chapter available at: http://cain.ulst.ac.uk/issues/sectarian/brewer.htm
2. It was technically the Civil Authorities (Special Powers) Act (Northern Ireland) 1922, but is known by its more informal title as the Special Powers Act.
3. Fionnuala Ni Aolain, *The Politics of Force*, Blackstaff Press, Belfast, 2000, p. 14.
4. Quoted in M. Farrell, *Northern Ireland: The Orange State*, Pluto Press, London, 1976, pp. 90–91.
5. ibid.
6. Quoted in Sunday Times Insight team, *Ulster*, Penguin, London, 1972.
7. Senator J. Barnhill, quoted in Farrell, *Northern Ireland*, p. 91.
8. Terence O'Neill, *Autobiography*, Hart Davis, London, 1972, p. 40.
9. David Gordon, *The O'Neill Years: Unionist politics 1963–69*, Athol Books, Belfast, 1989, p. 114.
10. *Belfast Telegraph*, 10 May 1969, p. 1.
11. Gordon, *The O'Neill Years*, p. 5.
12. K. Bloomfield, *Stormont in Crisis: A memoir*, Blackstaff Press, Belfast, 1994.
13. Lieutenant Colonel Robert Lundy was governor during the Siege of Derry in 1689. When thirteen young apprentices slammed the gates of the walled city closed against the advancing army of James II, a stand-off began with the majority in Derry who supported King William of Orange. It lasted 105 days and cost over 10,000 lives. Lundy advocated surrender to James but was resisted by the people and slunk out of the city in disgrace under the cover of darkness. His name became a byword within unionist folklore for betrayal, cowardice and treachery and a term of abuse that has been thrown at numerous unionist leaders ever since. Lundy's effigy is regularly burned on bonfires every December in Northern Ireland to commemorate his status as a unionist hate figure. His place in the history of the city is reflected in the fact that included in the programme of events for Derry's year as UK City of Culture in 2013 is the theatre production *The Trial of Lieutenant Colonel Robert Lundy*. As part of this interactive event, the public are able to vote on Lundy's guilt or innocence.
14. This quip was itself a paraphrase of the Leonard Cohen song 'Everybody Knows'.
15. The *Protestant Telegraph* was a weekly pamphlet and the mouthpiece of Paisley's Free Presbyterian Church.
16. E. Moloney and A. Pollak, *Paisley*, Poolbeg Press, Dublin, 1986, p. 159.
17. Quoted in J. Tonge, *Northern Ireland: Conflict and change*, Pearson, London, 2001, p. 44.
18. The Apprentice Boys is a Protestant fraternal association established in 1814 to commemorate the Siege of Derry. It is named after the apprentices who slammed the gates of the city closed against the advancing army of James II, after which the siege began.
19. Quoted in F. Cochrane, '"Meddling at the crossroads": The decline and fall of Terence O'Neill within the unionist community' in R. English and G. Walker (eds), *Unionism in Modern Ireland*, Macmillan, Basingstoke, 1996, p. 163.
20. O'Neill, *Autobiography*, p. 111.
21. Quoted in Tonge, *Northern Ireland*, p. 42.

22. Bardon, *History of Ulster*, p. 671.
23. Sunday Times Insight Team, *Ulster*, p. 139.
24. Faulkner died prematurely on 3 March 1977, aged fifty-six, when the horse he was riding bolted and hit a car. He had been awarded a life peerage only twenty-four days earlier – one of the shortest life peerages in modern British history.
25. D. Kennelly and E. Preston, *Belfast, August 1971 – a case to be answered*, Independent Labour Party, London, 1971, p. 39.
26. ibid., p. 71.
27. See 'Massacre at Derry', published by NICRA and available on the CAIN website at: http://cain.ulst.ac.uk/events/bsunday/mad.htm
28. It would be another thirty-eight years before the Saville Inquiry reported, in June 2010, that the Parachute Regiment had been responsible for the deaths that occurred. It concluded that none of the victims was armed, that soldiers gave no warnings before opening fire, and that the shootings were a 'catastrophe' for Northern Ireland. It also took this length of time for the British government, in the shape of Prime Minister David Cameron, to admit that innocent people had been unnecessarily killed: 'What happened on Bloody Sunday was both unjustified and unjustifiable. It was wrong. These are shocking conclusions to read and shocking words to have to say. But you do not defend the British army by defending the indefensible.'
29. ibid., at: http://cain.ulst.ac.uk/events/bsunday/mad2.htm#said
30. ibid., at: http://cain.ulst.ac.uk/events/bsunday/mad2.htm#said
31. Quoted in Bardon, *History of Ulster*, p. 688.
32. E. McCann, *What Happened in Derry*, Socialist Worker pamphlet, London, 1972, p. 11.
33. Sunday Times Insight Team, *Ulster*, p. 213.

## CHAPTER 3: THE RATIONALITY OF WAR, 1972–74

1. 'We' is used in the collective rather than personal sense here.
2. We were very lucky to be friends with a Jesuit priest studying for his PhD at Lancaster University at the time, Fr Kifle Wansamo SJ, who saved the day; we remain eternally grateful to him for marrying us.
3. C. Carson, 'Belfast Confetti' in *The Irish for No*, Wake Forest University Press, Winston-Salem, 1987.
4. Moloney and Pollak, *Paisley*, p. 352.
5. Farrell, *Northern Ireland*, p. 296.
6. Quoted in Bloomfield, *Stormont in Crisis*, p. 165.
7. C. Ryder, 'William Craig Obituary', *Guardian*, 26 April 2011, available at: http://www.guardian.co.uk/uk/2011/apr/26/william-craig-obituary
8. C. Smyth, *Ian Paisley: Voice of Protestant Ulster*, Scottish Academic Press, Edinburgh, 1987, p. 37.
9. P. Bishop and E. Mallie, *The Provisional IRA*, Corgi Books, London, 1987, pp. 139–40.
10. One of Whitelaw's reported negotiating techniques was to allow people to think him dim, to lull his adversaries into a false sense of security (a strategy since taken to new heights by the Conservative mayor of London, Boris Johnson, who has used it to great political effect). See I. Aitkin, 'Loyal to a fault', Guardian, 11 September 2002, available at: http://www.guardian.co.uk/politics/2002/sep/11/past.conservatives
11. Peter Taylor, *Loyalists*, Bloomsbury, London, 1999, p. 108.
12. Available (as reproduced) on the CAIN website, at: http://cain.ulst.ac.uk/events/bfriday/nio/nio72.htm
13. It would take another thirty years for the Provisional IRA to make an apology to the victims. The thirtieth anniversary of Bloody Friday was marked by the IRA in its in-house *An Phoblacht* newspaper with the following statement:

Sunday 21 July marks the 30th anniversary of an IRA operation in Belfast in 1972 which resulted in nine people being killed and many more injured. While it was not our intention to injure or kill non-combatants, the reality is that on this and on a number of other occasions, that was the consequence of our actions. It is therefore appropriate on the anniversary of this tragic event, that we address all of the deaths and injuries of non-combatants caused by us. We offer our sincere apologies and condolences to their families.

It is doubtful whether the adjectives 'remorseful' or 'contrite' could be attached to this statement, but it does indicate at some level that the IRA was aware of the impact of its actions and of the damage it did. It went beyond the 'I'm sorry you feel that way' nature of previous admissions of regret, but little further.

14. House of Commons Debate, 24 July 1972, Hansard, Vol. 841, cc1326–90, available at: http://hansard.millbanksystems.com/commons/1972/jul/24/northern-ireland
15. Bardon, *History of Ulster*, p. 698.
16. ibid.
17. ibid.
18. ibid., p. 699.
19. John McGuffin, *The Guineapigs*, Penguin, London, 1974, p. 65.
20. Peter Taylor, *Beating the Terrorists*, Penguin, London, 1980, pp. 25–6.
21. Brice Dickson, 'Counter-insurgency and human rights in Northern Ireland', *Journal of Strategic Studies*, 32 (2009), pp. 492–3.

CHAPTER 4: DIRECT RULE AND THE GROWTH OF INFORMAL POLITICS, 1974–90

1. Wilson was given the 'Pipe-smoker of the Year' award in 1976, despite the fact that he reportedly preferred to smoke cigars away from the cameras.
2. Bardon, *History of Ulster*, p. 706.
3. Moloney and Pollak, *Paisley*, p. 358.
4. P. Bew and G. Gillespie, *Northern Ireland: A chronology of the troubles 1968–1993*, Gill & Macmillan, Dublin, 1993, p. 86.
5. Bloomfield, *Stormont in Crisis*, p. 219.
6. Bardon, *History of Ulster*, pp. 708–9.
7. The word 'Taig' is one of the many derogatory terms in Northern Ireland employed as a form of sectarian shorthand. It is used by some Protestant loyalists as an offensive word for Catholics and derives from the Irish Gaelic name Tadhg. During the 1980s, loyalist prisoners in the Maze prison had a mural in one of the 'H-Blocks' which contained the wording: 'Yabba-Dabba-Doo, Any Taig Will Do'.
8. A second bomb exploded in the Seven Stars pub, though it had been evacuated and no one was injured.
9. See http://news.bbc.co.uk/onthisday/hi/dates/stories/october/5/newsid_2492000/2492543.stm
10. A. Hill, 'Paddy Hill: "All I think about is shooting police. I am traumatised', *Guardian*, 4 November 2010, available at: http://www.guardian.co.uk/law/2010/nov/04/paddy-hill-birmingham-six-counselling
11. G. Peirce, 'The Birmingham Six: Have we learned from our disgraceful past?', *Guardian*, 12 March 2011, available at: http://www.guardian.co.uk/theguardian/2011/mar/12/gareth-peirce-birmingham-six
12. Dum-dum bullets are also known as 'expanding' or hollow-point bullets. Developed by the British army in India during the nineteenth century, they are designed to flatten on impact and to cause greater haemorrhaging. They are still used by 'anti-terrorist' police today to quickly incapacitate targets. In 2005, the innocent Brazilian Jean Charles de Menezes was shot in the head seven times by police in London using these bullets.
13. All three were eventually released from jail under the terms of the 1998 Good Friday Agreement.
14. G. Adams, *Free Ireland: Towards a lasting peace*, Brandon Books, Dublin, 1986, p. 63.
15. Quoted in A. Pollak (ed.), *A Citizen's Inquiry: The Opsahl Report on Northern Ireland*, The Lilliput Press, Dublin, 1993, p. 13.
16. Pollak, *Citizen's Inquiry*, p. 13.

17. ibid.
18. C. Farrington (ed.), *Global Change, Civil Society and the Northern Ireland Peace Process*, Palgrave, Basingstoke, 2008, pp. 118–19.
19. *The View from the Castle*, BBC Northern Ireland, 1988.
20. G. Wheatcroft, 'A happy 80th birthday to the IRA's most deadly foe', *Daily Telegraph*, 18 April 2004, available at: http://www.telegraph.co.uk/comment/personal-view/3604965/A-happy-80th-birthday-to-the-IRAs-most-deadly-foe.html
21. ibid.
22. Farrington, *Global Change*, p. 124.
23. Quoted in F. Cochrane, *People Power? The role of the voluntary and community sector in the Northern Ireland conflict*, Cork University Press, Cork, 2002, p. 50.
24. M. Rees, *Northern Ireland: A personal perspective*, Methuen Press, London, 1985, p. 277.
25. Quoted in Bishop and Mallie, *Provisional IRA*, pp. 352–53.
26. L. Clarke, 'Did IRA hunger strikers believe Danny Morrison's spin?', *Belfast Telegraph*, 11 January 2011, available at: http://www.belfasttelegraph.co.uk/opinion/news-analysis/did-ira-hunger-strikers-believe-danny-morrisons-spin-15050183.html
27. Adams, *Free Ireland*, p. 79.
28. This allegedly acceded to three of the five demands, and effectively to a fourth, as the definition of 'prison work' was to be expanded to include educational and cultural pursuits. Richard O'Rawe made this allegation in his book *Blanketmen: An untold story of the H-Block hunger strike*, New Island Books, Dublin, 2005.
29. R. English, *Armed Struggle: The history of the IRA*, Macmillan, Basingstoke, 2003, pp. 224–25.
30. John Hewitt, *The Selected Poems of John Hewitt*, ed. Michael Longley and Frank Ormsby, Blackstaff Press, Belfast, 2007. Reproduced by permission of Blackstaff Press, on behalf of the estate of John Hewitt.
31. ibid. Reproduced by permission of Blackstaff Press, on behalf of the estate of John Hewitt.

## CHAPTER 5: TALKING TO THE ENEMY, 1993–95

1. John Major, quoted in F. Cochrane, *Ending Wars*, Polity Press, Cambridge, 2008, p. 78.
2. J. Major, *The Autobiography*, HarperCollins, London, 2000, p. 447.
3. E. Mallie and D. McKittrick, *Endgame in Ireland*, Hodder and Stoughton, London, 2001, p. 73.
4. Quoted in ibid.
5. ibid.
6. Gurney met John Major over twenty years later and gave him the firing pin from one of the mortars that he had defused.
7. P. Taylor, *Provos: The IRA & Sinn Fein*, Bloomsbury, London, 1997, pp. 321–22.
8. While John Major was the unfortunate victim of this attack, it had been in the planning stage for over six months, the original target being his immediate predecessor, Margaret Thatcher.
9. Sir Patrick Mayhew took over from Peter Brooke as secretary of state in 1992.
10. Pollak, *Citizen's Inquiry*, p. 11.
11. J. Powell, *Great Hatred, Little Room: Making peace in Northern Ireland*, Bodley Head, London, 2008, p. 71.
12. Mallie and McKittrick, *Endgame in Ireland*, p. 135.
13. ibid., p. 148.
14. Sean Kelly was convicted of the bombing but was released in 2000 under the terms of the Good Friday Agreement.
15. M. Connolly, 'Remembering a black week in our history', *Irish News*, 21 October 2003, available at http://www.nuzhound.com/articles/irish_news/arts2003/oct21_black_week_in_history.php
16. F. Cochrane, *Unionist Politics and the Politics of Unionism since the Anglo-Irish Agreement*, first edition, Cork University Press, Cork, 1997, p. 306.

17. Torrens Knight and two other members of the UFF received eight life sentences before being released under the terms of the Good Friday Agreement.
18. Mallie and McKittrick, *Endgame in Ireland*, p. 128.
19. B. Rowan, *Behind the Lines*, Blackstaff Press, Belfast, 1995, p. 91.
20. My italics. Reference to justice as well as peace was not insignificant and reflects the fact that Sinn Fein in particular saw these themes as inextricably linked.
21. ibid., p. 176.
22. Cochrane, *Unionist Politics* (first edition), p. 328.
23. Eighteen years later, on 18 June 2012, Ireland was again drawn to play Italy, this time in the group matches of Euro 2012. As a mark of respect for the victims of the Loughinisland shootings, the Ireland team received permission from UEFA to wear black armbands to mark the incident.
24. An inauspicious comparison, given that this deal had fallen apart amid mutual recriminations and Rabin's assassination by a Jewish extremist who was opposed to the deal.
25. Quoted in Powell, *Great Hatred*, p. 77.
26. Cochrane, *Unionist Politics* (first edition), p. 327.
27. G. McMichael, *An Ulster Voice*, Roberts Rinehart, Dublin, 1999, p. 63.
28. CLMC statement, quoted in McMichael, *An Ulster Voice*, p. 66.
29. Major ended the affair on his promotion to Margaret Thatcher's Cabinet in 1988 and it remained a secret until September 2002, when Edwina Currie (apparently stung after being passed over by Major when he became prime minister in 1990, and ignored by him in his own autobiography) serialized the affair in her own diaries.
30. Mallie and McKittrick, *Endgame in Ireland*, p. 177.
31. M. White, 'Leveson inquiry: Kelvin MacKenzie tells it like it was at the Sun', *Guardian*, 9 January 2012, available at: http://www.guardian.co.uk/media/2012/jan/09/leveson-inquiry-kelvin-mackenzie-lobbing
32. See Conflict Archive on the Internet (CAIN), available at: http://cain.ulst.ac.uk/issues/violence/paramilitary2.htm

## CHAPTER 6: BRINGING THE OUTSIDE IN: THE INTERNATIONAL DIMENSION, 1995–98

1. Quoted in T. Birney and J. O'Neill, *When the President Calls*, Guildhall Press, Derry, 1997, available at: http://cain.ulst.ac.uk/events/peace/docs/birney.htm
2. M. McGovern, 'Rhyming history with the man from Hope', *Peace Review*, 13:1 (2001), p. 81.
3. 'William J. Clinton: Remarks on lighting the city Christmas tree in Belfast', American Presidency Project website, available at: http://www.presidency.ucsb.edu/ws/?pid=50829
4. Mallie and McKittrick, *Endgame in Ireland*, p. 6.
5. ibid., p. 150.
6. ibid.
7. N. O'Dowd, 'Irish America played pivotal Northern role', *Sunday Business Post*, 7 August 2005, p. 4.
8. P. Arthur, *Special Relationships*, Blackstaff Press, Belfast, 2000, p. 136.
9. J. Dumbrell, ' "Hope and history": the US and peace in Northern Ireland' in M. Cox, A. Guelke and F. Stephen (eds), *A Farewell to Arms? From 'long war' to long peace in Northern Ireland*, Manchester University Press, Manchester, 2000, p. 219.
10. A. Guelke, 'Northern Ireland: international and north/south issues' in W. Crotty and D. Schmitt (eds), *Ireland and the Politics of Change*, Longman, London, 1998, p. 203.
11. ibid., p. 208.
12. These principles were named after Sean MacBride, a man with an impeccable pedigree in Irish nationalist and international politics. MacBride was the son of Irish revolutionary Maud Gonne, and his father was executed in 1916, along with James Connolly and the other leaders of the Easter Rising. He opposed the Anglo-Irish Treaty and was imprisoned on several occasions in Mountjoy jail. He became a member of the IRA and also studied law at University College Dublin. By the end of the 1930s, MacBride had become a barrister and frequently defended IRA prisoners. In 1947, he won a seat in the

Irish Dail Eireann, having founded a new republican socialist party, *Clann na Poblachta*, the previous year. He became the Irish minister of external affairs in 1948 and played a leading role in the Council of Europe and in the drafting of the European Convention on Human Rights. He was a founding member of Amnesty International and was also instrumental in the decision of the Free State to formally leave the British Commonwealth and become the Republic of Ireland in 1949. He later held a number of senior posts within the United Nations, including assistant secretary general and high commissioner for Namibia. MacBride was awarded the Nobel Peace Prize in 1974. He died in 1988 aged eighty-three.

13. B. Hanley, 'The politics of Noraid', *Irish Political Studies*, 19:1 (2004), p. 7.
14. Dumbrell, '"Hope and history"', p. 216.
15. ibid., p. 153.
16. C. O'Clery, *The Billionaire Who Wasn't: How Chuck Feeney made and gave away a fortune without anyone knowing*, Public Affairs, New York, 2007.
17. N. O'Dowd, 'Irish America Played Pivotal Northern Role', *Sunday Business Post*, 7 August 2005, p. 4.
18. Powell, *Great Hatred*, p. 78.
19. D. De Breadun, *The Far Side of Revenge*, Collins, Dublin, 2001, p.11.
20. Arthur, *Special Relationships*, p. 133.
21. Mallie and McKittrick, *Endgame in Ireland*, p. 159.
22. ibid., p. 169.
23. Mitchell headed up an international team that included Canadian General John de Chastelain (chosen by the British) and former Finnish Prime Minister Harri Holkeri (chosen by the Irish). Everyone was aware of the need to have a balanced ticket to avoid easy accusations of bias or partiality, which would undermine their credibility. This troika would become a semi-permanent fixture in Northern Ireland over the formal multi-party negotiations that took place from 1996 to 1998, and specifically over the issue of weapons decommissioning for most of the next decade.
24. ibid., p. 77–8.
25. ibid., p. 185.
26. G. Mitchell, *Making Peace*, Heinemann, London, 1999, p. 30.
27. ibid., p. 31.
28. ibid.
29. See http://news.bbc.co.uk/onthisday/hi/dates/stories/february/10/newsid_2539000/2539265.stm
30. De Breadun, *Far Side of Revenge*, p. 16.
31. Mitchell was joined by two co-chairmen, General John de Chastelain and Harri Holkeri.
32. Mitchell, *Making Peace*, p. 47.
33. 'New truce, disarmament rejected', *Chicago Tribune*, 6 June 1996, available at: http://articles.chicagotribune.com/1996-06-06/news/9606060145_1_ira-cease-fire-ira-statement-peace-talks
34. Mitchell, *Making Peace*, p. 50.
35. Cochrane, *Unionist Politics* (first edition), p. 360.
36. Powell, *Great Hatred*, p. 15.
37. S. McCaffery, 'Path to peace marked with clasp of hands', *Irish Examiner*, 28 June 2012, available at: http://www.irishexaminer.com/archives/2012/0628/ireland/path-to-peace-marked-with-clasp-of-hands-198941.html
38. T. Blair, *A Journey*, Hutchinson, London, 2010.
39. Mallie and McKittrick, *Endgame in Ireland*, p. 238.
40. Powell, *Great Hatred*, pp. 28–9.
41. *Sunday Tribune*, 5 April 1998, cited in F. Cochrane, *Unionist Politics and the Politics of Unionism since the Anglo-Irish Agreement*, second edition, Cork University Press, Cork, 2001, p. 375.
42. She went public with the news when tabloid journalists began commenting on her weight gain just before the general election, with *Daily Mail* columnist Lynda Lee-Potter cruelly comparing her to an 'only slightly effeminate Geordie Trucker'. The newspaper subsequently apologized when it was announced that this was the result of

her medical condition, but the image stuck and many Geordie truckers adopted Mowlam – to the extent that at one point, following a television interview in 1999, the Road Haulage Association had to contact the Northern Ireland Office for signed photographs of her, so numerous were the requests for her picture among lorry drivers. Ironically, Lee-Potter herself died of a brain tumour in October 2004.

43. Mitchell, *Making Peace*, p. 102.
44. 'Interview: Adam Ingram – Mo Mowlam and me', *Scotsman*, 2 February 2010, available at: http://www.scotsman.com/news/interview-adam-ingram-mo-mowlam-and-me-1-788921
45. G. Mitchell, 'Remarks by Senator George J. Mitchell', Organization for Security and Cooperation in Europe, Dublin, Ireland, 27 April 2012, p. 6, available at: http://www.osce.org/cio/90200
46. Mallie and McKittrick, *Endgame in Ireland*, p. 237.
47. 'Interview with Martha Pope and David Pozorski', Oral History Project, Digital Commons, 2009, available at: http://digitalcommons.bowdoin.edu/mitchelloralhistory/45/
48. Mallie and McKittrick, *Endgame in Ireland*, p. 236.
49. Quoted in Cochrane, *Unionist Politics* (second edition), p. 378.
50. Quoted in Cochrane, *Unionist Politics* (second edition), p. 375.
51. 'The Agreement', 10 April 1998, Belfast, p. 20, available at: http://www.nio.gov.uk/agreement.pdf
52. Mallie and McKittrick, *Endgame in Ireland*, p. 249.
53. Tony Blair letter to David Trimble, 10 April 1998, available at: http://cain.ulst.ac.uk/events/peace/docs/tb100498.htm
54. G. McLaughlin and S. Baker, *The Propaganda of Peace*, University of Chicago Press, Chicago, 2010, p. 21.
55. 'The Agreement', 10 April 1998, Belfast, available at: http://www.nio.gov.uk/agreement.pdf
56. Mitchell, *Making Peace*, p. 68.

## CHAPTER 7: THE INCOMPLETE AGREEMENT, 1998–2002

1. T. Blair, Press Conference, Belfast, 10 April 1998.
2. Statement by Sinn Fein President Gerry Adams at a post-GFA press conference, 10 April 1998, available at: http://www.sinnfein.org/releases/pr041098b.html
3. Eamon de Valera introduced a new written constitution to the Irish Free State in 1937. Article 2 defined the 'national territory' of Ireland as being all thirty-two counties, while Article 3 indicated a desire to exercise jurisdiction over the whole national territory. As a result of the Good Friday Agreement and the subsequent parliamentary legislation and referendum, both of these articles were diluted into aspirations rather than rights. The concept of the 'national territory' was reformulated into a right to belong to the Irish nation for those born on the island of Ireland, while people of Irish ancestry living abroad were to be cherished by the Irish nation. The critical reformulation in Article 3 was as follows: 'It is the firm will of the Irish Nation, in harmony and friendship, to unite all the people who share the territory of the island of Ireland, in all the diversity of their identities and traditions, recognising that a united Ireland shall be brought about only by peaceful means with the consent of a majority of the people, democratically expressed, in both jurisdictions in the island. Until then, the laws enacted by the Parliament established by this Constitution shall have the like area and extent of application as the laws enacted by the Parliament that existed immediately before the coming into operation of this Constitution.' See 'The Agreement', 10 April 1998, Belfast, p. 20, available at: http://www.nio.gov.uk/agreement.pdf
4. ibid., p. 1.
5. S. Elliot, 'The referendum and assembly elections in Northern Ireland', *Irish Political Studies*, 14 (1999), p. 141.
6. *Ireland on Sunday*, 12 April 1998, p. 4, quoted in Cochrane, *Unionist Politics* (second edition).

7. 'It's Right to Say "No"', Democratic Unionist Party referendum communication, Belfast, 1998, available at: http://irishelectionliterature.wordpress.com/2010/05/22/its-right-to-say-no-dup-good-friday-agreement/
8. 'Progress Union Peace – Yes', Progressive Unionist Party referendum communication, Belfast, 1998, available at: http://cain.ulst.ac.uk/issues/politics/docs/pup/pup220598.pdf
9. 'Agreement Our Shared Future – A Key Decision', SDLP referendum communication, Belfast, 1998 available at: http://cain.ulst.ac.uk/issues/politics/docs/sdlp/sdlp220598.pdf
10. N. Thompson, 'Ringmaster Noel bids fond farewell to political circus', *News Letter*, 21 June 2012, available at: http://www.newsletter.co.uk/news/headlines/ringmaster-noel-bids-fond-farewell-to-political-circus-1-3973348
11. Q. Oliver, *Working for 'Yes'*, The 'Yes' Campaign, Belfast, 1998, p. 81.
12. ibid., p. 21.
13. Mallie and McKittrick, *Endgame in Ireland*, p. 218.
14. ibid., p. 78.
15. Tonge, *Northern Ireland*, p. 190.
16. 'Resurrected Paisley belts out his hymn of victory', *Irish Independent*, 7 May 2005, available at: http://www.independent.ie/national-news/resurrected-paisley-belts-out-his-hymn-of-victory-258105.html
17. McLaughlin and Baker, *Propaganda of Peace*, p. 25.
18. http://news.bbc.co.uk/1/hi/events/northern_ireland/focus/96491.stm
19. ibid.
20. I. McAllister, B. Hayes and L. Dowds, 'The erosion of consent: Protestant disillusionment with the Agreement', *Ark Research Update*, 32 (January 2005), p. 2.
21. ibid.
22. 'A message from the prime minister, Tony Blair, following the Omagh bomb', 18 August 1998, available at: http://cain.ulst.ac.uk/events/peace/docs/tb18898.htm
23. See http://www.youtube.com/watch?v=8jzQ_Nb9GqM The song was written by American singer songwriter Julie Miller and appears on her 1991 album *He Walks Through Walls*. See also: http://news.bbc.co.uk/1/hi/events/northern_ireland/latest_news/156891.stm#
24. D. Murray, 'Sadness surrounding the NI crisis', BBC News, 8 February 2000, available at: http://news.bbc.co.uk/2/hi/uk_news/northern_ireland/631547.stm
25. '"We've done our bit. Now, Mr Adams, it's over to you"', *Observer*, 28 November 1999, available at: http://www.guardian.co.uk/uk/1999/nov/28/northernireland.johnofarrell
26. ibid.
27. Tonge, *Northern Ireland*, p. 194.
28. 'DUP pledges Stormont disruption', BBC News, 31 May 2000, available at: http://news.bbc.co.uk/1/hi/northern_ireland/770694.stm
29. P. Robinson, 'Defining moments on the road to devolution', First Minister Peter Robinson, John F. Kennedy Lecture, Institute of Irish Studies, University of Liverpool, 2011, available at: http://www.peterrobinson.org/MainNewsArticles.asp?ArticleNewsID=3870
30. 'Second chance for Ulster', *Guardian*, 29 May 2000, available at: http://www.guardian.co.uk/uk/2000/may/29/northernireland.guardianleaders
31. 'Trimble's offensive logic', *An Phoblacht*, 1 June 2000, available at: http://republican-news.org/archive/2000/June01/01trim.html
32. David Trimble resigned as leader of the UUP in 2005 after losing his Upper Bann seat at Westminster in the general election to the DUP's David Simpson.
33. Joe O'Donnell of the Belfast Interface Project. Interviewed by author, 22 February 2011.
34. P. Shirlow, 'Segregation, ethno-sectarianism and the "new" Belfast' in M. Cox, A. Guelke and F. Stephen, *A Farewell to Arms? Beyond the Good Friday Agreement*, Manchester University Press, Manchester, 2005, p. 226.
35. ibid., p. 228.

36. ibid., p. 229.
37. 'The Agreement', 10 April 1998, Belfast, p. 18, available at: http://www.nio.gov.uk/agreement.pdf
38. P. Dixon, *Northern Ireland: The politics of war and peace*, second edition, Palgrave, Basingstoke, 2007, p. 299.
39. D. Cronin, 'And the Europeans of the Year are . . .', EuropeanVoice.com, 5 December 2002, available (on subscription) at: http://www.europeanvoice.com/article/imported/-and-the-europeans-of-the-year-are-/46242.aspx
40. Noel Doran, editor, *Irish News*. Interviewed by author, 24 February 2011.
41. Brewer et al., *Religion, Civil Society and Peace*, pp. 61–2.
42. A. Troy, *Holy Cross: A personal experience*, Currach Press, Blackrock, 2005, pp. 69–70.
43. ibid., pp. 60–1.
44. Brewer et al., *Religion, Civil Society and Peace*, p. 63.
45. ibid.
46. 'The Agreement', 10 April 1998, Belfast, p. 5, available at: http://www.nio.gov.uk/agreement.pdf
47. B. Dickson, Address given to the Orange Order Conference on Human Rights, 13 April 2002, available at: http://www.findthatdoc.com/search-9210270-hDOC/download-documents-orange-address-02.doc.htm
48. 'Northern Ireland chronology: 2002', BBC News, 9 April 2003, available at: http://news.bbc.co.uk/1/hi/northern_ireland/2933949.stm
49. D. McKittrick, 'The spy's tale: The life and death of Denis Donaldson', *Independent*, 6 April 2006, available at: http://www.independent.co.uk/news/uk/this-britain/the-spys-tale-the-life-and-death-of-denis-donaldson-472992.html
50. This internal security unit within the IRA was named after its practice of shooting informers in the head. Ironically, a number of those who ran it, most famously Freddie 'Stakeknife' Scappaticci, were themselves paid British informers.
51. 'The big lie', *Irish Republican News*, 12 December 2005, available at: http://republican-news.org/current/news/2005/12/the_big_lie.html
52. 'Spy ring riddle', *Down Democrat*, 3 January 2006.

CHAPTER 8: DELIVERY, DELIVERY, DELIVERY, 1999–2010

1. Quintin Oliver, director of Stratagem. Interviewed by author, 26 February 2011. Stratagem is a public policy lobbying company, and its director was using the collective 'we' here to point out that the various paramilitary factions – and the wider communities on whose behalf they claim to act – are responsible for a much smaller amount of fatal violence than they were in the past. His reference to 104 out of 108 MLAs being in government starkly highlights the lack of any effective opposition in the process, as the vast majority of MLAs belong to one of the five parties who sit in permanent coalition in the governing Executive (DUP, UUP, Sinn Fein, SDLP and Alliance).
2. Between 2001 and 2011 (when 50–50 recruitment was discontinued), Catholic membership of the PSNI rose from around 8 per cent to over 27 per cent.
3. C. Helferty, president of the National Union of Students–Union of Students of Ireland (NUS–USI). Interviewed by author, 25 February 2011.
4. M. Holland, 'Anxious Irish eyes turn to McGuinness vital statistics', *Observer*, 5 December 1999, available at: http://www.guardian.co.uk/uk/1999/dec/05/northernireland.theobserver
5. C. Helferty interview, 2011.
6. At its most basic, the 'Notices' sections of the *News Letter* and *Irish News* were read by one community and not the other to see who had recently been born, got married or had died. The fact that neither community felt the need to check the notices in the 'other' paper is a marker of the level of community division that remains.
7. Noel Doran interview, 2011.
8. Office of the First Minister and Deputy First Minister, see http://www.ofmdfmni.gov.uk/

9. R. O'Reilly and B. McCaffrey, 'How Stormont cuts could decide what newspaper you read', *The Detail*, 1 April 2012, available at: http://www.thedetail.tv/issues/76/newspaper-advertising-story/how-stormont-cuts-could-decide-what-newspaper-you-read—3
10. ibid.
11. Conall McDevitt, SDLP Member of the Legislative Assembly (MLA). Interviewed by author, 23 February 2011.
12. G. McLaughlin and S. Baker, 'The media, the peace process and "bread and butter" politics', *Political Quarterly*, 83:2 (April–June 2012), p. 292.
13. 'Sofa, so good for new IKEA', *Belfast Telegraph*, 14 December 2007, available at: http://www.belfasttelegraph.co.uk/news/local-national/sofa-so-good-for-new-ikea-13501783.html
14. This is admittedly a rather stretched metaphor, as the behaviour of these particular caterpillars seems to be controlled by the wasp grubs, to the point that the former spend their dying hours protecting the wasp cocoons from attack by other predators. The analogy is also rather hard on the DUP, which could argue, with some justification, that the UUP devoured itself without much intervention.
15. 'Fair Deal Manifesto 2003', DUP election literature, Belfast, 2003, available at: http://cain.ulst.ac.uk/issues/politics/docs/dup/dup03man.pdf
16. 'Agenda for Government Clár Rialtais', Sinn Fein election literature, Belfast, 2003, available at: http://cain.ulst.ac.uk/issues/politics/docs/sf/sf03man.pdf
17. P. Robinson, 'Defining moments on the road to devolution', First Minister Peter Robinson, John F. Kennedy Lecture, Institute of Irish Studies, University of Liverpool, 2011, available at: http://www.peterrobinson.org/MainNewsArticles.asp?ArticleNewsID=3870
18. Powell, *Great Hatred*, p. 236.
19. Noel Doran interview, 2011.
20. This Robert McCartney had no connection to the Robert McCartney who was then leader of the UKUP.
21. Quoted in F. Cochrane, 'Irish-America, the end of the IRA's armed struggle and the utility of soft power', *Journal of Peace Research*, 44:2 (2007), p. 215.
22. Martin McGuinness, quoted in Dixon, *Northern Ireland*.
23. Paisley, quoted in Cochrane, *Ending Wars*, p. 183.
24. 'Martin McGuinness' speech in full', BBC News, 8 May 2007, available at: http://news.bbc.co.uk/1/hi/northern_ireland/6636227.stm
25. Quintin Oliver interview, 2011.
26. My thanks go to Professor David Denver of Lancaster University, who had the onerous task of marking this exam answer several years ago.
27. Stephen Farry, Alliance Party MLA, Minister for Employment and Learning. Interviewed by author, 24 February 2011.
28. Conall McDevitt interview, 2011.
29. Peter Weir, DUP MLA. Interviewed by author, 21 February 2011.
30. 'About us', Traditional Unionist Voice website, available at: http://www.tuv.org.uk/tuv/about/
31. 'Iris Robinson's toy boy lover Kirk McCambley "feigned testicular cancer to end affair"', *Daily Mail*, 13 January 2010, available at: http://www.dailymail.co.uk/news/article-1242090/Iris-Robinsons-toy-boy-lover-Kirk-McCambley-feigned-testicular-cancer-end-affair.html
32. http://www.publications.parliament.uk/pa/cm200708/cmgeneral/nigc/080617/80617s02.htm
33. David Ford, Alliance Party leader, MLA and justice minister. Interviewed by author, 21 February 2011.
34. Peter Weir interview, 2011.
35. David Ford interview, 2011.
36. Stephen Farry interview, 2011.
37. Nigel Smyth, Director-General, Northern Ireland CBI. Interviewed by author, 25 February 2011.
38. 'Platform for Change', available at: http://www.platformforchange.net/documents/Platform%20for%20Change%20Extended.pdf

39. ibid.
40. Northern Ireland Executive, *Programme for Government*, available at: http://www.northern ireland.gov.uk/pfgfinal.pdf
41. P. Nolan, *Northern Ireland Peace Monitoring Report Number One*, Community Relations Council, Belfast, 2012, p. 117.
42. D. Murray, 'Beyond Westminster', BBC Radio 4, 20 February 2010, available at: http://www.bbc.co.uk/iplayer/episode/b00qvqcs/Beyond_Westminster_20_02_2010/
43. 'Our vision is of . . . stable, cohesive government', NICVA website, 7 April 2011, available at: http://www.nicva.org/policy-manifesto-2011/government
44. OFMDFM, 'Programme for cohesion, sharing and integration: Consultation document', available at: http://www.ofmdfmni.gov.uk/reformatted_final_print_version_csi_-_26.07.10.pdf
45. Available at: http://www.ofmdfmni.gov.uk/policy-strategic-framework-good-relations.pdf
46. J. Todd and J. Ruane, *From 'A Shared Future' to 'Cohesion, Sharing and Integration': An analysis of Northern Ireland's policy framework documents*, Joseph Rowntree Charitable Trust, York, 2010.
47. Conall McDevitt interview, 2011.
48. Chartered Institute of Housing, 'Shared Housing: The building block for cohesion, sharing and integration', October 2010, p. 2, available at: http://www.ofmdfmni.gov.uk/csiresponses2010_chartered_institute_of_housing.pdf
49. Rural Community Network, 'Programme for Cohesion, Sharing and Integration: Response to the Consultation by Rural Community Network', October 2010, p. 4, available at: http://www.community-relations.org.uk/fs/doc/RCNCSI%20Consultation%20Response%20final%20draft.pdf
50. Joe O'Donnell interview, 2011.
51. N. Jarman, 'Security and segregation: interface barriers in Belfast', *Shared Space* (2005), available at: http://www.community-relations.org.uk/fs/doc/shared-space-neil-jarmon.pdf
52. David Ford interview, 2011.
53. Noel Doran interview, 2011.

CHAPTER 9: DISSENTING VOICES, 2010–12

1. '"I hope he listens now" – mum ordered to bring son to be shot', *Derry Journal*, 30 April 2012, available at: http://www.derryjournal.com/news/local/i-hope-he-listens-now-mum-ordered-to-bring-son-to-be-shot-1-3789831#
2. 'Mothers who tell RAAD – MOVE ON', *Derry Journal*, 1 May 2012, available at: http://www.derryjournal.com/news/local/mothers-who-tell-raad-move-on-1-3794156
3. 'Punishment shootings in Derry', *Woman's Hour*, BBC Radio 4, 25 May 2012, available at: http://www.bbc.co.uk/programmes/p00t4544
4. PSNI, 'Security situation statistics: monthly update', 16 March 2012, p. 4, available at: http://www.psni.police.uk/security_situation_statistics_-_by_district_and_area__april_2011_-_february_2012.pdf
5. R. Cowan, 'Adair's son takes his punishment: a shooting sanctioned by his father', *Guardian*, 9 August 2002, available at: http://www.guardian.co.uk/uk/2002/aug/09/northernireland.rosiecowan1
6. 'Uncle who refused to condemn bomb bid on niece "an eejit", says Gerry Adams', *Belfast Telegraph*, 9 August 2010, available at: http://www.belfasttelegraph.co.uk/news/local-national/northern-ireland/uncle-who-refused-to-condemn-bomb-bid-on-n.html—lsquoan-eejitrsquo-says-gerry-adams-14902447.html
7. The 'dissidents' is an umbrella term for a range of diverse actors, the common thread being that they still support the use of violence in pursuit of Irish reunification. The groups largely object to the term 'dissident', as it suggests that they are political 'outsiders'. Within their own logic, they have remained constant, while the Provisional IRA and Sinn Fein have changed direction.

8. The Workers' Party traces its lineage back to the formation of Sinn Fein in 1905, but owes its current form to the split in the IRA in 1970. It was on the Southern Marxist side of the argument, supporting an end to Sinn Fein's abstention policy and rejecting the increasing militancy of those who went on to form the Provisional IRA. In 1977, Official Sinn Fein adopted the name 'Sinn Fein: The Workers' Party', and in 1982 the metamorphosis was completed when it became known simply as the Workers' Party.

9. L. Bowman-Grieve and M. Conway, 'Exploring the form and function of dissident Irish republican online discourses', *Media, War and Conflict*, 5:1 (2012), p. 73.

10. Nolan, *Northern Ireland Peace Monitoring Report*, pp. 43–4.

11. M. Frampton, *The Return of the Militants: Violent dissident republicanism*, ICSR, London, 2010, p. 2.

12. Nolan, *Northern Ireland Peace Monitoring Report*, p. 44.

13. 'Security forces warned over internet dangers', *News Letter*, 13 January 2012, available at: http://www.newsletter.co.uk/news/headlines/security-forces-warned-over-internet-dangers-1-3415780

14. 'NI violence "organised on social networking sites"', BBC Newsbeat, 26 January 2010, available at: http://www.bbc.co.uk/newsbeat/10005113

15. Bowman-Grieve and Conway, 'Exploring the form and function', p. 71.

16. ibid., p. 75.

17. C. Corrigan, 'Real IRA, other dissidents use social nets to catch teenagers', Irish Central website, 23 April 2009, last accessed on 10 September 2010 at: www.IrishCentral.com

18. 'The militarist campaign: "Who's pulling the strings?" asks ex-POW Bobby Storey', *An Phoblacht*, 2 July 2010, available at: http://www.anphoblacht.com/contents/106

19. Some studies have resorted to the phrase 'violent dissident republicans' (VDRs) to differentiate between those who still advocate 'armed struggle' and those who – while remaining just as critical of Sinn Fein and the Provisional IRA's strategic shift to non-violence – do not.

20. Bowman-Grieve and Conway, 'Exploring the form and function', p. 77.

21. A. McIntyre, quoted in *Fortnight*, March 2009, p. 29.

22. Jonathan Evans, 'Address at the Worshipful Company of Security Professionals by the Director General of the Security Service', 16 September 2010, available at: https://www.mi5.gov.uk/home/about-us/who-we-are/staff-and-management/director-general/speeches-by-the-director-general/the-threat-to-national-security.html

23. J. Evans and J. Tonge, 'Menace without mandate? Is there any sympathy for "dissident" Irish republicanism in Northern Ireland?', *Terrorism and Political Violence*, 24:1 (2012), pp. 61–78.

24. East Belfast loyalist paramilitary, quoted in L. Smithey, *Unionists, Loyalists and Conflict Transformation in Northern Ireland*, Oxford University Press, Oxford, 2011, p. 152.

25. C. Steenkamp, 'Loyalist paramilitary violence after the Belfast agreement', *Ethnopolitics*, 7:1 (2008), p. 159.

26. Quoted in Nolan, *Northern Ireland Peace Monitoring Report*, p. 46.

27. C. Mitchell, 'The limits of legitimacy: former loyalist combatants and peace-building in Northern Ireland', *Irish Political Studies*, 23:1 (2008), p. 4.

28. ibid.

29. The Historical Enquiries Team (HET) is a unit within the PSNI that was established in 2005 to investigate over 3,000 unsolved killings during the period 1968–98. Its methods have resulted in some criticism that it gives preferential treatment to soldiers than to non-military suspects, and this led to a review of its practices in April 2012. See Patricia Lundy, 'Research brief: Assessment of HET review processes and procedures in Royal Military Police investigation cases', University of Ulster, 2012, available at: http://eprints.ulster.ac.uk/21809/

30. Nolan, *Northern Ireland Peace Monitoring Report*, p. 49.

31. P. Shirlow, 'A prosperity of thought in an age of austerity: The case of Ulster loyalism', *Political Quarterly*, 83:2 (April–June 2012).

32. The police ombudsman launched an investigation into allegations of collusion between the PSNI and the UVF over the murder of Bobby Moffett in October 2012.

33. 'Bomb defused in Northern Ireland would have caused devastation', Reuters, 28 April 2012, available at: http://uk.reuters.com/article/2012/04/28/uk-irish-bombs-idUKBRE 83R0AJ20120428
34. 'Government will not talk to dissident republicans, says Northern Ireland Secretary Owen Patterson', *Guardian*, 9 August 2010, available at: http://www.guardian.co.uk/politics/2010/aug/09/government-will-not-talk-to-dissident-republicans
35. Nolan, *Northern Ireland Peace Monitoring Report*, p. 42.
36. IMC, *Twenty-sixth and final report of the Independent Monitoring Commissioning: 2004– 2011: Changes, impact and lessons*, 2011, pp. 55–6, available at: http://www.justice.ie/en/JELR/Final%20IMC%20Report.pdf/Files/Final%20IMC%20Report.pdf
37. This pin denotes that the wearer has conversational Irish.
38. David Ford interview, 2011.

## CHAPTER 10: LOOKING TO THE FUTURE, 2012–13

1. *The Nolan Show*, BBC Northern Ireland Television, 23 May 2012.
2. E. McCann on *The Nolan Show*, BBC Northern Ireland Television, 23 May 2012.
3. 'Alliance pulls out of Stormont's "shared future" group', BBC News, 24 May 2012, available at: http://www.bbc.co.uk/news/uk-northern-ireland-18186505
4. Both the DUP and Sinn Fein denied that any deal had been struck which linked these two policies.
5. 'Caledon 1968 – Girdwood 2012!', *Republican Socialist News*, 30 May 2012, available at: http://www.irsp.ie/news/?p=848
6. This line was quoted by Deputy First Minister Seamus Mallon in a speech welcoming President Bill Clinton to Northern Ireland on 3 September 1998 and was spoken by Maya Angelou herself when she delivered her 'Inaugural Poem' at President Clinton's inauguration in Washington on 20 January 1993, see: http://cain.ulst.ac.uk/events/peace/docs/sm3998.htm
7. *Healing Through Remembering Project* http://www.healingthroughremembering.org/news/article/365/
8. Nigel Smyth interview, 2011.
9. R. Wilson and E. Meehan, 'Can Northern Ireland become normal? Attitudes to the role of government in Northern Ireland', *ARK Research Update*, 57 (June 2008), p. 4.
10. ibid.
11. Northern Ireland Life and Times Survey, available at: http://www.ark.ac.uk/nilt/2010/Political_Attitudes/NIGOVDO1.html
12. ibid., available at: http://www.ark.ac.uk/nilt/2010/Political_Attitudes/COMPREC.html
13. ibid., available at: http://www.ark.ac.uk/nilt/2010/Community_Relations/RLRELAGO.html
14. Noel Doran interview, 2011.
15. 'Changing Voices', BBC Northern Ireland Eyewitness website, undated, available at: http://www.bbc.co.uk/northernireland/learning/eyewitness/changing/voices/giles.shtml
16. A previous effort had been made to do this with the publication of *We Will Remember Them*, compiled by the recently appointed 'victims commissioner', Sir Kenneth Bloomfield. This imaginative report was published in April 1998, though it was rather overtaken by events, as the political process lurched from crisis to crisis over the next several years. See: http://cain.ulst.ac.uk/issues/victims/docs/bloomfield98.pdf
17. The word ex-combatant has come into vogue in recent years and is favoured most by those who used to be called 'terrorists' by some or 'paramilitaries' by others. It is also used by academics who advocate restorative justice programmes and who favour the neutrality of the term.
18. M. Nesbitt, Victims and Survivors – private members' business debate, Northern Ireland Assembly, 8 May 2012, available at: http://www.theyworkforyou.com/ni/?id= 2012-05-08.3.1

19. F. Molloy, Victims and Survivors – private members' business debate, Northern Ireland Assembly, 8 May 2012, available at: http://www.theyworkforyou.com/ni/?id=2012-05-08.3.1

20. The H-Blocks, which include the prison hospital where ten republicans died on hunger strike in 1981, are now listed buildings and would be the centrepiece of any commemorative museum or conflict centre of this type.

21. Reference to Maze/Long Kesh contains undertones connected with the conflict itself. Long Kesh was the name of the prison during the period when special category status existed in the 1970s. When this status was removed in 1976 in order to criminalize the inmates, the prison was renamed the Maze (after the local area outside Belfast). Thus, to call it Long Kesh is, by extension, a recognition of the demand for political status. To refer to it as the Maze prison may indicate an acceptance of the British criminalization policy and a rejection of the 'political status' of the prisoners. Such linguistic nuances are not always observed, but republicans and loyalists still refer to the prison as Long Kesh, and the fact that the abbreviation MLK has been settled upon by the current devolved government is itself a reflection of their different readings of the past.

22. OFMDFM, 'Maze/Long Kesh Development Corporation: Information pack for chair and board members', March 2012, p. 3, available at: www.ofmdfmni.gov.uk/mlk_dc_chair___board__information_pack_March_2012.docx

23. S. Hoggart, 'David Cameron's statement on the Bloody Sunday report was pitch-perfect', *Guardian*, 16 June 2010, available at: http://www.guardian.co.uk/politics/2010/jun/16/david-cameron-bloody-sunday-statement?intcmp=239

24. This event was also attended by Robinson's wife Iris. This was the first time she had appeared at a public occasion since her much-publicized affair with a nineteen-year-old man and her subsequent medical treatment for depression.

25. S. Bates and H. McDonald, 'Queen gives Ireland closest royals have come to apology for Britain's actions', *Guardian*, 19 May 2011, available at: http://www.guardian.co.uk/uk/2011/may/18/queen-ireland-apology-britains-actions

26. 'Queen's visit to Ireland "extraordinary moment in history"', *Daily Telegraph*, 16 May 2011, available at: http://www.telegraph.co.uk/news/uknews/theroyalfamily/8515165/Queens-visit-to-Ireland-extraordinary-moment-in-history.html

27. 'Queen offers sympathy to Irish victims of troubles', BBC News, 19 May 2011, available at: http://www.bbc.co.uk/news/world-europe-13447236

28. Conall McDevitt interview, 2011.

29. T. McCusker, Speech at the 'No More Them and Us' conference, Titanic Building, 16 May 2012.

30. D. Ford, MLA and Justice Minister, Speech at the 'No More Them and Us' conference, Titanic Building, 16 May 2012.

31. ibid.

32. Northern Ireland Executive, *Programme for Government 2011–15*, available at: http://www.northernireland.gov.uk/pfg-2011-2015-final-report.pdf

33. Taylor, R. (ed.), *Consociational Theory: McGarry and O'Leary and the Northern Ireland conflict*, Routledge, London, 2009, p. 46.

34. J. McGarry (ed.), *Northern Ireland and the Divided World*, Oxford University Press, Oxford, 2001, p. 122.

35. Mark Durkan speech to the British-Irish Association, Oxford University, 5 September 2008.

36. Peter Weir interview, 2011.

37. David Ford interview, 2011.

38. While McCallister lost the UUP leadership election, he had a more important victory just days before the vote, when he managed to deliver his wife's baby on the bathroom floor of their home after she went into labour a week early. He commented afterwards that 'maybe if I lose on Saturday I can retrain as a midwife'. He lost out in the end to former local television journalist Mike Nesbitt, which has set the likelihood of this move into opposition back for the moment.

39. Margaret Ritchie's speech to the 2010 SDLP Annual Conference, 6 November 2010, available at: http://www.sdlp.ie/index.php/newsroom_media/speech/a_new_ireland_for_all_-_leaders_speech_to_conference_2010/

40. P. Robinson, 'Reflections on Irish Unionism', Edward Carson Lecture, Dublin, 29 March 2012.

41. Northern Ireland Tourist Board, 'Derry–Londonderry named as one of the top cities in the world for 2013', press release, 23 October 2012. My thanks go to Margaret Duffy for the link to this story, which is available at: http://www.nitb.com/NewsMedia/LatestNews/tabid/180/EntryId/342/Derry~Londonderry-named-as-one-of-the-top-cities-in-the-world-for-2013.aspx

42. R. Meredith, 'MTV Europe Music awards generated £22m for Belfast', BBC News, available at: http://www.bbc.co.uk/news/uk-northern-ireland-19289581

43. N. Sayee, 'Belfast in National Geographic top 10 destinations', BBC News, 24 November 2011, available at: http://www.bbc.co.uk/news/uk-northern-ireland-15872225

44. C. Weir, 'Suddenly the world wants to visit Northern Ireland', *Belfast Telegraph*, 21 April 2012, available at: http://www.belfasttelegraph.co.uk/news/local-national/northern-ireland/suddenly-the-world-wants-to-visit-northern-ireland-16148091.html

45. Paddywagon is a deliberately ironic name and derives from the Irish-American diaspora. It was used as a slang term for police vans in the US at the beginning of the twentieth century.

46. See http://www.paddywagontours.com/viewtour.php?id=26&&day=09&&month=01&&year=2009

47. Allen's Tours, http://www.allensbelfastbustours.com/belfastbustours.php

48. P. Robinson, 'Reflections on Irish Unionism', Edward Carson Lecture, Dublin, 29 March 2012.

## POSTSCRIPT

1. M. Purdy, 'Martin McGuinness' journey from IRA leader to meeting the Queen', BBC News, 22 June 2012, available at: http://www.bbc.co.uk/news/uk-northern-ireland-18549981

2. A. McIntyre, 'By shaking the Queen's hand, Martin McGuinness accepts her sovereignty', *Guardian*, 26 June 2012, available at: http://www.guardian.co.uk/commentisfree/2012/jun/26/shaking-queen-hand-martin-mcguinness

3. ibid.

# BIBLIOGRAPHY

Adams, G., *Free Ireland: Towards a lasting peace*, Brandon Books, Dublin, 1986

Arthur, P., *The Government and Politics of Northern Ireland*, Longman, Harlow, 1984

——, *Special Relationships*, Blackstaff Press, Belfast, 2000

Bardon, J., *A History of Ulster*, Blackstaff Press, Belfast, 1992

Bew, P. and G. Gillespie, *Northern Ireland: A chronology of the troubles 1968–1993*, Gill & Macmillan, Dublin, 1993

Birney, T. and J. O'Neill, *When the President Calls*, Guildhall Press, Derry, 1997, available at: http://cain.ulst.ac.uk/events/peace/docs/birney.htm

Bishop, P. and E. Mallie, *The Provisional IRA*, Corgi Books, London, 1987

Blair, T., *A Journey*, Hutchinson, London, 2010

Bloomfield, K., *Stormont in Crisis: A memoir*, Blackstaff Press, Belfast, 1994

Bowman-Grieve, L. and M. Conway, 'Exploring the form and function of dissident Irish republican online discourses', *Media, War and Conflict*, 5:1 (2012)

Brewer, J. and G. Higgins, *Anti-Catholicism in Northern Ireland 1600–1998*, Macmillan, Basingstoke, 1998, available at: http://cain.ulst.ac.uk/issues/sectarian/brewer.htm

Brewer, J., G. Higgins and F. Teeney, *Religion, Civil Society and Peace in Northern Ireland*, Oxford University Press, Oxford, 2011

Buckland, P., *James Craig*, Gill & Macmillan, Dublin, 1980

Carson, C., 'Belfast Confetti' in *The Irish for No*, Wake Forest University Press, Winston-Salem, 1987

Cochrane, F., ' "Meddling at the crossroads": The decline and fall of Terence O'Neill within the unionist community' in R. English and G. Walker (eds), *Unionism in Modern Ireland*, Macmillan, Basingstoke, 1996

——, *Unionist Politics and the Politics of Unionism since the Anglo-Irish Agreement*, first edition, Cork University Press, Cork, 1997

——, *Unionist Politics and the Politics of Unionism since the Anglo-Irish Agreement*, second edition, Cork University Press, Cork, 2001

——, *People Power? The role of the voluntary and community sector in the Northern Ireland conflict*, Cork University Press, Cork, 2002

——, 'Irish-America, the end of the IRA's armed struggle and the utility of soft power', *Journal of Peace Research*, 44:2 (2007)

——, *Ending Wars*, Polity Press, Cambridge, 2008

Cox, M., A. Guelke and F. Stephen (eds), *A Farewell to Arms? Beyond the Good Friday Agreement*, second edition, Manchester University Press, Manchester, 2006

Crawford, R., *Loyal to King Billy: A portrait of the Ulster Protestants*, Gill & Macmillan, Dublin, 1987

De Breadun, D., *The Far Side of Revenge*, Collins, Dublin, 2001

Defoe, D., *The Parallel; or Persecution of Protestants the shortest way to prevent the growth of Popery in Ireland*, London, 1704

Dickson, Brice, 'Counter-insurgency and human rights in Northern Ireland', *Journal of Strategic Studies*, 32 (2009), pp. 475–93

Dixon, P., *Northern Ireland: The politics of war and peace*, second edition, Palgrave, Basingstoke, 2007

Dumbrell, J., '"Hope and history": the US and peace in Northern Ireland' in M. Cox, A. Guelke and F. Stephen (eds), *A Farewell to Arms? From 'long war' to long peace in Northern Ireland*, Manchester University Press, Manchester, 2000

Elliot, S., 'The referendum and assembly elections in Northern Ireland', *Irish Political Studies*, 14 (1999)

English, R., *Armed Struggle: The history of the IRA*, Macmillan, Basingstoke, 2003

Ervine, St John, *Craigavon*, Ulsterman, London, 1949

Evans, J. and J. Tonge, 'Menace without mandate? Is there any sympathy for "dissident" Irish republicanism in Northern Ireland?', *Terrorism and Political Violence*, 24:1 (2012), pp. 61–78

Farrell, M., *Northern Ireland: The Orange State*, Pluto Press, London, 1976

Farrington, C. (ed.), *Global Change, Civil Society and the Northern Ireland Peace Process*, Palgrave, Basingstoke, 2008

Foster, R.F., *Modern Ireland 1600–1972*, Penguin, London, 1989

Frampton, M., *The Return of the Militants: Violent dissident republicanism*, ICSR, London, 2010

Gordon, D., *The O'Neill Years: Unionist politics 1963–69*, Athol Books, Belfast, 1989

Guelke, A., 'Northern Ireland: international and north/south issues' in W. Crotty and D. Schmitt (eds), *Ireland and the Politics of Change*, Longman, London, 1998

Hanley, B., 'The politics of Noraid', *Irish Political Studies*, 19:1 (2004)

Hewitt, John, *The Selected Poems of John Hewitt*, ed. Michael Longley and Frank Ormsby, Blackstaff Press, Belfast, 2007

Jarman, N., 'Security and segregation: interface barriers in Belfast', *Shared Space* (2005), available at: http://www.community-relations.org.uk/fs/doc/shared-space-neil-jarmon.pdf

Kennelly, D. and E. Preston, *Belfast, August 1971 – a case to be answered*, Independent Labour Party, London, 1971

Kinealy, C., *This Great Calamity: The Irish famine 1845–52*, Gill & Macmillan, Dublin, 2006

Lundy, P., 'Research brief: Assessment of HET review processes and procedures in Royal Military Police investigation cases', University of Ulster, 2012, available at: http://eprints.ulster.ac.uk/21809/

Major, J., *The Autobiography*, HarperCollins, London, 2000

Mallie, E. and D. McKittrick, *The Fight for Peace*, Hodder and Stoughton, London, 1997

——, *Endgame in Ireland*, Hodder and Stoughton, London, 2001

McAllister, I., B. Hayes and L. Dowds, 'The erosion of consent: Protestant disillusionment with the Agreement', *Ark Research Update*, 32 (January 2005)

McCann, E., *What Happened in Derry*, Socialist Worker pamphlet, London, 1972

McGarry, J. (ed.), *Northern Ireland and the Divided World*, Oxford University Press, Oxford, 2001

McGovern, M., 'Rhyming history with the man from Hope', *Peace Review*, 13:1 (2001)

McGuffin, J., *The Guineapigs*, Penguin, London, 1974

McIntyre, A., *Good Friday: The death of Irish republicanism*, Ausubo Press, New York, 2009

McLaughlin, G. and S. Baker, *The Propaganda of Peace*, University of Chicago Press, Chicago, 2010

——, 'The media, the peace process and "bread and butter" politics', *Political Quarterly*, 83:2 (April–June 2012)

McMichael, G., *An Ulster Voice*, Roberts Rinehart, Dublin, 1999

Mitchell, C., 'The limits of legitimacy: former loyalist combatants and peace-building in Northern Ireland', *Irish Political Studies*, 23:1 (2008)

Mitchell, G., *Making Peace*, Heinemann, London, 1999

——, 'Remarks by Senator George J. Mitchell', Organization for Security and Cooperation in Europe, Dublin, Ireland, 27 April 2012, p. 6, available at: http://www.osce.org/cio/90200

Moloney, E. and A. Pollak, *Paisley*, Poolbeg Press, Dublin, 1986

Ni Aolain, F., *The Politics of Force*, Blackstaff Press, Belfast, 2000

Nolan, P., *Northern Ireland Peace Monitoring Report Number One*, Community Relations Council, Belfast, 2012

O'Clery, C., *The Billionaire Who Wasn't: How Chuck Feeney made and gave away a fortune without anyone knowing*, Public Affairs, New York, 2007

Oliver, Q., *Working for 'Yes'*, The 'Yes' Campaign, Belfast, 1998

O'Neill, T., *Autobiography*, Hart Davis, London, 1972

O'Rawe, R., *Blanketmen: An untold story of the H-Block hunger strike*, New Island Books, Dublin, 2005

Pollak, A., *A Citizen's Inquiry: The Opsahl Report on Northern Ireland*, The Lilliput Press, Dublin, 1993

Powell, J., *Great Hatred, Little Room: Making peace in Northern Ireland*, Bodley Head, London, 2008

Rees, M., *Northern Ireland: A personal perspective*, Methuen Press, London, 1985

Rowan, B., *Behind the Lines*, Blackstaff Press, Belfast, 1995

Shirlow, P., 'Segregation, ethno-sectarianism and the "new" Belfast' in M. Cox, A. Guelke and F. Stephen, *A Farewell to Arms? Beyond the Good Friday Agreement*, Manchester University Press, Manchester, 2005

——, 'A prosperity of thought in an age of austerity: The case of Ulster loyalism', *Political Quarterly*, 83:2 (April–June 2012)

Smithey, L., *Unionists, Loyalists and Conflict Transformation in Northern Ireland*, Oxford University Press, Oxford, 2011

Smyth, C., *Ian Paisley: Voice of Protestant Ulster*, Scottish Academic Press, Edinburgh, 1987

Steenkamp, C., 'Loyalist paramilitary violence after the Belfast agreement', *Ethnopolitics*, 7:1 (2008)

Stewart, A.T.Q., *The Ulster Crisis*, Faber, London, 1969

Sunday Times Insight Team, *Ulster*, Penguin, London, 1972

Taylor, P., *Beating the Terrorists*, Penguin, London, 1980

——, *Provos: The IRA & Sinn Fein*, Bloomsbury, London, 1997

——, *Loyalists*, Bloomsbury, London, 1999

Taylor, R. (ed.), *Consociational Theory: McGarry and O'Leary and the Northern Ireland conflict*, Routledge, London, 2009

Todd, J. and J. Ruane, *From 'A Shared Future' to 'Cohesion, Sharing and Integration': An analysis of Northern Ireland's policy framework documents*, Joseph Rowntree Charitable Trust, York, 2010

Tonge, J., *Northern Ireland: Conflict and change*, Pearson, London, 2001

Troy, A., *Holy Cross: A personal experience*, Currach Press, Blackrock, 2005

Wilford, R. (ed.), *Aspects of the Belfast Agreement*, Oxford University Press, Oxford, 2001

Wilson, R and E. Meehan, 'Can Northern Ireland become normal? Attitudes to the role of government in Northern Ireland', *ARK Research Update*, 57 (June 2008), pp. 1–5

INTERVIEWS CITED

Doran, Noel, editor, *Irish News* (interviewed by author, 24 February 2011)

Farry, Stephen, MLA, Alliance Party of Northern Ireland (interviewed by author, 24 February 2011)

Ford, David, MLA, Justice Minister, Alliance Party of Northern Ireland (nterviewed by author, 21 February 2011)

Helferty, Ciarnan, President National Union of Students–Union of Students of Ireland (NUS–USI) (interviewed by author, 25 February 2011)

McDevitt, Conall, MLA, SDLP (interviewed by author, 23 February 2011)
O'Donnell, Joe, Belfast Interface Project (interviewed by author, 22 February 2011)
Oliver, Quintin, Director, Stratagem (interviewed by author, 26 February 2011)
Smyth, Nigel, Director-General, Northern Ireland CBI (interviewed by author, 25 February 2011)
Weir, Peter, MLA, DUP (interviewed by author, 21 February 2011)

# INDEX